Rites of Passage

Rites of Passage

Judie Rae
American River College, Sierra College

Catherine Fraga
California State University, Sacramento

*Australia • Canada • Mexico • Singapore • Spain •
United Kingdom • United States*

HEINLE & HEINLE
THOMSON LEARNING™

Publisher: Michael Rosenberg
Development Editor: Jill Johnson
Project Manager, Editorial Production: Barrett Lackey
Print/Media Buyer: Marcia Locke
Permissions Editor: Beverly Wyatt
Production Service: G&S Typesetters, Inc.
Copy Editor: Cynthia Lindlof
Cover Image: Doug Bowles
Cover Printer: Malloy Lithographing
Compositor: G&S Typesetters, Inc.
Printer: Malloy Lithographing

Printed in the United States of America

1 2 3 4 5 6 7 05 04 03 02 01

For more information about our products, contact us at:
Thomson Learning Academic Resource Center
1-800-423-0563

For permission to use material from this text, contact us by:
Phone: 1-800-730-2214
Fax: 1-800-730-2215
Web:
http://www.thomsonrights.com

ISBN: 0-15-506122-4

Thomson Learning
60 Albert Street, #15-01
Albert Complex
Singapore 189969

Australia
Nelson Thomson Learning
102 Dodds Street
South Melbourne, Victoria 3205
Australia

Canada
Nelson Thomson Learning
1120 Birchmount Road
Toronto, Ontario M1K 5G4
Canada

Europe/Middle East/Africa
Thomson Learning
Berkshire House
168-173 High Holborn
London WC1 V7AA
United Kingdom

Latin America
Thomson Learning
Seneca, 53
Colonia Polanco
11560 Mexico D.F.
Mexico

Spain
Paraninfo Thomson Learning
Calle/Magallanes, 25
28015 Madrid, Spain

This book is dedicated to our students,
who teach us

Contents

Rhetorical Modes

DESCRIPTION AND NARRATION

PERSUASION AND ARGUMENT

ANALYSIS

DEFINITION

COMPARISON AND CONTRAST

CAUSE AND EFFECT

DIVISION AND CLASSIFICATION

EXAMPLE AND ILLUSTRATION

Preface

As college English instructors, we feel passionate about finding ways to reach our students and guide them toward becoming proficient writers. However, over the years we have found ourselves on the first day of class reminding students that, above all else, we would like to witness them becoming better thinkers. In this new century of accelerated lifestyles, not a lot of validation is given to slowing down and analyzing the events around us.

Consequently, we realized the need for a reader that teaches critical thinking skills by introducing students to readings on topics meaningful to them. *Rites of Passage* is a single-theme reader that examines how various cultures celebrate and honor life-shaping events. By viewing life as a process, as a collection of meaningful moments, we can give direction and meaning to our lives.

UNIQUENESS

This book differs from other readers in that it relies heavily (though not exclusively) on short stories to present the thematically arranged material. We deliberately weighted the text this way because in many cultures, some of which are represented in the reader, stories are used not only to entertain but also to instruct and even to discipline. Stories allow us to see one thing in terms of another, which is a key aspect of critical thinking. They also allow us to enter worlds we might not visit ordinarily.

Ritual and storytelling are parts of our everyday experience. This text introduces students, in a systematic yet enjoyable format, to the importance of myth and how it allows us to develop a deeper awareness of ourselves. Our academic intent is for students ultimately to realize that what happens to the character in any story is not important; rather, the intent of the work is to awaken aspects of the character within themselves. Just as a hero would remain stuck at the beginning of his tale if he refused the challenges of separation, initiation, and return, so too the student must pass through comparable thresholds of experience.

Rites of Passage is a multicultural reader that takes into consideration different language communities: ethnic, racial, and sociological. This is a text that combines the study of composition with the study of anthropology, psychology, and child development, so that students gain practice in reading across disciplines. Our goal is to prepare students for the larger role they are to assume as they enter society. We want to prepare them not only as educated beings but also as people sensitive to the collection of images we study for inspiration and hope.

APPARATUS

This reader consists of 76 readings divided into seven sections. The organization of the text reflects the human growth process: childhood; fairy tales and myths; adolescence; adulthood; love, marriage, and birth; family; and the mature years.

Each reading echoes a familiar need of all humanity: how to find meaning and a place in the world. Certainly the stories we tell and listen to shape who we are. In the selections here, a wide variety of writers share their beliefs and experiences. Joy Harjo writes about the power of the past to influence the future in "Three Generations of Native American Women's Birth Experience." Among many others are two points of view regarding educating our young, one from John Holt ("Three Kinds of Discipline") and one from Jennifer Boroquez ("Spare the Chores, Spoil the Child"). Other selections include very different views of euthanasia, useful for the teaching of argument.

A very student-approachable introduction explains why the study of rites of passage is useful in all of our lives. The introduction also offers a guide to reading, thinking, and writing about rites of passage, a brief review of how to formulate a thesis statement, and tips on planning and organizing an essay. We also include both a rough draft and revised version of a sample student essay on the topic of rites of passage.

For each reading, we include the following:

- **Journal Prompt:** Encourages honest, thoughtful response based on personal experience
- **Collaborative Exercise:** Helps to facilitate classroom discussion
- **Essay Assignments:** Offers opportunities to examine the topic more closely and provide assertions that must be supported using the text or outside research

At the end of each chapter, you will find additional essay assignments as well as research-based essay prompts. Several prompts ask students to link two or more readings in their analysis.

ANCILLARIES

An Instructor's Manual accompanies *Rites of Passage* and features film suggestions for each chapter, to be used in conjunction with the readings in the text. Because film is a genre that speaks to today's college student, and perhaps more importantly, because film borrows from dramatic structure, we have included movies we believe suitable for a rites of passage study—works that, if viewed through a symbolic lens, provide life lessons for us all.

While the central element connecting all of the films is a call to adventure, the mythic dimensions of these works are readily apparent. Many of the movies are quest stories; something about each one draws us into an engagement with the characters. Though our students may not battle dragons, symbolic dragons await us all: possible divorce, illness, financial upsets, and loss of loved ones.

Additional exercise prompts for the films are also included. The intent of these exercises is to offer instructors opportunities to further discuss the readings as they relate to philosophical, anthropological, social, and ethical issues presented in film.

A brief overview of archetypal criticism and its usefulness as background material for teaching *Rites of Passage* is an integral part of the Instructor's Manual. Other helpful material includes an extensive bibliography of reading suggestions for both student and instructor.

ACKNOWLEDGMENTS

We are indebted to so many colleagues and friends who provided suggestions, advice, and emotional support. First we would like to thank our husbands, Will and Michael, for their patience and kind reassurance through the process of creating this text. Our children—Tiffany Rae Looney, Brooke Rae Felmar, and Taylor and Patrick Fraga Mahony—were most gracious while their mothers' efforts were directed elsewhere. Special thanks to son-in-law Rich Looney, who more than once restored a notional computer to proper working order. Bill Brisick has been a continuous, solid source of advice as well as a cheerleader urging us on. We would also like to thank Robert Frew from American River College, and John Rush, Michelle Johnson, Marcelle Strong, Sue McNichols, Pam Garibaldi, Pam Wilson, Marilyn Errett, Danita Rayhbuck, and Shelley Shaver for their aid and friendship. A special note of thanks to composition student Tina Limón for her generous contribution.

Julie McBurney acted as our acquisitions editor and was a major player in seeing this project become a reality. Thanks also go to the publisher, Michael Rosenberg. It is to Jill Johnson, our development editor, that we owe the greatest thank you; her advice, humor, and continuous help through two years of work kept us on track.

Additional thank yous are owed to Barrett Lackey at Thomson Learning and to Gretchen Otto, production coordinator, and the staff of G&S Typesetters. Ms. Otto kept us apprised of the production process and did so with unfailing good humor. Copyeditor Cynthia Lindlof, with her incredibly diligent and helpful proofreading, was invaluable to us.

Much appreciation to the following reviewers for their very wise suggestions and for their encouragement: Debbie Barberousse, Montgomery Community College; John Boly, Marquette University; John J. Desjarlais, Kishwaukee College; Sarah Dye, Elgin Community College; John Esperian, Community College of Southern Nevada; Candy Henry, Seton Hill College; James Knox, Roane State Community College; Jack Miller, Normandale Community College; Cindy Moore, Indiana University–Purdue University, Fort Wayne; and Fran O'Connor, Nassau Community College.

And finally, a thank you to our students, whose wisdom is a constant source of surprise and delight. Without them, there would be no book.

1

Reading and Writing about Rites of Passage

INTRODUCTION: WHY THIS BOOK?

The person who lives without myth lives without roots, without links to the collective self which is finally what we are all about. He is literally isolated from reality. The person who lives with a myth gains "a sense of wider meaning" to his existence and is raised "beyond mere getting and spending."

—Carl Jung

So much has been written about Western culture's mania for "getting and spending" and about our disenfranchised population—a society often described as rootless, without hope for the future—that we are almost inured to the message. Typically blamed are the media, two-income households, and our society's easy access to weapons. Jungian psychologists, artists, writers, and poets point fingers at a society out of touch with our past, with the stories and rituals that nourish the soul and keep us human.

This thematic reader touches on these very issues. If, as some claim, we are a culture without community, how then do we create one for ourselves? We know that ritual (a ceremonial act customarily repeated) satisfies many human needs. It uplifts people and community. It lends meaning to our lives and helps us recognize the natural flow of life. It attunes us to the past.

Before humans could read or write, they had rites to honor those who preceded them. Ritual, then, is about interconnectedness. A rite of passage is a ritual event that celebrates a passage in life from one stage to another; it is an action whose intention is transformation: of the body as well as the spirit. It answers the deep need to be in a common place by connecting us to all who came before.

We are in no way advocating the return to, or the practice of, ritualistic initiation rites found in some primitive cultures, rites that today do little more than horrify most of us; nonetheless, we do believe there is a need to acknowledge the confusing process of maturation in the modern world, for many of our current difficulties are situational and very much rooted in modern culture.

Traditional people avoid these problems by inculcating their young into cultures steeped with meaning. While researching material for this book, we came across an African saying that verifies this reality. "Before we send our young men off to war," an African Elder says, "we teach them how to dance." In other words, these young men are prepared for any of the life experiences that await them.

Our young are without a dance to call their own, one that attaches them to the sacred past. Instead we see adolescents who sport tattoos and navel rings; they engage in borrowed ritualistic behavior, but it is devoid of meaning. In contrast, the scarification ritual of a tribal male announces to his contemporaries that he has withstood a physical, psychological, and spiritual testing; his scars are proof that he has cast off childhood ways and has been born again into an honored position as a member of his tribe.

Mircea Eliade, author of *Rites and Symbols,* describes the importance of these initiation rites in a broad context:

> Initiation represents one of the most significant spiritual phenomena in the history of humanity. It is an act that involves not only the religious life of the individual, in the modern meaning of the word "religion"; it involves his entire life. It is through initiation that, in primitive and archaic societies, man becomes what he is and what he should be—a being open to the life of the spirit, hence one who participates in the culture into which he was born. (3)

Eliade claims then, that the task of initiands is "to attain the status of human beings" (3). In traditional societies, people prepare their children for the future by telling stories. Frances Harwood, an anthropologist, once asked a Sioux Elder why people tell stories. "In order to become human beings," he answered.

"Aren't we human beings already?" she asked him.

He smiled. "Not everyone makes it."

How to become fully actualized human beings when our own mythological and cultural traditions are no longer clear to us is the task at hand. Some of the authors included in this text (E. B. White for one) suggest the power of spiritual connection rests in nature; that myth and love and human longing are the wisdom we seek, the quest on which we embark. As Joseph Campbell suggests, we must all become the heroes of our own narratives.

"As Campbell makes clear, these narratives are really instructions for individual and group behavior in the grand rites of passage that mark the thresholds of life: birth, naming, puberty, marriage, and death" (Frederick Turner, *Beyond Geography* 116).

With this in mind, we have divided the text to coincide with the major life transformations Campbell addresses, to explain them, to understand them, and ultimately, to honor them. If, as Campbell claims, the purpose of rites of passage is transformation, let us hope that contained within them is the potential to connect and transform us all.

Finally, we have seen that all rites of passage involve initiation. Initiation means to begin. Let us begin, then, a new adventure in reading and writing and storytelling.

READING AND THINKING ABOUT RITES OF PASSAGE

Reading . . . does not win huge sums of money or applause, or give joy and solace to others. What it does offer is a delectable exercise for the mind. . . .

—LYNNE SHARON SCHWARTZ

Several years ago, while I was teaching a creative writing course, one very eager student approached after class wanting me to read the first chapters of a mystery novel she had written. After reading it, I was faced with an uncomfortable situation, for her characters were flat: one-dimensional and unfocused. The writing, too, was dreadful.

Treading gently, I asked her what mystery novels she had read to date. The look on her face said it all. Incredulous, she responded curtly, "I don't read books. I'm a writer. I write books."

Great writers are great readers. The two activities, reading and writing, cannot be separated, something the student had not yet realized. They are inextricably interwoven. Every writer, student or professional, must commit to reading to give his or her writing shape, tone, and voice, for effective reading produces effective writing.

Even a matter as mundane as grammar can be learned through reading. A good reader may not know the rule that a semicolon connects two related independent clauses, yet if he or she reads enough, the information is understood *intuitively*, for the reader has seen the punctuation used correctly thousands of times. The reader's own writing, then, benefits from his or her reading.

Reading can refine your own style as a writer. You note how an author puts words together, how ideas are expressed.

How does one become a good reader? Unless you are reading purely for pleasure, it is important to read every assignment at least twice: once to get the *feel* of the piece—how a particular author uses language—and a second time to read critically, attempting to understand the points the author is trying to convey. It is in this important second reading where you develop your understanding of the work, analyzing carefully how the material is developed, how the work is organized. A good way to do this is with pencil in hand. (I suspect most English teachers feel a book is only as good as the notes in the margins.)

What to write in those margins? To begin, make note of your response to the piece. Do you agree? Disagree? Is there a concept you don't understand? A word you've never seen before? *Write it down. Underline.* This process of note taking is called **annotating.**

Even before you annotate, scan the material, asking yourself what you know about the author. Is the author a contemporary? Have you read other pieces by this person? Can you tell by the title what the piece is about? Do you already know something about the subject? What is the reading's genre? Is it poetry, a short story, a nonfiction piece? We sometimes read different genres differently. With poetry, we may ask, "Is it beautiful? Did it touch me?" With nonfiction, "Does it move by logical connection? Do all the parts hold together?" After scanning the work, you should know whether you can read the material in one sitting or whether you should plan to break up the reading into parts.

Now you are ready to begin annotating. The following are a few suggestions to keep in mind as you read the text.

1. What is the author's thesis, or main point? Is it stated directly or implied?
2. How does the author support the main point? Do the supporting ideas relate to the thesis? How? (Mark statements that seem to you to summarize the theme; in fact, mark anything that strikes you as relevant.)
3. How is the essay structured?
4. To whom is the author addressing this piece? (Ask yourself: Is this written for someone who knows nothing about the subject, or is the author presupposing that his or her audience has some awareness of what it is he or she is writing about?)
5. What is the tone of the work? Is it sarcastic, humorous, ironic, objective, or hostile?
6. Are there any patterns or evolving themes?
7. What passages stand out and why?
8. What strategies does the author use to develop his or her piece (i.e., what are the rhetorical modes in use)?
9. Does the strategy he or she chooses fit the work?
10. Finally, how effective did you find the essay?

Once you have asked yourself these questions, you are ready to make a final evaluation of the work. Reread your notes, as they will remind you of the important issues the work discusses. Take a look at the author's conclusion. Does it effectively summarize the thesis? A well-written expository conclusion offers the reader a sense of closure; it does not leave the reader hanging or confused.

The following two works have been annotated as examples for you. Read them, and consider the notes *you* might make in the margins.

This short narrative first served as an introduction to a chapter in *Cultural Anthropology,* a textbook written by the authors, professors at the State University of New York at Stony Brook. **DAVID HICKS** has received numerous research awards, including a National Science Foundation award. **MARGARET GWYNNE** works as a consultant in the eastern Caribbean for the World Health Organization.

DAVID HICKS AND
MARGARET A. GWYNNE

A PRIMITIVE RITUAL

title clue to subject matter?

Setting

(The professor in a big introductory course in anthropology at a state university often illustrated his lectures with ethnographic films.) Most films portrayed events in the lives of people living in small-scale societies in faraway parts of the world. Over the course of the semester, students in the class saw Inuit hunters celebrating a successful seal hunt with drumming, dancing, and singing; a group of Middle Eastern nomads walking hundreds of miles to take their sheep to new pastures; Balinese dancers performing a religious drama to the eerie accompaniment of strange-looking stringed instruments; and opposing groups of Pacific islanders, wearing elaborate feather headdresses, fighting each other with homemade spears. The reaction of the students to these films was mixed. Some viewers were intrigued, others were bored, and still others admitted that at times they were shocked or even repelled. In general, however, the students were more struck by the strangeness of what they saw on the screen than by similarities between the filmed scenes and events in their own lives.

look up

Examples of primitive rituals

Student reactions

Use of narrative mode

One day, toward the end of the semester, the professor dimmed the lecture hall lights for yet another film. This one, like several of the others, began with a darkened screen and the heavy thump of distant drumming, and some students groaned inwardly at the thought of having to sit through what they anticipated would be another strange, incomprehensible, or even repellent dance, drama, sacrifice, or other ritual. As the screen slowly brightened, shadowy human figures became visible—moving shapes with flapping clothing and grotesque, voluminous hairdos.

> Smoke swirled around the silhouetted figures who bounced up and down rhythmically to the faint but steady beat of the drums. *Tone is humorous*
>
> *Thesis is implied, not direct*
>
> As the sound track gradually grew louder and musical tones surfaced above the percussive thumping, the students began to listen more intently, for they thought they recognized something familiar. Soon the screen brightened, and they began to laugh, for this footage, far from showing a primitive rite filmed in some remote land, had been filmed at a popular nightclub near the campus, and the mysterious figures gyrating rhythmically to the music were none other than the students themselves.
>
> *Thesis: the rituals of American society bear a striking resemblance to those of small-scale societies elsewhere*
>
> *effective conclusion points to implied thesis*

Annotating a short story differs from annotating nonfiction in that setting, characters, conflict, and point of view are also matters of importance. Ask yourself the following questions.

1. Who are the characters in the story?
2. How do they change as the story develops?
3. What is the subject matter of the story? (The title sometimes helps with this, but not always.)
4. What is the theme? (In a short story, the theme is implied, not stated directly.)
5. What is the conflict? (Is it internal, an individual against himself or herself; or external—an individual against another person, society, or nature?)
6. Is the conflict resolved by story's end?
7. Where does the story take place?
8. What is the time frame of the work?
9. Is place important to understanding the story?
10. Who tells the story?
11. Is the narrator a character in the piece or an observer?

How language is used in a work of fiction is also relevant. Imagery, metaphor, figurative language, and irony all serve to create a rich, evocative environment the reader inhabits for the brief time he or she is engaged with the work. The following paragraphs are taken from Tim O'Brien's short story, "On the Rainy River." The narrator recalls his young adult years and the moral freeze he experienced when his draft notice arrived, calling him to serve in the Vietnam War. Early on in the piece, the author writes:

> *Moral view of narrator at younger age*
>
> All of us, I suppose, like to believe that in a moral emergency we will behave like the heroes of our youth, bravely and forthrightly, without thought of personal loss or discredit. . . . If the stakes ever became high enough—if the evil were evil enough, if the good were good enough—I would simply tap a secret reservoir of courage that had been accumulat-

> ing inside me over the years. Courage, I seemed to think, comes to us in finite quantities, like an inheritance, and by being frugal and stashing it away and letting it earn interest, we steadily increase our moral capital in preparation for that day when the account must be drawn down. It was a comforting theory. It dispensed with all those bothersome little acts of daily courage; it offered hope and grace to the repetitive coward; it justified the past while amortizing the future.

In another passage the narrator describes his summer job at a meatpacking plant. This evocative paragraph, though written about something ostensibly unrelated, reveals his internal struggle and feelings about the war.

> I spent the summer of 1968 working in an Armour meatpacking plant in my hometown of Worthington, Minnesota. The plant specialized in pork products, and for eight hours a day I stood on a quarter-mile assembly line—more properly, a disassembly line—removing blood clots from the necks of dead pigs. My job title, I believe, was Declotter. After slaughter, the hogs were decapitated, split down the length of the belly, pried open, eviscerated, and strung up by the hind hocks on a high conveyer belt. Then gravity took over. By the time a carcass reached my spot on the line, the fluids had mostly drained out, everything except for thick clots of blood in the neck and upper chest cavity. To remove the stuff, I used a kind of water gun. The machine was heavy, maybe eighty pounds, and was suspended from the ceiling by a heavy rubber cord. There was some bounce to it, an elastic up-and-down give, and the trick was to maneuver the gun with your whole body, not lifting with the arms, just letting the rubber cord do the work for you. At one end was a trigger; at the muzzle end was a small nozzle and a steel roller brush. As a carcass passed by, you'd lean forward and swing the gun up against the clots and squeeze the trigger, all in one motion, and the brush would whirl and water would come shooting out and you'd hear a quick splattering sound as the clots dissolved into a fine red mist. It was not pleasant work. Goggles were a necessity, and a rubber apron, but even so it was like standing for eight hours a day under a lukewarm blood-shower. At night I'd go home smelling of pig. I couldn't wash it out. Even after a hot bath, scrubbing hard, the stink was always there—like old bacon, or sausage, a dense greasy pig-stink that soaked deep into my skin and hair. Among other things, I remember, it was tough getting dates that summer. I felt isolated; I spent a lot of time alone. And there was also that draft notice tucked away in my wallet.

After a great deal of moral confusion, the protagonist of this tale makes the decision to head north; he contemplates going to Canada to avoid the war.

nice description

> Though it was still August, the air already had the smell of October, football season, piles of yellow-red leaves, everything crisp and clean. I remember a huge blue sky. Off to my right was the Rainy River, wide as a lake in places, and beyond the Rainy River was Canada.

He comes to an old fishing resort called the Tip Top Lodge, a place in disrepair and abandoned for the season.

> The main building, which stood in a cluster of pines on high ground, seemed to lean heavily to one side, like a cripple, the roof sagging toward Canada.

Description leads the Reader; narrat is an emotional cripple at this point

---

At the Tip Top, the character meets Elroy Berdahl, the eighty-one-year-old owner of the lodge. In the six days they spend together, Elroy

Elroy acts as conscience of narrator

> never pried. He never put me in a position that required lies or denials. To an extent, I suppose, his reticence was typical of that part of Minnesota, where privacy still held value, and even if I'd been walking around with some horrible deformity—four arms and three heads—I'm sure the old man would've talked about everything except those extra arms and heads. Simple politeness was part of it. But even more than that, I think, the man understood that words were insufficient. The problem had gone beyond discussion.

On their last day together Elroy takes the young man out on the river, ostensibly to fish, but Canada is now within swimming distance. It is here that the narrator makes his decision.

> I would not swim away from my hometown and my country and my life. I would not be brave. That old image of myself as a hero, as a man of conscience and courage, all that was just a theadbare pipe dream.

disillusioned narrator

On the boat he experiences a hallucination and he sees a parade.

litany of watchers matches his confusion

many war references

> All my aunts and uncles were there, and Abraham Lincoln, and Saint George, and a nine-year-old girl named Linda who had died of a brain tumor back in fifth grade, and several members of the United States Senate, and a blind poet scribbling notes, and LBJ, and Huck Finn, and Abbie Hoffman, and all the dead soldiers back from the grave, and the many thousands who were later to die—villagers with terrible burns, little kids without arms or legs—yes, and the Joint Chiefs of Staff were there, and a

he, too, runs away

> couple of popes, and a first lieutenant named Jimmy Cross, and the last surviving veteran of the American Civil War, and Jane Fonda dressed up as Barbarella, and an old man sprawled beside a pigpen, and my grandfather, and Gary Cooper, and a kind-faced woman carrying an umbrella and a copy of Plato's *Republic,* and a million ferocious citizens waving flags of all shapes and colors—people in hard hats, people in headbands—they were all whooping and chanting and urging me toward one shore or the other.

story's conflict is internal

At that moment, he makes his decision.

ironic view of bravery?

> Even in my imagination, the shore just twenty yards away, I couldn't make myself be brave. It had nothing to do with morality. Embarrassment, that's all it was.
>
> And right then I submitted.
>
> I would go to war—I would kill and maybe die—because I was embarrassed not to.

The story ends with the narrator leaving the Tip Top Lodge and Elroy Berdahl.

> I washed up the breakfast dishes, left his two hundred dollars on the kitchen counter, got into the car, and drove south toward home.
>
> The day was cloudy. I passed through towns with familiar names, through the pine forests and down to the prairie, and then to Vietnam, where I was a soldier, and then home again. I survived, but it's not a happy ending. I was a coward. I went to war.

Conflicts with our standard perception of a coward

Remembering that reading and writing are interwoven, think about how you would annotate the material that follows. And ask yourself, after the critical reading of a piece, have you found techniques, strategies, and ideas you might want to incorporate into your own writing?

WRITING ABOUT RITES OF PASSAGE

Most of the material a writer works with is acquired before the age of fifteen.

—Willa Cather

As you begin to write essays about rites of passage, remember that you have already collected an impressive amount of material. Just as our interpretation of what we read relies heavily on our life experiences and observations, our writing takes shape based on our life histories. How we respond in written form to something we read is very much a product of who we are. The rites of passage you have participated in or observed—first day of school, bar mitzvah, first date, wedding, and so on—will all contribute to the content, expression, and analysis of your writing.

Throughout this book you will find readings on rites of passage that you can view as models for your own writing, or as subjects to which you might respond, assignments for writing critical essays, and group activities and research projects to help you sort out and analyze a wide variety of life events.

THE WAY WRITERS WORK

However great a man's natural talent may be, the art of writing cannot be learned all at once.

JEAN JACQUES ROUSSEAU

Several years ago, while I was explaining the process of writing to my freshman composition students, one of the students appeared very anxious. Finally, she spoke up: "But you gave me an A on my last essay, and I never planned it. I never wrote a rough draft. I just *wrote* it!"

Her statement seemed to contradict everything I had just written on the chalkboard: *Plan your essay! Organize your ideas! Write a first draft! Revise, revise, and revise!*

This student's experience with writing an essay, granted a rare occurrence for most writers, was one that I used very successfully to illustrate and support the main idea of our discussion: Good writing that is clear, focused, and well supported and that offers an interesting and perhaps provocative perspective requires planning, a lot of thinking, and a series of revisions.

To my student, I acknowledged aloud that I believed her, yet I had a few questions. During the course of my questioning, she rather sheepishly admitted to several things.

- Yes, from the moment the essay was assigned, she had been narrowing her focus and formulating a thesis statement.
- Yes, on the way to and from work, she had created a list of main supports.
- Yes, while she did the laundry, she eliminated the weaker supports and selected four strong supports that would form a convincing argument.

In short, she had lived and breathed the essay for two weeks. Certainly it is not the usual scenario for most of us—planning and composing an essay without ever putting pen to paper. She had, nonetheless, gone through a specific, almost methodical process of preparation to write. Most of us, however, must commit to more tangible planning time in order to write a competent, interesting essay.

PLANNING YOUR ESSAY

Before you begin to write, be sure you understand the essay prompt and what is being asked. Read the prompt over several times, and take note of the words that direct you to a particular task: **explore, examine, argue, address, analyze, explain, comment, debate, discuss** are a few examples.

Rewrite the prompt in your own words. Notice how composition student Tina Limon rewrote the prompt in her own words. Articulating the assigned prompt so it is clear to you, the writer, is essential in the beginning stages of a writing assignment.

Example:

Original Prompt:

Write about a rite of passage you have experienced or observed (or both). Include the circumstances surrounding the event, as well as your reactions and those of others whose lives were changed either directly or indirectly by this experience. Your rite of passage may have a cultural frame of reference (such as a quinceañera or a bar mitzvah) or a universal frame of reference (such as graduating from high school or leaving home). If one of these frames of reference is used, read about what others have to say about the subject and respond to their commentary.

Rewritten in Your Own Words:

Write about a rite of passage I've experienced. Who was there? How did I respond? What were others' reactions, and how did the event change their lives? Do professionals have anything to say about this particular rite of passage?

Once you understand the assignment, you may want to try a strategy called **focused freewriting.** This is a way to discover all you know about a topic to determine how much material you have and how much research you may have to do, if required.

Example:

Leaving home for college (both my sister and I) triggered some big changes for everyone in the family. Mindy left first, and that was the most difficult. My parents felt lost, and although I gained more room in the house, I missed her, too. There were numerous phone calls to Mindy, at least at first. Everyone felt a bit awkward and uneasy with Mindy gone. We were all used to the four of us together.

By the time I left, my parents' response was drastically different. They seemed eager to see me go. No sad goodbyes, no tears. They turned my bedroom into a library in less than a week of my leaving!

Lots of researchers have written about this "empty-nest syndrome" and the effects on all family members, especially the parents. It is something that both parents and adolescents must face—with all its uncertainty, fear, disbelief, and joy. All adolescents must face the passage into adulthood, and leaving home for college is one of the more well-known methods of gaining independence.

Another discovery strategy is **listing.** Making lists can help a writer sort out ideas, discover new ideas, or elaborate on thoughts from freewriting.

Example:

Family's reaction to Mindy leaving; very difficult to accept

Interview Mom, Dad, and Mindy

Include my feelings

What happened when I left?

Parents adapted very quickly to my absence

What the experts say about the empty-nest syndrome

What does it mean if the children really want to leave the parents?

A yearning for independence, freedom

Home is never the same for parents after child leaves

After you feel you have a direction, you will need to formulate a **working thesis statement.** Many writers are more comfortable referring to the thesis statement as a *working thesis* because it leaves open the possibility that it may change somewhat as the essay progresses.

The purpose of the essay determines whether or not a thesis is necessary. A list of requirements to get into a college or a straight description of how a computer works usually will not need a thesis. However, when you want to express a point of view or uphold the validity of an opinion, you will need a thesis to express the idea you are presenting. Most essays you will write in college classes will ask you to do exactly that: to adopt a point of view and try to convince your readers to at least consider your point of view as logical and well articulated.

What a good thesis is:

- Restricted: no vague or general terms
- Specific: use of names, places, and facts
- Complete: a grammatically complete sentence

What a good thesis is *not:*

- Not a title
- Not an announcement of the subject
- Not a summary of the essay, story, or poem
- Not wordy
- Not a statement of absolute fact (it must be an assertion!)

As you can see, the most important quality of a good thesis is its forecasting ability, or its ability to show a reader what to expect in an essay. Let's look at a few sample thesis statements.

1. Because an open visitation policy in dormitories may interfere with studies, cause roommate problems, and pose security difficulties, the university should not adopt an open-visitation policy.
2. Open-visitation dorm policies are bad.

Sentence 1 is the better thesis because it shows specifically how the essay will unfold. Sentence 2 makes a judgment, but it is not specific about *how* the open-visitation policy is bad, or even what *bad* means.

Let's look at another set of thesis statements.

1. There's no reason why you have to have excessive debt; this problem can be avoided.
2. Here are three easy steps for debt avoidance.

Sentence 2 is the better thesis because it shows *how* the essay will be developed. Sentence 1 is more general. *Ideally, the two should be used in combination, with 1 preceding 2.*

In Tina's case, her first attempt at a thesis statement was workable and helped her get started in a focused direction, but she eventually reworked it to eliminate unnecessary words and phrases and commentary belonging elsewhere in the essay.

Example (working thesis)

There are a variety of challenges that accompany children and parents when leaving home for college, and each perspective is handled differently to cope with a child fleeing the nest.

Example (revised thesis)

A variety of challenges accompany both children and parents when children leave home for college.

Once you have written your working thesis statement, and if you have spent considerable time narrowing your topic, you should feel as if approximately 50 percent of your work has already been completed. You now have a clear direction for your essay, and you know what is expected of you as the writer.

Writing a Draft

As you write your first draft, it is very important to remember your reading **audience.** Of course, your instructor is part of the audience, but you will probably be working in class with other students acting as peer editors. Consider the following when determining your audience.

- How much does your audience know about your topic?
- What are the value systems of your readers?
- What are the various ages, ethnic backgrounds, work experiences, and educational backgrounds of your readers?

While it is often dangerous to make generalizations without acknowledging that there are exceptions, it is often advantageous to make some educated guesses about your audience, their backgrounds, and their knowledge about particular subjects or issues.

Spend some time determining how you will **organize** your essay. The following are the two most common ways of organizing your essay.

1. Organize your supportive evidence from the least important to the most important, or in the case of an argument, from the least convincing to the most convincing. For example:

   Mindy leaves home for college

   My reaction and parents' reaction

   Mindy's reaction

   I leave home (how I feel about it)

   My parents' reaction to my leaving

   How parents prepare for when a child leaves home

   Empty-nest syndrome explained and discussed

   Why leaving home is important transition to adult life

   Need for parental support during transition

   Concluding remarks (summary of adjustments for both parents and children)

2. Organize your supportive evidence from the most important to the least convincing.

   Consider the listing in #1 above and reverse it. Begin with outside research and statistics and conclude with a narrative of personal experiences and observations.

Think of a slender thread running down the center of your essay. Your goal is to make that thread as taut as possible. If the thread is too relaxed, your reader is bound to get lost and become disinterested. How do you keep your reader from becoming bored and distracted? One way is to **use transitional words or phrases** to guide your reader from one idea to the next, whether it is within a paragraph or between paragraphs.

It is easy to get in the habit of using the same two or three transitional markers, and soon your essay may become tedious. Try some of the following transitions when you feel "stuck."

Category	*Transitions*
In addition	additionally, again, also, as well, besides, beyond, equally important, first (second, third, fourth, finally, last, lastly, etc.), for one thing, furthermore, likewise, moreover, next, now, on top of that, over and above
Emphasis	above all, certainly, especially, in any event, in fact, in particular, indeed, most important, surely
Comparison	in the same way, likewise, similarly
Contrast	after all, although, and yet, be that as it may, but, even so, for all that, however, in contrast, in other circumstances, in spite of that, nevertheless, nonetheless, on the contrary, on the other hand, otherwise, still, this may be true, yet
Exemplification	as an example, as an illustration, for example, for instance, in other words, in particular, that is
Place	above that, at this point, below that, beyond that, here, nearby, next to that, on the other side, outside, within
Reason	for this purpose, for this reason, to this end
Result	accordingly, as a consequence, as a result, consequently, for that reason, hence, inevitably, necessarily, that being the case, then, therefore, thus
Summary	as has been noted, as I have said, finally, in brief, in other words, in short, in sum, lastly, on the whole, to be sure, to sum up
Time	after a while, afterward, at last, at length, at once, briefly, by degrees, eventually, finally, first (second, third, etc.), gradually, immediately, in a short time, in the future, in the meantime, instantaneously, later, meanwhile, promptly, soon, suddenly

Revising Your Essay

If possible, after you write your first draft, refrain from looking at it again for a day or so. When you return to the draft, you will probably notice weak areas right away. Your peer editors and your instructor will serve as valuable sources of feedback, too.

Ask yourself the following questions to guide you in the process of revision.

Issues of Content and Organization

- Is my paper focused? Is the thesis concise? Does my essay address the thesis statement specifically and fully?
- Do I have a clear understanding of the purpose of my paper? Have I communicated that purpose clearly to my readers?
- Does each of my paragraphs deal with one idea, and does each paragraph flow easily from one to the next?
- Does every paragraph say something specific to support the idea it expresses (examples, details, reasons)?
- Have I considered the values, opinions, knowledge, and abilities of my audience?
- Does my opening paragraph really "grab" the reader's attention? Is it written in such a way that it serves as an invitation to the reader to continue reading? An introduction dictates to the writer what explanation or evidence must be provided. It may also indicate both the tone and the nature of the diction to be expected in the remaining essay. Some techniques of successfully appealing to the reader include starting with a striking fact or statistic, posing a problem or question, using narrative details, beginning with a rejection of widely accepted opinions or an authority to startle or provoke the reader, and using descriptive details that catch in concrete terms the essence of your thesis.

Example:

Here's an early version of Tina's opening paragraph, as well as a revised version. Note the changes she made in her second effort to draw the reader more effectively into her paper. Wordiness and too much information all at once usually distract and even bore a reader.

Introductory Paragraph (rough draft)

Living at home with a mother, a father, and a sister I got to experience both the joy and the sorrow of someone leaving home. I was there when my parents felt the emptiness of my sister's absence, and I believe it was one of the most traumatizing milestones of my family's lives. On the other hand, I have also left for college and I remember coming home for a visit to discover my room had been turned into a library. For parents, it is the end of an era, and for teenagers it is a beginning, and for both there is a sudden vast hole in our lives and in our hearts. There are a variety of challenges that accompany children and parents when leaving home for college, and each perspective is handled differently to cope with a child fleeing the nest.

Introductory Paragraph (revised)

Ups and downs occur in every family; however, nothing prepared me for the most traumatizing period of my family's lives. When my older sister, Mindy, left home for college, life was never quite the same for my parents and me. Interestingly, I also left for college a few years later, yet my parents' reaction was very different than it was when my sister left. For parents it is the end of an era, for teenagers it is a rite of passage into adulthood, and for both there is a sudden void that is both painful and exhilarating. A variety of adjustments accompany both children and parents when adolescents leave home for college.

- In my concluding paragraph (or concluding remarks), did I provide an original analysis, solution, evaluation, or insight? Remember that a successful conclusion does more than simply summarize what you've already said. Successful conclusions do *not* introduce a new subject but rather propose a solution or suggest that further research might be needed.

Example:

When Tina began the process of revision, she realized her concluding remarks were wordy and hard to follow, even overly repetitive.

Concluding Paragraph (rough draft)

The feeling for children when they leave home can be overwhelming; they can suddenly not feel as grown up as they did in the previous days of preparation. There is a compelling sense of adventure mixed with the uncertainty and not fear, but trepidation, and it is here when we take the leap into the abyss of independence and adulthood. On the other hand, parents take a different stand of the departure, whether it is empty or just emptier, the nest is never the same once a child flies. It makes the house an empty place and it is here when parents realize that a part of their children gets frozen in their minds at a certain age. Perhaps it is when the child first really connects with their parents with a personality separate from their own, and becomes an independent person. It is usually a painful experience, but there comes a time when children get closer to the edge and they are ready to fly.

Concluding Paragraph (revised)

For adolescents, leaving home can be overwhelming; they can suddenly not feel as grown up as they did in the previous days of preparation. A compelling sense of adventure is mixed with the uncertainty. On the other hand, parents must adjust to the empty nest—physically, psychologically, and emotionally. Parents suddenly realize a previously held image of their child is frozen in their minds, and they will need to adjust to their child's passage into adulthood. It is usually a sobering experience for everyone involved, but all children inch closer to the edge and sooner than later, it is time to take off.

Issues of Tone and Style

- Have I selected words with care, considering both the denotation (dictionary meaning) as well as the connotation (the emotional tones readers often attach to words)?
- Have I avoided repetitive words and phrases unless I am using repetition to effectively emphasize my point?
- Have I tried to stay in active voice throughout my essay? (I know that passive-voice sentences are those in which the subject is acted upon rather than doing the acting. For example: **Passive voice:** The meeting was monitored by the president of the school board. **Active voice:** The president of the school board monitored the meeting.)
- Have I eliminated awkward word choices or words that are long and pretentious when a more concise word conveys my meaning just as well?

Issues of Grammar and Mechanics

- Are there any sentence fragments?
- Are there any comma splices or run-on sentences (where I have joined two complete thoughts with only a comma or have written two or more complete thoughts with no punctuation at all)?
- Do all my subjects and verbs agree?
- Is the tense of verbs consistent throughout the paper except when I intentionally changed tense to indicate a change of time?
- Are all punctuation marks used correctly?
- Are all words spelled correctly?

After spending two weeks or more on an out-of-class essay assignment, you may find it very challenging to revisit your work. It is just as important to be a good editor and proofreader as it is to be a successful writer. Try reading your essay from the last paragraph to the first. This will naturally slow you down and help you find careless errors you may have missed. Many students also find it helpful to read their essays aloud. Amazingly, problems such as sentence fragments, awkward word choices, and punctuation errors will "jump" out at us when we actually hear them.

The following paragraph is taken from Tina's rough draft and shows her editing work where she eliminated only mechanical and sentence-level errors.

Later, she eliminated wordiness, repetitiveness, and awkward sentences, as you will note in the final draft version. The care you take in putting the finishing touches on your essay in the revision process will make a very significant difference in the success of your paper.

It was then my turn to take that first flight from the nest and my experience was a lot different. Even though, I was only forty minutes away from home, it seemed like my parents were delighted to see me leave. It took me about two hours to pack up all my things, and I was ready to go. My mom did not even accompany my dad when he dropped me off, she just said her good-bye, gave me a hug, and off I went. The move happened so quickly, we unloaded all my things into my new apartment, and as soon as I got situated I reassured my dad that I was going to be fine, he then said good-bye and he was gone. It was so simple, it was almost too easy there were no big sighs, no tears, no awkward feelings, I felt like they were leaving me alone. When I returned home the next weekend to pick up a few things that I had left behind my parents had already started renovating my room in to the new library. I could not believe it; it was almost like they could not wait for me to leave. However, I do have to suffer through the phone calls, just so they feel that I am still alive. Finally, I now know what it feels like to be independent I began my own journey and the courageous leap out of the nest was well worth it.

Following is the final draft version of Tina's essay. Her revision work includes attention to sentence structure, as well as to wordiness and problems with focus.

Fleeing the Nest

Living at home with a mother, a father, and a sister I was able to experience both the joy and the sorrow of someone leaving home. I was there when my parents felt the emptiness of my older sister's absence when she left for college, and I believe it was one of the most traumatizing periods of my family's lives. Eventually, I also left for college and my parents' reaction was nothing like it had been during my sister's leaving. For parents it is the end of an era, for teenagers it is a rite of passage into adulthood, and for both there is a sudden void that is both painful and exhilarating. A variety of adjustments accompany both children and parents when children leave home for college.

"It was one of the longest drives of my life," my dad explained, as he recalled driving to San Diego to drop off my older sister, Mindy, at her new home at the University of California in San Diego. "I just wanted to stop and turn back for home, and tell her that she couldn't leave" (Manuel Limon). However, he knew that was impossible because this was a "dream come true" for my sister—to leave our small, quiet town

560 miles away—and he could not take that away from her. My mother, on the other hand, remained quiet for most the trip. She remembered thinking, "She hasn't even left us yet and there is already something missing" (Linda Limon).

As for myself, I remember being so excited, not only because I would have the whole house to call my own, and I would no longer have to share a bathroom, but also I looked forward to all the fun trips I would take to visit her in San Diego. Finally, seeing her leave put thoughts into my head about taking the voyage away from home myself.

For my sister, it was an entirely different feeling. "I had a strange feeling in my stomach. I remember being afraid of not knowing anyone; I was alone, but at the same time I felt so grown up. I finally felt like an individual, and I was overwhelmed by excitement." Mindy is now finishing her final year at UC, San Diego and is planning on making another daring move to Washington, D.C., for her first internship. When asked what empowered her to leave home initially, she explained, "It was not an option for me to stay home after high school graduation; it was my chance to see if I could survive and I took it. It was one of the biggest challenges I have ever faced, but I did it—I survived." I was curious about how she felt about departing her family. She answered, "It was difficult to do, but the bond that I share with my family will always be with me wherever I go. The most important aspect about leaving for me was to be sure that all of you had faith in me, and it made coping that much easier" (Mindy Limon).

Leaving my sister in San Diego was difficult for my parents and me, but I think the biggest challenge was yet to come. On the quiet drive back home, my dad would occasionally take a deep breath and let out a long sigh of discomfort, and my mother sniffled as she hid her teary eyes behind a pair of sunglasses. I was still ecstatic thinking about how I was going to arrange my things into my sister's empty room, which just a few days ago was filled with all Mindy's possessions: her clothes, her furniture, her memories, her stuff. But now it all remained empty, along with her side of the bathroom sink, her favorite spot on the couch, and the most obvious, the deserted place next to me in the backseat of the car.

The days following were occupied with the same awkwardness, and of course, the many phone calls made by my parents just to check up on my sister. Yet, as days evolved into months, things started to return to normal, and we all got used to the eerie, almost mysterious void in our house; even the phone calls began to decrease. I took a couple of wild trips to visit my sister, and I could tell she did not miss home very much, maybe not even at all. As a matter of fact, she seemed to belong there and the more I visited her over the years, the greater the urge I harbored to discover what it felt like to be on my own and free from parental eyes.

Sooner than even I expected, it was my turn to take that first flight from the nest. This time, my going did not mirror Mindy's leaving at all. Even though I was only forty minutes away from home, my parents appeared delighted to see me leave. It took me about two hours to pack up all my things, and I was ready to go. My mom did not even accompany my dad when he dropped me off; she just said her good-bye, gave me a hug, and off I went. We unloaded all my things into my new apartment, and as soon as I was situated, I reassured my dad that I was going to be fine. He said his quick good-bye and he was gone. It was simple—it was almost too easy. No big sighs, no tears, no awkward feelings. When I returned home the next weekend to pick up a few things I had left behind, my parents had already started renovating my room into a library. I could scarcely believe it; it was as if they could not wait for me to leave. However, I did have to suffer through the phone calls, just so they knew I was still alive. Finally, I knew how it felt to be truly independent as I began my own journey into adulthood. The courageous leap out of the nest was well worth it.

"Many parents are emotionally unprepared for the time when their children leave home," explains Professor Lee Handy, an educational psychologist at the University of Calgary. "They say, 'I thought this parenting business was never going to end and the next day it was gone'" (McLean 35). Still, he says parents who suffer the depression known as "empty-nest syndrome" should not be too hard on themselves. Nevertheless, the professor emphasizes that it is unrealistic not to see the "empty nest" as one of life's rites of passage. He continues, "There is nothing wrong with parents letting their offspring know they are having difficulty with the separation," yet he recommends parents draw upon their own coping skills rather than intrude on their children's newfound freedom. "The point to remember," cautions Handy, "is that children only fly the nest if the parents have done a good job" (McLean 35).

The process of leaving home is an important part of the transition to adult life. Whereas in the past leaving home was usually associated with marriage, now the move from the parental home is increasingly concerned with need for independence. A study done by F. Goldscheider in 1993 states, "In most families, however, the direction of generational disagreement is likely to be reversed: Children are likely to be ahead of their parents in expecting to leave home before marriage." Goldscheider also goes on to explain, "Young adults have been leaving home at earlier ages through much of the 20th century, and they have been increasingly leaving home not to get married but for premarital residential independence, alone or with roommates" (858). In addition, Nicholas Buck and Jacqueline Scott state in the *Journal of Marriage & the Family,* "Fewer parents expected premarital independence for their children than their children did for themselves" (871).

Another important aspect for children leaving the nest is the need for continuous parental support. Parental support should reinforce the effects of their children's expectations about routes to residential independence. "Increasing parental support for leaving home is very important in the trend toward earlier residential independence" (Buck 865). Also, researchers Lynn White and Naomi Lacy state, "Leaving home for school, presumably with high achievement, regardless of the age, requires continuous parental support. Children's status attainment is maximized if they continue to receive substantial parental sponsorship into their early 20s. Regardless of the pathway from home, children's education will benefit from continued support" (984).

For adolescents, leaving home can be overwhelming; they can suddenly not feel as grown up as they did in the previous days of preparation. A compelling sense of adventure is mixed with the uncertainty. On the other hand, parents must adjust to the empty nest—physically, psychologically, and emotionally. Parents suddenly realize a previously held image of their child is frozen in their minds, and they will need to adjust to their child's passage into adulthood. It is usually a sobering experience for everyone involved, but all children inch closer to the edge and sooner than later, it is time to take off.

Works Cited

Buck, Nicholas, and Jacqueline Scott. "She's Leaving Home: But Why? An Analysis of Young People Leaving the Parental Home." *Journal of Marriage & the Family* (Nov. 1993): 863–875.

Goldscheider, F. *Leaving Home before Marriage.* Madison: University of Wisconsin Press, 1993.

Limon, Linda. Personal Interview. 27 February 2001.

Limon, Manuel. Personal Interview. 27 February 2001.

Limon, Mindy. Personal Interview. 28 February 2001.

McLean, Candice. "What Happens When They Leave Home." *Newsmagazine* 21 Sept. 1998: 35–36.

White, Lynn, and Naomi Lacy. "The Effects of Age at Home Leaving and Pathways from Home on Educational Attainment." *Journal of Marriage & the Family* (Nov. 1997): 982–996.

2

CHILDHOOD

When we speak of rites of passage, we refer to ritual acts observed by a particular group to mark life's major transformations. Childhood rites of passage include physical milestones: a baby's first steps, a child's first words and first day of school, no doubt more important to the parent than to the youngster whose achievements are noted in baby books or captured on film. The writers in this unit comment on the past, some from a parent's perspective witnessing a child's growth and maturity, and others from the perspective of adults looking back on childhood and now recognizing defining moments in their lives.

Many of these works are anchored in the writers' early experiences. Reliving these archetypal moments in childhood helps reveal who the writers are and how they became who they are. For many of the writers, an archetypal experience of growing up has meant moving away from the safe world of childhood to a new world of possibilities, both intriguing and sobering.

In "Rites of Passage," poet Sharon Olds recounts her young son's birthday party and observes the slow, yet startling, transformation of boys into men. Both "The First Day" and "My Papa's Waltz" suggest the significance of childhood memories and the volatile relationship with parents, and how the two can shape our lives in irreversible ways.

This passage is an excerpt from JOHN HOLT's *Freedom and Beyond,* published in 1972. Holt, a former schoolteacher, is the author of several books on alternative education, including *How Children Fail* (1964) and *How Children Learn* (1967), in which he investigates and challenges the American educational system. Holt died in 1985.

JOHN HOLT

THREE KINDS OF DISCIPLINE

A child, in growing up, may meet and learn from three different kinds of disciplines. The first and most important is what we might call the Discipline of Nature or of Reality. When he is trying to do something real, if he does the wrong thing or doesn't do the right one, he doesn't get the result he wants. If he doesn't pile one block right on top of another, or tries to build on a slanting surface, his tower falls down. If he hits the wrong key, he hears the wrong note. If he doesn't hit the nail squarely on the head, it bends, and he has to pull it out and start with another. If he doesn't measure properly what he is trying to build, it won't open, close, fit, stand up, fly, float, whistle, or do whatever he wants it to do. If he closes his eyes when he swings, he doesn't hit the ball. A child meets this kind of discipline every time he tries to *do* something, which is why it is so important in school to give children more chances to do things, instead of just reading or listening to someone talk (or pretending to). This discipline is a good teacher. The learner never has to wait long for his answer; it usually comes quickly, often instantly. Also it is clear, and very often points toward the needed correction; from what happened he can not only see that what he did was wrong, but also why, and what he needs to do instead. Finally, and most important, the giver of the answer, call it Nature, is impersonal, impartial, and indifferent. She does not give opinions, or make judgments: she cannot be wheedled, bullied, or fooled; she does not get angry or disappointed; she does not praise or blame; she does not remember past failures or hold grudges; with her one always gets a fresh start, this time is the one that counts.

The next discipline we might call the Discipline of Culture, of Society, of What People Really Do. Man is a social, a cultural animal. Children sense around them this culture, this network of agreements, customs, habits, and rules binding the adults together. They want to understand it and be a part of it. They watch very carefully what people around them are doing and want to do the same. They want to do right, unless they become convinced they can't do right. Thus children rarely misbehave seriously in church, but sit as quietly as they can. The example of all those grownups is contagious. Some mysterious ritual is going on, and children, who like rituals, want to be part of it. In the same way, the little children that I see at concerts or operas, though they may fidget a little, or perhaps take a nap now and then, rarely make any disturbance. With all those grownups sitting there, neither moving nor talking, it is the most natural thing in the world to imitate them. Children who live among adults who are habitually courteous to each other, and to them, will soon learn to be courteous. Children who live surrounded by people who speak a certain way will speak that way, however much we may try to tell them that speaking that way is bad or wrong.

The third discipline is the one most people mean when they speak of discipline—the Discipline of Superior Force, of sergeant to private, of "you do what I tell you or I'll make you wish you had." There is bound to be some of this in a child's life. Living as we do surrounded by things that can hurt children, or that children can hurt, we cannot avoid it. We can't afford to let a small child find out from experience the danger of playing in a busy street, or of fooling with the pots on the top of a stove, or of eating up the pills in the medicine cabinet. So, along with other precautions, we say to him, "Don't play in the street, or touch things on the stove, or go into the medicine cabinet, or I'll punish you." Between him and the danger too great for him to imagine we put a lesser danger, but one he can imagine and maybe therefore wants to avoid. He can have no idea of what it would be like to be hit by a car, but he can imagine being shouted at, or spanked, or sent to his room. He avoids these substitutes for the greater danger until he can understand it and avoid it for its own sake. But we ought to use this discipline only when it is necessary to protect the life, health, safety, or well-being of people or other living creatures, or to prevent destruction of things that people care about. We ought not to assume too long, as we usually do, that a child cannot understand the real nature of the danger from which we want to protect him. The sooner he avoids the danger, not to escape our punishment, but as a matter of good sense, the better. He can learn that faster than we think. In Mexico, for example, where people drive their cars with a good deal of spirit, I saw many children no older than five or four walking unattended on the streets. They understood about cars, they knew what to do. A child whose life is full of the threat and fear of punishment is locked into babyhood. There is no way for him to grow up, to learn to take responsibility for his life and acts. Most important of all, we should not assume that having to yield to the threat of our superior force is good for the child's character. It is never good for *anyone*'s character. To bow to superior force makes us feel impotent and cowardly for not having had the strength or courage to resist. Worse, it makes us resentful and vengeful. We can hardly wait to make someone pay for our humiliation, yield to us as we were once made to yield. No, if we cannot always avoid using the discipline of Superior Force, we should at least use it as seldom as we can.

There are places where all three disciplines overlap. Any very demanding human activity combines in it the disciplines of Superior Force, of Culture, and of Nature. The novice will be told, "Do it this way, never mind asking why, just do it that way, that is the way we always do it." But it probably *is* just the way they always do it, and usually for the very good reason that it is a way that has been found to work. Think, for example, of ballet training. The student in a class is told to do this exercise, or that; to stand so; to do this or that with his head, arms, shoulders, abdomen, hips, legs, feet. He is constantly corrected. There is no argument. But behind these seemingly autocratic demands by the teacher lie many decades of custom and tradition, and behind that, the necessities of dancing itself. You cannot make the moves of classical ballet unless over many years you have acquired, and renewed every day, the needed strength and suppleness in scores of muscles and joints. Nor can you do the difficult motions, making them look easy, unless you have learned hundreds of easier ones first. Dance teachers may not always agree on all the details of teaching these strengths and skills. But no novice could learn them all by himself. You could not go for a night or two to watch the ballet and then, without any other knowledge at all, teach yourself how to do it. In the same way, you would be unlikely to learn any complicated and difficult human activity without drawing heavily on the experience of those who know it better. But the point is that the authority of these experts or teachers stems from, grows out of their greater competence and experience, the fact that what they do *works,* not the fact that they happen to be the teacher and as such have the power to kick a student out of the class. And the further point is that children are always and everywhere attracted to that competence, and ready and eager to submit themselves to a discipline that grows out of it. We hear constantly that children will never do anything unless compelled to by bribes or threats. But in their private lives, or in extracurricular activities in school, in sports, music, drama, art, running a newspaper, and so on, they often submit themselves willingly and wholeheartedly to very intense disciplines, simply because they want to learn to do a given thing well. Our Little-Napoleon football coaches, of whom we have too many and hear far too much, blind us to the fact that millions of children work hard every year getting better at sports and games without coaches barking and yelling at them.

JOURNAL PROMPT:

Write about a time you experienced or witnessed one of Holt's three kinds of discipline. What was your reaction?

COLLABORATIVE EXERCISE:

Working in small groups, first list five situations where a child might encounter one of Holt's three kinds of discipline. (Examples: stealing from the corner grocery store, cheating on a test at school, lying, talking back, etc.) Then, discuss why Holt might recommend a particular kind of discipline and how he would envision the learning process unfolding. Be specific (i.e., nature or reality, culture or society, superior force, or all three).

ESSAY ASSIGNMENT:

1. Holt's essay invites the reader to consider the issue of child rearing as it relates to how a child learns. Does Holt's "Three Kinds of Discipline" support the need for a rite of passage from innocence and childhood to autonomy and adolescence?
2. Interview your grandparents (or older relatives or friends), asking them about the type of discipline they experienced as a child. Then, interview your parents or someone from your parents' generation. Ask them the

same questions. As you compare the different generations, do you note a change in parenting styles? If so, to what do you attribute the change?

3. Devise a lesson for preschool or early elementary classes (math, science, or language arts) that provides students the opportunity to learn from natural consequences. (Note: In explaining your lesson, define your terms, number your instructions, and put the steps in chronological order.)

Poet SHARON OLDS was born in 1942 in San Francisco, and educated at Stanford University and Columbia University. She has received many prestigious awards for her work, including the Lamont Poetry Selection for 1983 and the National Book Critics Circle Award for her collection *The Dead and the Living,* from which this poem is taken. She teaches poetry workshops at New York University and at Goldwater Hospital in New York. Her most recent publication is *The Wellspring,* a collection of poems that explores childhood, sexual awakening, childbirth, parenthood, and adult love.

SHARON OLDS

Rites of Passage

As the guests arrive at my son's party
they gather in the living room—
short men, men in first grade
with smooth jaws and chins.
Hands in pockets, they stand around
jostling, jockeying for place, small fights
breaking out and calming. One says to another
How old are you? Six. I'm seven. So?
They eye each other, seeing themselves
tiny in the other's pupils. They clear their
throats a lot, a room of small bankers,
they fold their arms and frown. *I could beat you*
up, a seven says to a six,
the dark cake, round and heavy as a
turret, behind them on the table. My son,
freckles like specks of nutmeg on his cheeks,
chest narrow as the balsa keel of a
model boat, long hands
cool and thin as the day they guided him

out of me, speaks up as a host
for the sake of the group.
We could easily kill a two-year-old,
he says in his clear voice. The other
men agree, they clear their throats
like Generals, they relax and get down to
playing war, celebrating my son's life.

JOURNAL PROMPT:

Why do you suppose the author chose to title her poem "Rites of Passage"?

COLLABORATIVE EXERCISE:

Record all the words and phrases Olds uses to suggest combat, competition, and stereotypical male mannerisms. How do these contribute to the theme or purpose of the poem? In your opinion, is she successful in getting her point across?

ESSAY ASSIGNMENT:

1. The poem invites a consideration of the nature vs. nurture issue as it relates to child rearing. How much influence do you think parents have on how their children are raised?
2. Do you think it's possible to create an environment for children fairly free of gender bias? Why or why not?
3. Write a letter to the editor of your local newspaper in which you argue for or against the marketing of war toys.

EDWARD P. JONES was nominated for a 1992 National Book Award. This selection is from *Lost in the City,* a collection of short stories that centers on the lives of African Americans living in Washington, D.C. The nearly universal rite of passage of a child's first day of school is the focus of this particular piece, as the author invites the reader to revisit the moment in which we first felt separate from a parent or guardian.

EDWARD P. JONES

THE FIRST DAY

On an otherwise unremarkable September morning, long before I learned to be ashamed of my mother, she takes my hand and we set off down New Jersey

Avenue to begin my very first day of school. I am wearing a checkered-like blue-and-green cotton dress, and scattered about these colors are bits of yellow and white and brown. My mother has uncharacteristically spent nearly an hour on my hair that morning, plaiting and replaiting so that now my scalp tingles. Whenever I turn my head quickly, my nose fills with the faint smell of Dixie Peach hair grease. The smell is somehow a soothing one now and I will reach for it time and time again before the morning ends. All the plaits, each with a blue barrette near the tip and each twisted into an uncommon sturdiness, will last until I go to bed that night, something that has never happened before. My stomach is full of milk and oatmeal sweetened with brown sugar. Like everything else I have on, my pale green slip and underwear are new, the underwear having come three to a plastic package with a little girl on the front who appears to be dancing. Behind my ears, my mother, to stop my whining, has dabbed the stingiest bit of her gardenia perfume, the last present my father gave her before he disappeared into memory. Because I cannot smell it, I have only her word that the perfume is there. I am also wearing yellow socks trimmed with thin lines of black and white around the tops. My shoes are my greatest joy, black patent-leather miracles, and when one is nicked at the toe later that morning in class, my heart will break.

I am carrying a pencil, a pencil sharpener, and a small ten-cent tablet with a black-and-white speckled cover. My mother does not believe that a girl in kindergarten needs such things, so I am taking them only because of my insistent whining and because they are presented from our neighbors, Mary Keith and Blondelle Harris. Miss Mary and Miss Blondelle are watching my two younger sisters until my mother returns. The women are as precious to me as my mother and sisters. Out playing one day, I have overheard an older child, speaking to another child, call Miss Mary and Miss Blondelle a word that is brand new to me. This is my mother: When I say the word in fun to one of my sisters, my mother slaps me across the mouth and the word is lost for years and years.

All the way down New Jersey Avenue, the sidewalks are teeming with children. In my neighborhood, I have many friends, but I see none of them as my mother and I walk. We cross New York Avenue, we cross Pierce Street, and we cross L and K, and still I see no one who knows my name. At I Street, between New Jersey Avenue and Third Street, we enter Seaton Elementary School, a timeworn, sad-faced building across the street from my mother's church, Mt. Carmel Baptist.

Just inside the front door, women out of the advertisements in *Ebony* are greeting other parents and children. The woman who greets us has pearls thick as jumbo marbles that come down almost to her navel, and she acts as if she had known me all my life, touching my shoulder, cupping her hand under my chin. She is enveloped in a perfume that I only know is not gardenia. When, in answer to her question, my mother tells her that we live at 1227 New Jersey Avenue, the woman first seems to be picturing in her head where we live. Then she shakes her head and says that we are at the wrong school, that we should be at Walker-Jones.

My mother shakes her head vigorously. "I want her to go here," my mother says. "If I'da wanted her some-place else, I'da took her there." The woman continues to act as if she has known me all my life, but she tells my mother that we live beyond the area that Seaton serves. My mother is not convinced and for several more minutes she questions the woman about why I cannot attend Seaton. For as many Sundays as I can remember, perhaps even Sundays when I was in her womb, my mother has pointed across I Street to Seaton as we come and go to Mt. Carmel. "You gonna go there and learn about the whole world." But one of the guardians of that place is saying no, and no again. I am learning this about my mother: The higher up on the scale of respectability a person is—and teachers are rather high up in her eyes—the less she is liable to let them push her around. But finally, I see in her eyes the closing gate, and she takes my hand and we leave the building. On the steps, she stops as people move past us on either side.

"Mama, I can't go to school?"

She says nothing at first, then takes my hand again and we are down the steps quickly and nearing New Jersey Avenue before I can blink. This is my mother: She says, "One monkey don't stop no show."

Walker-Jones is a larger, new school and I immediately like it because of that. But it is not across the street from my mother's church, her rock, one of her connections to God, and I sense her doubts as she absently rubs her thumb over the back of her hand. We find our way to the crowded auditorium where gray metal chairs are set up in the middle of the room. Along the wall to the left are tables and other chairs. Every chair seems occupied by a child or adult. Somewhere in the room a child is crying, a cry that rises above the buzz-talk of so many people. Strewn about the floor are dozens and dozens of pieces of white paper, and people are walking over them without any thought of picking them up. And seeing this lack of concern, I am all of a sudden afraid.

"Is this where they register for school?" my mother asks a woman at one of the tables.

The woman looks up slowly as if she has heard this question once too often. She nods. She is tiny, almost as small as the girl standing beside her. The woman's hair is set in a mass of curlers and all of those curlers are made of paper money, here a dollar bill, there a five-dollar bill. The girl's hair is arrayed in curls, but some of them are beginning to droop and this makes me happy. On the table beside the woman's pocketbook is a large notebook, worthy of someone in high school, and looking at me looking at the notebook, the girl places her hand possessively on it. In her other hand she holds several pencils with thick crowns of additional erasers.

"These the forms you gotta use?" my mother asks the woman, picking up a few pieces of the paper from the table. "Is this what you have to fill out?"

The woman tells her yes, but that she need fill out only one.

"I see," my mother says, looking about the room. Then: "Would you help me with this form? That is, if you don't mind."

The woman asks my mother what she means.

"This form. Would you mind helpin' me fill it out?"

The woman still seems not to understand.

"I can't read it. I don't know how to read or write, and I'm askin' you to help me." My mother looks at me, then looks away. I know almost all of her looks, but this one is brand new to me. "Would you help me, then?"

The woman says "Why sure," and suddenly she appears happier, so much more satisfied with everything. She finishes the form for her daughter and my mother and I step aside to wait for her. We find two chairs nearby and sit. My mother is now diseased, according to the girl's eyes, and until the moment her mother takes her and the form to the front of the auditorium, the girl never stops looking at my mother. I stare back at her. "Don't stare," my mother says to me. "You know better than that."

Another woman out of the *Ebony* ads takes the woman's child away. Now, the woman says upon returning, let's see what we can do for you two.

My mother answers the questions the woman reads off the form. They start with my last name, and then on to the first and middle names. This is school, I think. This is going to school. My mother slowly enunciates each word of my name. This is my mother: As the questions go on, she takes from her pocketbook document after document, as if they will support my right to attend school, as if she has been saving them up for just this moment. Indeed, she takes out more papers than I have ever seen her do in other places: my birth certificate, my baptismal record, a doctor's letter concerning my bout with chicken pox, rent receipts, records of immunization, a letter about our public assistance payments, even her marriage license—every single paper that has anything even remotely to do with my five-year-old life. Few of the papers are needed here, but it does not matter and my mother continues to pull out the documents with the purposefulness of a magician pulling out a long string of scarves. She has learned that money is the beginning and end of everything in this world, and when the woman finishes, my mother offers her fifty cents, and the woman accepts it without hesitation. My mother and I are just about the last parent and child in the room.

My mother presents the form to a woman sitting in front of the stage, and the woman looks at it and writes something on a white card, which she gives to my mother. Before long, the woman who has taken the girl with the drooping curls appears from behind us, speaks to the sitting woman, and introduces herself to my mother and me. She's to be my teacher, she tells my mother. My mother stares.

We go into the hall, where my mother kneels down to me. Her lips are quivering. "I'll be back to pick you up at twelve o'clock. I don't want you to go nowhere. You just wait right here. And listen to every word she say." I touch her lips and press them together. It is an old, old game between us. She puts my hand down at my side, which is not part of the game. She stands and looks a second at the teacher, then she turns and walks away. I see where she has darned one of her socks the night before. Her shoes make loud sounds in the hall. She passes through the doors and I can still hear the loud sounds of her shoes. And even when the teacher turns me toward the classrooms and I hear what must be the singing and talking of all the children in the world, I can still hear my mother's footsteps above it all.

JOURNAL PROMPT:

Recall a time when, as a child, you were separated from a loved one: a parent, grandparent, sibling, or close friend. How did you handle the feelings engendered by the separation?

COLLABORATIVE EXERCISE:

Discuss at least three new things the young girl discovers about her mother on the first day of school. In what ways will these things change her relationship with her mother? Be specific.

ESSAY ASSIGNMENT:

1. Write an essay about your memories of the first day of school. Include details such as what you wore and who took you to school. Was the separation painful? What were some of your fears and expectations?
2. As a young child, were you ever ashamed of a parent or guardian? Describe the circumstances and how you felt at the time. Have your feelings changed now that time has passed?
3. What are some of the things a parent can do to lessen a child's separation anxiety?

KIERNAN EGAN, an associate professor of education at Simon Fraser University, is the author of *Educational Development,* from which this selection was taken. He is interested in engaging children in learning by examining the four stages of educational development: mythic, romantic, philosophic, and ironic. This selection focuses on children four to ten years of age in the first stage of development. Writing primarily for educators of young children, the author suggests that in order to interest children in learning, it is important to understand that "children's major intellectual tools and categories are not rational and logical but emotional and moral. . . . The most effective teaching will be that which provides best access to the world, by organizing what is to be known in terms that children can best absorb and use."

KIERNAN EGAN

THE MYTHIC STAGE

Characteristics

WHAT CHILDREN KNOW BEST

It is a truism that in educating young children, we should start from what they know best and expand outward from that. This notion, so obvious to us today, is relatively new. When James Boswell asked Dr. Johnson what children should learn first, Johnson replied:

> there is no matter what children should learn first, any more than what leg you shall put into your breeches first. Sir, you may stand disputing which is best to put in first, but in the meantime your backside is bare. Sir, while you stand considering which of two things you should teach your child first, another boy has learnt 'em both.[1]

We still tend to stand disputing while our educational backside is bare, but, these days, we do have some grounds for thinking it is important that children should learn certain things first and that there is a certain sequence in which things should be introduced.

Acceptance of the truism that one should begin from what children know best has led to various forms of the expanding horizons curriculum. Take, for example, the social studies curriculum that is dominant throughout North America and, increasingly, in Great Britain. We may infer at a glance what its designers assume children know best. It begins with units on families, homes, communities, and so on, those things children have daily contact with. Children, it is assumed, will have developed a concept of family, which can be used as the basis for the content of a unit that expands that concept. That is, despite rhetoric about inquiry-based curricula, the implicit question about what children know best is answered *in terms of content.*

Proponents of a child-centered curriculum propose "relevance to the child's needs" as one of the principles to be used in constructing the curriculum. A teacher might use the child's experience of shopping in a supermarket as a starting point for a unit; and this might lead to lessons on such topics as the typical layout of a supermarket, the sources of various products, the means by which the products are brought to the shelves, making change, the structure of

---

[1] James Boswell, *London Journal, 1762–1763,* ed. Frederick A. Pottle (New York: McGraw Hill, 1950), p. 323.

neighborhoods, and other kinds of shops. That is, the child's needs are interpreted in terms of specific content to be learned. Even the more radical approach to early education that claims to construct a curriculum out of children's expressed interests seeks and accepts expression of these interests in terms of content. What alternative is there?

Instead of focusing on such content, we might examine those things that most engage children's interest (for example, fairy stories and games) and try to see "through" their content to the main mental categories children seem to use in making sense of them. I will consider stories and games in more detail below, but even a casual view from this perspective suggests that what children know best when they come to school are love, hate, joy, fear, good, and bad. That is, they know best the most profound human emotions and the bases of morality. Children, for instance, have direct access to the wildest flights of fantasy—to princesses, monsters, and witches in bizarre places and once upon a times. Typical fairy stories are built on vivid and dramatic conflicts involving love, hate, joy, fear, good, bad, and so on. Their engaging power derives from their being the purest embodiments of the most basic emotions and moral conflicts.

This simple observation undermines the foundation of the typical expanding horizons curriculum, allowing us to see that children's access to the world need not be, as it were, along lines of content associations moving gradually out from families, homes, communities, and daily experience, or from things judged relevant on grounds of some kind of physical proximity. Far from condemning ourselves to provincial concerns in the early grades, we may provide direct access to anything in the world that can be connected with basic emotions and morality. We will see what effect this may have on the design of lessons, units, and curricula after considering some characteristics of children's thinking.

MYTHIC THINKING

I call this first stage of educational development mythic because young children's thinking shares important features with the kind of thinking evident in the stories of myth-using people. I will consider four roughly parallel features.

First, a main function of myth is to provide its users with intellectual security. It does this by providing absolute accounts of why things are the way they are and by fixing the meaning of events by relating them to sacred models.[2] All people look for intellectual security amid the changes of life in the world, and

---

[2] For some analyses of mythic thinking useful in this context see Bronislaw Malinowski, "Myth in Primitive Psychology," *Magic, Science and Religion and Other Essays* (New York: Doubleday, 1954); Mircea Eliade, *Myth and Reality* (New York: Harper and Row, 1963); Claude Lévi-Strauss, *The Savage Mind* (Chicago: University of Chicago Press, 1966); Claude Lévi-Strauss, *Structural Anthropology* (New York: Basic Books, 1963); and Claude Lévi-Strauss, *The Raw and the Cooked* (New York: Harper and Row, 1969).

young children in western industrial societies seem to establish a first security in a manner not dissimilar from that evident in myth stories. They seek absolute accounts of things, and they want precise, fixed meanings Young children have great difficulty deriving meaning from the ambiguous and complex. For reasons I will discuss later, children need to know how to feel about a thing in order for that thing to be clear and meaningful; they need to establish some personal and affective relationship with what is being learned.

Second, myth stories and children lack what has been generally called a sense of otherness—concepts of historical time, physical regularities, logical relationships, causality, and geographical space. Some analysts of myth suggest one of myth's functions is to obliterate history, to assert that nothing has changed in the world since the sacred beginning, thus providing a kind of eternally valid charter for things as they are. Children's lack of the concepts of otherness, however, may be accounted for simply as a lack of experience and knowledge of change and causality on a historical scale in a geographical arena.

A third feature of mythic thinking is its, lack of a clear sense of the world as autonomous and objective. The conception of the world as an impersonal, objective entity is the achievement of a mature rationality. The child's world is full of entities charged with and given meaning by those things the child knows best: love, hate, joy, fear, good, bad. The world is, as it were, absorbed into the child's vivid mental life. Much more than is the case for an adult, children's imaginative life colors and charges their environment with a meaning derived from within. Piaget has expressed this well in the observation that at this age there is "a sort of confusion between the inner and the outer, or a tendency to fix in objects something which is the result of the activity of the thinking subject."[3]

Fourth, myth stories tend to be articulated on binary oppositions. In the case of myth stories, the oppositions may be between important elements in the life of their users: nature/culture, life/death, raw/cooked, honey/ashes. In the mental life of children, important basic oppositions include big/little, love/hate, security/fear, courage/cowardice, good/bad. Typical fairy stories are built on sets of such binary opposites, and children tend initially to make sense of things in binary terms, using only a couple of concepts at one time. These binary opposites are then elaborated by a process of mediation between the binary poles. For example, the concepts of hot and cold will normally be learned as the first temperature distinctions. These will then be mediated by warm or by quite hot and quite cold. Thereafter, children may learn to mediate between cold and warm, and warm and hot, leading gradually to a set of concepts along the temperature continuum. Attempts to mediate between other binary opposites perceived in their environments lead to more than simple conceptual elaborations along continua of size, speed, temperature. When the same process tries to

---

[3] Jean Piaget, "Children's Philosophies," *Handbook of Child Psychology*, ed. C. Murchison (Worcester, Mass.: Clark University Press, 1931), pp. 377–91.

mediate between humans and animals, we get those dressed and talking bears, dogs, rabbits that play so prominent a part in children's imaginations. Attempts to mediate between life and death give us ghosts and spirits of various kinds—things that are both alive and dead, as things warm are both hot and cold.

This is not to suggest that children at the mythic stage can understand things *only* if they are put in terms of binary opposites. Greater or lesser elaboration between binary opposites will have been achieved depending on the degree of progress they have made through the stage. However, binary opposites are still fundamental to children's thinking at this mythic stage; even though considerable elaboration from the initial binary terms may have been achieved, meaning derives most clearly from the basic binary distinctions. That is, if something is to be most clearly meaningful, it should be built on and elaborated from clear binary opposites.

Claude Lévi-Strauss concludes that myth stories are also built on or elaborated from basic binary opposites perceived in their users' environments.[4] Lévi-Strauss has also argued, drawing on Roman Jacobson's work in phonetics, that the kind of binary thinking I have alluded to is basic to all thought and reflects a basic structure of the human mind. Whether or not this is the case, it is evident that such binary structures are prominent in young children's thinking.

These four characteristics of young children's thinking, then, are important because they influence profoundly how children can derive meaning from the world, how they learn, and what they can learn. Taken together, these characteristics help to explain the power of stories in the mental life of young children and lead to clear conclusions for teaching, learning, and motivation. The ability of stories to engage children's interest is worth dwelling on a little more, because features that give stories their power can also be used in engaging children's enthusiasm in learning about the world. First, though, we should consider the general *process* whereby the characteristics of children's thinking outlined above are used in their learning. That is, we should characterize in a general way *how* children learn at the mythic stage.

PROJECTION AND ABSORPTION: LEARNING, FEELING, AND MEANING

Learning at the mythic stage involves making sense of the unknown world without in terms of the known world within. The things children have available to learn with are those things they know best[:] love, hate, joy, fear, good, bad. These are the intellectual tools and conceptual categories that children can employ in making sense of the outside world. The process of learning at the mythic stage involves projecting these known things onto the outside world and, as it were, absorbing the world to them.

---

[4] See Lévi-Strauss, "The Structural Study of Myths," *Structural Anthropology;* Lévi-Strauss, *The Savage Mind;* and Lévi-Strauss, *The Raw and the Cooked.*

Initially, the world becomes known in terms of the basic forms and characteristics of children's mental life. It could hardly be otherwise. Learning is a matter of connecting the known categories to the outside world and fitting the things in the world to them. The clearer the connection between categories and things in the world, the more successful will be the learning. As children develop through the mythic stage, knowledge about the world expands the initial set of mental categories. The world provides not only knowledge as such, but the things in the world that the child-perceives and experiences become concepts the child thinks *with;* that is, the child uses the world to think with. I will discuss this in more detail at the beginning of the next chapter when considering the move from the mythic to the romantic stage.

The confusion between inner and outer that Piaget observed, which I have described as the result of making sense of the unknown world without in terms appropriate to the child's mental life, is not a confusion restricted to children. It persists in all of us to a greater or lesser degree, though, in at least one dimension, we measure development in terms of the clarity with which we can distinguish between what is true about the world and what we think about the world. This confusion is also a common feature of myth-using people's thinking.[5] It is not, then, simply an error to be overcome, it is a valid way of making sense of the world and of one's place in it. For young children, it is a *necessary* way of making sense of things and of learning.

This is a point I will repeat in different ways for each stage; we must be sensitive to the changing character of children's thinking and learning and must not see any of the stages as confusions or errors. They are stages of development, and the achievement of further development does not come by hurrying children to make sense of things in more sophisticated ways. The first requirement for educational development is that children develop the characteristics of each stage as fully as possible.

Young children's thinking and learning are in important qualitative ways different from adults'. Children's major intellectual tools and categories are not rational and logical but emotional and moral. This is not a casual nor insignificant difference. It means that access to the world must be provided in the terms of emotion and morality, or knowledge will be simply meaningless. It will always be possible to make children store things in memory and repeat them on request, but such knowledge will remain inert and will contribute nothing toward the development of children's understanding of the world or their place in it. True learning at this stage must involve their being able to absorb the world to the categories of their own vivid mental life and to dialectically use the world to expand the intellectual categories they have available. The most effective teaching will be that which provides best access to the world, by organizing what is to be known in terms that children can best absorb and use.

---

[5] See Lévi-Strauss, *The Savage Mind.*

Now we need to see how the characteristics of children's thinking that we have considered lead to principles for organizing knowledge in terms that children can best absorb and use. First, though, let us return to stories and see what clues their engaging power offers towards clarifying such principles.

THE NECESSITY OF THE STORY FORM

It is worth noting that analyses of the fairy stories that most powerfully engage children's interest suggest underlying characteristics similar to those outlined above as the basic characteristics of children's thinking.[6] The Grimm-type stories lack realistic concepts of action, place, change, causality; they make little call on the simultaneous combination of ideas; the number of characters is small and homogeneous; the characters are composed from one or two out standing characteristics (big and bad, beautiful and industrious, etc.); the characters are differentiated by simple contrasts, or binary opposites (rich or poor, big or little, obedient or disobedient, clever or stupid); meaning is always clear, in the sense that it is always understood who is to be approved of or disapproved of and what one should feel about the events.

The similarities are hardly surprising, though, given the close relationship between fairy stories, folktales, and myth stories. Like myth stories, fairy stories derive their power from being more or less pure reflections or embodiments of those characteristics basic to children's thinking. These are preeminently the terms in which children can make sense of things; they *understand* things put in these terms.

However, we need to ask what is a story? Perhaps the most important feature of a story is that it is the linguistic unit that can ultimately fix the meaning of the events that compose it. Take, for example, the event, "He shot Tom." By itself the event is not very meaningful; we don't know how or why or where he shot Tom, or who he and Tom are, or, most important, whether to feel glad or sorry that he shot Tom. The only linguistic unit that can finally answer all these questions is the story. The story, as Aristotle[7] pointed out, has a beginning that sets up expectations, a middle that complicates them, and an end that satisfies them. The meaning of an event in history cannot be fixed in any ultimate way because history has not ended—no one can establish finally that it was good or bad that, say, the French Revolution took place. As new things happen, we constantly reassess the meaning of all past events. We especially reassess how we *feel*—whether it was good or bad, whether we are glad or sorry that this or that happened. With a story, however, the meaning of events may be ultimately fixed. Each event has a place in the whole, and we know we have reached the end of a story when we know what to feel about all the events that compose it.

---

[6] See Karl Bühler, *The Mental Development of the Child,* trans. Oscar Oeser (London: Routledge and Kegan Paul, 1930).

[7] *Poetics.*

Another way of saying that the most important feature of stories is that they fix meaning is to say that the most important feature of stories is that they come to an end. That is, they don't just stop. The end involves satisfying the expectations set up in the beginning, thus creating a whole, a unit, within which meaning and feeling are bound together and ultimately fixed.[8]

If a necessary condition of best engaging children's interest in and understanding of knowledge is that it be organized into the kind of unit that fixes meaning and coheres with the other characteristics of children's thinking we have noted, then the story form is not something educators can ignore as significant only for fiction. Indeed, it must lie at the heart of all attempts to make the world meaningful to young children.

Before going on to consider how these characteristics common to simple stories and children's thinking yield principles for how to organize lessons and units, it is important to observe a basic distinction between stories and the story form. Stories are composed of fictional content. The story form refers to the abstract structure that underlies the content. This form/content distinction is a little unreal, but it serves to emphasize that my concern is not with the *content* of stories, but with the story *form*. That is, I am *not* advocating that we should tell children stories *about* whatever is to be learned; I am advocating something much more radical—that we use the main features of the simple story form to organize whatever is to be learned.

GAMES

This brief analysis of some underlying features of the story form and, by extension, children's thinking may seem to be leading somewhere if we have social studies content in mind. It may, however, appear quite opaque if we try to relate it to the physical sciences or mathematics. The connection between the characteristics of children's thinking and these subjects may become a little clearer when we consider that the features we have found underlying stories are also fundamental to children's games.

That is, young children's games have beginnings, middles, and ends. As with stories, they are thus able to reduce and limit reality, providing an arena within which children may feel secure because they know the rules. Within the limits of the game, the meaning of behavior is established clearly and precisely. In the imaginative content of games, binary opposites—fairies and witches, cops and robbers, war and team games—are common. As with fairy stories, the basic concepts of good, bad, fear, security, love, hate are basic to these games.

The importance of play and games in young children's learning is increasingly being recognized. What is not adequately recognized by educators, however, are the changing characteristics of children's games and the features of the

---

[8] See Frank Kermode, *The Sense of an Ending* (Oxford: Oxford University Press, 1966).

games that are most significant for encouraging learning at different stages of children's educational development. This theory may help to make a few useful initial distinctions in the appropriate characteristics for educational games at different stages.

JOURNAL PROMPT:

What is your favorite memory of play? Try to recall how old you were. Did you play alone or with others?

COLLABORATIVE EXERCISE:

Discuss how a detailed knowledge of the mythic stage might be helpful to a parent or teacher. In what specific ways might this information be utilized to improve the communication between adult and child?

ESSAY ASSIGNMENT:

1. Compare Egan's assertions about children, the mythic stage, and the learning process with those of another early childhood expert. (Suggestions: Maria Montessori, Jean Piaget, Rudolf Steiner, etc.)
2. Explore some of the imaginary games of childhood you have participated in or observed your own children enjoying. Offer details of those games, and respond to Egan's suggestion that "the basic concepts of good, bad, fear, security, love, hate are basic to these games."
3. Why is play so important to a child's development?

THEODORE ROETHKE was a prolific American poet, winner of the Pulitzer Prize (1953) and the National Book Award (1964). His evocative poems are a blend of introspection and landscape imagery, most noted for his accounts of childhood memories.

THEODORE ROETHKE

MY PAPA'S WALTZ

The whiskey on your breath
Could make a small boy dizzy;
But I hung on like death:
Such waltzing was not easy.

We romped until the pans
Slid from the kitchen shelf;
My mother's countenance
Could not unfrown itself.

The hand that held my wrist
Was battered on one knuckle;
At every step you missed
My right ear scraped a buckle.

You beat time on my head
With a palm caked hard by dirt,
Then waltzed me off to bed
Still clinging to your shirt.

JOURNAL PROMPT:

For many readers this poem resonates on a personal level, as it brings back memories of their own families. Write about your earliest memory of a relationship with a close relative.

COLLABORATIVE EXERCISE:

Readers are often divided about what Roethke's intent was in this poem. Is this poem a loving moment between father and son, or is it a scene of child abuse? Working in small groups, record supportive evidence for both sides. Rely only on the poem and not on personal experience.

ESSAY ASSIGNMENT:

1. Consider the poem in relationship to the extraordinary number of children who are now being raised by only one parent, usually the mother. The poem appears to record a fond memory of a father/child relationship. Research current statistics on children being raised without a father.
2. What are some of the possible drawbacks and consequences of being raised by only one parent?
3. Write an opinion piece in which you urge prospective parents to avail themselves of parenting classes.

JENNIFER BOJORQUEZ offers readers a provocative look at a book by Brown University professor William Damon, a child development specialist. Damon appears incredulous that parents today are raising their children with little discipline, which he believes must start with "something as simple as household chores." He suggests that baby boomers are more interested in preserving their children's self-esteem than instilling in them a sense of responsibility.

JENNIFER BOJORQUEZ

Spare the Chores, Spoil the Child

This article was published in the Sacramento Bee, *8/21/95.*

A few years ago, William Damon attended an international conference for child development experts in Germany and heard something that shocked him.

Household chores for children are out of fashion.

This news was delivered to the group by an expert who had completed a study on children and household chores. He said things-to-do lists hanging on the refrigerator door are from another era. The proportion of children doing chores—especially in Western countries—is decreasing, according to the study. That means that soon there might be no more nagging your kid to take out the garbage or to vacuum the living room. No more hassles over the cleaning of their rooms.

The expert then gave the reason: Parents have simply given up.

Damon, listening as the expert spoke with an approving voice, noticed that the other people in the room seemed to agree that the study's findings were positive. One person said it was about time that adults realize that kids' time is valuable, too.

"The parents said it was easier to do the chores themselves than to get their kids to do them," says Damon. "I couldn't believe it. . . . Everybody was acting as if this was right."

Damon says he then stood and listed the benefits of having children do household chores. But when he started talking about the work ethic, responsibility and the importance of helping in the community, he noticed that few seemed to agree with him.

"Everybody looked at me as if I was from Mars," says Damon. "It hit me: We have come too far. Our children are running our homes, and in the long run, it hurts them. We are bringing up a generation of self-indulgent, spoiled kids who whine to get their way. . . . Parents are giving in to this type of behavior because child care experts have told them that's the way it should be, and it starts with something as simple as household chores."

Damon himself is one of those experts. He is a professor in the education department at Brown University, and is considered a leader in his field. That conference, however, convinced him that there is something very wrong with the way we are bringing up our kids.

In his 246-page, highly praised book, *Greater Expectations,* Damon argues that dangerous misconceptions about children's developmental needs have resulted in an increase in youth violence, suicide, delinquency, teen pregnancies, poor social conduct and low academic achievement.

"Children need discipline. They need to be told 'no,'" he says in an interview. "But parents are afraid of hurting their children's self-esteem or hurting their feelings. . . . This is what they've been told by popular culture child care experts, and they are wrong."

Damon argues that children thrive on challenges because their abilities are tested, that children are capable of understanding serious discussions, that children must be taught morals early and that parental discipline, when applied thoughtfully, is good.

In other words, instead of lowering standards, we should increase standards, and have greater expectations of our children.

Our children, he argues, will adjust accordingly.

"Despite what parents may hear, children will not be scarred for life if you tell them 'no,'" says Damon. He emphasizes that he recognizes that there is abuse—that too many parents put too much pressure on their kids—but says that in the majority of the cases, parents and educators have lowered standards.

He particularly criticizes the self-esteem movement.

"We are telling children that they are great, but they haven't earned it. Yes, it's important to tell your children positive things, but telling your child everything he does is great is not good for him. It lowers his expectations and instills a sense of entitlement."

Damon's views are shared by a growing number of people in the child development community.

"We are telling them they are great for doing the minimal," says Daina Bluett, child development specialist for In-Charge, a national program that teaches parenting skills. "Children develop this sense that they are great and they are owed something without working for it. . . . The end result is that they feel they are entitled to $90 tennis shoes."

Damon blames a lot of this on baby boomers' belief that children should have the freedom to make their own decisions. Damon says a certain amount of such freedom is good, but it has gone too far. He says parents must return to a common-sense approach.

"I'm a parent. I know it's not easy. . . . but we as a society can't afford this. But it is something we can change."

"The next time your child tries to get out of a chore," he says, "talk to him or her about why it's important to do it. And make them do it. . . . Be consistent. After a while, probably a shorter time than most parents think, children will change."

And they'll be cleaning their rooms themselves.

JOURNAL PROMPT:

Did you have chores to do as a child? What were they?

COLLABORATIVE EXERCISE:

Working in small groups, share how you feel about assigning tasks to children. At what age do you think children should be responsible for helping around the house? Rely on your own childhood experience and/or your experience as a parent.

ESSAY ASSIGNMENT:

1. William Damon is critical of the self-esteem movement as the cause (in part) for children developing a sense that they are "owed something without working for it." Do you agree with his assessment?
2. Damon also blames baby boomers for a lowering of the expectations we have of children. Develop an argument, based upon what you know about baby boomers, in which you either agree with Damon's assessment or disagree.
3. Part of being an adult is accepting responsibility. Write about some ways, other than having a child do household chores, that parents can instill responsibility.

New England poet **ANNE SEXTON** (1928–1974) studied poetry under Robert Lowell at Boston University. Many scholars recognize her as an introspective writer who explored life through confessional poetry. In this poem, originally published in her collection *Live or Let Die* (1966), Sexton adopts the wise voice of a mother observing her daughter's passage into adolescence.

ANNE SEXTON

PAIN FOR A DAUGHTER

Blind with love, my daughter
has cried nightly for horses,
those long-necked marchers and churners
that she has mastered, any and all,

reigning them in like a circus hand—
the excitable muscles and the ripe neck;
tending this summer, a pony and a foal.
She who is too squeamish to pull
a thorn from the dog's paw,
watched her pony blossom with distemper,
the underside of the jaw swelling
like an enormous grape.
Gritting her teeth with love,
she drained the boil and scoured it
with hydrogen peroxide until pus
ran like milk on the barn floor.

Blind with loss all winter,
in dungarees, a ski jacket and a hard hat,
she visits the neighbors' stable,
our acreage not zoned for barns;
they who own the flaming horses
and the swan-whipped thoroughbred
that she tugs at and cajoles,
thinking it will burn like a furnace
under her small-hipped English seat.

Blind with pain she limps home.
The thoroughbred has stood on her foot.
He rested there like a building.
He grew into her foot until they were one.
The marks of the horseshoe printed
into her flesh, the tips of her toes
ripped off like pieces of leather,
three toenails swirled like shells
and left to float in blood in her riding boot.

Blind with fear, she sits on the toilet,
her foot balanced over the washbasin,
her father, hydrogen peroxide in hand,
performing the rites of the cleansing.
She bites on a towel, sucked in breath,
sucked in and arched against the pain,
her eyes glancing off me where
I stand at the door, eyes locked
on the ceiling, eyes of a stranger,
and then she cries . . .
Oh my God, help me!

Where a child would have cried *Mama!*
Where a child would have believed *Mama!*
she bit the towel and called on God
and I saw her life stretch out . . .
I saw her torn in childbirth,
and I saw her, at that moment,
in her own death and I knew that she
knew.

JOURNAL PROMPT:

As children, we responded to physical pain with tears, loud vocalizations, and fear of treatment. At some point we became more stoic when faced with physical discomfort. Reflect on this change in your own life. Include a comparison of an event in childhood with one much later. How were they different?

COLLABORATIVE EXERCISE:

Each stanza begins in a similar way: "Blind with love," "Blind with loss," "Blind with pain," "Blind with fear." How does each of these phrases reflect a gradual loss of innocence? Additionally, how do the last lines emphasize the impact of this life change on her daughter?

ESSAY ASSIGNMENT:

1. Both this work and "The First Day" have as one of their themes the issue of separation from a child that most parents experience numerous times throughout their lives. Compare how the theme of parent/child separation is communicated in these two works. Include a discussion of tone, vocabulary, imagery, and writer's voice.
2. Write about one of the first times in your life when you felt the weight of adult responsibility. How old were you? Did you feel ready to accept the seriousness of your responsibility?
3. The event detailed in "Pain for a Daughter" marked a significant turning point in the girl's life. Write about an intense change or initiation in your own life. What was the occasion? Student responses to this prompt will not be shared in class.

This excerpt, taken from the 1989 *Washington Post* series by reporter MICHELE L. NORRIS, follows the life of six-year-old Dooney Waters. It is a haunting portrayal of a youngster's life in the drug-infested inner city.

MICHELE L. NORRIS

A CHILD OF CRACK

Dooney Waters, a thickset 6-year-old missing two front teeth, sat hunched over a notebook, drawing a family portrait. First he sketched a stick-figure woman smoking a pipe twice her size. A coil of smoke rose from the pipe, which held a white square he called a "rock." Above that, he drew a picture of himself, another stick figure with tears falling from his face.

"Drugs have wrecked my mother," Dooney said as he doodled. "Drugs have wrecked a lot of mothers and fathers and children and babies. If I don't be careful, drugs are going to wreck me too."

His was a graphic rendering of the life of a child growing up in what police and social service workers have identified as a crack house, an apartment in Landover where people congregated to buy and use drugs. Dooney's life was punctuated by days when he hid behind his bed to eat sandwiches sent by teachers who knew he would get nothing else. Nights when Dooney wet his bed because people were "yelling and doing drugs and stuff." And weeks in which he barely saw his 32-year-old mother, who spent most of her time searching for drugs.

Addie Lorraine Waters, who described herself as a "slave to cocaine," said she let drug dealers use her apartment in exchange for the steady support of her habit. The arrangement turned Dooney's home into a modern-day opium den where pipes, spoons and needles were in supply like ketchup and straws at a fast-food restaurant.

The apartment was on Capital View Drive, site of more than a dozen slayings last year. Yet, the locks were removed from the front door to allow an unyielding tide of addicts and dealers to flow in and out. Children, particularly toddlers, commonly peered inside to ask: "Is my mommy here?" or "Have you seen my mommy?"

While he was living in the crack house, Dooney was burned when a woman tossed boiling water at his mother's face in a drug dispute, and his right palm was singed when his 13-year-old half brother handed him a soft drink can that had been used to heat crack cocaine on the stove.

Teachers said that Dooney often begged to be taken to their homes, once asking if he could stay overnight in his classroom. "I'll sleep on the floor," Dooney told an instructor in Greenbelt Center Elementary School's after-school counseling and tutorial program. "Please don't make me go home. I don't want to go back there."

Dooney was painfully shy or exhaustively outgoing, depending largely upon whether he was at home or in school—the one place where he could relax. In class, he played practical jokes on friends and passed out kisses and hugs to teachers. But his mood darkened when he boarded a bus for home. In Washington Heights, a community of federally subsidized apartments, he invariably plodded around with his chin on his chest, dragging his feet and sucking his thumb.

The violence that surrounded Dooney at home was, in most cases, a byproduct of the bustling drug trade. Washington Heights was host to one of the county's largest open-air drug markets until a series of police raids last winter drove the problem indoors, spawning several interior drug centers like the one where Dooney lived.

On Saturday, April 29, Dooney was sitting in the living room near his mother when a 15-year-old drug dealer burst in and tossed a pan of boiling water, a weapon that anybody with a stove could afford. Dooney, his mother and two neighbors recalled that the dealer then plopped down on a sofa and watched as Dooney's weeping mother soothed the burns on her shoulder and neck. Dooney also was at home when another adolescent enforcer leaned through an open window on Sunday, May 14, and pitched a blend of bleach and boiling water in the face of 19-year-old Clifford E. Bernard, a regular in the apartment. The right side of Bernard's face became a twisted mass of pink and brown scars, the price for ignoring a $150 debt.

"People around here don't play when you owe them money," said Sherry Brown, 25, a friend of Addie Waters who frequents the apartment. "These young boys around here will burn you in a minute if you so much as look at them the wrong way. I'm telling you sure as I'm sitting here, crack has made people crazy," said Brown, who said she smokes crack every day and has given birth to two crack-addicted babies in the last three years.

Almost everyone was welcome at "Addie's place." Her patrons included some unlikely characters, but as one said, "Addie don't turn nobody away." Not the 15-year-old who in May burned her furniture and clothing intentionally with a miniature blow torch. Not even the 21-year-old man who "accidentally" shot her 13-year-old son, Frank Russell West, five inches above the heart on Dec. 16. Police ascribed the shooting to a "drug deal gone bad."

Dooney was sleeping when Russell, shot in the left shoulder, stumbled back into the apartment. Dooney will not talk about the night his brother was shot except to say, "Russell was shot 'cause of drugs." His mother said that Dooney watched quietly, sucking his thumb as she wept and rocked her oldest son in her arms while they waited for an ambulance.

Waters did not press charges against Edward "June" Powell, the man police charged with shooting Russell. Powell, whose trial has been continued because he did not have an attorney, is out on bail. "He didn't mean to do it," said Waters, who still refers to Powell as a close friend of the family. "It was an accident. He meant to kill someone else."

Dooney's mother and others who congregated in her apartment were bound by a common desperation for drugs. The majority, in their late twenties or early thirties, described themselves as "recreational" drug users until they tried the highly addictive crack. Many said they had swapped welfare checks, food stamps, furniture and sexual favors to support their craving for crack. They had lost jobs, spouses, homes and self-respect. Nearly all were in danger of losing children, too.

The Prince George's County Department of Social Services was investigating charges of parental neglect against many of the people who frequented Waters's apartment. But they rarely took the county's investigations seriously. Some would joke about timid caseworkers who were too "yellow" to visit Washington Heights or would pass around letters in which officials threatened to remove children from their custody. The problem, as in Dooney's case, was that the county's threats lacked teeth. Caseworkers were usually so overloaded that they rarely had time to bring cases to court, even after they had corroborated charges of abuse and neglect.

Prince George's County police said they know about Waters's operation but have never found enough drugs in the apartment to charge her or others. "The problem is that drugs don't last long up there," said Officer Alex Bailey, who patrols the Washington Heights neighborhood. "They use them up as soon as they arrive."

Such explanations seemed lost on Dooney.

"Everybody knows about the drugs at my house," he said with a matter-of-fact tone not common to a first-grader. Each sentence was accompanied by an adult-like gesture. One second he threw his right palm in the air, the next moment the hand slammed down on his desktop and his eyes rolled up toward the top of his forehead. "The police know, too, but they don't do nothing about it. Don't nobody do nothing about it," he said.

Police did raid Dooney's apartment on Saturday, May 13, after they were called there by a neighbor who complained about noise. "They were looking for the drugs," Dooney said during an interview two days later, as his eyes grew full of tears. "They took all the clothes out of my mother's closets. They threw it all on my mother. They called my mother names."

Dooney also said he was afraid of the police, and when asked why, he inquired, "How do you spell the word 'shoot'?" Supplied with a notebook and pen, he wrote the word slowly in large, shaky letters and then repeatedly punched the pen into the paper to form a circle of black marks. Pausing a minute, he drew a person holding a pipe, a smiling face atop a body with a circle in her belly. "That's my mother," Dooney said, pointing to the figure's face. He moved his finger toward the circle. "And that's a bullet hole."

Around the apartment, Dooney was constantly on guard, watchful for signs of a ruckus or a raid. "Don't stand too close," he told a visitor standing near the front door, warning that the lockless door was often kicked open.

Since kindergarten, Dooney has pulled himself out of bed almost every school morning without the help of adults or alarm clocks, said his mother, who boasts about his independence. Asked how he gets himself up in the morning,

Dooney tapped a finger to his forehead and said, "My brain wakes me up. I get up when it gets light outside."

Dooney rarely bathed or brushed his hair before he went to school while he was living with his mother. The bathroom was inoperable during the period that *The Washington Post* regularly visited. The toilet overflowed with human waste. Stagnant water stood in the bathtub. There was no soap, no shampoo, no toilet paper or toothpaste.

When Dooney did wash, he used a yellow dishpan that doubled as a washtub for rinsing out his clothes. Without a working toilet in the apartment, Dooney went across the hall when he needed to use the bathroom. If he couldn't wait, or if the neighbors weren't home, Dooney went outside in the bushes or urinated in the bathtub. He reasons that this is the root of his bed-wetting. "I didn't want to get up [at night] to go to the bathroom and now I pee in my bed every night," he said.

Dooney's mother moved to Washington Heights in 1977, a time when the complex advertised "luxury apartments." During Dooney's preschool years, Waters said, the complex was "a nice, clean place full of working class folks." Even then, marijuana, speed, powder cocaine and other drugs circulated through the community.

But the introduction of crack swept in a new era. Nothing before it had spawned so rapid and so wrenching an addiction.

Not all Washington Heights residents are involved in the drug trade. Many families take pains to shield themselves and their children from drugs and violence. But the vast numbers that started using crack tell similar tales about addictions that rapidly exceeded their incomes.

Three years ago, Dooney's father worked as an electrician's apprentice. His mother was a typist for the Prince George's County Board of Education and took night courses in interior design at Prince George's County Community College.

"We had two incomes, two kids, all the things that you dream about in a marriage," Waters said. "There was always food in the refrigerator and money in the bank. We did drugs then, but only at night and on weekends."

Dooney's parents were introduced to crack shortly after their separation, and their drug use became less recreational. Dooney's father said he became a small-time drug dealer to support his crack habit and spent six months in jail in 1988 for selling drugs. Dooney's mother said she has traded away most of the family's belongings—and all of her sons' toys—to buy drugs.

Waters, who has no criminal record, said she lost her job with the Armed Forces Benefit and Relief Association in the District early last year, a few months after she was hired, because she kept falling asleep on the job after smoking crack all night. With an abundance of time and a circle of drug-addicted neighbors, Waters's occasional crack use became an insatiable ache. She said she began selling crack to support her mounting habit by buying one large rock, smoking some and selling the rest.

At that point, Dooney's apartment became a crack house. "All of a sudden, they just set up shop," his mother said. "I told people never to keep more than

$100 worth in my house. Smoking is one thing but for the police to walk up in your house and have people selling, that's two charges."

The children's lives declined in step with their parents. Dooney's teachers at Greenbelt Center Elementary School said he has had increasing emotional and academic problems since he entered kindergarten almost two years ago.

Both of Waters's sons have begged her to seek help and she maintained that she wanted to kick her addiction. She said she wanted to move away from Washington Heights to a place where "people leave your house when you tell them to." But Waters won't enter a treatment program, even though she has been referred by social workers. "I'm doing rehabilitation on my own self," she said.

In the last three years, addiction has whittled her body from a size 16 to a size 5. Her eyes were sunken, underlined by tufts of purplish skin. Her complexion, which she said was once "the envy" of her three sisters, was lifeless, almost like vinyl. Waters did not own a comb during the period that *The Washington Post* visited her home. When she wanted to fix her hair, she borrowed one from a neighbor.

Pictures in a blue photo album she kept in her living room show a more attractive Addie L. Waters—a buxom woman with radiant eyes, bright red lipstick and a voluminous hairdo. Dooney paged through the photo album on a Sunday afternoon and said, "My mother used to be pretty."

Dooney comes from a family with a legacy of addiction. His mother said she bought her first bag of drugs, a $5 sack of marijuana, from her alcoholic father in the late '70s. Now she said she buys crack occasionally from her 13-year-old son.

Dooney's father said he started smoking marijuana in high school and moved on to using PCP, speed and powder cocaine. Dooney's parents both described themselves as "recreational drug users" when they were married on May 28, 1981.

When she first started smoking crack, Waters said, she would lock herself in the bathroom to hide from her two sons. The charade didn't last long. One evening Russell threw open the bathroom door and discovered his mother with a plastic pipe in her mouth.

"I tried to hide it and he saw me," said Waters, who went on to describe how Russell, then in the fifth grade, slapped her several times and flushed the drugs down the toilet. "By him seeing me, it really affected me," Waters said. "I left it alone for about an hour."

Eventually, she said, Russell's reactions became less extreme, and he got involved with the drug trade himself by selling soap chips on the street to unsuspecting buyers.

In early interviews, Waters called herself a good parent, a claim her two sons disputed. By Waters's admission, she rarely woke up with Dooney when he got ready for school and only occasionally cooked meals for him. During the two months a reporter and photographer visited the apartment, Waters never checked Dooney's homework after school and in interviews couldn't remember his kindergarten or first-grade teachers' names.

Over time, Waters backed away from her earlier descriptions of herself. "I can't be the kind of mother I should be when I'm smoking crack," she said. "If I could do it all over again I would not do drugs."

Waters will take the blame for Russell, but she maintains that it would not be her fault if Dooney started using or selling drugs.

"If he does, it won't be because of me," Waters said: "I learned with Russell so I tell [Dooney] not to smoke or sell drugs. It's my fault that I'm doing it but I think [Dooney] knows better. I tell him all the time that he don't want to live like me."

Waters said that Dooney had seen her smoke crack "hundreds" of times. "He would always tell me, 'Mommy, say no to drugs' and I would say 'Okay, baby.'" She eventually stopped trying to hide her crack habit from Dooney and began smoking crack in front of him the way many parents nurture strong cigarette habits.

Dooney said he hates drugs and what they have done to his life. Yet he seems to view the drug trade as an inevitable calling in the way that some children look at the steel mills and coal mines in which their forebears have worked. They may not like the idea of working in the factory or mine, but for many, it is the most reliable and accessible source of income. In Dooney's neighborhood, the industry is drugs.

Asked if he will sell or use drugs when he grows up, Dooney shook his head violently and wrinkled his nose in disgust. But the expression faded, and Dooney looked at the floor. "I don't want to sell drugs, but I will probably have to."

JOURNAL PROMPT:

As this essay so realistically illustrates, drugs often force a child to grow up much too quickly. Do you think this young boy has a chance of ever escaping the downward spiral of his life?

COLLABORATIVE EXERCISE:

What evidence do we have that this child is living the life of an adult? How does Dooney use language? How and where does his speech contradict his age? Cite specific examples.

ESSAY ASSIGNMENT:

1. Write an essay that examines Dooney's behavior, appearance, and belief that he will end up selling drugs just like his mother.
2. Describe the living conditions of Dooney Waters. How do you think growing up in such an environment affects the development of a child?

3. In paragraph 16 the author discusses the role of the Department of Social Services. What recommendations would you make for changing social service departments so that children like Dooney Waters do not become victims a second time, victims of a vast bureaucracy?

In this piece the author explores how a perfect childhood is, in many ways, a burden to be cast off before one moves on in life. The author poses the question: Do we ever escape our childhoods, even the happy ones? MARY CANTWELL is the author of *Manhattan, When I Was Young*. This selection was originally published in *The New York Times* in February 1998.

MARY CANTWELL

THE BURDEN OF A HAPPY CHILDHOOD

The New York Times, *2/1/98 (permission of author)*

Every time I described the house to friends—the two porches, the bay windows, the balcony over the front door, the stone tubs on either side of the front steps that, before they crumbled, always held geraniums—they said, "It sounds wonderful."

"No, it's not wonderful," I'd protest. "It's too narrow, even if it runs deep, and why in a town of beautiful houses my grandfather had to buy that one. . . ." Then I'd stop, partly because no amount of words could disabuse my listeners of the notion that all big Victorian houses resembled the charmer in "Meet Me in St. Louis," and partly out of guilt. How could I say such things about three tall stories of white clapboard that had housed my grandparents, a widowed great-aunt, an aunt, the husband she acquired at 56, my parents, my sister, myself and, on occasion, whatever distant relatives were passing through.

Oh, yes, I forgot. Until I was 19, there was a cocker spaniel named Judy and in my earliest childhood a series of canaries, all of which were named Dickie and all of which flew away because my aunt trusted them to stay on their perches when she cleaned their cages out of doors.

My grandfather bought the house in 1920. My mother's wedding reception was in the backyard; my aunt's, when she finally married, on the first floor; my sister's, on the second. I remember coffins in the first-floor bay window (there is nothing like an old-fashioned New England upbringing to acquaint you with life's realities) and, in the same place, the narrow bed in which my father died. It was there so he could have a view of the main street. My grandmother and I loved that view. When I was little we would sit in the window, she in her rocker, I in a hard cut-velvet-upholstered chair, and monitor the passersby.

The house was across the street from a little beach, and after our morning dip our grandfather sluiced my sister and me with the garden hose. Years later my aunt's husband sluiced my daughters and, eventually, my niece after their dips. In my grandfather's day the garden was beautiful. After his death my grandmother, who was not one for gardening, said there was nothing nicer than a nice green lawn. Perhaps there isn't, but I have always missed his rosebushes and peonies and his patches of sweet william and pansies.

Recently, after 77 years as one family's residence, the house was sold. "How dreadful for you!" friends said. Not at all. What in my childhood had been not only my home but also my fortress, because outside of it lurked every grade-school classmate who didn't like me, had become my prison. As long as it was the place to which I fled whenever my life as an adult became too hard to bear, I was immured in childhood. I was also incapable of calling the apartments in which I lived with my husband and, later, my children "home." Home was where members of my family, some of whom were long gone, were forever baking apple pies, smoking pipes while patting the dog, reading *The Providence Evening Bulletin* and crocheting elaborate bedspreads.

An unhappy childhood can cripple, but so can one as blessed as mine. You go through life with the sense that something has been mislaid, something you think that, with luck, you can find again. Only you can't, because what you're looking for is unconditional love. My family was too strict to spoil a child, but I knew, even before I knew the words, that they would betray me only by dying. As long as they lived, my cradle would never fall.

If you're smart you give up the search early on, but that is hard when the house in which you lived your joy is still yours for the wandering. Furthermore, the ghost I met in every room was not that of a grandparent or the father who died when I was 20 but of my past self. In most particulars she was pretty much the person I am today. But I have lost forever, and mourn, the innocence that had her greeting every morning as if it were the world's first.

Today, though, the house is gone and with it a sadness I wore as a turtle wears its shell. The old radiators are in the side yard and a big hose is hanging out the third-floor window. Its buyers are updating the heating system, gutting the attic. The door on which I had painted "Artist's Den, Keep Out" has disappeared, and once the painters move in, my family's fingerprints will disappear too. But when its new occupants first toured the house, the real-estate agent reported that they said it had "good vibes." So the family that once owned it is still there, not only in my memory but in its laths and beams and solid—oh, so solid—foundation.

JOURNAL PROMPT:

Have you ever felt trapped in childhood—by a rich family life that calls you back (as is the author's case), by a parent who creates dependencies, or by memories of a "happier time"?

COLLABORATIVE EXERCISE:

Working in small groups, explore the contradictions inherent in the title of this piece. How can a happy childhood be a burden?

ESSAY ASSIGNMENT:

1. One of the themes of Cantwell's essay deals with her search for unconditional love. Do you believe such a love is possible? Explain.
2. Explore how the author uses details to create a mood. Select a passage you consider illustrative of the tone of the piece. Does Cantwell maintain that tone consistently throughout the essay?

In this first-person narrative, San Francisco poet and short-story writer DEVORAH MAJOR recalls a childhood friendship. She writes that "we were little girls reaching to be women." This essay was first published in the anthology *California Childhood: Recollections and Stories of the Golden State* (1988), edited by Gary Soto.

DEVORAH MAJOR

LITTLE GIRL DAYS

The first time I met Lora she was getting her hair pressed. Her mother had just singed a lock, and the bright yellow kitchen smelled of oil and dry smoke as it crackled. Whining, Lora pulled away as her ear collided with the thick slate-gray comb. I was a welcome relief, if only so her mom would put down the comb and complete the introductions. We would be, we were told, good friends because we were almost the same age. Charlotte, already preened with an air of knowing sophistication I would later envy, seemed to see me as snot and bruises, two characteristics I did seem always to carry, one from allergies and the other from my determination to prove that "pretty" and "awkward" were not self-canceling adjectives. After the brief introductions were ended and the birthdays arranged in a linear fashion, we were done. That was it. No, I was not to play with the landlord's children that day, just to meet them. Anyway, Lora had seemed to immediately lose interest in us as her mother reached over the stove again, brandishing the smoking hair iron.

Lora had more than a little spunk. While the hot comb made her mean, the music in her home made her swirl. She was for me a wonder. She could hula-hoop from her neck, do one-arm cartwheels, and blow gum bubbles as large as her head. All of this at six or seven. I, with rash crevices at every fold of skin, counted dancing and jacks as my only accomplishments. The dancing was mostly in mirrors and hallways, waiting for lessons that hadn't yet come, and the jacks were played along on the linoleum flowered kitchen floor. I could run fast, too, but I wasn't supposed to because of my lungs, so I didn't let many people know.

Lora knew more than me about most things. When she and David and Charlotte pushed me into the closet with Junius, she knew what kind of kissing we were supposed to be doing, and it wasn't bird pecks. When we only hugged and giggled, she also knew we didn't do our part and tried to push us back. Instead we decided to write love letters full of hearts and flowers. Of course, Lora colored better than me too. She always stayed inside the lines, making a thick hard border, and was undeniably neat.

Lora was always game and I liked to play. So we became adventurers, light and dark caramels running through Golden Gate Park, rolling down hills, chasing White Russians (weren't they all white?) and calling them "pasty" and "whitey"—tame words against their ugly screeches of "nigger." At the park we found seventeen different ways to get to the glass house and disturb its humid silence with races across the wooden bridges. Sometimes on the way home, when we were lucky, we would see an almost-grown-up guy laying on top of his girlfriend and getting ready to do it. We, wanting more than anything to be noticed, would pretend to sneak closer until, unable to deny our presence any longer he would jump up and shake his fist and growl, and occasionally even start to chase us. We would bellow out laughter as we ran for the safety of our homes to share a grape soda and laugh at how red they got.

We knew the best hills to roll down and where to fly kites without having them snatched by trees, and we had traveled through time in the furniture rooms at the De Young, becoming princesses and madams as we debated stepping over the red corded rope to actually sit on the shrunken hard bed. We were asked to leave the museum by a gray guard with a face that would crumble if it remembered youth.

It was the two us, bored with a long, fogged-in summer, who elected to investigate the local Russian Orthodox Church. It was big and lovely and opened to a large somber chapel. We walked around the room, being overly quiet, looking at the windows and icons that lined the walls, and commenting on the women who spent the day on their knees praying for unknown miracles or at least relief. When we found ourselves seduced by the flickering candles, we began with care and young-girl ritual to light them one by one. Taking a new one, as we had seen others do, we leaned its tip to the fire and made a wish and then another wish and then another. Some of the women grabbed up their prayer shawls and looked at us with scorn, but we ignored them. They were, after all, the same ones whose children called us hurtful names. They certainly had no more dominion over magic and candles than us! So we lit each golden fire, making a little more heat with each until a halo of light appeared, when a slim wrinkled hand reached out and touched mine. A nun in long dark clothes and wirestrung top said, "No more."

"We weren't hurting anything."

"These are prayer candles."

"Well, we were praying."

And then I could see it coming. Lora expected us to just get kicked out and was ready for the Hop-Along-Cassidy run. But I had a mother who gave me long sorrowful looks whenever I erred and rarely raised a hand. So I knew the very serious look-at-me-when-I-talk-to-you lecture. The litany rolled over me, full of reason and patience and far too much religion. I knew we hadn't sinned or made a "scalidge." Finally when we had twisted and flinched enough, the nun led us to the door, and we bolted out with wind-blown "sorrys." The fog was thick and cold by that time and the try-and-be-cool skip home wasn't quite worth all the trouble. But Lora and I had, as our parents directed, become friends—get chicken-pox-together, watch-for-signs-of-growing-titties, and talk-about-preferred-forms-of-punishment friends.

I was what was later to be named a "latch key" child, while Lora had a mother who made magnificent cakes with an electric mixer that even turned the bowl by itself, and then heaped them with thick frothy icings, even when it wasn't anybody's birthday. Lora always had desserts, ice cream, cookies, jello, something. Even though their vegetables came from cans, eating at her house was a special treat with sugar and forbidden Wonder Bread. They also had television. My parents listened to jazz; later I discovered that her dad actually played it. Her mom looked at Jack La Lanne and Ed Sullivan and Disney, and we were allowed to sit on the floor and marvel. Lora always spoke on my behalf as we invaded her parents' bedroom while my parents sat upstairs debating the wisdom of no television set against the reality of children who seemed to be trying to relocate downstairs.

Lora and I never fought, or when we did, it wasn't for long. I suppose that could have been because we were two of the few black girls in the neighborhood, but I think it was because I was peaceable and she was fun. Other than our hair—mine was wild and "good," impossibly messy most of the times; hers was kinky and "bad," excruciatingly neat even on the windiest days—we really had little about which to argue. But one day we found something which was just big enough to set up a spark and we, with cajoling from my brother and hisses from her sister, entered the garage where we began to wail at each other, pulling hair and circling around each other as our siblings rooted us on, offering tips for tight punches, hard kicks and good slaps. They laughed and would not allow us to stop the fight although I stood biting my lips and wincing, forgetting what the issue had been but knowing I was supposed to be mad and trying hard to show it.

And then we didn't speak for a long time. She must have won because I wasn't serious and really couldn't fight unless enraged to the point of insanity, in which case I foamed at the mouth, cried, and in my usual smart-mouth way, let loose with a shadow of the verbal epithets I heard flowing from my father whenever his steel lightning-fast hand collided with the side of my equally hard if fragile head.

After a respectable spell it was over. After a number of days of not playing together at recess, not walking home with each other, not skating together, not borrowing each other's skate key, not searching the gutters for lost pennies, and not having a best friend, we were friends again. We were sitting on the stoop. I finally had gotten the wide petticoat I had pined for. Lora already had three. "Come on," she said as I lifted my dress to show the lace, and she took me by the hand to her dining room at the back of the flat, where no one seemed to ever eat, except on Christmas or Easter, and where the record player lived. She put on a forty-five and we began to dance. First we twirled around the table as the cloth swirled and floated above our ashy legs. Leaping and prancing we performed circles around the wide oak table and began to spin each other under and around each other's arms playing the record again and again, melting in giggles at our fantasy dance hall. Oiling the floor, we were little girls reaching to be women, laughing as our skirts flew around our spindle legs as her father's record beat out lick after lick of happy talk.

JOURNAL PROMPT:

Describe your best friend from childhood. How were you alike? How were you different?

COLLABORATIVE EXERCISE:

Working in small groups, discuss how childhood relationships between young children are different from many adolescent and adult relationships. How do issues such as age, peer influence, priorities, goals, social status, and career/educational choices affect friendships at certain stages in our lives?

ESSAY ASSIGNMENT:

1. The narrator of "Little Girl Days" refers to herself as a "latch key" child. Speculate about what some of the repercussions—both good and bad—of being left alone a few hours each day might be for a child. (Consider also at what age—in general—you think a child can safely be left alone.)

2. Describe the relationship between Lora and the narrator. Be specific and use details from the narrative. Also, include your own memory of a childhood relationship and discuss how it was similar or different from Major's experience.
3. Write about a disagreement you had with a childhood friend. Describe this disagreement. Now that time has passed, do you still think that you were right about the matter, or can you see the issue from your friend's perspective?

This essay is adapted from **KAY S. HYMOWITZ**'s book *Ready or Not* (1999). Hymowitz is an affiliate scholar at the Institute of American Values. She is also a senior fellow at the Manhattan Institute, as well as contributing editor at *City Journal.* This article takes a look at advertisers who push products to pre-teens.

KAY S. HYMOWITZ

THE TEENING OF CHILDHOOD

"A kid's gotta do what a kid's gotta do!" raps a cocksure tyke on a 1998 television ad for the cable children's network Nickelodeon. She is surrounded by a large group of hip-hop-dancing young children in baggy pants who appear to be between the ages of three and eight. In another 1998 ad, this one appearing in magazines for the Gap, a boy of about eight in a T-shirt and hooded sweatshirt, his meticulously disheveled hair falling into his eyes and spilling onto his shoulders, winks ostentatiously at us. Is he neglected (he certainly hasn't had a haircut recently) or is he just street-smart? His mannered wink assures us it's the latter. Like the kids in the Nickelodeon ad, he is hip, aware, and edgy, more the way we used to think of teenagers. Forget about what Freud called latency, a period of sexual quiescence and naïveté; forget about what every parent encounters on a daily basis—artlessness, shyness, giggling jokes, cluelessness. These media kids have it all figured out, and they know how to project the look that says they do.

The media's darling is a child who barely needs childhood. In the movies, in magazines, and most of all on television, children see image upon irresistible image of themselves as competent sophisticates wise to the ways of the world. And maybe that's a good thing too, since their parents and teachers appear as weaklings, narcissists, and dolts. That winking 8-year-old in the Gap ad tells the story of his generation. A gesture once reserved for adults to signal to gullible children that a joke was on its way now belongs to the child. This child gets it; it's the adults who don't.

There are plenty of signs that the media's deconstruction of childhood has been a rousing success. The enthusiastic celebration of hipness and attitude has helped to socialize a tough, "sophisticated" consumer child who can assert himself in opposition to the tastes and conservatism of his parents. The market aimed at children has skyrocketed in recent years, and many new products, particularly those targeting the 8- to 12-year-olds whom marketers call tweens, appeal to their sense of teen fashion and image consciousness. Moreover, kids have gained influence at home. In part, this is undoubtedly because of demographic changes that have "liberated" children from parental supervision. But let's give the media their due. James McNeal, who has studied childhood consumerism for many decades, proclaims the United States a "filiarchy," a bountiful kingdom ruled by children.

Lacking a protected childhood, today's media children come immediately into the noisy presence of the media carnival barkers. Doubtless, they learn a lot from them, but their sophistication is misleading. It has no relation to a genuine worldliness, an understanding of human hypocrisy or life's illusions. It is built on an untimely ability to read the glossy surfaces of our material world, its symbols of hipness, its image-driven brands and production values. Deprived of the concealed space in which to nurture a full and independent individuality, the media child unthinkingly embraces the dominant cultural gestures of ironic detachment and emotional coolness. This is a new kind of sophistication, one that speaks of a child's diminished expectations and conformity rather than worldliness and self-knowledge.

Nowadays when people mourn the media's harmful impact on children, they often compare the current state of affairs to the Brigadoon of the 1950s. Even those who condemn the patriarchal complacency of shows like *Father Knows Best* or *Ozzie and Harriet* would probably concede that in the fifties parents did not have to fret over rock lyrics like *Come on bitch . . . lick up the dick* or T-shirts saying Kill Your Parents. These were the days when everyone, including those in the media, seemed to revere the protected and long-lived childhood that had been the middle-class ideal since the early 19th century.

But the reality of fifties media was actually more ambiguous than the conventional wisdom suggests. The fifties saw the rise of television, a medium that quickly opened advertisers' and manufacturers' eyes to the possibility of promoting in children fantasies of pleasure-filled freedom from parental control, which in turn fertilized the fields for liberationist ideas that came along in the next decade. American parents had long struggled to find a balance between their children's personal drives and self-expression and the demands of common life, but television had something else in mind. It was fifties television that launched the media's two-pronged attack on the pre-conditions of traditional childhood, one aimed directly at empowering children, the other aimed at undermining the parents who were trying to civilize them. By the end of the decade, the blueprint for today's media approach to children was in place.

The first prong of attack was directed specifically at parents—or, more precisely, at Dad. Despite the assertions of those who see in *Father Knows Best* and *Ozzie and Harriet* evidence that the fifties were a patriarchal stronghold, these shows represent not the triumph of the old-fashioned family but its feeble swan song.[1] Dad, with his stodgy ways and stern commandments, had been having a hard time of it since he first stumbled onto television. An episode of *The Goldbergs,* the first television sitcom and a remake of a popular radio show featuring a Jewish immigrant family, illustrates his problem: Rosalie, the Goldbergs' 14-year-old daughter, threatens to cut her hair and wear lipstick. The accent-laden Mr. Goldberg tries to stop her, but he is reduced to impotent blustering: "I am the father in the home, or am I? If I am, I want to know!" It is the wise wife who knows best in this house; she acts as an intermediary between this old-world patriarch and the young country he seems unable to understand. "The world is different now," she soothes.[2] If this episode dramatizes the trans-generational tension inevitable in a rapidly changing immigrant country, it also demonstrates how television tended to resolve that tension at Dad's blushing expense. The man of the fifties television house was more likely to resemble the cartoon character Dagwood Bumstead ("a joke which his children thoroughly understand" according to one critic)[3] than Robert Young of *Father Knows Best.* During the early 1950s, articles began to appear decrying TV's "male boob" with titles like "What Is TV Doing to MEN?" and "Who Remembers Papa?" (an allusion to another early series called *I Remember Mama*).[4] Even *Ozzie and Harriet* was no *Ozzie and Harriet.* Ozzie, or Pop, as he was called by his children, was the Americanized and suburbanized papa who had been left behind in city tenements. Smiling blandly as he, apparently jobless, wandered around in his cardigan sweater, Ozzie was the dizzy male, a portrait of grinning ineffectuality. It is no coincidence that *Ozzie and Harriet* was the first sitcom to showcase the talents of a child character, when Ricky Nelson began his career as a teen idol. With parents like these, kids are bound to take over.

Still, the assumption that the first years of television were happy days for the traditional family has some truth to it. During the early fifties, television was widely touted as about the best thing that had ever happened to the family—surely one of the more interesting ironies of recent social history. Ads for the strange new appliance displayed a beaming mom and dad and their big-eyed kids gathered together around the glowing screen. It was dubbed the "electronic hearth." Even intellectuals were on board; early sociological studies supported the notion that television was family-friendly. Only teenagers resisted its lure. They continued to go to the movies with their friends, just as they had since the 1920s; TV-watching, they said, was family stuff, not an especially strong recommendation in their eyes.

In order to turn television into the children's oxygen machine that it has become, television manufacturers and broadcasters during the late forties and early fifties had to be careful to ingratiate themselves with the adults who actually had to purchase the strange new contraption. Families never had more than one television in the house, and it was nearly always in the living room, where everyone could watch it. Insofar as the networks sought to entice children to watch their shows, they had to do so by convincing Mom that television was good for them. It was probably for these reasons that for a few short years children's television was more varied and of higher quality than it would be for a long time afterward. There was little to offend, but that doesn't mean it was bland. In an effort to find the best formula to attract parents, broadcasters not only showed the familiar cowboy and superhero adventure series but also experimented with circus and science programs, variety shows, dramas, and other relatively highbrow fare, for example, Leonard Bernstein's *Young People's Concerts*. Ads were sparse. Since the networks had designed the earliest children's shows as a lure to sell televisions to parents, they were not thinking of TV as a means of selling candy and toys to kids; almost half of those shows had no advertising at all and were subsidized by the networks. At any rate, in those days neither parents nor manufacturers really thought of children as having a significant role in influencing the purchase of anything beyond, perhaps, cereal, an occasional cupcake, or maybe a holiday gift.

This is not to say that no one had ever thought of advertising to children before. Ads targeting youngsters had long appeared in magazines and comic strips. Thirties radio shows like *Little Orphan Annie* and *Buck Rogers in the Twenty-Fifth Century* gave cereal manufacturers and the producers of the ever-popular Ovaltine a direct line to millions of children. But as advertisers and network people were gradually figuring out, when it came to transporting messages directly to children, radio was a horse and buggy compared to the supersonic jet known as television, and this fact changed everything. By 1957, American children were watching TV an average of an hour and a half each day. And as television became a bigger part of children's lives, its role as family hearth faded. By the mid-fifties, as television was becoming a domestic necessity, manufacturers began to promise specialized entertainment. Want to avoid those family fights over whether to watch the football game or Disneyland? the ads queried. You need a *second* TV set. This meant that children became a segregated audience in front of the second screen, and advertisers were now faced with the irresistible opportunity to sell things to them. Before television, advertisers had no choice but to tread lightly around children and to view parents as judgmental guardians over the child's buying and spending. Their limited appeals to kids had to be more than balanced by promises to parents, however spurious, of health and happiness for their children.

That balance changed once television had a firm foothold in American homes and advertisers could begin their second prong of attack on childhood. With glued-to-the-tube children now segregated from adults, broadcasters soon went about pleasing kids without thinking too much about parents. The first industry outside of the tried-and-true snacks and cereals to capitalize on this opportunity was, predictably, toys.[5] By the mid-fifties, forward-looking toy manufacturers couldn't help but notice that Walt Disney was making a small fortune selling Mickey Mouse ears and Davy Crockett coonskin hats to the viewers of his *Disneyland* and *The Mickey Mouse Club*. Ruth and Eliot Handler, the legendary owner-founders of Mattel Toys, were the first to follow up. They risked their company's entire net worth on television ads during *The Mickey Mouse Club* for a toy called "the burp gun"; with 90 percent of the nation's kids watching, the gamble paid off bigger than anyone could ever have dreamed.

It's important to realize, in these days of stadium-sized toy warehouses, that until the advent of television, toys were nobody's idea of big business. There simply was not that big a market out there. Parents themselves purchased toys only as holiday or birthday presents, and they chose them simply by going to a specialty or department store and asking advice from a salesperson. Depression-traumatized grandparents, if they were still alive, were unlikely to arrive for Sunday dinner bearing Baby Alive dolls or Nerf baseball bats and balls. And except for their friends, children had no access to information about new products. At any rate, they didn't expect to own all that many toys. It's no wonder toy manufacturers had never shown much interest in advertising; in 1955 the "toy king" Louis Marx had sold fifty million dollars' worth of toys and had spent the grand total of $312 on advertising.

The burp gun ad signaled the beginning of a new era, a turning point in American childhood and a decisive battle in the filiarchal revolution. Toy sales almost tripled between 1950 and 1970. Mattel was now a boom company with sales rising from $6 million in 1955 to $49 million in 1961.[6] Other toy manufacturers who followed Mattel onto television also watched their profits climb.

But the burp gun ad was also a watershed moment, because it laid the groundwork for today's giant business of what Nickelodeon calls "kid kulture," a phenomenon that has helped to alter the dynamic between adults and children. Television transformed toys from a modest holiday gift enterprise mediated by parents into an ever-present, big-stakes entertainment industry enjoyed by kids. Wholesalers became less interested in marketing particular toys to adults than in the manufacturer's plans for promotional campaigns to seduce children. In short, the toy salesman had pushed open the front door, had crept into the den while Mom and Dad weren't looking, and had whispered to Dick and Jane, without asking their parents' permission, of all the happiness and pleasure they could have in exchange for several dollars of the family's hard-earned money.

That the burp gun had advanced more power to children became more apparent by 1959, when Mattel began to advertise a doll named Barbie. Barbie gave a hint as to just how far business was ready to take the filiarchal revolution that had been set in motion by the wonders of television. Regardless of the promotional revolution it had unleashed, the burp gun was a familiar sort of toy, a quirky accessory to the battlefield games always enjoyed by boys. But Barbie was something new. Unlike the baby dolls that encouraged little girls to imitate Mommy, Barbie was a swinger, a kind of Playboy for little girls. She had her own Playboy Mansion, called Barbie's Dream House, and she had lots of sexy clothes, a car, and a boyfriend. The original doll had pouty lips—she was redesigned for a more open California look in the sixties—and she was sold in a leopard skin bathing suit and sunglasses, an accessory whose glamour continues to have iconic status in the children's market. In fact, though it isn't widely known, Barbie was copied from a German doll named Lili, who was in turn modeled on a cartoon prostitute. Sold in bars and tobacco shops, Lili was a favorite of German men, who were suckers for her tight (removable) sweater and short (removable) miniskirt.

Barbie has become so familiar that she is seen as just another citizen of the toy chest, but it's no exaggeration to say that she is one of the heroes in the media's second prong of attack on childhood. She proved not only that toy manufacturers were willing to sell directly to children, bypassing parents entirely, but that they were willing to do so by undermining the forced and difficult-to-sustain latency of American childhood. According to marketing research, mothers without exception *hated* Barbie. They believed she was too grown-up for their 4-to-12-year-old daughters, the toy's target market. The complaint heard commonly today—that by introducing the cult of the perfect body Barbie promotes obsessive body consciousness in girls, often resulting in eating disorders—is actually only a small part of a much larger picture. Barbie symbolized the moment when the media and the businesses it promoted dropped all pretense of concern about maintaining childhood. They announced, first, that they were going to flaunt for children the very freedom, consumer pleasure, and sex that parents had long been trying to delay in their lives. And, second, they were going to do this by initiating youngsters into the cult of the teenager. If this formula sounds familiar, it's because it remains dominant today. Barbie began the media's teening of childhood; today's media images and stories are simply commentary.

Ads targeting children make perfect companion pieces to stories of family rot and children savvy enough to roll their eyes amusingly through all the misery. In ads today, the child's image frequently appears in extreme close-up—the child as giant. Appealing to children's fantasies of omnipotent, materialistic freedom, advertisers portray an anarchic world of misrule in which the pleasure-seeking child reigns supreme.[7] Spot, the red dot on the logo of containers of 7 Up, comes to life, escapes from the refrigerator, and tears through the house causing riotous havoc.[8] A Pepsi ad shows screaming teens and preteens gorging themselves with cake, pouring Pepsi over their heads, and jumping on the bed with an electric guitar. "Be young, have fun, drink Pepsi," says the voice-over.[9] Adult characters—even adult voice-overs and on-camera spokespeople—have been banished in favor of adolescent voices in the surfer-dude mode.[10] Any old folks left standing should prepare to be mocked. Perceived as carping, droning old-timers who would deny the insiders their pleasure or fun, adults are the butts of the child-world joke. They are, as the *New York Times'* Charles McGrath noted after surveying Saturday morning cartoons, "either idiots, like the crazed geek who does comic spots on 'Disney's 1 Saturday Morning,' or meanies, like the crochety, incompetent teachers and principals on the cartoons 'Recess' and 'Pepper Ann.'"[11] Teachers are, of course, citizens of the adult geekville as well: In one typical snack food ad, kids break out of the halls of their school or behind the back of dimwitted teachers droning on at the chalk-board.[12]

The misleading notion that children are autonomous figures free from adult influence is on striking display in ads like these. Children liberated from parents and teachers are only released into new forms of control. "Children will not be liberated," wrote one sage professor. "They will be dominated."[13] Nineteenth-century moralists saw in the home a haven from the increasingly harsh and inhuman marketplace. The advantage of hindsight allows us to see how this arrangement benefited children. The private home and its parental guardians could exercise their influence on children relatively unchallenged by commercial forces. Our own children, on the other hand, are creatures—one is tempted to say slaves—of the marketplace almost immediately.

The same advertisers who celebrate children's independence from the stodgy adult world and all its rules set out to educate children in its own strict regulations. They instruct children in the difference between what's in and what's out, what's hip and what's nerdy—or, to quote the inimitable Beavis and Butthead, "what's cool and what sucks." Giving new meaning to the phrase *hard sell,* today's ads demonstrate for children the tough posture of the sophisticated child who is savvy to the current styles and fashions. In a contest held by Polaroid for its Cool Cam promotion, the winning entry, from a Manassas, Virginia, girl, depicted a fish looking out a fishbowl at the kids in the house and sneering, "The only thing cool about these nerds is that they have a Cool Cam." Polaroid marketed the camera with a pair of sunglasses, the perennial childhood signifier of sophistication.

It should be clear by now that the pose the media has in mind for children—cool, tough, and sophisticated independence—is that of the teenager. The media's efforts to encourage children to identify with the independent and impulsive consumer teen—efforts that began tentatively, as we saw, with Barbie—have now gone into overdrive. Teenagers are everywhere in children's media today. Superheroes like Mighty Morphin Power Rangers and Teenage Mutant Ninja Turtles are teenagers. Dolls based on the TV character Blossom; her suggestively named friend, Six; and her brother, Joey, portray teenagers, as do the dolls based on the TV series *Beverly Hills 90210,* not to mention the ever-popular Barbie herself. Even the young children dressed in baggy pants who sing *A kid's gotta do what a kid's gotta do* for Nickelodeon are, for all intents and purposes, teenagers.

By populating kids' imaginative world with teenagers, the media simultaneously flatters children's fantasies of sophistication and teaches them what form those fantasies should take. Thus, the media's "liberation" of children from adults also has the mischievous effect of binding them more closely to the peer group. In turn, the peer group polices its members' dress and behavior according to the rules set by this unrecognized authority. In no time at all, children intuit that teens epitomize the freedom, sexiness, and discretionary income—not to mention independence—valued in our society. Teens do not need their mommies to tell them what to wear or eat or how to spend their money, nor do they have sober responsibilities to restrain them from impulse buying.

These days, the invitation to become one of the teen in-crowd arrives so early that its recipients are still sucking their thumbs and stroking their blankies. During the preschool lineup on Nickelodeon one morning, there was a special Nickelodeon video for a song entitled "I Need Mo' Allowance." In this video the camera focuses on a mock heavy metal rock band consisting of three teenaged boys in baggy pants and buzz cuts who rasp a chorus that includes lines like *Mo' allowance to buy CDs!* A dollar sign flashes repeatedly on the screen. This video was followed by an ad for a videotape of *George of the Jungle.* "This George rides around in a limo, baby, and looks great in Armani," jeers the dude announcer. "It's not your parents' *George of the Jungle!*" Change the channel to *Sesame Street,* and although the only ads you'll get are for the letter *H* or the number 3, you may still see an imitation MTV video with a group of longhaired, bopping, stomping muppets singing *I'm so cool, cool, cool!* That few 3-year-olds know the first thing about Armani, limos, or even cool is irrelevant; it's time they learned.

Many companies today have "coolhunters" or "street teams," that is, itinerant researchers who hang out in clubs, malls, and parks and look for trends in adolescent styles in clothes, music, and slang to be used in educating younger consumer trainees. Advertisers can then broadcast for children an aesthetic to emblazon their peer group identity. Even ads for the most naive, childlike products are packed with the symbols of contemporary cool. The Ken doll, introduced in 1993, has hair tinted with blond streaks and wears an earring and a thick gold chain around his neck. The rock and roll which accompanies many of these ads is the pulsing call to generational independence now played for even the youngest tot. The Honey Comb Bear (in sunglasses) raps the virtues of his eponymous cereal. The 1998 Rugrats movie is accompanied by musicians like Elvis Costello and Patti Smith. With a name like Kool-Aid, how could the drink manufacturer continue its traditional appeal to parents and capture today's child sophisticate as well? The new Mr. Kool Aid raps his name onto children's brains.

As math or geography students, American children may be mediocre, but as consumers they are world-class. They learn at prodigiously young ages to obey the detailed sumptuary laws of the teen material world, a world in which status emanates out of the cut of a pair of jeans or the stitching of a sneaker. M/F Marketing Research found that kids make brand decisions by the age of four.[14] *Marketing to and Through Kids* recounts numerous stories of kids under 10 unwilling to wear jeans or sneakers without a status label. One executive at Converse claims that dealers inform him that children as young as two are "telling their parents what they want on their feet." Another marketing executive at Nike notes, "The big shift we've been seeing is away from unbranded to more sophisticated branded athletic shoes at younger and younger ages." At Nike the percentage of profit attributable to young children grew from nothing to 14 percent by the early nineties.[15]

Nowhere has the success of media education been more dramatically apparent than among 8-to-12-year-old "tweens." The rise of the tween has been sudden and intense. In 1987 James McNeal, perhaps the best-known scholar of the children's market, reported that children in this age group had an income of $4.7 billion. In 1992 in an article in *American Demographics* he revised that figure up to $9 billion, *an increase of almost 100 percent in five years.*[16] While children spent almost all their money on candy in the 1960s, they now spend two-thirds of their cash on toys, clothes, movies, and games they buy themselves.[17]

The teening of those we used to call preadolescents shows up in almost everything kids wear and do. In 1989 the Girl Scouts of America introduced a new MTV-style ad with rap music in order to, in the words of the organization's media specialist, "get away from the uniformed, goody-goody image and show that the Girl Scouts are a fun, mature, cool place to be." [18] Danny Goldberg, the chief executive officer of Mercury Records, concedes that teenagers have been vital to the music industry since the early days of Sinatra. "But now the teenage years seem to start at eight or nine in terms of entertainment tastes," he says. "The emotions are kicking in earlier." [19] A prime example is Hanson, a rock-and-roll group whose three members achieved stardom when they were between the ages of 11 and 17. Movie producers and directors are finding it increasingly difficult to interest children this age in the usual children's fare. Tweens go to *Scream,* a horror film about a serial killer, or *Object of My Affection,* a film about a young woman who falls in love with a homosexual man.[20] After the girl-driven success of *Titanic,* Buffy Shutt, president of marketing at Universal Pictures, marveled, "They're amazing consumers." [21] Mattel surely agrees, as evidenced by their Barbie ad. "You, girls, can do anything." Clothing retailers are scrambling for part of the tween action. All over the country companies like Limited Too, Gap Kids, Abercrombie and Fitch, and Gymboree have opened stores for 6-to-12-year-olds and are selling the tween look—which at this moment means bell bottoms, ankle-length skirts or miniskirts, platform shoes, and tank tops.[22] Advertisers know that kids can spot their generational signature in a nanosecond—the hard rock and roll, the surfer-dude voices, the baggy pants and bare midriffs shot by tilted cameras in vibrant hues and extreme close-ups—and they oblige by offering these images on TV, the Internet, in store displays, and in the growing number of kid magazines.[23]

The seduction of children with dreams of teen sophistication and tough independence, which began with Barbie and intensified markedly in the last decade, appears to have had the desired effect: It has undermined childhood by turning children into teen consumers. This new breed of children won't go to children's movies and they won't play with toys. One of the stranger ironies of the rise of the tween is that toy manufacturers, who with the introduction of Barbie began the direct hard sell to children and were the first to push the teening of American childhood, have been hoist with their own petard. The 1998–99 Toy Industry Factbook of the Toy Manufacturer's Association says that the industry used to think of kids between birth and 14 as their demographic audience, but with the emergence of tweens they have had to shrink that audience to birth to 10.[24] Even seven- and eight-year-olds are scorning Barbie.[25]

Who needs a doll when you can live the life of the teen vamp yourself? Cosmetic companies are finding a bonanza among this age group. Lines aimed at tweens include nail polish, hair mascara, lotions, and lip products like lipstick, lip gloss, "lip lix." Sweet Georgia Brown is a cosmetics line for tweens that includes body paints and scented body oils with come-hither names like Vanilla Vibe or Follow Me Boy. The Cincinnati design firm Libby Peszyk Kattiman has introduced a line of bikini underwear for girls. There are even fitness clubs and personal trainers for tweens in Los Angeles and New York.[26]

Marketers point at broad demographic trends to explain these changes in the child market, and they are at least partially correct. Changes in the family have given children more power over shopping decisions. For the simple reason that fewer adults are around most of the time, children in single-parent homes tend to take more responsibility for obtaining food and clothes. Market researchers have found that these kids become independent consumers earlier than those in two-parent homes.[27] Children of working mothers also tend to do more of the family shopping when at around age eight or nine they can begin to get to the store by themselves. Though candy, toy, and cereal manufacturers had long been well aware of the money potential of tween cravings, by the mid-eighties, even though their absolute numbers were falling, tweens began to catch the eye of a new range of businesses, and ads and marketing magazines started to tout the potential of this new niche. The reason was simple: Market research revealed that more and more children in this age group were shopping for their own clothes, shoes, accessories, and drug-store items—indeed, they were even shopping for the family groceries. Just as marketers had once targeted housewives, now they were aiming at kids.[28] Jeans manufacturer Jordache was one of the first companies to spot the trend. "My customers are kids who can walk into a store with either their own money or their mothers'," the company's director of advertising explained at the time. "The dependent days of tugging on Mom or Dad's sleeve are over." Now as the number of children is rising again, their appeal is even more irresistible. Packaged Facts, a division of the worldwide research firm Find/SVP, has said that the potential purchasing power of today's kids "is the greatest of any age or demographic group in our nation's history."[29]

And there is another reason for the increasing power of children as consumers: By the time they are tweens, American children have simply learned to expect a lot of stuff.[30] Many of them have been born to older mothers; the number of first babies born to women over 30 has quadrupled since 1970, and the number born to women over 40 doubled in the six years between 1984 and 1990. Older mothers are more likely to have established careers and to be in the kind of financial position that allows them to shower their kids with toys and expensive clothes.[31] Also, grandparents are living longer and more comfortably, and they often arrive with an armload of toys, sports equipment, and fancy dresses. (The products of the children's clothes company Osh Kosh B'Gosh are known in the trade as "granny bait.") Divorce has also helped to inflate the child market: Many American children divide their time between parents, multiplying by two the number of soccer balls and Big Bird toothbrushes they must own. But as we have seen before, impersonal social forces have found support in human decisions. Important as they are, demographics by themselves can't explain 10-year-olds who have given up dolls for mascara and body oil. The teening of childhood has been a consummation the media devoutly wished—and planned. The media has given tweens a group identity with its own language, music, and fashion. It has done this by flattering their sense of being hip and aware almost-teens rather than out-of-it little kids dependent on their parents. On discovering the rising number of child customers, Jordache Jeans did not simply run ads for kids; they ran ads showing kids saying things like "Have you ever seen your parents naked?" and "I hate my mother. She's prettier than me." When Bonne Bell cosmetics discovered the rising sales potential of younger shoppers, they did not merely introduce a tween line, which some parents might think bad enough; they introduced it with the kind of in-your-face language that used to send children to bed without dinner: "We know how to be cool. We have our own ideas. And make our own decisions. Watch out for us." Sassaby's "Watch your mouth, young lady" is a smirking allusion to old-fashioned childhood that is meant to sell a line of lip "huggers" and "gloss overs."

There is little reason to think that children have found the freedom and individuality that liberationists assumed they would find now that they have been liberated from old-fashioned childhood and its adult guards. The rise of the child consumer and the child market itself is compelling evidence that children will always seek out some authority for rules about how to dress, talk, and act. Today's school-age children, freed from adult guidance, turn to their friends, who in turn rely on a glamorous and flattering media for the relevant cultural messages. Recent studies have found that children are forming cliques at younger ages than in previous years and that those cliques have strict rules about dress, behavior, and leisure. By the fifth or sixth grade, according to *Peer Power: Preadolescent Culture and Identity,* girls are gaining status "from their success at grooming, clothes, and other appearance-related variables."[32] Teachers and principals also see an increasing number of 10- and 11-year-olds who have given up toys for hair mousse and name-brand jeans and who heckle those who do not. What matters to this new breed of child is, according to Bruce Friend, vice president of worldwide research and planning at Nickelodeon, "being part of the in-crowd" and "being the first to know what's cool."[33] These "free" children "are extremely fad conscious"; moreover, according to *American Demographics,* tweens' attraction to fads has "no saturation points."[34] Look for the tween consumer to become even more powerful.

A diminished home life and an ever more powerful media constitute a double blow against the conditions under which individuality flourishes. Whereas in the past eccentric or bookish children might have had the privacy of their home to escape the pressures of their media-crazed peers, today such refuge has gone the way of after-school milk and cookies. And if you think that at least such children have been freed of the pressure of yesterday's domineering fathers and frustrated mothers, you might want to reconsider. As Hannah Arendt once noted, "The authority of a group, even a child group, is always considerably stronger and more tyrannical than the severest authority of an individual person can ever be." The opportunity for an individual to rebel when bound to a group is "practically nil"; few adults can do it.[35] The truth is, yesterday's parent-controlled childhood protected children not only from sex, from work, and from adult decisions but also from the dominance of peers and from the market, with all its pressures to achieve, its push for status, its false lures, its passing fads.

But in the anticultural filiarchy which is replacing traditional childhood, adults no longer see their job as protecting children from the market. In fact, it is not that the child's hurried entrance into the market means that parents are increasingly failing to socialize children. It's the other way around. Children are viewed by manufacturers as the "opinion leaders in the household," according to a vice president at Keebler.[36] Manufacturers believe that children are exercising influence over family purchases never before remotely associated with the young. Holiday Inn and Delta Airlines have established marketing programs aimed at children, and *Sports Illustrated for Kids* publishes ads from American Airlines, IBM, and car manufacturers.[37]

While simply turning off the TV would help, at this point television is only one part of the picture. Kids learn of their sophisticated independence from retail displays and promotions, from magazines and direct mailings. With their captive audience, schools, too, have become an advertiser's promised land: Kids see ads in classrooms, on book order forms, on Channel One, on the Internet, on school buses, and now even in textbooks. Book order forms distributed in schools throughout the country from the putatively educational firm Scholastic look like cartoons and provide children with the opportunity to order stickers, autograph books, fan biographies, and books based on popular movies and television shows. Practically every Fortune 500 company has a school project, according to the *New York Times,* and many administrators expect that in the near future we will be seeing signs like CHEERLEADERS BROUGHT TO YOU BY REEBOK in school gyms.[38] "It isn't enough just to advertise on television," Carol Herman, a senior vice president of Grey Advertising, explains. "You've got to reach the kids throughout their day—in school, as they're shopping at the mall . . . or at the movies. You've got to become part of the fabric of their lives."[39]

The scorched earth policy in the name of the filiarchy requires that ever younger children be treated as potential customers, once again in the guise of education. When *Sesame Street* arrived on the airwaves in 1969, no one imagined that preschoolers could be a significant market segment. In fact, the improbability of preschool purchasing power was the reason *Sesame Street* had to appear on public television in the first place; no one wanted to put a lot of money into creating and broadcasting a program for kids who had no purchasing power. How shortsighted that was! By 1994 Children's Television Workshop was bringing in $120 million a year largely on the strength of its over 5,000 licensed products. The list includes not just educational items like books and audiotapes but bubble bath, pajamas, underwear, and Chef Boyardee Sesame Street pasta. Toy manufacturers gradually caught on to the power of the littlest people, especially where their education was concerned. The number of preschool toys exploded in the decades after *Sesame Street* was introduced, and many of them were stamped with a seal of approval from some expert or other—or with the image of Ernie or Big Bird, which in the minds of many amounted to the same thing.

And now *Teletubbies* has arrived to help carve out the *pre*-preschool market and to give power to the littlest people. *Teletubbies* was designed for one- and two-year-olds, and though no one has ever explained how it could possibly be educational for babies to watch television, it is clear that when toddlers see pictures of the four vividly hued plush and easily identified characters (with television screens on their stomachs) on bottles or bibs, they will cry for them and PBS will rake it in. In anticipation of opening up this new market segment, the media went into overdrive. Pictures of the characters appeared in ads in trade and consumer magazines and were plastered on buses in New York City and on a giant billboard in Times Square. The show was a topic on *Letterman, Today,* and *Nightline.* "If this isn't the most important toy at Christmas this year, then something desperately wrong will have happened," gloated Kenn Viselman, whose Itsy Bitsy Entertainment Company has the rights to *Teletubbies* products. "This show had more advance press than *Titanic.*" Wondered one critic, "Where does it end: A TV in the amniotic sac?" But marketers were thrilled: according to the president of another licensing company, before now "the one-to-two-year-old niche hasn't been filled very well."[40] The one-to-two-year-old niche? McNeal has said that children become aware of the market as early as two months of age.[41] There is no more unmistakable sign of the end of childhood as Americans have known it.

References

1. The history presented in this article is taken from Lynn Spigel, *Make Room for TV: Television and the Family Ideal in Postwar America* (Chicago: University of Chicago Press, 1992); Gerard Jones, *Honey I'm Home: Sitcoms: Selling the American Dream* (New York: Grove Weidenfeld, 1992): William Melody, *Children's Television: The*

Economics of Exploitation (New Haven, Conn.: Yale University Press, 1973); Cy Schneider, *Children's Television: The Art, the Business and How It Works* (Chicago: NTC Business Books, 1987); Mark Crispin Miller, "Deride and Conquer," in *Watching Television,* ed. Todd Gitlin (New York: Pantheon Books, 1986), traces the "long decline of Dad" (pp. 196ff.) and the triumph of the ironic tone.

2. Quoted in Jones, p. 42.

3. Arthur Asa Berger, *The Comic-Stripped American: What Dick Tracy, Blondie, Daddy Warbucks and Charlie Brown Tell Us About Ourselves* (New York: Walker, 1973), p. 103.

4. Spigel, p. 60.

5. The history of toy advertising and Barbie comes from Schneider, pp. 18–26; G. Wayne Miller, *Toy Wars: The Epic Struggle Between G. I. Joe, Barbie, and the Companies That Make Them* (New York: Random House, 1998), p. 67; Gary Cross, *Kids' Stuff: Toys and the Changing World of American Childhood* (Cambridge: Harvard University Press, 1997), chap. 6.

6. Cross, pp. 165–166.

7. Ellen Seiter, *Sold Separately: Parents and Children in the Consumer Culture* (New Brunswick, N.J.: Rutgers University Press, 1993), notes this same theme (in chap. 4), and several of my examples come from there. Seiter, like other academics today writing in the Ariès tradition, believes Kid Kulture can "express a resistance to the middle-class culture of parenting . . . that may be very healthy indeed" (p. 232). In other words, she finds ads genuinely subversive.

8. Example from Selina S. Guber and Jon Berry, *Marketing to and Through Kids* (New York: McGraw-Hill, 1993), p. 133.

9. Patricia Winters, "Pepsi Harkens Back to Youth," *Advertising Age,* January 25, 1993, p. 3.

10. Seiter (p. 130) quotes research, comparing boys' toy ads from the fifties and those of today which finds that the adult male voice-over or on-camera spokesman has almost entirely disappeared.

11. Charles McGrath, "Giving Saturday Morning Some Slack," *New York Times Magazine,* November 9, 1997, p. 54.

12. Seiter, p. 121.

13. John E. Coons, "Intellectual Liberty and the Schools," *Notre Dame Journal of Law, Ethics, and Public Policy,* vol. 1, 1985, p. 503.

14. "News/Trends—Kidpower," *Fortune,* March 30. 1987, pp. 9–10.

15. Guber and Berry, pp. 27, 78.

16. James McNeal, "Growing Up in the Market," *American Demographics,* October 1992, p. 47.

17. Figure cited in Lisa Bannon, "As Children Become More Sophisticated, Marketers Think Older," *Wall Street Journal,* October 13, 1998, p. A1. McNeal says that aggregate spending on or for children between ages four and twelve doubled every decade in the 1960s, 1970s, and 1980s. In the 1990s the children's market picked up more steam: between 1990 and 1997, it had already tripled.

18. Jane Weaver, "Girl Scout Campaign: Shedding Old Image for Media Cool," *Adweek,* September 11, 1989, p. 11.

19. Quoted in Bernard Weinraub, "Who's Lining Up at Box Office? Lots and Lots of Girls," *New York Times,* Arts Section, February 23, 1998, p. 1.

20. Bannon, p. A8; Michele Willens, "Young and in a Niche That Movies Neglect," *New York Times,* Arts and Leisure Section, June 14, 1998, pp. 13–14.
21. Quoted in Weinraub, p. 4.
22. Bannon, pp. A1, 8.
23. The number of magazines for children almost doubled between 1986 and 1991. S. K. List, "The Right Place to Find Children," *American Demographics,* February 1992, pp. 44–47.
24. Toy Industry Factbook at www.toy-tma.com/PUBLICATIONS/factbook98/economics.html.
25. Bannon, p. A1.
26. Laura Klepacki, "Courting the Tweenie' Boppers," *WWD,* February 27, 1998, p. 10; Becky Ebenkamp, "Packaging: Sara Lee Repackages Youthful Underwear to Better Draw Juniors," *Brandweek,* January 5, 1998, p. 36.
27. James McNeal and Chyon-Hwa Yeh, "Born to Shop," *American Demographics,* June 1993, p. 37.
28. Carrier Telegardin, "Growing Up Southern: The Kids Take Over," *Atlanta Journal-Constitution,* June 7, 1993, p. E1. According to Telegardin, "America's new housewife [is] the housekid."
29. Quoted in Toy Industry Factbook. See also "Generation Y," *Business Week,* February 15, 1999, pp. 80–88, for how this generation is changing the marketplace.
30. The psychologist Marilyn Bradford found that preschoolers ask for an average of 3.4 toys for Christmas and receive 11.6. Cited in Gary Cross, "Too Many Toys," *New York Times,* November 24, 1995, p. 35.
31. Lisa Gubernick and Marla Matzer, "Babies as Dolls," *Forbes,* February 27, 1995, p. 78.
32. Patricia A. Adler and Peter Adler, *Peer Power: Preadolescent Culture and Identity* (New Brunswick. N.J.: Rutgers University Press, 1998), p. 55. Tellingly, by 1991 shoes and clothing were the fastest-growing categories among children up to age twelve and accounted for 13 percent of their spending, up from an unmeasurably small amount in 1988, according to Susan Antilla, "'I Want' Now Gets," *New York Times,* Education Life, April 4, 1993, p. 17. See also Carol Pogash, "The Clothing Boom in the Land of the Little People," *Los Angeles Times,* August 29, 1995, p. 22.
33. Interview by the author, July 1998.
34. Judith Waldrop, "The Tween Scene." *American Demographics,* September 1992, p. 4.
35. Hannah Arendt, "Crisis in Education," *Partisan Review,* Fall 1958, p. 500.
36. Quoted in Guber and Berry, p. 84. See also Claire Collins, "Fighting the Holiday Advertising Blitz," *New York Times,* December 1, 1994, p. C4; Matt Murray, "Hey Kids! Marketers Want Your Help!" *Wall Street Journal,* May 6, 1997, pp. B1, 8; Antilla, p. 17; Steven A. Holmes, "Shoppers! Deciding? Just Ask Your Child," *New York Times,* Week in Review, January 8, 1995, p. 4; Becky Ebenkamp, Mike Beirne, and Christine Bittar, "Products for the Sophisticated Little Nipper," *Brandweek,* February 22, 1999, pp. 1, 53.
37. See Don Oldenberg, "Consummate Consumer: Children's Business: America's 90 Billion Plus Youth Market," *Washington Post,* July 6, 1995, p. C5.
38. Deborah Stead, "Classrooms and Commercialism," *New York Times,* Education Life, January 5, 1997, p. 30.

39. Quoted in Michael F. Jacobson and Laurie Ann Mazur, *Marketing Madness: A Survival Guide for a Consumer Society* (New York: Westview Press, 1995), p. 21. See also Carrie Goerne, "Marketers Try to Get More Creative at Reaching Teens," *Marketing News,* August 5, 1991, pp. 2, 6; Judann Dagnoli, "Consumer's Union Hits Kids Advertising," *Advertising Age,* July 23, 1990, p. 4.
40. Quoted in Lawrie Mifflin, "Critics Assail PBS over Plan for Toys Aimed at Toddlers," *New York Times,* April 20, 1998, p. A17.
41. Quoted in Oldenberg, p. C5. Mary Ellen Podmolik, "Kids' Clothing Boom," *Chicago Sun Times,* Financial Section, August 21, 1994, p. 1, quotes McNeal to the effect that 10 percent of a two-year-old's vocabulary is made up of brand names.

JOURNAL PROMPT:

When did you first become aware of the effects of advertising on your life?

COLLABORATIVE EXERCISE:

Hymowitz insists, "There are plenty of signs that the media's deconstruction of childhood has been a rousing success." Working in small groups, create a list of signs or indicators, however subtle, which illustrate that the teening of childhood is alive and well—in the media, outside the media, or perhaps in your own household or right next door.

ESSAY ASSIGNMENT:

1. Is consumerism in the schools an exercise in free speech, or a moral issue? Write an editorial in which you take a stance one way or the other.
2. The author claims that "today's ads demonstrate for children the tough postures of the sophisticated child who is savvy to the current styles and fashions." To what do you attribute our apparent need to be like everybody else?
3. Kay S. Hymowitz argues that marketing techniques aimed at youngsters have "undermined childhood by turning children into teen consumers." Do you agree or disagree with her assessment?

As a child, **MARIE WINN** immigrated with her parents to the United States from Czechoslovakia. She attended both Radcliffe College and Columbia University. A freelance writer, her work has been published in the *New York Book Review, Parade,* and *The New York Times Magazine.* Her novel, *Summer in Prague* (1973), won the American Library Association's award for notable book. Winn lives in New York.

MARIE WINN

THE END OF PLAY

Of all the changes that have altered the topography of childhood, the most dramatic has been the disappearance of childhood play. Whereas a decade or two ago children were easily distinguished from the adult world by the very nature of their play, today children's occupations do not differ greatly from adult diversions.

Infants and toddlers, to be sure, continue to follow certain timeless patterns of manipulation and exploration; adolescents, too, have not changed their free-time habits so very much, turning as they ever have towards adult pastimes and amusements in their drive for autonomy, self-mastery, and sexual discovery. It is among the ranks of school-age children, those six-to-twelve-year-olds who once avidly filled their free moments with childhood play, that the greatest change is evident. In the place of traditional, sometimes ancient childhood games that were still popular a generation ago, in the place of fantasy and make-believe play—"You be the mommy and I'll be the daddy"—doll play or toy-soldier play, jump-rope play, ball-bouncing play, today's children have substituted television viewing and, most recently, video games.

Many parents have misgivings about the influence of television. They sense that a steady and time-consuming exposure to passive entertainment might damage the ability to play imaginatively and resourcefully, or prevent this ability from developing in the first place. A mother of two school-age children recalls: "When I was growing up, we used to go out into the vacant lots and make up week-long dramas and sagas. This was during third, fourth, fifth grades. But my own kids have never done that sort of thing, and somehow it bothers me. I wish we had cut down on the TV years ago, and maybe the kids would have learned how to play."

The testimony of parents who eliminate television for periods of time strengthens the connection between children's television watching and changed play patterns. Many parents discover that when their children don't have television to fill their free time, they resort to the old kinds of imaginative, traditional "children's play." Moreover, these parents often observe that under such circumstances "they begin to seem more like children" or "they act more child-like." Clearly, a part of the definition of childhood, in adults' minds, resides in the nature of children's play.

Children themselves sometimes recognize the link between play and their own special definition as children. In an interview about children's books with four ten-year-old girls, one of them said: "I read this story about a girl my age growing up twenty years ago—you know, in 1960 or so—and she seemed so much younger than me in her behavior. Like she might be playing with dolls, or playing all sorts of children's games, or jump-roping or something." The other girls all agreed that they had noticed a similar discrepancy between themselves and fictional children in books of the past: those children seemed more like children. "So what do *you* do in your spare time, if you don't play with dolls or play make-believe games or jump rope or do things kids did twenty years ago?" they were asked. They laughed and answered, "We watch TV."

But perhaps other societal factors have caused children to give up play. Children's greater exposure to adult realities, their knowledge of adult sexuality, for instance, might make them more sophisticated, less likely to play like children. Evidence from the counterculture communes of the sixties and seventies adds weight to the argument that it is television above all that has eliminated children's play. Studies of children raised in a variety of such communes, all television-free, showed the little communards continuing to fill their time with those forms of play that have all but vanished from the lives of conventionally reared American children. And yet these counterculture kids were casually exposed to all sorts of adult matters—drug taking, sexual intercourse. Indeed, they sometimes incorporated these matters into their play: "We're mating," a pair of six-year-olds told a reporter to explain their curious bumps and grinds. Nevertheless, to all observers the commune children preserved a distinctly childlike and even innocent demeanor, an impression that was produced mainly by the fact that they spent most of their time playing. Their play defined them as belonging to a special world of childhood.

Not all children have lost the desire to engage in the old-style childhood play. But so long as the most popular, most dominant members of the peer group, who are often the most socially precocious, are "beyond" playing, then a common desire to conform makes it harder for those children who still have the drive to play to go ahead and do so. Parents often report that their children seem ashamed of previously common forms of play and hide their involvement with such play from their peers. "My fifth-grader still plays with dolls," a mother tells, "but she keeps them hidden in the basement where nobody will see them." This social check on the play instinct serves to hasten the end of childhood for even the least advanced children.

What seems to have replaced play in the lives of great numbers of preadolescents these days, starting as early as fourth grade, is a burgeoning interest in boy-girl interactions—"going out" or "going together." These activities do not necessarily involve going anywhere or doing anything sexual, but nevertheless are the first stage of a sexual process that used to commence at puberty or even later. Those more sophisticated children who are already involved in such manifestly unchildlike interests make plain their low opinion of their peers who still *play*. "Some of the kids in the class are real weird," a fifth-grade boy states. "They're not interested in going out just in trucks and stuff, or games pretending they're monsters. Some of them don't even *try* to be cool."

Video Games versus Marbles

Is there really any great difference, one might ask, between that gang of kids playing video games by the hour at their local candy store these days and those small fry who used to hang around together spending equal amounts of time playing marbles? It is easy to see a similarity between the two activities: each requires a certain amount of manual dexterity, each is almost as much fun to watch as to play, each is simple and yet challenging enough for that middle-childhood age group for whom time can be so oppressive if unfilled.

One significant difference between the modern pre-teen fad of video games and the once popular but now almost extinct pastime of marbles is economic: playing video games costs twenty-five cents for approximately three minutes of play; playing marbles, after a small initial investment, is free. The children who frequent video-game machines require a considerable outlay of quarters to subsidize their fun; two, three, or four dollars is not an unusual expenditure for an eight- or nine-year-old spending an hour or two with his friends playing Asteroids or Pac-Man or Space Invaders. For most of the children the money comes from their weekly allowance. Some augment this amount by enterprising commercial ventures—trading and selling comic books, or doing chores around the house for extra money.

But what difference does it make where the money comes from? Why should that make video games any less satisfactory as an amusement for children? In fact, having to pay for the entertainment, whatever the source of the money, and having its duration limited by one's financial resources changes the nature of the game, in a subtle way diminishing the satisfactions it offers. Money and time become intertwined, as they so often are in the adult world and as, in the past, they almost never were in the child's world. For the child playing marbles, meanwhile, time has a far more carefree quality, bounded only by the requirements to be home by suppertime or by dark.

But the video-game-playing child has an additional burden—a burden of choice, of knowing that the money used for playing Pac-Man could have been saved for Christmas, could have been used to buy something tangible, perhaps something "worthwhile," as his parents might say, rather than being "wasted" on video games. There is a certain sense of adultness that spending money imparts, a feeling of being a consumer, which distinguishes a game with a price from its counterparts among the traditional childhood games children once played at no cost.

There are other differences as well. Unlike child-initiated and child-organized games such as marbles, video games are adult-created mechanisms not entirely within the child's control, and thus less likely to impart a sense of mastery and fulfillment: the coin may get jammed, the machine may go haywire, the little blobs may stop eating the funny little dots. Then the child must go to the storekeeper to complain, to get his money back. He may be "ripped off" and simply lose his quarter, much as his parents are when they buy a faulty appliance. This possibility of disaster gives the child's play a certain weight that marbles never imposed on its light-hearted players.

Even if a child has a video game at home requiring no coin outlay, the play it provides is less than optimal. The noise level of the machine is high—too high, usually, for the child to conduct a conversation easily with another child. And yet, according to its enthusiasts, this very noisiness is a part of the game's attraction. The loud whizzes, crashes, and whirrs of the video-game machine "blow the mind" and create an excitement that is quite apart from the excitement generated simply by trying to win a game. A traditional childhood game such as marbles, on the other hand, has little built-in stimulation; the excitement of playing is generated entirely by the players' own actions. And while the pace of a game of marbles is close to the child's natural physiological rhythms, the frenzied activities of video games serve to "rev up" the child in an artificial way, almost in the way a stimulant or an amphetamine might, Meanwhile the perceptual impact of a video game is similar to that of watching television—the action, after all, takes place on a television screen—causing the eye to defocus slightly and creating a certain alteration in the child's natural state of consciousness.

Parents' instinctive reaction to their children's involvement with video games provides another clue to the difference between this contemporary form of play and the more traditional pastimes such as marbles. While parents, indeed most adults, derive open pleasure from watching children at play, most parents today are not delighted to watch their kids flicking away at the Pac-Man machine. This does not seem to them to be real play. As a mother of two school-age children anxiously explains, "We used to do real childhood sorts of things when I was a kid. We'd build forts and put on crazy plays and make up new languages, and just generally we *played.* But today my kids don't play that way at all. They like video games and of course they still go in for sports outdoors. They go roller skating and ice skating and skiing and all. But they don't seem to really *play.*"

Some of this feeling may represent a certain nostalgia for the past and the old generation's resistance to the different ways of the new. But it is more likely that most adults have an instinctive understanding of the importance of play in their own childhood. This feeling stokes their fears that their children are being deprived of something irreplaceable when they flip the levers on the video machines to manipulate the electronic images rather than flick their fingers to send a marble shooting towards another marble.

Play Deprivation

In addition to television's influence, some parents and teachers ascribe children's diminished drive to play to recent changes in the school curriculum, especially in the early grades.

"Kindergarten, traditionally a playful port of entry into formal school, is becoming more academic, with children being taught specific skills, taking tests, and occasionally even having homework," begins a report on new directions in early childhood education. Since 1970, according to the United States census, the proportion of three and four-year-olds enrolled in school has risen dramatically, from 20.5 percent to 36 percent towards academic acceleration in the early grades. Moreover, middle-class nursery schols in recent years have introduced substantial doses of academic material into their daily programs, often using those particular devices originally intended to help culturally deprived preschoolers in compensatory programs such as Headstart to catch up with their middle-class peers. Indeed, some of the increased focus on academic skills in nursery schools and kindergartens is related to the widespread popularity among young children and their parents of *Sesame Street,* a program originally intended to help deprived children attain academic skills, but universally watched by middle-class toddlers as well.

Parents of the *Sesame Street* generation often demand a "serious," skill-centered program for their preschoolers in school, afraid that the old-fashioned, play-centered curriculum will bore their alphabet-spouting, number-chanting four- and five-year-olds. A few parents, especially those whose children have not attended television classes or nursery school, complain of the high-powered pace of kindergarten these days. A father whose five-year-old daughter attends a public kindergarten declares: "There's a lot more pressure put on little kids these days than when we were kids, that's for sure. My daughter never went to nursery school and never watched *Sesame,* and she had a lot of trouble when she entered kindergarten this fall. By October, just a month and a half into the program, she was already flunking. The teacher told us our daughter couldn't keep up with the other kids. And believe me, she's a bright kid! All the other kids were getting gold stars and smiley faces for their work, and every day Emily would come home in tears because she didn't get a gold star. Remember when we were in kindergarten? We were *children* then. We were allowed just to play!"

A kindergarten teacher confirms the trend towards early academic pressure. "We're expected by the dictates of the school system to push a lot of curriculum," she explains. "Kids in our kindergarten can't sit around playing with blocks any more. We've just managed to squeeze in one hour of free play a week, on Fridays."

The diminished emphasis on fantasy and play and imaginative activities in early childhood education and the increased focus on early academic-skill acquisition have helped to change childhood from a play-centered time of life to one more closely resembling the style of adulthood: purposeful, success-centered, competitive. The likelihood is that these preschool "workers" will not metamorphose back into players when they move on to grade school. This decline in play is surely one of the reasons why so many teachers today comment that their third- or fourth-grades act like tired businessmen instead of like children.

What might be the consequences of this change in children's play? Children's propensity to engage in that extraordinary series of behaviors characterized as "play" is perhaps the single great dividing line between childhood and adulthood, and has probably been so throughout history. The make-believe games anthropologists have recorded of children in primitive societies around the world attest to the universality of play and to the uniqueness of this activity to the immature members of each society. But in those societies, and probably in Western society before the middle or late eighteenth century, there was always a certain similarity between children's play and adult work. The child's imaginative play took the form of imitation of various aspects of adult life, culminating in the gradual transformation of the child's play from make-believe work to *real* work. At this point, in primitive societies or in our own society of the past, the child took her or his place in the adult work world and the distinctions between adulthood and childhood virtually vanished. But in today's technologically advanced society there is no place for the child in the adult work world. There are not enough jobs, even of the most menial kind, to go around for adults, much less for children. The child must continue to be dependent on adults for many years while gaining the knowledge and skills necessary to become a working member of society.

This is not a new situation for children. For centuries children have endured a prolonged period of dependence long after the helplessness of early childhood is over. But until recent years children remained childlike and playful far longer than they do today. Kept isolated from the adult world as a result of deliberate secrecy and protectiveness, they continued to find pleasure in socially sanctioned childish activities until the imperatives of adolescence led them to strike out for independence and self-sufficiency.

Today, however, with children's inclusion in the adult world both through the instrument of television and as a result of a deliberately preparatory, integrative style of child rearing, the old forms of play no longer seem to provide children with enough excitement and stimulation. What then are these so-called children to do for fulfillment if their desire to play has been vitiated and yet their entry into the working world of adulthood must be delayed for many years? The answer is precisely to get involved in those areas that cause contemporary parents so much distress: addictive television viewing during the school years followed, in adolescence or even before, by a search for similar oblivion via alcohol and drugs; exploration of the world of sensuality and sexuality before achieving the emotional maturity necessary for altruistic relationships.

Psychiatrists have observed among children in recent years a marked increase in the occurrence of depression, a state long considered antithetical to the nature of childhood. Perhaps this phenomenon is at least somewhat connected with the current sense of uselessness and alienation that children feel, a sense that play may once upon a time have kept in abeyance.

JOURNAL PROMPT:

Write about an activity you engaged in as a child that you think the author would define as the type of play currently on the decline.

COLLABORATIVE EXERCISE:

Working in small groups, discuss children you know, either siblings, neighbors, or perhaps your own youngsters. Do these children engage in the type of play Winn describes as beneficial? Do they also partake in the activities she describes as harmful?

ESSAY ASSIGNMENT:

1. Winn writes, "It is among the ranks of school-age children, those six-to-twelve-year-olds who once avidly filled their free moments with childhood play, that the greatest change is evident." Do you believe there is a correlation between the claims of this author and Hymowitz's hypothesis in "The Teening of Childhood"?
2. According to the author, play seems to have been replaced by a "burgeoning interest in boy-girl interactions. . . . activities . . . that used to commence at puberty or even later." How do you feel about prepubescents engaged in "manifestly unchildlike interests"? What are some of the possible consequences of such behavior?
3. The author makes some basic assumptions about her subject matter, with which you may or may not agree. What are those assumptions? Do you believe them to be accurate?

ADDITIONAL ESSAY PROMPTS

1. In each of the readings "Pain for a Daughter," "Rites of Passage," and "The First Day," there is a change from childhood innocence to self-discovery. Compare these three works as they relate to that change.

2. Reread Mary Cantwell's description of her childhood, as well as Michele Norris's description of Dooney Waters's childhood in "A Child of Crack." Speculate on how Dooney will recall *his* earliest years.

3. Both John Holt in "Three Kinds of Discipline" and William Damon in "Spare the Chores, Spoil the Child" make a claim that children learn important lessons through the life experiences provided for them by the role models in their lives. Do you think Holt would agree with Damon that

children benefit from doing chores? Do you think Damon would agree with Holt's assessment of the different types of discipline? Explain.

4. During his discussion of the third discipline—The Discipline of Superior Force—John Holt explains: "A child whose life is full of the threat and fear of punishment is locked into babyhood. There is no way for him to grow up, to learn to take responsibility for his life and acts." How does Holt's philosophy reflect or contradict your own childhood experiences with discipline?
5. Reflect on the rewards—and dangers—of making the past the focus of your current life. What benefits do we gain from reflection, and what happens when the past prevents us from moving on?
6. Advertisers have obviously adjusted their focus to include a very particular group of children: preteens. Recall when you were first drawn to advertisements. How old were you? What were the items you wanted? How did your parents respond to these wishes?
7. Do you believe nostalgia to be a good or a bad thing? How does it differ from sentimentality?
8. Why do you think homeschooling is experiencing such popularity now?
9. Write about your childhood neighborhood. Does your sense of community derive from that early experience? Explain.
10. Did you have a pet as a child? Did this animal play an important role in your life? Explain.

ADDITIONAL RESEARCH QUESTIONS

1. What is "hands-on" learning? How does it correlate with John Holt's description of the Discipline of Nature?
2. How do you know if a child is ready for school? Research what educators look for in assessing a child's readiness.
3. What antidrug measures are being adopted in your community? Which of these seems to be the most effective?
4. Many public schools today receive additional revenues from corporations anxious to advertise their products to children, in a previously ad-free environment. Look for reasons why this situation exists. What are some ways parents, teachers, administrators, and the community can counteract the influence advertisers have over children?

5. Our drug laws don't seem to be particularly effective in curbing either drug use or drug sales. Write an essay in which you argue your views on solving this problem and why you think your plan might be more effective than current policy. (If you know someone who has been adversely impacted by drug use, you might want to use such personal knowledge to point out the main weaknesses of current laws.)

3

In Our Midst: The Importance of Fairy Tales in Our Lives

The adventures detailed in fairy tales mirror our own psychological journeys. We may not have to work as a scullery maid while our sisters play all day, but we can and do experience sibling rivalry in much the same way Cinderella did.

Fairy tales are loaded with symbolism; as we struggle to understand a story, meaning develops concurrent with our deeper awareness of ourselves. For example: The forest, a common motif in fairy tales, is a representation of our innermost fears. As characters go into the forest to conquer the monsters that reside there, so too do we confront shadowy places in our own psyches, and from these confrontations we learn.

Bruno Bettelheim, in his book *The Uses of Enchantment,* claims that "fairy tales . . . direct the child to discover his identity and calling, and they also suggest what experiences are needed to develop his character further. Fairy tales intimate that a rewarding, good life is within one's reach despite adversity—but only if one does not shy away from the hazardous struggles without which one can never achieve true identity."

The selections in this unit introduce students to rich and varied material. Critical-thinking skills are enhanced as the readers analyze and determine for themselves the symbolic intent of the stories included.

Anne Sexton was born in 1928 to a prominent New England family. Shortly after the birth of a second daughter, she suffered a mental breakdown. Prompted by her psychiatrist, Sexton started writing poetry. Soon she was publishing in *The New Yorker* and other prestigious magazines. While her confessional poems earned her acclaim—as well as a Pulitzer Prize— Sexton was never able to overcome her fragile mental state, which saw her in and out of hospitals. In 1974, at the age of forty-five, she committed suicide.

ANNE SEXTON

Cinderella

You always read about it:
the plumber with twelve children
who wins the Irish Sweepstakes.
From toilets to riches.
That story.

Or the nursemaid,
some luscious sweet from Denmark
who captures the oldest son's heart.
From diapers to Dior.
That story.

Or a milkman who serves the wealthy,
eggs, cream, butter, yogurt, milk,
the white truck like an ambulance
who goes into real estate
and makes a pile.
From homogenized to martinis at lunch.

Or the charwoman
who is on the bus when it cracks up
and collects enough from the insurance.
From mops to Bonwit Teller.
That story.

Once
the wife of a rich man was on her deathbed
and she said to her daughter Cinderella:
Be devout. Be good. Then I will smile
down from heaven in the seam of a cloud.
The man took another wife who had
two daughters, pretty enough
but with hearts like blackjacks.
Cinderella was their maid.
She slept on the sooty hearth each night
and walked around looking like Al Jolson.
Her father brought presents home from town,

jewels and gowns for the other women
but the twig of a tree for Cinderella.
She planted that twig on her mother's grave
and it grew to a tree where a white dove sat.
Whenever she wished for anything the dove
would drop it like an egg upon the ground.
The bird is important, my dears, so heed him.

Next came the ball, as you all know.
It was a marriage market.
The prince was looking for a wife.
All but Cinderella were preparing
and gussying up for the big event.
Cinderella begged to go too.
Her stepmother threw a dish of lentils
into the cinders and said: Pick them
up in an hour and you shall go.
The white dove brought all his friends;
all the warm wings of the fatherland came,
and picked up the lentils in a jiffy.
No, Cinderella, said the stepmother,
you have no clothes and cannot dance.
That's the way with stepmothers.

Cinderella went to the tree at the grave
and cried forth like a gospel singer:
Mama! Mama! My turtledove,
send me to the prince's ball!
The bird dropped down a golden dress
and delicate little gold slippers.
Rather a large package for a simple bird.
So she went. Which is no surprise.

Her stepmother and sisters didn't
recognize her without her cinder face
and the prince took her hand on the spot
and danced with no other the whole day.

As nightfall came she thought she'd better
get home. The prince walked her home
and she disappeared into the pigeon house
and although the prince took an axe and broke
it open she was gone. Back to her cinders.
These events repeated themselves for three days.

However on the third day the prince
covered the palace steps with cobbler's wax
and Cinderella's gold shoe stuck upon it.

Now he would find whom the shoe fit
and find his strange dancing girl for keeps.
He went to their house and the two sisters
were delighted because they had lovely feet.
The eldest went into a room to try the slipper on
but her big toe got in the way so she simply
sliced it off and put on the slipper.
The prince rode away with her until the white dove
told him to look at the blood pouring forth.
That is the way with amputations.
They don't just heal up like a wish.
The other sister cut off her heel
but the blood told as blood will.
The prince was getting tired.
He began to feel like a shoe salesman.
But he gave it one last try.
This time Cinderella fit into the shoe
like a love letter into its envelope.

At the wedding ceremony
the two sisters came to curry favor
and the white dove pecked their eyes out.
Two hollow spots were left
like soup spoons.

Cinderella and the prince
lived, they say, happily ever after,
like two dolls in a museum case
never bothered by diapers or dust,
never arguing over the timing of an egg,
never telling the same story twice,
never getting a middle-aged spread,
their darling smiles pasted on for eternity.
Regular Bobbsey Twins.
That story.

JOURNAL PROMPT:

Explore how Sexton's poem "Cinderella" differs from the story you remember from childhood. Be specific.

COLLABORATIVE EXERCISE:

The class should be divided into groups of four or five. In your group, choose one person to be the recorder. Each group should pick one of the following points of view: Rewrite the Cinderella story from the point of view of the prince, the stepmother, the stepsisters, the rat who is turned into the coachman, or the mice who are turned into horses.

ESSAY ASSIGNMENT:

1. Consider Sexton's use of sarcasm. In particular, what do you suppose she is suggesting about the male/female relationship? While her description of self-mutilation seems exaggerated, explore some of the lengths men and women go to today to attract a mate.
2. In *The Uses of Enchantment,* child psychologist Bruno Bettelheim claims that the fairy tale "Cinderella" is a story of sibling rivalry—one reason, he says, for the tale's continuing popularity. Do you think this story reflects society's image of stepparents today?

MONA VAN DUYN is the first woman named poet laureate of the United States. Born in Iowa in 1921, Van Duyn is a 1991 Pulitzer Prize winner. Some of her works include *Bedtime Stories; A Time of Bees; To See, to Take;* and *Letter from a Father* (1987), from which this poem is taken.

MONA VAN DUYN

CINDERELLA'S STORY

To tell you the truth, the shoe pinched.
I had no way of knowing, you see,
that I was the girl he'd dreamed of.
Imagination had always consoled me,
but I'd tried to use it with care.
My sisters, I'd always thought, were the family
romantics, expecting nice clothes to do the trick
instead of the beholder's transforming eye.
All that dancing I would have to have done,
if it *was* me, had made my feet swollen.
But I didn't know I'd been dancing, I thought him a dreamer.
He had everything—looks, loneliness,

the belief that comforting and love could cure
even an advanced neurosis.
I didn't know whether or not
he was deluded, but I was sure
he was brave. I wanted to have worn the slipper.

And that's all there was to the first transformation,
something that happened so fast I nearly lost it
with one disclaiming murmur, but something
that did happen, that he made me believe.

None of my skills but love was the slightest use
to my husband. Others did well at keeping
the home fires damped or hot.
And so I began to learn the sleeping
senses. I learned wholly to love
the man in the prince, what didn't dance:
bad breath in the morning, sexual clumsiness,
a childlike willingness to let the old queen
dominate. That was easy. And I read a lot.
Snarled in ideas, heading for the unseen,
I heard the wise men snicker when I spoke.
I learned that I had some beauty and, wearing
one gown or another for my husband's sake,
I learned of its very real enhancement.
That was a little harder. I had a ball
before I learned to use what beauty I had
with kindness and honor. That was hardest of all.
Our son was born, and I went to the child
through a clutter of nursemaids to tell him
how it feels to be poor. I started to grow old.
My husband saw everything and was grateful.
Thickening a bit at the waist, he firmed
and stayed, always, faithful.

And that was the second transformation,
slow and solid.
We were happy together.

Everything comes in three's, they say,
and I'm stuck in the third transformation,
flopping like a fish who's out of the life-saving
everyday water. I starve now for a ration
of dreams, I've never learned to live

without dreams. All through the filth and anger
of childhood I ate them like a calming sugar,
my sweet secret. I move through the palace,
gripping its ghostly furniture
till my fingers ache. I guess
that it is real, that I am living,
but what is there left to dream of?
I dream, day and night, of giving.

Prince, soon to be king,
we've made all our lovely exchanges
and my years as your princess are ending.
Couldn't there be, for me,
just one more fairytale?
More fiercely than the silliest clubwoman
in the kingdom, I try to hold onto my looks
because I dream that there was someone
warted, once upon a time,
waiting a kiss to tell him he too
could be beloved. My frog,
my frog, where shall I find you?

JOURNAL PROMPT:

Who first read to you or told you stories?

COLLABORATIVE EXERCISE:

What *is* Van Duyn's third transformation? Discuss some possibilities.

ESSAY ASSIGNMENT:

1. Explore similar "Cinderella" stories from other cultures. What are the similarities and differences? Use the German (the Brothers Grimm) version as your basis for comparison.
2. Consider the male/female relationships in a sampling of fairy tales you are familiar with, including "Snow White," "Sleeping Beauty," and of course, "Cinderella." To adult readers, what makes these fairy tales so unrealistic in terms of current relationship patterns?

The following Japanese folktale describes how the Japanese people came to venerate and honor their elders.

AUTHOR UKNOWN

The Mountain Where Old People Were Abandoned

Long ago when people had reached the age of sixty and were unable to do anything, they were thrown into a mountain canyon. This was known as "sixty canyon abandonment."

In a certain village there was a farmer who became sixty years old. Since the lord of the country had commanded it, the time had arrived for him to be thrown into the mountain canyon. The man's son took him on his back and set off for the mountains. They continued farther and farther into the mountains. As they went along, the old man, riding on his son's back, broke off the tips of tree branches in order to mark the trail. "Father, father, what are you doing that for? Is it so you can find your way back home?" asked the son.

"No, it would be too bad if you were unable to find your way home," replied the father, "so I am marking the trail for you."

When he heard this the son realized how kindhearted his father was, and so he returned home with him. They hid the old man under the porch so that the lord would know nothing about it.

Now the lord of the country sometimes commanded his subjects to do very difficult things. One day he gathered all the farmers of the village together and said, "You must each bring me a rope woven from ashes."

All the farmers were very troubled, knowing that they could not possibly weave a rope from ashes. The young farmer whom we just mentioned went back home, called to his father under the porch, and said, "Today the lord commanded that everyone bring a rope woven from ashes. How can we do this?"

"You must weave a rope very tightly, then carefully burn it until it turns to ashes; then you can take it to the lord," said the old man.

The young farmer, happy to get this advice, did just as he was told. He made a rope of ashes and took it to the lord. None of the other farmers were able to do it, and so this farmer alone had carried out the lord's instructions. For this the lord praised him highly.

Next the lord commanded, "Everyone must bring a conch shell with a thread passed through it."

The young farmer went to his father again and asked him what he should do. "Take a conch shell and point the tip toward the light; then take a thread and stick a piece of rice on it. Give the rice to an ant and make it crawl into the mouth of the shell; in this way you can get the thread through."

The young farmer did as he was told, and so got the thread through the conch shell. He took the shell to the lord, who was much impressed. "How were you able to do such a difficult thing?" he asked.

The young farmer replied: "Actually I was supposed to throw my old father down into the mountain canyon, but I felt so sorry for him that I brought him back home and hid him under the porch. The things that you asked us to do were so difficult that I had to ask my father how to do them. I have done them as he told me, and brought them to you," and he honestly told what had happened.

When the lord heard this he was very much impressed and realized that old people are very wise and that they should be well taken care of. After that he commanded that the "sixty canyon abandonment" be stopped.

JOURNAL PROMPT:

Draft a letter to family members informing them in specific detail how you wish to live your final years if you are unable to live alone and care for yourself independently.

COLLABORATIVE EXERCISE:

In your groups, discuss the following:

1. List the alternatives available to elderly men or women as they become unable to care for themselves.
2. Explore in detail what you and other group members know about the nursing-home situation in the United States. What are the positive and negative aspects of these environments? Include any personal experiences you may have regarding nursing homes or senior care centers.

ESSAY ASSIGNMENT:

1. Explore the similarities and/or differences between the treatment of the elderly in the United States and in another country of your choice. Include an examination of each country's general attitude toward and sensibility about older people.
2. Years ago grandparents were cared for by an extended family with whom they lived until they died. Why have things changed, and what changes have you observed or read about that account for the ways in which we now treat our aging population?

ROBERT BLY is a storyteller, poet, and lecturer. He won the 1967 National Book Award for his second volume of poetry, *The Light around the Body.* Bly plays a primary role as organizer of the men's liberation movement, running retreats for men designed to aid them in discovering the truth about the pervasive stereotypes of masculinity in this society. This selection is an excerpt from his 1990 work, *Iron John: A Book about Men.*

ROBERT BLY

IRON JOHN

We talk a great deal about "the American man," as if there were some constant quality that remained stable over decades, or even within a single decade.

The men who live today have veered far away from the Saturnian, old-man-minded farmer, proud of his introversion, who arrived in New England in 1630, willing to sit through three services in an unheated church. In the South, an expansive, motherbound cavalier developed, and neither of these two "American men" resembled the greedy railroad entrepreneur that later developed in the Northeast, nor the reckless I-will-do-without culture settlers of the West.

Even in our own era the agreed-on model has changed dramatically. During the fifties, for example, an American character appeared with some consistency that became a model of manhood adopted by many men: the Fifties male.

He got to work early, labored responsibly, supported his wife and children, and admired discipline. Reagan is a sort of mummified version of this dogged type. This sort of man didn't see women's souls well, but he appreciated their bodies; and his view of culture and America's part in it was boyish and optimistic. Many of his qualities were strong and positive, but underneath the charm and bluff there was, and there remains, much isolation, deprivation, and passivity. Unless he has an enemy, he isn't sure that he is alive.

The Fifties man was supposed to like football, be aggressive, stick up for the United States, never cry, and always provide. But receptive space or intimate space was missing in this image of a man. The personality lacked some sense of flow. The psyche lacked compassion in a way that encouraged the unbalanced pursuit of the Vietnam war, just as, later, the lack of what we might call "garden" space inside Reagan's head led to his callousness and brutality toward the powerless in El Salvador, toward old people here, the unemployed, schoolchildren, and poor people in general.

The Fifties male had a clear vision of what a man was, and what male responsibilities were, but the isolation and one-sidedness of his vision were dangerous.

During the sixties, another sort of man appeared. The waste and violence of the Vietnam war made men question whether they knew what an adult male really was. If manhood meant Vietnam, did they want any part of it? Meanwhile, the feminist movement encouraged men to actually look at women, forcing them to become conscious of concerns and sufferings that the Fifties male labored to avoid. As men began to examine women's history and women's sensibility, some men began to notice what was called their *feminine* side and pay attention to it. This process continues to this day, and I would say that most contemporary men are involved in it in some way.

There's something wonderful about this development—I mean the practice of men welcoming their own "feminine" consciousness and nurturing it—this is important—and yet I have the sense that there is something wrong. The male in the past twenty years has become more thoughtful, more gentle. But by this process he has not become more free. He's a nice boy who pleases not only his mother but also the young woman he is living with.

In the seventies I began to see all over the country a phenomenon that we might call the "soft male." Sometimes even today when I look out at an audience, perhaps half the young males are what I'd call soft. They're lovely, valuable people—I like them—they're not interested in harming the earth or starting wars. There's a gentle attitude toward life in their whole being and style of living.

But many of these men are not happy. You quickly notice the lack of energy in them. They are life-preserving but not exactly life-giving. Ironically, you often see these men with strong women who positively radiate energy.

Here we have a finely tuned young man, ecologically superior to his father, sympathetic to the whole harmony of the universe, yet he himself has little vitality to offer.

The strong or life-giving women who graduated from the sixties, so to speak, or who have inherited an older spirit, played an important part in producing this life-preserving, but not life-giving, man.

I remember a bumper sticker during the sixties that read "WOMEN SAY YES TO MEN WHO SAY NO." We recognize that it took a lot of courage to resist the draft, go to jail, or move to Canada, just as it took courage to accept the draft and go to Vietnam. But the women of twenty years ago were definitely saying that they preferred the softer receptive male.

So the development of men was affected a little in this preference. Nonreceptive maleness was equated with violence, and receptive maleness was rewarded.

Some energetic women, at that time and now in the nineties, chose and still choose soft men to be their lovers and, in a way, perhaps, to be their sons. The new distribution of "yang" energy among couples didn't happen by accident. Young men for various reasons wanted their harder women, and women began to desire softer men. It seemed like a nice arrangement for a while, but we've lived with it long enough now to see that it isn't working out.

I first learned about the anguish of "soft" men when they told their stories in early men's gatherings. In 1980, the Lama Community in New Mexico asked me to teach a conference for men only, their first, in which about forty men participated. Each day we concentrated on one Greek god and one old story, and then late in the afternoons we gathered to talk. When the younger men spoke it was not uncommon for them to be weeping within five minutes. The amount of grief and anguish in these younger men was astounding to me.

Part of their grief rose out of remoteness from their fathers, which they felt keenly, but partly, too, grief flowed from trouble in their marriages or relationships. They had learned to be receptive, but receptivity wasn't enough to carry their marriages through troubled times. In every relationship something *fierce* is needed once in a while: both the man and the woman need to have it. But at the point when it was needed, often the young man came up short. He was nurturing, but something else was required—for his relationship, and for his life.

The "soft" male was able to say, "I can feel your pain, and I consider your life as important as mine, and I will take care of you and comfort you." But he could not say what he wanted, and stick by it. *Resolve* of that kind was a different matter.

In *The Odyssey,* Hermes instructs Odysseus that when he approaches Circe, who stands for a certain kind of matriarchal energy, he is to lift or show his sword. In these early sessions it was difficult for many of the younger men to distinguish between showing the sword and hurting someone. One man, a kind of incarnation of certain spiritual attitudes of the sixties, a man who had actually lived in a tree for a year outside Santa Cruz, found himself unable to extend his arm when it held a sword. He had learned so well not to hurt anyone that he couldn't lift the steel, even to catch the light of the sun on it. But showing a sword doesn't necessarily mean fighting. It can also suggest a joyful decisiveness.

The journey many American men have taken into softness, or receptivity, or "development of the feminine side," has been an immensely valuable journey, but more travel lies ahead. No stage is the final stop.

Finding Iron John

One of the fairy tales that speak of a third possibility for men, a third mode, is a story called "Iron John" or "Iron Hans." Though it was first set down by the Grimm brothers around 1820, this story could be ten or twenty thousand years old.

As the story starts, we find out that something strange has been happening in a remote area of the forest near the king's castle. When hunters go into this area, they disappear and never come back. Twenty others go after the first group and do not come back. In time, people begin to get the feeling that there's something weird in that part of the forest, and they "don't go there anymore."

One day an unknown hunter shows up at the castle and says, "What can I do? Anything dangerous to do around here?"

The King says: "Well, I could mention the forest, but there's a problem. The people who go out there don't come back. The return rate is not good."

"That's just the sort of thing I like," the young man says. So he goes into the forest and, interestingly, he goes there *alone,* taking only his dog. The young man and his dog wander about in the forest and they go past a pond. Suddenly a hand reaches up from the water, grabs the dog, and pulls it down.

The young man doesn't respond by becoming hysterical. He merely says, "This must be the place."

Fond as he is of his dog and reluctant as he is to abandon him, the hunter goes back to the castle, rounds up three more men with buckets, and then comes back to the pond to bucket out the water. Anyone who's ever tried it will quickly note that such bucketing is very slow work.

In time, what they find, lying on the bottom of the pond, is a large man covered with hair from head to foot. The hair is reddish—it looks a little like rusty iron. They take the man back to the castle, and imprison him. The King puts him in an iron cage in the courtyard, calls him "Iron John," and gives the key into the keeping of the Queen.

Let's stop the story here for a second.

When a contemporary man looks down into his psyche, he may, if conditions are right, find under the water of his soul, lying in an area no one has visited for a long time, an ancient hairy man.

The mythological systems associate hair with the instinctive and the sexual and the primitive. What I'm suggesting, then, is that every modern male has, lying at the bottom of his psyche, a large, primitive being covered with hair down to his feet. Making contact with this Wild Man is the step the Eighties male or the Nineties male has yet to take. That bucketing-out process has yet to begin in our contemporary culture.

As the story suggests very delicately, there's more than a little fear around this hairy man, as there is around all change. When a man begins to develop the receptive side of himself and gets over his initial skittishness, he usually finds the experience to be wonderful. He gets to write poetry and go out and sit by the ocean, he doesn't have to be on top all the time in sex anymore, he becomes empathetic—it's a new, humming, surprising world.

But going down through water to touch the Wild Man at the bottom of the pond is quite a different matter. The being who stands up is frightening, and seems even more so now, when the corporations do so much work to produce the sanitized, hairless, shallow man. When a man welcomes his responsiveness, or what we sometimes call his internal woman, he often feels warmer, more companionable, more alive. But when he approaches what I'll call the "deep male," he feels risk. Welcoming the Hairy Man *is* scary and risky, and it requires a different sort of courage. Contact with Iron John requires a willingness to descend into the male psyche and accept what's dark down there, including the *nourishing* dark.

For generations now, the industrial community has warned young businessmen to keep away from Iron John, and the Christian church is not too fond of him either.

Freud, Jung, and Wilhelm Reich are three investigators who had the courage to go down into the pond and to accept what they found there. The job of contemporary men is to follow them down.

Some men have already done this work, and the Hairy Man has been brought up from the pond in their psyches, and lives in the courtyard. "In the courtyard" suggests that the individual or the culture has brought him into a sunlit place where all can see him. That is itself some advance over keeping the Hairy Man in a cellar, where many elements in every culture want him to be. But, of course, in either place, he's still in a cage.

The Loss of the Golden Ball

Now back to the story.

One day the King's eight-year-old son is playing in the courtyard with the golden ball he loves, and it rolls into the Wild Man's cage. If the young boy wants the ball back, he's going to have to approach the Hairy Man and ask him for it. But this is going to be a problem.

The golden ball reminds us of that unity of personality we had as children—a kind of radiance, or wholeness, before we split into male and female, rich and poor, bad and good. The ball is golden, as the sun is, and round. Like the sun, it gives off a radiant energy from the inside.

We notice that the boy is eight. All of us, whether boys or girls, lose something around the age of eight. If we still have the golden ball in kindergarten, we lose it in grade school. Whatever is still left we lose in high school. In "The Frog Prince," the princess's ball fell into a well. Whether we are male or female, once the golden ball is gone, we spend the rest of our lives trying to get it back.

The first stage in retrieving the ball, I think, is to accept—firmly, definitely—that the ball has been lost. Freud said: "What a distressing contrast there is between the radiant intelligence of the child and the feeble mentality of the average adult."

So where is the golden ball? Speaking metaphorically, we could say that the sixties culture told men they would find their golden ball in sensitivity, receptivity, cooperation, and nonaggressiveness. But many men gave up all aggressiveness and still did not find the golden ball.

The Iron John story says that a man can't expect to find the golden ball in the feminine realm, because that's not where the ball is. A bridegroom secretly asks his wife to give him back the golden ball. I think she'd give it to him if she could, because most women in my experience do not try to block men's growth. But she can't give it to him, because she doesn't have it. What's more, she's lost her own golden ball and can't find that either.

Oversimplifying, we could say that the Fifties male always wants a woman to return his golden ball. The Sixties and Seventies man, with equal lack of success, asks his interior feminine to return it.

The Iron John story proposes that the golden ball lies within the magnetic field of the Wild Man, which is a very hard concept for us to grasp. We have to accept the possibility that the true radiant energy in the male does not hide in, reside in, or wait for us in the feminine realm, nor in the macho/John Wayne realm, but in the magnetic field of the deep masculine. It is protected by the *instinctive* one who's underwater and who has been there we don't know how long.

In "The Frog Prince" it's the frog, the un-nice one, the one that everyone says "Ick!" to, who brings the golden ball back. And in the Grimm brothers version the frog himself turns into the prince only when a hand throws him against the wall.

Most men want some nice person to bring the ball back, but the story hints that we won't find the golden ball in the force field of an Asian guru or even the force field of gentle Jesus. Our story is not anti-Christian but pre-Christian by a thousand years or so, and its message is still true—getting the golden ball back is incompatible with certain kinds of conventional tameness and niceness.

The kind of wildness, or un-niceness, implied by the Wild Man image is not the same as macho energy, which men already know enough about. Wild Man energy, by contrast, leads to forceful action undertaken, not with cruelty, but with resolve.

The Wild Man is not opposed to civilization; but he's not completely contained by it either. The ethical superstructure of popular Christianity does not support the Wild Man, though there is some suggestion that Christ himself did. At the beginning of his ministry, a hairy John, after all, baptized him.

When it comes time for a young male to talk with the Wild Man he will find the conversation quite distinct from a talk with a minister, a rabbi, or a guru. Conversing with the Wild Man is not talking about bliss or mind or spirit or "higher consciousness," but about something wet, dark, and low—what James Hillman would call "soul."

The first step amounts to approaching the cage and asking for the golden ball back. Some men are ready to take that step, while others haven't yet bucketed the water out of the pond—they haven't left the collective male identity and gone out into the unknown area alone, or gone with only their dog.

The story says that after the dog "goes down" one has to start to work with buckets. No giant is going to come along and suck out all the water for you: that magic stuff is not going to help. And a weekend at Esalen won't do it. Acid or cocaine won't do it. The man has to do it bucket by bucket. This resembles the slow discipline of art: it's the work that Rembrandt did, that Picasso and Yeats and Rilke and Bach did. Bucket work implies much more discipline than most men realize.

The Wild Man, as the writer Keith Thompson mentioned to me, is not simply going to hand over the golden ball either. What kind of story would it be if the Wild Man said: "Well, okay, here's your ball"?

Jung remarked that all successful requests to the psyche involve deals. The psyche likes to make deals. If part of you, for example, is immensely lazy and doesn't want to do any work, a flat-out New Year's resolution won't do any good. The whole thing will go better if you say to the lazy part: "You let me work for an hour, then I'll let you be a slob for an hour—deal?" So in "Iron John," a deal is made: the Wild Man agrees to give the golden ball back if the boy opens the cage.

The boy, apparently frightened, runs off. He doesn't even answer. Isn't that what happens? We have been told so often by parents, ministers, grade-school teachers, and high-school principals that we should have nothing to do with the Wild Man that when he says "I'll return the ball if you let me out of the cage," we don't even reply.

Maybe ten years pass now. On "the second day" the man could be twenty-five. He goes back to the Wild Man and says, "Could I have my ball back?" The Wild Man says, "Yes, if you let me out of the cage."

Actually, just returning to the Wild Man a second time is a marvelous thing; some men never come back at all. The twenty-five-year-old man hears the sentence all right, but by now he has two Toyotas and a mortgage, maybe a wife and a child. How can he let the Wild Man out of the cage? A man usually walks away the second time also without saying a word.

Now ten more years pass. Let's say the man is now thirty-five . . . have you ever seen the look of dismay on the face of a thirty-five-year-old man? Feeling overworked, alienated, empty, he asks the Wild Man with full heart this time: "Could I have my golden ball back?"

"Yes," the Wild Man says, "If you let me out of my cage."

Now something marvelous happens in the story. The boy speaks to the Wild Man, and continues the conversation. He says, "Even if I wanted to let you out, I couldn't, because I don't know where the key is."

That's so good. By the time we are thirty-five we don't know where the key is. It isn't exactly that we have forgotten—we never knew where it was in the first place.

The story says that when the King locked up the Wild Man, "he gave the key into the keeping of the Queen," but we were only about seven then, and in any case our father never told us what he had done with it. So where is the key?

I've heard audiences try to answer that one:

"It's around the boy's neck."

No.

"It's hidden in Iron John's cage."

No.

"It's inside the golden ball."

No.

"It's inside the castle . . . on a hook inside the Treasure Room."

No.

"It's in the Tower. It's on a hook high up on the wall!"

No.

The Wild Man replies, "The key is under your mother's pillow."

The key is not inside the ball, nor in the golden chest, nor in the safe . . . the key is under our mother's pillow—just where Freud said it would be.

Getting the key back from under the mother's pillow is a troublesome task. Freud, taking advice from a Greek play, says that a man should not skip over the mutual attraction between himself and his mother if he wants a long life. The mother's pillow, after all, lies in the bed near where she makes love to your father. Moreover, there's another implication attached to the pillow.

Michael Meade, the myth teller, once remarked to me that the pillow is also the place where the mother stores all her expectations for you. She dreams: "My son the doctor." "My son the Jungian analyst." "My son the Wall Street genius." But very few mothers dream: "My son the Wild Man."

On the son's side, he isn't sure he wants to take the key. Simply transferring the key from the mother's to a guru's pillow won't help. Forgetting that the mother possesses it is a bad mistake. A mother's job is, after all, to civilize the boy, and so it is natural for her to keep the key. All families behave alike: on this planet, "The King gives the key into the keeping of the Queen."

Attacking the mother, confronting her, shouting at her, which some Freudians are prone to urge on us, probably does not accomplish much—she may just smile and talk to you with her elbow on the pillow. Oedipus' conversations with Jocasta never did much good, nor did Hamlet's shouting.

A friend mentioned that it's wise to steal the key some day when your mother and father are gone. "My father and mother are away today" implies a day when the head is free of parental inhibitions. That's the day to steal the key. Gioia Timpanelli, the writer and storyteller, remarked that, mythologically, the theft of the key belongs to the world of Hermes.

And the key has to be *stolen.* I recall talking to an audience of men and women once about this problem of stealing the key. A young man, obviously well trained in New Age modes of operation, said, "Robert, I'm disturbed by this idea of stealing the key. Stealing isn't right. Couldn't a group of us just go to the mother and say, 'Mom, could I have the key back?'"

His model was probably consensus, the way the staff at the health food store settles things. I felt the souls of all the women in the room rise up in the air to kill him. Men like that are as dangerous to women as they are to men.

No mother worth her salt would give the key anyway. If a son can't steal it, he doesn't deserve it.

"I want to let the Wild Man out!"

"Come over and give Mommy a kiss."

Mothers are intuitively aware of what would happen if he got the key: they would lose their boys. The possessiveness that mothers typically exercise on sons—not to mention the possessiveness that fathers typically exercise on daughters—can never be underestimated.

The means of getting the key back varies with each man, but suffice it to say that democratic or nonlinear approaches will not carry the day.

One rather stiff young man danced one night for about six hours, vigorously, and in the morning remarked, "I got some of the key back last night."

Another man regained the key when he acted like a whole-hearted Trickster for the first time in his life, remaining fully conscious of the tricksterism. Another man stole the key when he confronted his family and refused to carry any longer the shame for the whole family.

We could spend days talking of how to steal the key in a practical way. The story itself leaves everything open, and simply says, "One day he stole the key, brought it to the Wild Man's cage, and opened the lock. As he did so, he pinched one of his fingers." The Wild Man is then free at last, and it's clear that he will go back to his own forest, far from "the castle."

What Does the Boy Do?

At this point a number of things could happen. If the Wild Man returns to his forest while the boy remains in the castle, the fundamental historical split in the psyche between primitive man and the civilized man would reestablish itself in the boy. The boy, on his side, could mourn the loss of the Wild Man forever. Or he could replace the key under the pillow before his parents got home, then say he knows nothing about the Wild Man's escape. After that subterfuge, he could become a corporate executive, a fundamentalist minister, a tenured professor, someone his parents could be proud of, who "has never seen the Wild Man."

We've all replaced the key many times and lied about it. Then the solitary hunter inside us has to enter into the woods once more with his body dog accompanying him, and then the dog gets pulled down again. We lose a lot of "dogs" that way.

We could also imagine a different scenario. The boy convinces, or imagines he could convince, the Wild Man to stay in the courtyard. If that happened, he and the Wild Man could carry on civilized conversations with each other in the tea garden, and this conversation would go on for years. But the story suggests that Iron John and the boy cannot be united—that is, cannot experience their initial union—in the castle courtyard. It's probably too close to the mother's pillow and the father's book of rules.

We recall that the boy in our story, when he spoke to the Wild Man, told him he didn't know where the key was. That's brave. Some men never address a sentence to the Wild Man.

When the boy opened the cage, the Wild Man started back to his forest. The boy in our story, or the thirty-five-year-old man in our mind—however you want to look at it—now does something marvelous. He speaks to the Wild Man once more and says, "Wait a minute! If my parents come home and find you gone, they will beat me." That sentence makes the heart sink, particularly if we know something about child-rearing practices that have prevailed for a long time in northern Europe.

As Alice Miller reminds us in her book *For Your Own Good,* child psychologists in nineteenth-century Germany warned parents especially about *exuberance.* Exuberance in a child is bad, and at the first sign of it, parents should be severe. Exuberance implies that the wild boy or girl is no longer locked up. Puritan parents in New England often punished children severely if they acted in a restless way during the long church services.

"If they come home and find you gone, they will beat me."

The Wild Man says, in effect, "That's good thinking. You'd better come with me."

So the Wild Man lifts the boy up on his shoulders and together they go off into the woods. That's decisive. We should all be so lucky.

As the boy leaves for the forest, he has to overcome, at least for the moment, his fear of wildness, irrationality, hairiness, intuition, emotion, the body, and nature. Iron John is not as primitive as the boy imagines, but the boy—or the mind—doesn't know that yet.

Still, the clean break with the mother and father, which the old initiators call for, now has taken place. Iron John says to the boy, "You'll never see your mother and father again. But I have treasures, more than you'll ever need." So that is that.

JOURNAL PROMPT:

What is your definition of masculinity?

COLLABORATIVE EXERCISE:

Working in small groups, find some of the hasty generalizations Bly makes about men. How do these generalizations serve the author's purpose?

ESSAY ASSIGNMENT:

1. The fairy tale detailed in this essay follows the traditional pattern of separation, initiation, and return, a pattern that, according to Bly, must be followed by modern men if they are to become fully actualized human beings. How do you interpret, then, Iron John's comment to the boy, "You'll never see your mother and father again. But I have treasures, more than you'll ever need"?
2. Differentiate between the concept of the "Wild Man" as explained by the author and your understanding of "macho energy."
3. Pick one male role (for example, husband, father, worker), and explore how that role in America has changed in the past century.

DAVE BARRY is a Pulitzer Prize–winning humorist and syndicated columnist. In this piece he explores the lure of the *Star Wars* films.

DAVE BARRY

Feeling the Force

It's coming! Put your ear to the page and listen . . .

BOM-bom! Bom bom bom BOM-bom! Bom bom bom BOM bom! Bom bom bom bom . . .

That's right: It's the theme from "Star Wars," the movie series that gave the world a whole new lexicon, including such phrases as "the Force," "Death Star," "light saber," "lexicon" and "licensed merchandise."

"Star Wars" has become an important and cherished part of our shared cultural heritage, like Starbucks and Pez. And soon another chapter will be added to the "Star Wars" legend with the release of the long-awaited new installment in the series, entitled "Episode I: The Empire Gets a Building Permit." On the day this movie is released, millions of Americans will flock to movie theaters to share in the excitement and wonder of being told that the theater is sold out through October because all the tickets have been snapped up by crazed drooling "Star Wars" geeks wearing officially licensed Han Solo underwear.

What explains the powerful appeal of the "Star Wars" series? Speaking as one who saw "Return of the Jedi" on video at least 14,000 times when my son was 4 and refused to watch anything else but also refused to be left alone with Jabba the Hutt, I would say that the key element is the theme of Good vs. Evil. Good is of course represented by Luke Skywalker (Mark Hamill), who has the Force, a mystical, universal power that causes him to be attracted to his sister. Fortunately, Luke gets over that and meets a wise Jedi master named Yoda (Raymond Burr) who trains Luke to harness the awesome power of the Force so that he can speak lines of really bad dialogue without laughing.

Along the way Luke meets many memorable characters, including Han Solo (Indiana Jones), Chewbacca (Sonny Bono), Princess Leia (Prince) and two quirky, lovable robots, C-3PO (Tony Danza) and R2-D2 (F7-Z9). After many hair-raising adventures, Luke finally goes to the Death Star (Marlon Brando) where he confronts Evil in the form of his father, Darth Vader (voice by Perry Como) and, in a heart-warming scene of reconciliation, beats him up. The dramatic climax comes when Luke removes the helmet from the dying Vader and gazes, at last, into the eyes of the person beneath the harsh, forbidding mask (Martha Stewart). In the end, Good triumphs over Evil, and Luke and his friends celebrate on the planet of the Ewoks, a race of fun-loving, short, hairy creatures (Robin Williams).

As humans, we relate to this timeless story because we all go through the same kind of moral struggle in our own lives. We have a Force within us, and sometimes we use it for Good, as when we decide to have a salad instead of a cheeseburger and fries; but sometimes we turn toward the Dark Side, as when we load up our salad with a fatty ranch dressing, or we take all the remaining artichoke segments from the salad bar, leaving none for the next person in line (Nick Nolte).

These timeless themes explain why we are all so excited that director George Lucas (Inc.) has decided, despite the very real risk that he will make billions of dollars, to come out with a new episode of "Star Wars." Until recently, specific information about the new episode was "Top Secret"—nobody knew the plot except Lucas, the actors, and of course the government of China. Fortunately, however, I have obtained, from high-level sources who asked not to be identified (Al and Tipper Gore), specific details on the plot. If you don't want me to spoil the shocking surprise ending (Liam Neeson gets killed), stop reading right now, because here is . . .

The plot: There is big trouble brewing in the universe (California). The evil and greedy Trade Federation (Microsoft) is planning to invade the tiny planet of Naboo (Naboo), which is inhabited by a race of strange frog-like beings (the House Judiciary Committee). Two Jedi knights, Obi-Wan and Qui-Gon Jinn (Siegfried and Roy) go to Naboo, where, after overcoming numerous special effects, they are joined by the Naboo queen (Dennis Rodman). They escape in a space ship, but when the "D"-cell batteries in their light sabers run low, they are forced to land on the evil, Hutt-controlled planet of Tatooine (New Jersey). There they meet 9-year-old Anakin Skywalker (Danny DeVito), and they realize that he has the Force when he is able, without physically touching it, to raise and lower a garage door. After a meeting with the ancient Jedi Council (the Rolling Stones), Anakin and the others return to Naboo for a climactic finale in which Siegfried (Roy) battles with the evil warlord Darth Maul (Marv Albert) to determine who will ultimately control the tie-in rights for Star Wars collectibles (Pepsi). As the movie ends, we see the young Anakin preparing to face an uncertain future consisting of at least 14 more sequels, and we hear the stirring sound of . . .

BOM-bom! Bom bom bom BOM-bom! Bom bom bom BOM bom! Bom bom bom bom . . .

. . . and we feel the Force welling up from deep inside ourselves. And so we burp.

JOURNAL PROMPT:

Did you see any of the *Star Wars* trilogy? What was it you liked or disliked about the films?

COLLABORATIVE EXERCISE:

Working in small groups, decide what it is about Dave Barry's writing that makes it humorous. What do you think are some of the elements of humor? How does Barry make use of these?

ESSAY ASSIGNMENT:

1. Although Dave Barry takes a humorous look at the *Star Wars* phenomenon, he claims the movie *works* because we face similar moral struggles in our own lives. Explain the parallels between the metaphorical *Star Wars* trilogy and problems that occur in "real" life.
2. Try writing a humorous review of the last movie you saw.

This selection is from BRUNO BETTELHEIM's famous work *The Uses of Enchantment: The Meaning and Importance of Fairy Tales* (1977). Bettelheim was recognized as a great child psychologist. Born in Vienna in 1903, he received his doctorate from the University of Vienna. Bettelheim spent time in the Nazi concentration camps. In 1939, he came to America, where he was a distinguished professor of education at the University of Chicago, well known for his work with autistic children. Dr. Bettelheim died in 1990.

BRUNO BETTELHEIM

LIFE DIVINED FROM THE INSIDE

"Little Red Riding Hood was my first love. I felt that if I could have married Little Red Riding Hood, I should have known perfect bliss." This statement by Charles Dickens indicates that he, like untold millions of children all over the world throughout the ages, was enchanted by fairy tales. Even when world-famous, Dickens acknowledged the deep formative impact that the wondrous figures and events of fairy tales had had on him and his creative genius. He repeatedly expressed scorn for those who, motivated by an uninformed and petty rationality, insisted on rationalizing, bowdlerizing, or outlawing these stories, and thus robbed children of the important contributions fairy tales could make to their lives. Dickens understood that the imagery of fairy tales helps children better than anything else in their most difficult and yet most important and satisfying task: achieving a more mature consciousness to civilize the chaotic pressures of their unconscious.[1]

Today, as in the past, the minds of both creative and average children can be opened to an appreciation of all the higher things in life by fairy tales, from

---

[1] Taken from Angus Wilson, *The World of Charles Dickens* (London: Secker and Warburg, 1970); and Michael C. Kotzin, *Dickens and the Fairy Tale* (Bowling Green: Bowling Green University Press, 1972).

which they can move easily to enjoying the greatest works of literature and art. The poet Louis MacNeice, for example, tells that "Real fairy stories always meant much to me as a person, even when I was at a public school where to admit this meant losing face. Contrary to what many people say even now, a fairy story, at least of the classical folk variety, is a much more solid affair than the average naturalistic novel, whose hooks go little deeper than a gossip column. From folk tales and sophisticated fairy tales such as Hans Andersen's or Norse mythology and stories like the *Alice* books and *Water Babies* I graduated, at about the age of twelve, to the *Faerie Queene*."[2] Literary critics such as G. K. Chesterton and C. S. Lewis felt that fairy stories are "spiritual explorations" and hence "the most life-like" since they reveal "human life as seen, or felt, or divined from the inside."[3]

Fairy tales, unlike any other form of literature, direct the child to discover his identity and calling, and they also suggest what experiences are needed to develop his character further. Fairy tales intimate that a rewarding, good life is within one's reach despite adversity—but only if one does not shy away from the hazardous struggles without which one can never achieve true identity. These stories promise that if a child dares to engage in this fearsome and taxing search, benevolent powers will come to his aid, and he will succeed. The stories also warn that those who are too timorous and narrow-minded to risk themselves in finding themselves must settle down to a humdrum existence—if an even worse fate does not befall them.

Past generations of children who loved and felt the importance of fairy tales were subjected to the scorn only of pedants, as happened to MacNeice. Today many of our children are far more grievously bereaved—because they are deprived of the chance to know fairy stories at all. Most children now meet fairy tales only in prettified and simplified versions which subdue their meaning and rob them of all deeper significance—versions such as those on films and TV shows, where fairy tales are turned into empty-minded entertainment.

Through most of man's history, a child's intellectual life, apart from immediate experiences within the family, depended on mythical and religious stories and on fairy tales. This traditional literature fed the child's imagination and stimulated his fantasizing. Simultaneously, since these stories answered the child's most important questions, they were a major agent of his socialization. Myths and closely related religious legends offered material from which children formed their concepts of the world's origin and purpose, and of the social ideals a child could pattern himself after. These were the images of the unconquered hero Achilles and wily Odysseus; of Hercules, whose life history showed

---

[2] Louis MacNeice, *Varieties of Parable* (New York: Cambridge University Press, 1965).

[3] C. K. Chesterton, *Orthodoxy* (London: John Lane, 1909). C. S. Lewis, *The Allegory of Love* (Oxford: Oxford University Press, 1936).

that it is not beneath the dignity of the strongest man to clean the filthiest stable; of St. Martin, who cut his coat in half to clothe a poor beggar. It is not just since Freud that the myth of Oedipus has become the image by which we understand the ever new but age-old problems posed to us by our complex and ambivalent feelings about our parents. Freud referred to this ancient story to make us aware of the inescapable cauldron of emotions which every child, in his own way, has to manage at a certain age.

In the Hindu civilization, the story of Rama and Sita (part of the *Ramayana*), which tells of their peaceable courage and their passionate devotion to each other, is the prototype of love and marriage relationships. The culture, moreover, enjoins everyone to try to relive this myth in his or her own life; every Hindu bride is called Sita, and as part of her wedding ceremony she acts out certain episodes of the myth.

In a fairy tale, internal processes are externalized and become comprehensible as represented by the figures of the story and its events. This is the reason why in traditional Hindu medicine a fairy tale giving form to his particular problem was offered to a psychically disoriented person, for his meditation. It was expected that through contemplating the story the disturbed person would be led to visualize both the nature of the impasse in living from which he suffered, and the possibility of its resolution. From what a particular tale implied about man's despair, hopes, and methods of overcoming tribulations, the patient could discover not only a way out of his distress but also a way to find himself, as the hero of the story did.

But the paramount importance of fairy tales for the growing individual resides in something other than teachings about correct ways of behaving in this world—such wisdom is plentifully supplied in religion, myths, and fables. Fairy stories do not pretend to describe the world as it is, nor do they advise what one ought to do. If they did, the Hindu patient would be induced to follow an imposed pattern of behavior—which is not just bad therapy, but the opposite of therapy. The fairy tale is therapeutic because the patient finds his *own* solutions, through contemplating what the story seems to imply about him and his inner conflicts at this moment in his life. The content of the chosen tale usually has nothing to do with the patient's external life, but much to do with his inner problems, which seem incomprehensible and hence unsolvable. The fairy tale clearly does not refer to the outer world, although it may begin realistically enough and have everyday features woven into it. The unrealistic nature of these tales (which narrow-minded rationalists object to) is an important device, because it makes obvious that the fairy tales' concern is not useful information about the external world, but the inner processes taking place in an individual.

In most cultures, there is no clear line separating myth from folk or fairy tale; all these together form the literature of preliterate societies. The Nordic languages have only one word for both: *saga*. German has retained the word *Sage* for myths, while fairy stories are called *Märchen*. It is unfortunate that both the English and French names for these stories emphasize the role of fairies in them—because in most, no fairies appear. Myths and fairy tales alike attain a definite form only when they are committed to writing and are no longer subject to continuous change. Before being written down, these stories were either condensed or vastly elaborated in the retelling over the centuries; some stories merged with others. All became modified by what the teller thought was of greatest interest to his listeners, by what his concerns of the moment or the special problems of his era were.

Some fairy and folk stories evolved out of myths; others were incorporated into them. Both forms embodied the cumulative experience of a society as men wished to recall past wisdom for themselves and transmit it to future generations. These tales are the purveyors of deep insights that have sustained mankind through the long vicissitudes of its existence, a heritage that is not revealed in any other form as simply and directly, or as accessibly, to children.

Myths and fairy tales have much in common. But in myths, much more than in fairy stories, the culture hero is presented to the listener as a figure he ought to emulate in his own life, as far as possible.

A myth, like a fairy tale, may express an inner conflict in symbolic form and suggest how it may be solved—but this is not necessarily the myth's central concern. The myth presents its theme in a majestic way; it carries spiritual force; and the divine is present and is experienced in the form of superhuman heroes who make constant demands on mere mortals. Much as we, the mortals, may strive to be like these heroes, we will remain always and obviously inferior to them.

The figures and events of fairy tales also personify and illustrate inner conflicts, but they suggest ever so subtly how these conflicts may be solved, and what the next steps in the development toward a higher humanity might be. The fairy tale is presented in a simple, homely way; no demands are made on the listener. This prevents even the smallest child from feeling compelled to act in specific ways, and he is never made to feel inferior. Far from making demands, the fairy tale reassures, gives hope for the future, and holds out the promise of a happy ending. That is why Lewis Carroll called it a "love-gift"—a term hardly applicable to a myth.*

---

* Child of the pure unclouded brow
And dreaming eyes of wonder!
Though time be fleet, and I and thou
Are half a life asunder,
Thy loving smile will surely hail
The love-gift of a fairy-tale.

C. L. Dodgson (Lewis Carroll), in *Through the Looking-Glass*

Obviously, not every story contained in a collection called "Fairy Tales" meets these criteria. Many of these stories are simply diversions, cautionary tales, or fables. If they are fables, they tell by means of words, actions, or events—fabulous though these may be—what one ought to do. Fables demand and threaten—they are moralistic—or they just entertain. To decide whether a story is a fairy tale or something entirely different, one might ask whether it could rightly be called a love-gift to a child. That is not a bad way to arrive at a classification.

To understand how a child views fairy tales, let us consider as examples the many fairy stories in which a child outwits a giant who scares him or even threatens his life. That children intuitively understand what these "giants" stand for is illustrated by the spontaneous reaction of a five-year-old.

Encouraged by discussion about the importance fairy tales have for children, a mother overcame her hesitation about telling such "gory and threatening" stories to her son. From her conversations with him, she knew that her son already had fantasies about eating people, or people getting eaten. So she told him the tale of "Jack the Giant Killer."[4] His response at the end of the story was: "There aren't any such things as giants, are there?" Before the mother could give her son the reassuring reply which was on her tongue—and which would have destroyed the value of the story for him—he continued, "But there are such things as grownups, and they're like giants." At the ripe old age of five, he understood the encouraging message of the story: although adults can be experienced as frightening giants, a little boy with cunning can get the better of them.

This remark reveals one source of adult reluctance to tell fairy stories: we are not comfortable with the thought that occasionally we look like threatening giants to our children, although we do. Nor do we want to accept how easy they think it is to fool us, or to make fools of us, and how delighted they are by this idea. But whether or not we tell fairy tales to them, we *do*—as the example of this little boy proves—appear to them as selfish giants who wish to keep to ourselves all the wonderful things which give us power. Fairy stories provide reassurance to children that they can eventually get the better of the giant—i.e., they can grow up to be like the giant and acquire the same powers. These are "the mighty hopes that make us men."[5]

---

[4] "Jack the Giant Killer" and various other stories in the Jack cycle are printed in Katherine M. Briggs, *A Dictionary of British Folk Tales,* 4 volumes (Bloomington: Indiana University Press, 1970). British folk tales mentioned in this book can be found there. Another important collection of English fairy tales is that of Joseph Jacobs: *English Fairy Tales* (London: David Nutt, 1890), and *More English Fairy Tales* (London: David Nutt, 1895).

[5] "The mighty hopes that make us men." A. Tennyson, "In Memoriam" LXXXV.

Most significantly, if we parents tell such fairy stories to our children, we can give them the most important reassurance of all: that we approve of their playing with the idea of getting the better of these giants. Here reading is not the same as being told the story, because while reading alone the child may think that only some stranger—the person who wrote the story or arranged the book—approves of outwitting and cutting down the giant. But when his parents *tell* him the story, a child can be sure that they approve of his retaliating in fantasy for the threat which adult dominance entails.

JOURNAL PROMPT:

After having read this selection, do you plan on reading fairy tales to your children if and when you become a parent? Why or why not?

COLLABORATIVE EXERCISE:

Working in small groups, discuss your favorite fairy tale. Analyze why you think the story held power for you as a child.

ESSAY ASSIGNMENT:

1. The author makes the distinction between the "prettified and simplified" versions of fairy tales presented to children today in films and the force of a well-constructed, well-read fairy tale. Read a Grimm's fairy tale. Compare and contrast the story itself with the film version. Is it true—as Bettelheim claims—that moviemakers have turned once powerful tales into "empty-minded entertainment"?
2. Bettelheim writes, "The fairy tale clearly does not refer to the outer world, although it may begin realistically enough and have everyday features woven into it. The unrealistic nature of these tales (which narrow-minded rationalists object to) is an important device, because it makes obvious the fairy tales' concern is not useful information about the external world, but the inner processes taking place in an individual." Pick a favorite fairy tale, and trace how the story could suggest internal dynamics in the human psyche.
3. According to Bettelheim, how does a child view a fairy tale?

CLARISSA PINKOLA ESTES is a Jungian psychologist, as well as a storyteller. In her work *Women Who Run with the Wolves,* she uses myths and fairy tales to aid women in reconstructing a healthy connection with the "Wild Woman" archetype. Estes claims that these motifs describe the female psyche and by exploring and examining them, women can transform their lives. "Sealskin, Soulskin" is a selection from her book.

CLARISSA PINKOLA ESTES

SEALSKIN, SOULSKIN

During a time that once was, is now gone forever, and will come back again soon, there is day after day of white sky, white snow . . . and all the tiny specks in the distance are people or dogs or bear.

Here, nothing thrives for the asking. The winds blow hard so the people have come to wear their parkas and *mamleks,* boots, sideways on purpose now. Here, words freeze in the open air, and whole sentences must be broken from the speaker's lips and thawed at the fire so people can see what has been said. Here, the people live in the white and abundant hair of old Annuluk, the old grandmother, the old sorceress who is Earth herself. And it was in this land that there lived a man . . . a man so lonely that over the years, tears had carved great chasms into his cheeks.

He tried to smile and be happy. He hunted. He trapped and he slept well. But he wished for human company. Sometimes out in the shallows in his kayak when a seal came near he remembered the old stories about how seals were once human, and the only reminder of that time was their eyes, which were capable of portraying those looks, those wise and wild and loving looks. And sometimes then he felt such a pang of loneliness that tears coursed down the well-used cracks in his face.

One night he hunted past dark but found nothing. As the moon rose in the sky and the ice floes glistened, he came to a great spotted rock in the sea, and it appeared to his keen eye that upon that old rock there was movement of the most graceful kind.

He paddled slow and deep to be closer, and there atop the mighty rock danced a small group of women, naked as the first day they lay upon their mothers' bellies. Well, he was a lonely man, with no human friends but in memory—and he stayed and watched. The women were like beings made of moon milk, and their skin shimmered with little silver dots like those on the salmon in springtime, and the women's feet and hands were long and graceful.

So beautiful were they that the man sat stunned in his boat, the water lapping, taking him closer and closer to the rock. He could hear the magnificent women laughing . . . at least they seemed to laugh, or was it the water laughing at the edge of the rock? The man was confused, for he was so dazzled. But somehow the loneliness that had weighed on his chest like wet hide was lifted away, and almost without thinking, as though he was meant, he jumped up onto the rock and stole one of the sealskins laying there. He hid behind an outcropping and he pushed the sealskin into his *qutnguq,* parka.

Soon, one of the women called in a voice that was the most beautiful he'd ever heard . . . like the whales calling at dawn . . . or no, maybe it was more like the newborn wolves tumbling down in the spring . . . or but, well no, it was something better than that, but it did not matter because . . . what were the women doing now?

Why, they were putting on their sealskins, and one by one the seal women were slipping into the sea, yelping and crying happily. Except for one. The tallest of them searched high and searched low for her sealskin, but it was nowhere to be found. The man felt emboldened—by what, he did not know. He stepped from the rock, appealing to her, "Woman . . . be . . . my . . . wife. I am . . . a lonely . . . man."

"Oh, I cannot be wife," she said, "for I am of the other, the ones who live *temeqvanek,* beneath."

"Be . . . my . . . wife," insisted the man. "In seven summers, I will return your sealskin to you, and you may stay or you may go as you wish."

The young seal woman looked long into his face with eyes that but for her true origins seemed human. Reluctantly she said, "I will go with you. After seven summers, it shall be decided."

So in time they had a child, whom they named Ooruk. And the child was lithe and fat. In winter the mother told Ooruk tales of the creatures that lived beneath the sea while the father whittled a bear in whitestone with his long knife. When his mother carried the child Ooruk to bed, she pointed out through the smoke hole to the clouds and all their shapes. Except instead of recounting the shapes of raven and bear and wolf, she recounted the stories of walrus, whale, seal, and salmon . . . for those were the creatures she knew.

But as time went on, her flesh began to dry out. First it flaked, then it cracked. The skin of her eyelids began to peel. The hairs of her head began to drop to the ground. She became *naluaq,* palest white. Her plumpness began to wither. She tried to conceal her limp. Each day her eyes, without her willing it so, became more dull. She began to put out her hand in order to find her way, for her sight was darkening.

And so it went until one night when the child Ooruk was awakened by shouting and sat upright in his sleeping skins. He heard a roar like a bear that was his father berating his mother. He heard a crying like silver rung on stone that was his mother.

"You hid my sealskin seven long years ago, and now the eighth winter comes. I want what I am made of returned to me," cried the seal woman.

"And you, woman, would leave me if I gave it to you," boomed the husband.

"I do not know what I would do. I only know I must have what I belong to."

"And you would leave me wifeless, and the boy motherless. You are bad."

And with that her husband tore the hide flap of the door aside and disappeared into the night.

The boy loved his mother much. He feared losing her and so cried himself to sleep . . . only to be awakened by the wind. A strange wind . . . it seemed to call to him, "Oooruk, Ooorukkkk."

And out of bed he climbed, so hastily that he put his parka on upside down and pulled his mukluks only halfway up. Hearing his name called over and over, he dashed out into the starry, starry night.

"Ooooooorukkk."

The child ran out to the cliff overlooking the water, and there, far out in the windy sea, was a huge shaggy silver seal . . . its head was enormous, its whiskers drooped to its chest, its eyes were deep yellow.

"Ooooooorukkk."

The boy scrambled down the cliff and stumbled at the bottom over a stone—no, a bundle—that had rolled out of a cleft in the rock. The boy's hair lashed at his face like a thousand reins of ice.

"Ooooooorukkk."

The boy scratched open the bundle and shook it out—it was his mother's sealskin. Oh, and he could smell her all through it. And as he hugged the sealskin to his face and inhaled her scent, her soul slammed through him like a sudden summer wind.

"Ohhh," he cried with pain and joy, and lifted the skin again to his face and again her soul passed through his. "Ohhh," he cried again, for he was being filled with the unending love of his mother.

And the old silver seal way out . . . sank slowly beneath the water.

The boy climbed the cliff and ran toward home with the sealskin flying behind him, and into the house he fell. His mother swept him and the skin up and closed her eyes in gratitude for the safety of both.

She pulled on her sealskin, "Oh, mother, no!" cried the child.

She scooped up the child, tucked him under her arm, and half ran and half stumbled toward the roaring sea.

"Oh, mother, don't leave me!" Ooruk cried.

And at once you could tell she wanted to stay with her child, she *wanted* to, but something called her, something older than she, older than he, older than time.

"Oh, mother, no, no, no," cried the child. She turned to him with a look of dreadful love in her eyes. She took the boy's face in her hands, and breathed her sweet breath into his lungs, once, twice, three times. Then, with him under her arm like a precious bundle, she dove into the sea, down, and down, and down, and still deeper down, and the seal woman and her child breathed easily under water.

And they swam deep and strong till they entered the underwater cove of seals where all manner of creatures were dining and singing, dancing and speaking, and the great silver seal that had called to Ooruk from the night sea embraced the child and called him grandson.

"How fare you up there, daughter?" asked the great silver seal.

The seal woman looked away and said, "I hurt a human . . . a man who gave his all to have me. But I cannot return to him, for I shall be a prisoner if I do."

"And the boy?" asked the old seal. "My grandchild?" He said it so proudly his voice shook.

"He must go back, father. He cannot stay. His time is not yet to be here with us." And she wept. And together they wept.

And so some days and nights passed, seven to be exact, during which time the luster came back to the seal woman's hair and eyes. She turned a beautiful dark color, her sight was restored, her body regained its plumpness, and she swam uncrippled. Yet it came time to return the boy to land. On that night, the old grandfather seal and the boy's beautiful mother swam with the child between them. Back they went, back up and up and up to the topside world. There they gently placed Ooruk on the stony shore in the moonlight.

His mother assured him, "I am always with you. Only touch what I have touched, my firesticks, my *ulu,* knife, my stone carvings of otters and seal, and I will breathe into your lungs a wind for the singing of your songs."

The old silver seal and his daughter kissed the child many times. At last, they tore themselves away and swam out to sea, and with one last look at the boy, they disappeared beneath the waters. And Ooruk, because it was not his time, stayed.

As time went on, he grew to be a mighty drummer and singer and a maker of stories, and it was said this all came to be because as a child he had survived being carried out to sea by the great seal spirits. Now, in the gray mists of morning, sometimes he can still be seen, with his kayak tethered, kneeling upon a certain rock in the sea, seeming to speak to a certain female seal who often comes near the shore. Though many have tried to hunt her, time after time they have failed. She is known as *Tanqigcaq,* the bright one, the holy one, and it is said that though she be a seal, her eyes are capable of portraying those human looks, those wise and wild and loving looks.

Loss of Sense of Soul as Initiation

The seal is one of the most beautiful of all symbols for the wild soul. Like the instinctual nature of women, seals are peculiar creatures who have evolved and adapted over eons. Like the seal woman, actual seals only come onto the land in order to breed and nurse. The mother seal is intensely devoted to her pup for about two months, loving, guarding, and feeding it solely from her own body stores. During this time, the thirty-pound pup quadruples in weight. Then the mother swims out to sea and the now viable and grown pup begins an independent life.

Among ethnic groups throughout the world, including many in the circumpolar region and West Africa, it is said that humans are not truly animated until the soul gives birth to the spirit, tenders and nurses it, filling it up with strength. Eventually the soul is believed to retreat to a farther home while the spirit begins its independent life in the world.

The symbol of seal for soul is all the more compelling because there is a "docility" about seals, an accessibility well known to those who live near them. Seals have a sort of dogness about them; they are naturally affectionate. A kind of purity radiates from them. But they can also be very quick to react, retreat, or retort if threatened. The soul is like that too. It hovers near. It nurses the spirit. It does not run away when it perceives something new or unusual or difficult.

But sometimes, especially when a seal is not used to humans and just lies about in one of those blissful states that seals seem to enter from time to time, she does not anticipate human ways. Like the seal woman in the story, and like the souls of young and/or inexperienced women, she is unaware of the intentions of others and potential harm. And that is always when the sealskin is stolen.

I have come to the sense over the years of working with "capture" and "theft of treasure" tales, and from analyzing many men and women, that there is in the individuation processes of almost everyone at least a one-time and significant theft. Some people characterize it as a theft of their "great opportunity" in life. Others define it as a larceny of love, or a robbing of one's spirit, a weakening of the sense of self. Some describe it as a distraction, a break, an interference or interruption of something vital to them: their art, their love, their dream, their hope, their belief in goodness, their development, their honor, their strivings.

Most of the time this major theft creeps up on the person from their blind side. It comes upon women for the same reasons it occurs in this Inuit story: because of naïveté, poor insight into the motives of others, inexperience in projecting what might happen in the future, not paying attention to all the clues in the environment, and because fate is always weaving lessons into the weft.

People who have been thusly robbed are not bad. They are not wrong. They are not stupid. But they are, in some major way, inexperienced or in a kind of psychic slumber. It would be a mistake to attribute such states only to the young. They can exist in anyone, regardless of age, ethnic affiliation, years of schooling, or even good intentions. It is clear that being stolen from most definitely evolves into a mysterious archetypal initiation opportunity for those who are caught up in it . . . which is almost everyone.

The process of retrieving the treasure and figuring out how to replenish oneself develops four vital constructs in the psyche. When this dilemma is met head-on, and the descent to the *Rio Abajo Rio,* river beneath the river, is made, it fiercely strengthens our resolve to strive for conscious reclamation. It clarifies, over time, what it is that is most important to us. It fills us up with the need to have a plan for freeing ourselves psychically or otherwise and to enact our newly found wisdom. Finally, and most importantly, it develops our medial nature, that wild and knowing part of psyche that can also traverse the world of soul and the world of humans.

The "Sealskin, Soulskin" story is extremely valuable, for it gives clear and pithy directions for the exact steps we must take in order to develop and find our way through this archetypal task. One of the central and most potentially destructive issues women face is that they begin various psychological initiation processes without initiators who have completed the process themselves. They have no seasoned persons who know how to proceed. When initiators are incompletely initiated themselves, they omit important aspects of the process without realizing it, and sometimes visit great abuse on the initiate, for they are working with a fragmentary idea of initiation, one that is often tainted in one way or another.

At the other end of the spectrum is the woman who has experienced theft, and who is striving for knowledge and mastery of the situation, but who has run out of directions and does not know there is more to practice in order to complete the learning, and so repeats the first stage, that of being stolen from, over and over again. Through whatever circumstances, she has gotten tangled in the reins. Essentially, she is without instruction. Instead of discovering the requirements of a healthy wildish soul, she becomes a casualty of an uncompleted initiation.

Because matrilineal lines of initiation—older women teaching younger women certain psychic facts and procedures of the wild feminine—have been fragmented and broken for so many women and over so many years, it is a blessing to have the archeology of the fairy tale to learn from. We can reconstruct all we need to know from those deep templates or compare our own ideas on women's integral psychological processes to those found in tales. In this sense, fairy tales and mythos are our initiators; they are the wise ones who teach those who have come after.

So, it is the incompletely initiated or half-initiated women for whom the dynamics in "Sealskin, Soulskin" are most valuable. By knowing all the steps to take to complete the cyclical return to home, even a botched initiation can be untangled, reset, and completed properly. Let us see how this story instructs us to proceed.

Losing One's Pelt

The development of knowing, as in versions of "Bluebeard," "Rapunzel," "Devil's Midwife," and "Briar Rose" and others, results from first being unaware, then tricked in one way or another, and thence finding one's way to power again. The theme of a fateful catching that tests consciousness and ends in a deep knowing is a timeless one in fairy tales with female protagonists. Such tales carry dense instruction to all of us about what our work is if and when we are captured, and how to come back from it with the ability *pasar atravez del basque como una loba,* to slip through the forest like a wolf, *con un ojo agudo,* with a piercing eye.

"Sealskin, Soulskin" has a retrograde motif. Storytellers call such tales "backward stories." In most fairy tales, a human is enchanted and turned into an animal. But here we have the opposite: a creature led into a human life. The story produces an insight into the structure of the female psyche. The seal maiden, like the wildish nature in women's psyches, is a mystical combination that is creatural and at the same time able to live among humans in a resourceful manner.

The pelt in this story is not so much an article as the representation of a feeling state and a state of being—one that is cohesive, soulful, and of the wildish female nature. When a woman is in this state, she feels entirely in and of herself instead of out of herself and wondering if she is doing right, acting right, thinking well. Though this state of being "in one's self" is one she occasionally loses touch with, the time she has previously spent there sustains her while she is about her work in the world. The return to the wildish state periodically is what replenishes her psychic reserves for her projects, family, relationships, and creative life in the topside world.

Eventually every woman away from her soul-home tires. This is as it should be. Then she seeks her skin again in order to revive her sense of self and soul, in order to restore her deep-eyed and oceanic knowing. This great cycle of going and returning, going and returning, is reflexive within the instinctual nature of women and is innate to all women for all their lives, from throughout girlhood, adolescence, and young adulthood through being a lover, through motherhood, through being a craftswoman, a wisdom-holder, an elderwoman, and beyond. These phases are not necessarily chronological, for mid-age women are often newborn, old women are intense lovers, and little girls know a good deal about cronish enchantment.

Over and over we lose this sense of feeling we are wholly in our skins by means already named as well as through extended duress. Those who toil too long without respite are also at risk. The soulskin vanishes when we are not paying attention to what we are really doing, and particularly the cost to us.

We lose the soulskin by becoming too involved with ego, by being too exacting, perfectionistic, or unnecessarily martyred, or driven by a blind ambition, or by being dissatisfied—about self, family, community, culture, world—and not saying or doing anything about it, or by pretending we are an unending source for others, or by not doing all we can to help ourselves. Oh, there are as many ways to lose the soulskin as there are women in the world.

The only way to hold on to this essential soulskin is to retain an exquisitely pristine consciousness about its value and uses. But, since no one can consistently maintain acute consciousness, no one can keep the soulskin absolutely every moment day and night. But we can keep the theft of it to a bare minimum. We can develop that *ojo agudo,* the piercing eye that watches the conditions all around and guards our psychic territory accordingly. The "Sealskin, Soulskin" story, however, is about an instance of what we might call aggravated theft. This big theft can, with consciousness, be mediated in the future if we will pay attention to our cycles and the call to take leave and return home.

Every creature on earth returns to home. It is ironic that we have made wildlife refuges for ibis, pelican, egret, wolf, crane, deer, mouse, moose, and bear, but not for ourselves in the places where we live day after day. We understand that the loss of habitat is the most disastrous event that can occur to a free creature. We fervently point out how other creatures' natural territories have become surrounded by cities, ranches, highways, noise, and other dissonance, as though we are not surrounded by the same, as though we are not affected also. We know that for creatures to live on, they must at least from time to time have a home place, a place where they feel both protected and free.

We traditionally compensate for loss of a more serene habitat by taking a vacation or a holiday, which is supposed to be the giving of pleasure to oneself, except a vacation is often anything but. We can compensate our workaday dissonance by cutting down on the things we do that cause us to tense our deltoids and trapeziuses into painful knots. And all this is very good, but for the soul-self-psyche, vacation is not the same as refuge. "Time out" or "time off" is not the same as returning to home. Calmness is not the same as solitude.

We can contain this loss of soul by keeping close to the pelt to begin with. For instance, I see in the talented women in my practice that soulskin theft can come through relationships that are not in their rightful skins themselves, and some relationships are downright poisonous. It takes will and force to overcome these relationships, but it can be done, especially if, as in the story, one will awaken to the voice calling from home, back to the core self where one's immediate wisdom is whole and accessible. From there, a woman can decide with clear-seeing what it is she must have, and what it is she wants to do.

The aggravated theft of the sealskin also occurs far more subtly through the theft of a woman's resources and of her time. The world is lonely for comfort, and for the hips and breasts of women. It calls out in a thousand-handed, million-voiced way, waving to us, plucking and pulling at us, asking for our attention. Sometimes it seems that everywhere we turn there is a someone or a something of the world that needs, wants, wishes. Some of the people, issues, and things of the world are appealing and charming; others may be demanding and angry; and yet others seem so heartrendingly helpless that, against our wills, our empathy overflows, our milk runs down our bellies. But unless it is a life-and-death matter, take the time, make the time, to "put on the brass brassiere." Stop running the milk train. Do the work of turning toward home.

Though we see that the skin can be lost through a devastating and wrong love, it may also be lost in a right and deepest love. It is not exactly the rightness of a person or thing or its wrongness that causes the theft of our soulskins, it is the cost of these things to us. It is what it costs us in time, energy, observation, attention, hovering, prompting, instructing, teaching, training. These motions of psyche are like cash withdrawals from the psychic savings account. The issue is not about these energic cash withdrawals themselves, for these are an important part of life's give and take. But it is being *overdrawn* that causes the loss of the skin, and the paling and dulling of one's most acute instincts. It is lack of further deposits of energy, knowledge, acknowledgment, ideas, and excitement that causes a woman to feel she is psychically dying.

In the story, when the young seal woman loses her pelt, she is involved in a beautiful pursuit, in the business of freedom. She dances and dances, and does not pay attention to what is going on about her. When we are in our rightful wildish nature, we all feel this bright life. It is one of the signs that we are close to Wild Woman. We all enter the world in a dancing condition. We always begin with our own pelts intact.

Yet, at least till we become more conscious, we all go through this stage in individuation. We all swim up to the rock, dance, and don't pay attention. It is then that the more tricksterish aspect of the psyche descends, and somewhere down the road we suddenly look for and can no longer find what belongs to us or to what we belong. Then our sense of soul is mysteriously missing, and more so, it is hidden away. And so we wander about partially dazed. It is not good to make choices when dazed, but we do.

We know poor choice occurs in various ways. One woman marries too early. Another becomes pregnant too young. Another goes with a bad mate. Another gives up her art to "have things." Another is seduced by any number of illusions, another by promises, another by too much "being good" and not enough soul, yet another by too much airiness and not enough earth. And in cases where the woman goes with her soulskin half on and half gone, it is not necessarily because her choices are wrong so much as that she stays away from her soul-home too long and dries out and is rather of little use to anyone, least of all herself. There are hundreds of ways to lose one's soulskin.

If we delve into the symbol of animal hide, we find that in all animals, including ourselves, piloerection—hair standing on end—occurs in response to things seen as well as to things sensed. The rising hair of the pelt sends a "chill" through the creature and rouses suspicion, caution, and other protective traits. Among the Inuit it is said that both fur and feathers have the ability to see what goes on far off in the distance, and that is why an *angakok,* shaman, wears many furs, many feathers, so as to have hundreds of eyes to better see into the mysteries. The sealskin is a symbol of soul that not only provides warmth, but also provides an early warning system through its vision as well.

In hunting cultures, the pelt is equal to food as the most important product for survival. It is used to make boots, to line parkas, for waterproofing to keep ice hoar away from the face and wrists. The pelt keeps little children safe and dry, protects and warms the vulnerable human belly, back, feet, hands, and head. To lose the pelt is to lose one's protections, one's warmth, one's early warning system, one's instinctive sight. Psychologically, to be without the pelt causes a woman to pursue what she thinks she should do, rather than what she truly wishes. It causes her to follow whoever or whatever impresses her as strongest—whether it is good for her or not. Then there is much leaping and little looking. She is jocular instead of incisive, laughs things off, puts things off. She pulls back from taking the next step, from making the necessary descent and holding herself there long enough for something to happen.

So you can see that in a world that values driven women who go, go, go, the stealing of soulskins is very easy, so much so that the first theft occurs somewhere between the ages of seven and eighteen. By then, most young women have begun to dance on the rock in the sea. By then most will have reached for the soulskin but not found it where they left it. And, though this initially seems meant to cause the development of a medial structure in the psyche—that is, an ability to learn to live in the world of spirit and in the outer reality as well—too often this progression is not accomplished, nor is any of the rest of the initiatory experience, and the woman wanders through life skinless.

Though we may have tried to prevent a recurrence of theft by practically sewing ourselves into our soulskins, very few women reach the age of majority with more than a few tufts of the original pelt intact. We lay aside our skins while we dance. We learn the world, but lose our skins. We find that without our skins we begin to slowly dry away. Because most women were raised to bear these things stoically, as their mothers did before them, no one notices there is a dying going on, until one day . . .

When we are young and our soul-lives collide with the desires and requirements of culture and the world, indeed we feel stranded far from home. However, as adults we continue to drive ourselves even farther from home as a result of our own choices about who, what, where, and for how long. If we were never taught return to the soul-home in childhood, we repeat the "theft and wandering around lost" pattern ad infinitum. But, even when it is our own dismal choices that have blown us off course—too far from what we need—hold faith, for within the soul is the homing device. We all can find our way back.

JOURNAL PROMPT:

Write about a time in your life when, in the author's words, you were "too involved with ego . . . or driven by a blind ambition."

COLLABORATIVE EXERCISE:

List some of the reasons why we leave home. Estes says, "Every creature on earth returns to home." Obviously, this isn't meant solely as a physical place. Discuss ways in which we replace home with other places, people, or comforts.

ESSAY ASSIGNMENT:

1. The author uses this myth as metaphor for loss of a sense of self, as well as loss of a sense of purposefulness in our lives. Erik Erikson, a renowned psychologist and expert on child development, discusses stages of development. Research these stages. Does this tale of separation, initiation, and return parallel his theory?

2. Telling stories is an age-old art form, one that both instructs and entertains. How do you think other art forms—painting, basket making, music, drama, etc.—also instruct? Refer to examples from your own experience with other creative arts.

The sealskin myth appears in many different forms among northern peoples, perhaps because at different times in our lives all of us leave a home we have known well; here is another version.

AN ICELANDIC FOLKTALE

The Seal's Skin

There was once some man from Myrdal in Eastern Iceland who went walking among the rocks by the sea one morning before anyone else was up. He came to the mouth of a cave, and inside the cave he could hear merriment and dancing, but outside it he saw a great many sealskins. He took one skin away with him, carried it home, and locked it away in a chest. Later in the day he went back to the mouth of the cave; there was a young and lovely woman sitting there, and she was stark naked, and weeping bitterly. This was the seal whose skin it was that the man had taken. He gave the girl some clothes, comforted her, and took her home with him. She grew very fond of him, but did not get on so well with other people. Often she would sit alone and stare out to sea.

After some while the man married her, and they got on well together, and had several children. As for the skin, the man always kept it locked up in the chest, and kept the key on him wherever he went. But after many years, he went fishing one day and forgot it under his pillow at home. Other people say that he went to church one Christmas with the rest of his household, but that his wife was ill and stayed at home; he had forgotten to take the key out of the pocket of his everyday clothes when he changed. Be that as it may, when he came home again the chest was open, and both wife and skin were gone. She had taken the key and examined the chest, and there she had found the skin; she had been unable to resist the temptation, but had said farewell to her children, put the skin on, and flung herself into the sea.

The Seal's Skin

Before the woman flung herself into the sea, it is said that she spoke these words:

Woe is me! Ah, woe is me!
I have seven bairns on land,
And seven in the sea.

It is said that the man was broken-hearted about this. Whenever he rowed out fishing afterwards, a seal would often swim round and round his boat, and it looked as if tears were running from its eyes. From that time on, he had excellent luck in his fishing, and various valuable things were washed ashore on his beach. People often noticed, too, that when the children he had had by this woman went walking along the seashore, a seal would show itself near the edge of the water and keep level with them as they walked along the shore, and would toss them jellyfish and pretty shells. But never did their mother come back to land again.

JOURNAL PROMPT:

What is it about human nature that explains the man's desire to keep the sealskin hidden?

COLLABORATIVE EXERCISE:

In this story the wife ultimately leaves her husband and seven children to return to the sea, where her other seven children await. Discuss in your groups who you believe is most responsible for her departure. Consider how this woman would be judged in this century.

ESSAY ASSIGNMENT:

1. Find other versions of this tale, and comment on the similarities and differences among them.
2. Peter Stillman in his book *Introduction to Myth* makes the claim that "there is a distinct danger connected with the study of mythology: once you discover that myths are not mere stories but the *story* of humankind—the lens through which we have always seen and understood the world—you are bound to find everywhere, in dreams, rituals, nursery rhymes, and any and all art forms, a mythic perspective." Based on your reading to date, write a response to Stillman's claim.

This selection is from LINDA SEGER's book *Making a Good Script Great* (1987). In it she claims that the key to a successful screenplay is knowledge of how archetypes infuse our lives. Seger is a script consultant and author, who gives filmmaking seminars worldwide.

LINDA SEGER

Creating the Myth

All of us have similar experiences. We share in the life journey of growth, development, and transformation. We live the same stories, whether they involve the search for a perfect mate, coming home, the search for fulfillment, going after an ideal, achieving the dream, or hunting for a precious treasure. Whatever our culture, there are universal stories that form the basis for all our particular stories. The trappings might be different, the twists and turns that create suspense might change from culture to culture, the particular characters may take different forms, but underneath it all, it's the same story, drawn from the same experiences.

Many of the most successful films are based on these universal stories. They deal with the basic journey we take in life. We identify with the heroes because we were once heroic (descriptive) or because we wish we could do what the hero does (prescriptive). When Joan Wilder finds the jewel and saves her sister, or James Bond saves the world, or Shane saves the family from the evil ranchers, we identify with the character, and subconsciously recognize the story as having some connection with our own lives. It's the same story as the fairy tales about getting the three golden hairs from the devil, or finding the treasure and winning the princess. And it's not all that different a story from the caveman killing the woolly beast or the Roman slave gaining his freedom through skill and courage. These are our stories—personally and collectively—and the most successful films contain these universal experiences.

Some of these stories are "search" stories. They address our desire to find some kind of rare and wonderful treasure. This might include the search for outer values such as job, relationship, or success; or for inner values such as respect, security, self-expression, love, or home. But it's all a similar search.

Some of these stories are "hero" stories. They come from our own experiences of overcoming adversity, as well as our desire to do great and special acts. We root for the hero and celebrate when he or she achieves the goal because we know that the hero's journey is in many ways similar to our own.

We call these stories *myths*. Myths are the common stories at the root of our universal existence. They're found in all cultures and in all literature, ranging from the Greek myths to fairy tales, legends, and stories drawn from all of the world's religions.

A myth is a story that is "more than true." Many stories are true because one person, somewhere, at some time, lived it. It is based on fact. But a myth is more than true because it is lived by all of us, at some level. It's a story that connects and speaks to us all.

Some myths are true stories that attain mythic significance because the people involved seem larger than life, and seem to live their lives more intensely than common folk. Martin Luther King, Jr., Gandhi, Sir Edmund Hillary, and Lord Mountbatten personify the types of journeys we identify with, because we've taken similar journeys—even if only in a very small way.

Other myths revolve around make-believe characters who might capsulize for us the sum total of many of our journeys. Some of these make-believe characters might seem similar to the characters we meet in our dreams. Or they might be a composite of types of characters we've met.

In both cases, the myth is the "story beneath the story." It's the universal pattern that shows us that Gandhi's journey toward independence and Sir Edmund Hillary's journey to the top of Mount Everest contain many of the same dramatic beats. And these beats are the same beats that Rambo takes to set free the MIAs, that Indiana Jones takes to find the Lost Ark, and that Luke Skywalker takes to defeat the Evil Empire.

In *Hero with a Thousand Faces,* Joseph Campbell traces the elements that form the hero myth. "In their own work with myth, writer Chris Vogler and seminar leader Thomas Schlesinger have applied this criteria to *Star Wars*. The myth within the story helps explain why millions went to see this film again and again."

The hero myth has specific story beats that occur in all hero stories. They show who the hero is, what the hero needs, and how the story and character interact in order to create a transformation. The journey toward heroism is a process. This universal process forms the spine of all the particular stories, such as the *Star Wars* trilogy.

The Hero Myth

1. In most hero stories, the hero is introduced in ordinary surroundings, in a mundane world, doing mundane things. Generally, the hero begins as a nonhero; innocent, young, simple, or humble. In *Star Wars,* the first time we see Luke Skywalker, he's unhappy about having to do his chores, which consists of picking out some new droids for work. He wants to go out and have fun. He wants to leave his planet and go to the Academy, but he's stuck. This is the setup of most myths. This is how we meet the hero before the call to adventure.
2. Then something new enters the hero's life. It's a catalyst that sets the story into motion. It might be a telephone call, as in *Romancing the Stone,* or the German attack in *The African Queen,* or the holograph of Princess Leia in *Star Wars*. Whatever form it takes, it's a new ingredient that pushes the hero into an extraordinary adventure. With this call, the stakes are established, and a problem is introduced that demands a solution.

3. Many times, however, the hero doesn't want to leave. He or she is a reluctant hero, afraid of the unknown, uncertain, perhaps, if he or she is up to the challenge. In *Star Wars,* Luke receives a double call to adventure. First, from Princess Leia in the holograph, and then through Obi-Wan Kenobi, who says he needs Luke's help. But Luke is not ready to go. He returns home, only to find that the Imperial Stormtroopers have burned his farmhouse and slaughtered his family. Now he is personally motivated, ready to enter into the adventure.
4. In any journey, the hero usually receives help, and the help often comes from unusual sources. In many fairy tales, an old woman, a dwarf, a witch, or a wizard helps the hero. The hero achieves the goal because of this help, and because the hero is receptive to what this person has to give.

   There are a number of fairy tales where the first and second son are sent to complete a task, but they ignore the helpers, often scorning them. Many times they are severely punished for their lack of humility and unwillingness to accept help. Then the third son, the hero, comes along. He receives the help, accomplishes the task, and often wins the princess.

   In *Star Wars,* Obi-Wan Kenobi is a perfect example of the "helper" character. He is a kind of mentor to Luke, one who teaches him the Way of the Force and whose teachings continue even after his death. This mentor character appears in most hero stories. He is the person who has special knowledge, special information, and special skills. This might be the prospector in *The Treasure of the Sierra Madre,* or the psychiatrist in *Ordinary People,* or Quint in *Jaws,* who knows all about sharks, or the Good Witch of the North who gives Dorothy the ruby slippers in *The Wizard of Oz.* In *Star Wars,* Obi-Wan gives Luke the light saber that was the special weapon of the Jedi Knight. With this, Luke is ready to move forward and do his training and meet adventure.
5. The hero is now ready to move into the special world where he or she will change from the ordinary into the extraordinary. This starts the hero's transformation, and sets up the obstacles that must be surmounted to reach the goal. Usually, this happens at the first Turning Point of the story, and leads into Act Two development. In *Star Wars,* Obi-Wan and Luke search for a pilot to take them to the planet of Alderan, so that Obi-Wan can deliver the plans to Princess Leia's father. These plans are essential to the survival of the Rebel Forces. With this action, the adventure is ready to begin.
6. Now begin all the tests and obstacles necessary to overcome the enemy and accomplish the hero's goals. In fairy tales, this often means getting past witches, outwitting the devil, avoiding robbers,

or confronting evil. In Homer's *Odyssey,* it means blinding the Cyclops, escaping from the island of the Lotus-Eaters, resisting the temptation of the singing Sirens, and surviving a shipwreck. In *Star Wars,* innumerable adventures confront Luke. He and his cohorts must run to the *Millennium Falcon,* narrowly escaping the Stormtroopers before jumping into hyperspace. They must make it through the meteor shower after Alderan has been destroyed. They must evade capture on the Death Star, rescue the Princess, and even survive a garbage crusher.

7. At some point in the story, the hero often hits rock bottom. He often has a "death experience," leading to a type of rebirth. In *Star Wars,* Luke seems to have died when the serpent in the garbage-masher pulls him under, but he's saved just in time to ask R2D2 to stop the masher before they're crushed. This is often the "black moment" at the second turning point, the point when the worst is confronted, and the action now moves toward the exciting conclusion.
8. Now, the hero seizes the sword and takes possession of the treasure. He is now in charge, but he still has not completed the journey. Here Luke has the Princess and the plans, but the final confrontation is yet to begin. This starts the third-act escape scene, leading to the final climax.
9. The road back is often the chase scene. In many fairy tales, this is the point where the devil chases the hero and the hero has the last obstacles to overcome before really being free and safe. His challenge is to take what he has learned and integrate it into his daily life. He *must* return to renew the mundane world. In *Star Wars,* Darth Vader is in hot pursuit, planning to blow up the Rebel Planet.
10. Since every hero story is essentially a transformation story, we need to see the hero changed at the end, resurrected into a new type of life. He must face the final ordeal before being "reborn" as the hero, proving his courage and becoming transformed. This is the point, in many fairy tales, where the Miller's Son becomes the Prince or the King and marries the Princess. In *Star Wars,* Luke has survived, becoming quite a different person from the innocent young man he was in Act One.

    At this point, the hero returns and is reintegrated into his society. In *Star Wars,* Luke has destroyed the Death Star, and he receives his great reward.

This is the classic "Hero Story." We might call this example a *mission* or *task myth,* where the person has to complete a task, but the task itself is not the real treasure. The real reward for Luke is the love of the Princess and the safe, new world he had helped create.

A myth can have many variations. We see variations on this myth in James Bond films (although they lack much of the depth because the hero is not transformed), and in *The African Queen,* where Rose and Allnutt must blow up the *Louisa,* or in *Places in the Heart,* where Edna overcomes obstacles to achieve family stability.

The *treasure myth* is another variation on this theme, as seen in *Romancing the Stone.* In this story, Joan receives a map and a phone call which forces her into the adventure. She is helped by an American bird catcher and a Mexican pickup truck driver. She overcomes the obstacles of snakes, the jungle, waterfalls, shootouts, and finally receives the treasure, along with the "prince."

Whether the hero's journey is for a treasure or to complete a task, the elements remain the same. The humble, reluctant hero is called to an adventure. The hero is helped by a variety of unique characters. S/he must overcome a series of obstacles that transform him or her in the process, and then faces the final challenge that draws on inner and outer resources.

The Healing Myth

Although the hero myth is the most popular story, many myths involve healing. In these stories, some character is "broken" and must leave home to become whole again.

The universal experience behind these healing stories is our psychological need for rejuvenation, for balance. The journey of the hero into exile is not all that different from the weekend in Palm Springs, or the trip to Hawaii to get away from it all, or lying still in a hospital bed for some weeks to heal. In all cases, something is out of balance and the mythic journey moves toward wholeness.

Being broken can take several forms. It can be physical, emotional, or psychological. Usually, it's all three. In the process of being exiled or hiding out in the forest, the desert, or even the Amish farm in *Witness,* the person becomes whole, balanced, and receptive to love. Love in these stories is both a healing force and a reward.

Think of John Book in *Witness.* In Act One, we see a frenetic, insensitive man, afraid of commitment, critical and unreceptive to the feminine influences in his life. John is suffering from an "inner wound" which he doesn't know about. When he receives an "outer wound" from a gunshot, it forces him into exile, which begins his process of transformation.

At the beginning of Act Two, we see John delirious and close to death. This is a movement into the unconscious, a movement from the rational, active police life of Act One into a mysterious, feminine, more intuitive world. Since John's "inner problem" is the lack of balance with his feminine side, this delirium begins the process of transformation.

Later in Act Two, we see John beginning to change. He moves from his highly independent life-style toward the collective, communal life of his Amish hosts. John now gets up early to milk the cows and to assist with the chores. He uses his carpentry skills to help with the barn building and to complete the birdhouse. Gradually, he begins to develop relationships with Rachel and her son, Samuel. John's life slows down and he becomes more receptive, learning important lessons about love. In Act Three, John finally sees that the feminine is worth saving, and throws down his gun to save Rachel's life. A few beats later, when he has the opportunity to kill Paul, he chooses a nonviolent response instead. Although John doesn't "win" the Princess, he has nevertheless "won" love and wholeness. By the end of the film, we can see that the John Book of Act Three is a different kind of person from the John Book of Act One. He has a different kind of comradeship with his fellow police officers, he's more relaxed, and we can sense that somehow, this experience has formed a more integrated John Book.

Combination Myths

Many stories are combinations of several different myths. Think of *Ghostbusters,* a simple and rather outrageous comedy about three men saving the city of New York from ghosts. Now think of the story of "Pandora's Box." It's about the woman who let loose all manner of evil upon the earth by opening a box she was told not to touch. In *Ghostbusters,* the EPA man is a Pandora figure. By shutting off the power to the containment center, he inadvertently unleashes all the ghosts upon New York City. Combine the story of "Pandora's Box" with a hero story, and notice that we have our three heroes battling the Marshmallow Man. One of them also "gets the Princess" when Dr. Peter Venkman finally receives the affections of Dana Barrett. By looking at these combinations, it is apparent that even *Ghostbusters* is more than "just a comedy."

Tootsie is a type of reworking of many Shakespearean stories where a woman has to dress as a man in order to accomplish a certain task. These Shakespearean stories are reminiscent of many fairy tales where the hero becomes invisible or takes on another persona, or wears a specific disguise to hide his or her real qualities. In the stories of "The Twelve Dancing Princesses" or "The Man in the Bearskin," disguise is necessary to achieve a goal. Combine these elements with the transformation themes of the hero myth where a hero (such as Michael) must overcome many obstacles to his success as an actor and a human being. It's not difficult to understand why the *Tootsie* story hooks us.

Archetypes

A myth includes certain characters that we see in many stories. These characters are called *archetypes.* They can be thought of as the original "pattern" or "character type" that will be found on the hero's journey. Archetypes take many forms, but they tend to fall within specific categories.

Earlier, we discussed some of the helpers who give advice to help the hero—such as the *wise old man* who possesses special knowledge and often serves as a mentor to the hero.

The female counterpart of the wise old man is the *good mother.* Whereas the wise old man has superior knowledge, the good mother is known for her nurturing qualities, and for her intuition. This figure often gives the hero particular objects to help on the journey. It might be a protective amulet, or the ruby slippers that Dorothy receives in *The Wizard of Oz* from the Good Witch of the North. Sometimes in fairy tales it's a cloak to make the person invisible, or ordinary objects that become extraordinary, as in "The Girl of Courage," an Afghan fairy tale about a maiden who receives a comb, a whetstone, and a mirror to help defeat the devil.

Many myths contain a *shadow figure.* This is a character who is the opposite of the hero. Sometimes this figure helps the hero on the journey; other times this figure opposes the hero. The shadow figure can be the negative side of the hero which could be the dark and hostile brother in "Cain and Abel," the stepsisters in "Cinderella," or the Robber Girl in "The Snow Queen." The shadow figure can also help the hero, as the whore with the heart of gold who saves the hero's life, or provides balance to his idealization of woman.

Many myths contain *animal archetypes* that can be positive or negative figures. In "St. George and the Dragon," the dragon is the negative force which is a violent and ravaging animal, not unlike the shark in *Jaws.* But in many stories, animals help the hero. Sometimes there are talking donkeys, or a dolphin which saves the hero, or magical horses or dogs.

The *trickster* is a mischievous archetypical figure who is always causing chaos, disturbing the peace, and generally being an anarchist. The trickster uses wit and cunning to achieve his or her ends. Sometimes the trickster is a harmless prankster or a "bad boy" who is funny and enjoyable. More often, the trickster is a con man, as in *The Sting,* or the devil, as in *The Exorcist,* who demanded all the skills of the priest to outwit him. The "Till Eulenspiegel" stories revolve around the trickster, as do the Spanish picaresque novels. Even the tales of Tom Sawyer have a trickster motif. In all countries, there are stories that revolve around this figure, whose job it is to outwit.

"Mythic" Problems and Solutions

We all grew up with myths. Most of us heard or read fairy tales when we were young. Some of us may have read Bible stories, or stories from other religions or other cultures. These stories are part of us. And the best way to work with them is to let them come out naturally as you write the script.

Of course, some filmmakers are better at this than others. George Lucas and Steven Spielberg have a strong sense of myth and incorporate it into their films. They both have spoken about their love of the stories from childhood, and of their desire to bring these types of stories to audiences. Their stories create some of the same sense of wonder and excitement as myths. Many of the necessary psychological beats are part of their stories, deepening the story beyond the ordinary action-adventure.

Myths bring depth to a hero story. If a filmmaker is only thinking about the action and excitement of a story, audiences might fail to connect with the hero's journey. But if the basic beats of the hero's journey are evident, a film will often inexplicably draw audiences, in spite of critics' responses to the film.

Take *Rambo* for instance. Why was this violent, simple story so popular with audiences? I don't think it was because everyone agreed with its politics. I do think Sylvester Stallone is a master at incorporating the American myth into his filmmaking. That doesn't mean it's done consciously. Somehow he is naturally in sync with the myth, and the myth becomes integrated into his stories.

Clint Eastwood also does hero stories, and gives us the adventure of the myth and the transformation of the myth. Recently Eastwood's films have given more attention to the transformation of the hero, and have been receiving more serious critical attention as a result.

All of these filmmakers—Lucas, Spielberg, Stallone, and Eastwood—dramatize the hero myth in their own particular ways. And all of them prove that myths are marketable.

Application

It is an important part of the writer's or producer's work to continually find opportunities for deepening the themes within a script. Finding the myth beneath the modern story is part of that process.

To find these myths, it's not a bad idea to reread some of Grimm's fairy tales or fairy tales from around the world to begin to get acquainted with various myths. You'll start to see patterns and elements that connect with our own human experience.

Also, read Joseph Campbell and Greek mythology. If you're interested in Jungian psychology, you'll find many rich resources within a number of books on the subject. Since Jungian psychology deals with archetypes, you'll find many new characters to draw on for your own work.

With all of these resources to incorporate, it's important to remember that the myth is not a story to force upon a script. It's more a pattern which you can bring out in your own stories when they seem to be heading in the direction of a myth.

As you work, ask yourself:

> Do I have a myth working in my script? If so, what beats am I using of the hero's journey? Which ones seem to be missing?
>
> Am I missing characters? Do I need a mentor type? A wise old man? A wizard? Would one of these characters help dimensionalize the hero's journey?

Could I create new emotional dimensions to the myth by starting my character as reluctant, naive, simple, or decidedly "unheroic"?

Does my character get transformed in the process of the journey?

Have I used a strong three-act structure to support the myth, using the first turning point to move into the adventure and the second turning point to create a dark moment, or a reversal, or even a "near-death" experience?

Don't be afraid to create variations on the myth, but don't start with the myth itself. Let the myth grow naturally from your story. Developing myths are part of the rewriting process. If you begin with the myth, you'll find your writing becomes rigid, uncreative, and predictable. Working with the myth in the rewriting process will deepen your script, giving it new life as you find the story within the story.

JOURNAL PROMPT:

Write about one of your all-time favorite films. Does it follow the classic pattern discussed by Seger?

COLLABORATIVE EXERCISE:

Many films follow the patterns Seger outlines in her essay. Working in small groups, discuss at least two films not mentioned in her work and trace the archetypes, such as the shadow figure, the good mother, etc.

ESSAY ASSIGNMENT:

1. Choose from the following list of films one to watch outside of class. Identify the myths behind these modern stories. Explain how they follow Seger's description of universal journeys.

   The Wizard of Oz

   Tootsie

   Pretty Woman

   The Sting

   The Secret of Roan Inish

2. How did reading this essay affect your opinion of the films she discusses? Do you feel you have a better understanding of the films?
3. Joseph Campbell, in writing about the hero's quest, said, "Dream is the personalized myth, myth the depersonalized dream." Respond to his assertion, relying on a personal dream that held meaning for you.

ADDITIONAL ESSAY PROMPTS

1. Many of the concepts Robert Bly discusses in "Iron John" are similar to those used by Clarissa Pinkola Estes in "Sealskin, Soulskin." Compare the similarities in these two works.
2. What are some of the myths of Western contemporary society? Can you see in them some of the reasons we as a culture seem divorced from our roots?
3. Today's children often "watch" stories instead of reading or listening to them. Explain the difference between these two activities in terms of the development of the imagination.
4. Argue pro or con Max Fisch's statement, "Technology is the knack of so arranging the world that we do not experience it." Be sure to include a refutation, regardless of which position you choose to take.
5. Many mythologists believe that modern Western society has misappropriated the word *hero* and assigned that role to celebrities and sports figures. Can you think of instances where any so-called heroes of the last century have abused the role?
6. Write an essay in which you explain how the selections in this chapter, as well as supplemental readings, have affected or confirmed your understanding of the importance of myth in our lives.
7. Create your own myth with yourself as the hero or heroine. How does your "real self" compare to your hero character?
8. What do myths tell us about expectations associated with love, particularly romantic love?
9. J. F. Bierlein, author of *Living Myths: How Myth Gives Meaning to Human Experience,* asserts that myth affirms that there is a purpose to human existence. Do you think this is true? Explain.
10. Using Dave Barry's "Feeling the Force" as inspiration, write your own analysis of the *Star Wars* movies and their appeal to moviegoers.

ADDITIONAL RESEARCH QUESTIONS

1. Research Carl Jung's concept of archetypes, and then pick a favorite fairy tale and trace an archetype throughout the story.
2. Many cultures throughout the world have their own creation myths, which explain the story of creation. Research three creation myths, and compare

how each of them illustrates fundamental beliefs about gods, humans, and nature.

3. According to David Leeming and Jake Page, authors of *Myths, Legends, & Folktales of America: An Anthology,* "The expression of the hero concept among African Americans . . . reflected the restricted place of people of African descent in American society." The legends of black heroes, then, included rebellious leaders seeking justice. Research the African American legend of Nat Turner. In your opinion, who are the modern hero descendants of Nat Turner?

4. Select a fairy tale of your choice, and explore how the story depicts the lives of young girls: their values, self-esteem, and priorities.

5. Select at least three fairy tales, and discuss the role of men in each story. What expectations are placed on the men in the stories?

6. Look at Abraham Maslow's theory of development. Do you think fairy tales of separation, initiation, and return parallel his theory? If so, how?

4

Adolescence

No other time in our lives is marked by so many transitions. The transition from childhood to adulthood can be a painful experience for many, especially in a culture that does a poor job of preparing its young for the upheavals inherent in such a process. Contemporary society gives us differing and conflicting definitions of what manhood and womanhood are and how they might be achieved. Regardless of the ambiguities, we understand all too well that adolescence is a time focused on inner conflict, questioning, and experimentation with ideas and consequences.

This section takes a look at initiation rites practiced by other cultures, as well as our own. Sometimes initiation refers simply to life's pivotal moments that force us to cast off the old in order to become acquainted with the new.

Our literature is filled with initiation stories, with tales of separation from family, of growth, and of new awareness. Some of these tales have been included here. Each carries its own message. In his first-person narrative "Salvation," Langston Hughes begins his journey toward adulthood when he bases his belief system on his own experiences rather than on those of church or family members. Poet Dorianne Laux asks us to recall the times in our teen years when we challenged the forbidden. The central theme of all initiation rites presented here is a change in identity from the death of the old to the birth of the new.

Feminist writer Naomi Wolf, in this excerpt from her book by the same title, asks readers to seriously consider the way female adolescents are encouraged to define womanhood in terms of outward beauty instead of self-esteem and health. As an adolescent, Wolf suffered from anorexia, so she brings a startling dose of reality to the problem. In this excerpt, she not only addresses the tenuous, often confusing search for womanhood but also suggests viable solutions.

NAOMI WOLF

Promiscuities: The Secret Struggle toward Womanhood

"Third Base: Identity"

He and I could have been a poster couple for the liberal ideal of responsible teen sexuality—and, paradoxically, this was reflected in the lack of drama and meaning that I felt crossing this threshold. Conscientious students who were mapping out our college applications and scheduling our after-school jobs to save up for tuition, we were the sort of kids who Planned Ahead. But even the preparations for losing one's virginity felt barren of larger social significance.

When Martin and I went together to a clinic to arrange for contraception some weeks before the actual deed, no experience could have been flatter. He waited, reading old copies of *Scientific American,* while I was fitted for a diaphragm ("the method with one of the highest effectiveness levels if we are very careful, and the fewest risks to you," Martin had explained after looking it up). The offices were full of high school couples. If the management intended the mood to be welcoming to adolescents, they had done an excellent job. Cartoon strips about contraception were displayed in several rooms. The staff members were straight-talking, and they did not patronize. The young, bearded doctor who fitted me treated it all as if he were explaining to me a terrific new piece of equipment for some hearty activity such as camping or rock climbing.

In terms of the mechanics of servicing teenage desire safely in a secular, materialistic society, the experience was impeccable. The technology worked and was either cheap or free. But when we walked out, I still felt there was something important missing. It was weird to have these adults just hand you the keys to the kingdom, ask, "Any questions?" wave, and return to their paperwork. They did not even have us wait until we could show we had learned something concrete—until we could answer some of their questions. It was easier than getting your learner's permit to drive a car. Now, giving us a moral context was not their job. They had enough to handle, and they were doing so valiantly. Indeed, their work seems in retrospect like one of the few backstops we encountered to society's abdication of us within our sexuality. But from visiting the clinic in the absence of any other adults giving us a moral framework in which to learn about sexuality, the message we got was: "You can be adults without trying. The only meaning this has is the meaning you give it." There was a sense, I recall in retrospect, that the adults who were the gatekeepers to society had once again failed to initiate us in any way.

For not at the clinic, at school, in our synagogue, or anywhere in pop culture did this message come through clearly to us: sexual activity comes with responsibilities that are deeper than personal. If our parents did say this, it was scarcely reinforced outside the home. No one said, at the clinic, "You must use this diaphragm or this condom, not only because that is how you will avoid the personal disaster of unwanted pregnancy but because if you have sex without using protection you are doing something antisocial and morally objectionable. If you, boy or girl, initiate a pregnancy out of carelessness, that is dumb, regrettable behavior." Nothing morally significant about the transfer of power from adults to teenagers was represented in that technology. It was like going to the vet: as if we were being processed not on a social but on an animal level.

Unsurprisingly, the more forbidden women are to own their sexuality lest they become "sluts," the more inclined they are to project an out-of-control sexuality onto men. The more a woman's "appropriate" sexual persona is defined as being for others, the more the demon lover stands in her mind as promising a sexuality that can be, subversively, for herself.

"Fourth Base: How to Make a Woman"

Losing our virginity was supposed to pass for attaining sexual maturity. But it was too easy, what we did, and it didn't matter enough to satisfy us more than physically. The end of our virginity passed unmarked, neither mourned nor celebrated: the worldview we inherited told us that what we gained by becoming fully sexual was infinitely valuable and what we lost by leaving behind our virgin state was less than negligible. In other cultures I have looked at, older women, who upheld the values of femaleness, decided when a girl could join them in womanhood. Their decision was based on whether the girl had attained the level of wisdom and self-discipline that would benefit her, her family, and the society. Those older women alone, through their deliberations, had the power to bestow womanhood on the initiates.

In our culture, men were deciding for us if we were women. Heck: *teenage boys* were deciding for us if we were women.

Instead we should be telling girls what they already know but rarely see affirmed: that the lives they lead inside their own self-contained bodies, the skills they attain through their own concentration and rigor, and the unique phase in their lives during which they may explore boys and eroticism at their own pace—these are magical. And they constitute the entrance point to a life cycle of a sexuality that should be held sacred.

"The Time and the Place: 1996"

If one is allowed to grow up being proud of one's sexual womanhood as it develops day by day, one may acquire that "sureness" that Margaret Mead[1] spoke

---

[1] Margaret Mead (1901–1978) was an American anthropologist whose classic *Coming of Age in Samoa* (1928) describes adolescent girls in a largely noncompetitive and permissive culture.

of, and be far less susceptible to the blandishment of industries or ideologies that promise to bestow a sexual womanhood, as well as being less susceptible to the pressures in the marketplace that stand ready to stigmatize women for any hint of their sexuality.

Obviously, girls need better rites of passage in our culture. Such rituals, we have seen, require rigor, separation from males and from the daily environment, and the exchange of privileged information. It is important, in such rituals, for grown women outside the family to do the initiating. I'd like to propose that groups of friends with children sign one another up, upon the birth of a daughter, for the responsibility of becoming part of small groups—Womanhood Guides. Instead or in addition to the familiar role of godparent, someone who signs on for such a task will join with a few other women, and a small cohort of girls, in the girls' thirteenth year, for a retreat into the wilderness—something as simple as a trip to a state park, organized through the schools, church groups, or through individual family groups. There, amid stories, songs, and hikes the older women would pass on to the younger everything they have learned about womanhood, and answer *every single question* the girls want to ask—questions that will be far more trusting and substantive than those asked in the constrained, public environment of a sex education class. The older women can certainly, depending on the religious and cultural sensitivities of the group, show the girls birth control devices and explain how they work. They would explain a sexual ethic that, as women initiates, the girls would be asked to commit to—an ethic that might include committing never to do anything one does not fully consent to do; never to use sex to get something (love, status, money) that one should seek in other ways; never to have sex without consciousness—not to use drugs or alcohol to mask one's sexual intention and responsibility; to practice saying what one wants; to practice saying what one doesn't want; to seek conscientiously, with every means at one's disposal, to avoid having to undergo an abortion or to bring into the world a child one is not ready to parent; never to degrade or violate one's own sexuality, or tolerate others' degrading or violating it. But their most important task—one that the culture would value these women for undertaking—would be to explain to the girls, in clear, compassionate terms, just how to explore female sexual desire in such a way as to postpone intercourse until they are really, truly, feeling safe, sensually aware, and ready; until, that is, whether the marker is their eighteenth birthday or their engagement or their marriage, they feel ready to undertake such a profound step not as curious, passionate, half certain girls, but as *empowered, self-knowing, mature women.* When the retreat is over and the girls have proven to the older women that they have mastered some of the skills and knowledge of womanhood—the rudiments of taking care of themselves professionally and sexually, and understanding what it means to take care of children—they return to their neighborhoods and a great big party is thrown to welcome them back and celebrate their changed status.

In addition to the sexual education, a family's friends can commit to being part of a wisdom initiation: transmitting their professional skills to the girl whom they are assigned to guide. I have, for instance, such a commitment of exchange from the scientist parents of a two-year-old girl; as my daughter grows up, they have agreed to teach her about earth sciences, show her experiments, and explain to her the jobs that one can do in that field—something in which I have no expertise—and I in turn have committed to working with their daughter on writing. In this way, through these commitments of mentoring exchanges, girls feel specially valued not only by their families but by the extended community—the locus of the initiation tension, and the possibilities of what they might love and become good at expands, and these skills are undertaken at the special time when they begin to cross the border into womanhood. "Privilege knowledge" associated with becoming women need not be sexual; through adolescent exchange relationships, that hunger for a special women's wisdom is filled.

JOURNAL PROMPT:

Write about a person in your life who is a source of wisdom.

COLLABORATIVE EXERCISE:

Working in small groups, brainstorm and develop a wisdom initiation that you feel might give a young woman a greater sense of herself.

ESSAY ASSIGNMENT:

1. Research how another culture prepares a young girl for womanhood.
2. Kay Hymowitz in "The Teening of Childhood" claims that advertisers are deliberately turning youngsters into consumers. Do you think the media plays a role in prematurely sexualizing adolescents? Explore the effects of one medium on adolescents.
3. What is the author's thesis? What arguments does she give to advance this idea? Do you find her thesis convincing? Explain.

TEPILIT OLE SAITOTI grew up in Tanzania and worked as a farmer. He later moved to Germany and then to the United States. In 1971, his life experiences were recorded in a film, *Man of Serengeti,* produced by the National Geographic Society. In this essay he reveals the details of the coming-of-age ceremony for a young Maasai—how young men in Tanzania prove their bravery.

TEPILIT OLE SAITOTI

THE INITIATION OF A MAASAI WARRIOR

"Tepilit, circumcision means a sharp knife cutting into the skin of the most sensitive part of your body. You must not budge; don't move a muscle or even blink. You can face only one direction until the operation is completed. The slightest movement on your part will mean you are a coward, incompetent and unworthy to be a Maasai man. Ours has always been a proud family, and we would like to keep it that way. We will not tolerate unnecessary embarrassment, so you had better be ready. If you are not, tell us now so that we will not proceed. Imagine yourself alone remaining uncircumcised like the water youth [white people]. I hear they are not circumcised. Such a thing is not known in Maasailand; therefore, circumcision will have to take place even if it means holding you down until it is completed."

My father continued to speak and every one of us kept quiet. "The pain you will feel is symbolic. There is a deeper meaning in all this. Circumcision means a break between childhood and adulthood. For the first time in your life, you are regarded as a grownup, a complete man or woman. You will be expected to give and not just to receive. To protect the family always, not just to be protected yourself. And your wise judgment will for the first time be taken into consideration. No family affairs will be discussed without your being consulted. If you are ready for all these responsibilities, tell us now. Coming into manhood is not simply a matter of growth and maturity. It is a heavy load on your shoulders and especially a burden on the mind. Too much of this—I am done. I have said all I wanted to say. Fellows, if you have anything to add, go ahead and tell your brother, because I am through. I have spoken."

After a prolonged silence, one of my half-brothers said awkwardly, "Face it, man . . . it's painful. I won't lie about it, but it is not the end. We all went through it, after all. Only blood will flow, not milk." There was laughter and my father left.

My brother Lellia said, "Men, there are many things we must acquire and preparations we must make before the ceremony, and we will need the cooperation and help of all of you. Ostrich feathers for the crown and wax for the arrows must be collected."

"Are you *orkirekenyi?*" One of my brothers asked. I quickly replied no, and there was laughter. *Orkirekenyi* is a person who has transgressed sexually. For you must not have sexual intercourse with any circumcised woman before you yourself are circumcised. You must wait until you are circumcised. If you have not waited, you will be fined. Your father, mother, and the circumciser will take a cow from you as punishment.

Just before we departed, one of my closest friends said, "If you kick the knife, you will be in trouble." There was laughter. "By the way, if you have decided to kick the circumciser, do it well. Silence him once and for all." "Do it the way you kick a football in school." "That will fix him," another added, and we all laughed our heads off again as we departed.

The following month was a month of preparation. I and others collected wax, ostrich feathers, honey to be made into honey beer for the elders to drink on the day of circumcision, and all the other required articles.

Three days before the ceremony my head was shaved and I discarded all my belongings, such as my necklaces, garments, spear, and sword. I even had to shave my pubic hair. Circumcision in many ways is similar to Christian baptism. You must put all the sins you have committed during childhood behind and embark as a new person with a different outlook on a new life.

The circumciser came the following day and handed the ritual knives to me. He left drinking a calabash of beer. I stared at the knives uneasily. It was hard to accept that he was going to use them on my organ. I was to sharpen them and protect them from people of ill will who might try to blunt them, thus rendering them inefficient during the ritual and thereby bringing shame on our family. The knives threw a chill down my spine; I was not sure I was sharpening them properly, so I took them to my closest brother for him to check out, and he assured me that the knives were all right. I hid them well and waited.

Tension started building between me and my relatives, most of whom worried that I wouldn't make it through the ceremony valiantly. Some even snarled at me, which was their way of encouraging me. Others threw insults and abusive words my way. My sister Loiyan in particular was more troubled by the whole affair than anyone in the whole family. She had to assume my mother's role during the circumcision. Were I to fail my initiation, she would have to face the consequences. She would be spat upon and even beaten for representing the mother of an unworthy son. The same fate would befall my father, but he seemed unconcerned. He had this weird belief that because I was not particularly handsome, I must be brave. He kept saying, "God is not so bad as to have made him ugly and a coward at the same time."

Failure to be brave during circumcision would have other unfortunate consequences: the herd of cattle belonging to the family still in the compound would be beaten until they stampeded; the slaughtered oxen and honey beer prepared during the month before the ritual would go to waste; the initiate's food would be spat upon and he would have to eat it or else get a severe beating. Everyone would call him Olkasiodoi, the knife kicker.

Kicking the knife of the circumciser would not help you anyway. If you struggle and try to get away during the ritual, you will be held down until the operation is completed. Such failure of nerve would haunt you in the future. For example, no one will choose a person who kicked the knife for a position of leadership. However, there have been instances in which a person who failed to go through circumcision successfully became very brave afterwards because he was filled with anger over the incident; no one dares to scold him or remind him of it. His agemates, particularly the warriors, will act as if nothing had happened.

During the circumcision of a woman, on the other hand, she is allowed to cry as long as she does not hinder the operation. It is common to see a woman crying and kicking during circumcision. Warriors are usually summoned to help hold her down.

For women, circumcision means an end to the company of Maasai warriors. After they recuperate, they soon get married, and often to men twice their age.

The closer it came to the hour of truth, the more I was hated, particularly by those closest to me. I was deeply troubled by the withdrawal of all the support I needed. My annoyance turned into anger and resolve. I decided not to budge or blink, even if I were to see my intestines flowing before me. My resolve was hardened when newly circumcised warriors came to sing for me. Their songs were utterly insulting, intended to annoy me further. They tucked their wax arrows under my crotch and rubbed them on my nose. They repeatedly called me names.

By the end of the singing, I was fuming. Crying would have meant I was a coward. After midnight they left me alone and I went into the house and tried to sleep but could not. I was exhausted and numb but remained awake all night.

At dawn I was summoned once again by the newly circumcised warriors. They piled more and more insults on me. They sang their weird songs with even more vigor and excitement than before. The songs praised warriorhood and encouraged one to achieve it at all costs. The songs continued until the sun shone on the cattle horns clearly. I was summoned to the main cattle gate, in my hand a ritual cowhide from a cow that had been properly slaughtered during my naming ceremony. I went past Loiyan, who was milking a cow, and she muttered something, she was shaking all over. There was so much tension that people could hardly breathe.

I laid the hide down and a boy was ordered to pour ice-cold water, known as *engare entolu* (ax water), over my head. It dripped all over my naked body and I shook furiously. In a matter of seconds I was summoned to sit down. A large crowd of boys and men formed a semicircle in front of me; women are not allowed to watch male circumcision and vice-versa. That was the last thing I saw clearly. As soon as I sat down, the circumciser appeared, his knives at the ready. He spread my legs and said, "One cut," a pronouncement necessary to prevent an initiate from claiming that he had been taken by surprise. He splashed a white liquid, a ceremonial paint called *enturoto,* across my face. Almost immediately I felt a spark of pain under my belly as the knife cut through my penis' foreskin. I happened to choose to look in the direction of the operation. I continued to observe the circumciser's fingers working mechanically. The pain became numbness and my lower body felt heavy, as if I were weighed down by a heavy burden. After fifteen minutes or so, a man who had been supporting from behind pointed at something, as if to assist the circumciser. I came to learn later that the circumciser's eyesight had been failing him and that my brothers had been mad at him because the operation had taken longer than was usually necessary. All the same, I remained pinned down until the operation was over. I heard a call for milk to wash the knives, which signaled the end, and soon the ceremony was over.

With words of praise, I was told to wake up, but I remained seated. I waited for the customary presents in appreciation of my bravery. My father gave me a cow and so did my brother Lillia. The man who had supported my back and my brother-in-law gave me a heifer. In all I had eight animals given to me. I was carried inside the house to my own bed to recuperate as activities intensified to celebrate my bravery.

I laid on my own bed and bled profusely. The blood must be retained within the bed, for according to Maasai tradition, it must not spill to the ground. I was drenched in my own blood. I stopped bleeding after about half an hour but soon was in intolerable pain. I was supposed to squeeze my organ and force blood to flow out of the wound, but no one had told me, so the blood coagulated and caused unbearable pain. The circumciser was brought to my aid and showed me what to do, and soon the pain subsided.

The following morning, I was escorted by a small boy to a nearby valley to walk and relax, allowing my wound to drain. This was common for everyone who had been circumcised, as well as for women who had just given birth. Having lost a lot of blood, I was extremely weak. I walked very slowly, but in spite of my caution I fainted. I tried to hang on to bushes and shrubs, but I fell, irritating my wound. I came out of unconsciousness quickly, and the boy who was escorting me never realized what had happened. I was so scared that I told him to lead me back home. I could have died without there being anyone around who could have helped me. From that day on, I was selective of my company while I was feeble.

In two weeks I was able to walk and was taken to join other newly circumcised boys far away from our settlement. By tradition Maasai initiates are required to decorate their headdresses with all kinds of colorful birds they have killed. On our way to the settlement, we hunted birds and teased girls by shooting them with our wax blunt arrows. We danced and ate and were well treated wherever we went. We were protected from the cold and rain during the healing period. We were not allowed to touch food, as we were regarded as unclean, so whenever we ate we had to use specially prepared sticks instead. We remained in this pampered state until our wounds healed and our headdresses were removed. Our heads were shaved, we discarded our black cloaks and bird headdresses and embarked as newly shaven warriors, Irkeleani.

As long as I live I will never forget the day my head was shaved and I emerged a man, a Maasai warrior. I felt a sense of control over my destiny so great that no words can accurately describe it. I now stood with confidence, pride, and happiness of being, for all around me I was desired and loved by beautiful, sensuous Maasai maidens. I could now interact with women and even have sex with them, which I had not been allowed before. I was now regarded as a responsible person.

In the old days, warriors were like gods, and women and men wanted only to be the parent of a warrior. Everything else would be taken care of as a result. When a poor family had a warrior, they ceased to be poor. The warrior would go on raids and bring cattle back. The warrior would defend the family against all odds. When a society respects the individual and displays confidence in him the way the Maasai do their warriors, the individual can grow to his fullest potential. Whenever there was a task requiring physical strength or bravery, the Maasai would call upon their warriors. They hardly ever fall short of what is demanded of them and so are characterized by pride, confidence, and an extreme sense of freedom. But there is an old saying in Maasai: "You are never a free man until your father dies." In other words, your father is paramount while he is alive and you are obligated to respect him. My father took advantage of this principle and held a tight grip on all his warriors, including myself. He always wanted to know where we all were at any given time. We fought against his restrictions, but without success. I, being the youngest of my father's five warriors, tried even harder to get loose repeatedly, but each time I was punished severely.

Roaming the plains with other warriors in pursuit of girls and adventure was a warrior's pastime. We would wander from one settlement to another, singing, wrestling, hunting, and just playing. Often I was ready to risk my father's punishment for this wonderful freedom.

One clear day my father sent me to take sick children and one of his wives to the dispensary in the Korongoro Highlands. We rode in the L. S. B. Leakey lorry. We ascended the highlands and were soon attended to in the local hospital. Near the conservation offices I met several acquaintances, and one of them told me of an unusual circumcision that was about to take place in a day or two. All the local warriors and girls were preparing to attend it.

The highlands were a lush green from the seasonal rains and the sky was a purple-blue with no clouds in sight. The land was overflowing with milk, and the warriors felt and looked their best, as they always did when there was plenty to eat and drink. Everyone was at ease. The demands the community usually made on warriors during the dry season when water was scarce and wells had to be dug were now not necessary. Herds and flocks were entrusted to youths to look after. The warriors had all the time for themselves. But my father was so strict that even at times like these he still insisted on overworking us in one way or another. He believed that by keeping us busy, he would keep us out of trouble.

When I heard about the impending ceremony, I decided to remain behind in the Korongoro Highlands and attend it now that the children had been treated. I knew very well that I would have to make up a story for my father upon my return, but I would worry about that later. I had left my spear at home when I boarded the bus, thinking that I would be coming back that very day. I felt lighter but now regretted having left it behind; I was so used to carrying it wherever I went. In gales of laughter resulting from our continuous teasing of each other, we made our way toward a distant kraal. We walked at a leisurely pace and reveled in the breeze. As usual we talked about the women we desired, among other things.

The following day we were joined by a long line of colorfully dressed girls and warriors from the kraal and the neighborhood where we had spent the night, and we left the highland and headed to Ingorienito to the rolling hills on the lower slopes to attend the circumcision ceremony. From there one could see Oldopai Gorge, where my parents lived, and the Inaapi hills in the middle of the Serengeti Plain.

Three girls and a boy were to be initiated on the same day, an unusual occasion. Four oxen were to be slaughtered, and many people would therefore attend. As we descended, we saw the kraal where the ceremony would take place. All those people dressed in red seemed from a distance like flamingos standing in a lake. We could see lines of other guests heading to the settlements. Warriors made gallant cries of happiness known as *enkiseer*. Our line of warriors and girls responded to their cries even more gallantly.

In serpentine fashion, we entered the gates of the settlement. Holding spears in our left hands, we warriors walked proudly, taking small steps, swaying like palm trees, impressing our girls, who walked parallel to us in another line, and of course the spectators, who gazed at us approvingly.

We stopped in the center of the kraal and waited to be greeted. Women and children welcomed us. We put our hands on the children's heads, which is how children are commonly saluted. After the greetings were completed, we started dancing.

Our singing echoed off the kraal fence and nearby trees. Another line of warriors came up the hill and entered the compound, also singing and moving slowly toward us. Our singing grew in intensity. Both lines of warriors moved parallel to each other, and our feet pounded the ground with style. We stamped vigorously, as if to tell the next line and the spectators that we were the best.

The singing continued until the hot sun was overhead. We recessed and ate food already prepared for us by other warriors. Roasted meat was for those who were to eat meat, and milk for the others. By our tradition, meat and milk must not be consumed at the same time, for this would be a betrayal of the animal. It was regarded as cruel to consume a product of the animal that could be obtained while it was alive, such as milk, and meat, which was only available after the animal had been killed.

After eating we resumed singing, and I spotted a tall, beautiful *esiankiki* (young maiden) of Masiaya whose family was one of the largest and richest in our area. She stood very erect and seemed taller than the rest.

One of her breasts could be seen just above her dress, which was knotted at the shoulder. While I was supposed to dance generally to please all the spectators, I took it upon myself to please her especially. I stared at and flirted with her, and she and I danced in unison at times. We complemented each other very well.

During a break, I introduced myself to the *esiankiki* and told her I would like to see her after the dance. "Won't you need a warrior to escort you home later when the evening threatens?" I said. She replied, "Perhaps, but the evening is still far away."

I waited patiently. When the dance ended, I saw her departing with a group of other women her age. She gave me a sidelong glance, and I took that to mean come later and not now. With so many others around, I would not have been able to confer with her as I would have liked anyway.

With another warrior, I wandered around the kraal killing time until the herds returned from pasture. Before the sun dropped out of sight, we departed. As the kraal of the *esiankiki* was in the lowlands, a place called Enkoloa, we descended leisurely, our spears resting on our shoulders.

We arrived at the woman's kraal and found that cows were now being milked. One could hear the women trying to appease the cows by singing to them. Singing calms cows down, making it easier to milk them. There were no warriors in the whole kraal except for the two of us. Girls went around into warriors' houses as usual and collected milk for us. I was so eager to go and meet my *esiankiki* that I could hardly wait for nightfall. The warriors' girls were trying hard to be sociable, but my mind was not with them. I found them to be childish, loud, bothersome, and boring.

As the only warriors present, we had to keep them company and sing for them, at least for a while, as required by custom. I told the other warrior to sing while I tried to figure out how to approach my *esiankiki*. Still a novice warrior, I was not experienced with women and was in fact still afraid of them. I could flirt from a distance, of course. But sitting down with a woman and trying to seduce her was another matter. I had already tried twice to approach women soon after my circumcision and had failed. I got as far as the door of one woman's house and felt my heart beating like a Congolese drum; breathing became difficult and I had to turn back. Another time I managed to get in the house and succeeded in sitting on the bed, but then I started trembling until the whole bed was shaking, and conversation became difficult. I left the house and the woman, amazed and speechless, and never went back to her again.

Tonight I promised myself I would be brave and would not make any silly, ridiculous moves. "I must be mature and not afraid," I kept reminding myself, as I remembered an incident involving one of my relatives when he was still very young and, like me, afraid of women. He went to a woman's house and sat on a stool for a whole hour; he was afraid to awaken her, as his heart was pounding and he was having difficulty breathing.

When he finally calmed down, he woke her up, and their conversation went something like this:

"Woman, wake up."

"Why should I?"

"To light the fire."

"For what?"

"So you can see me."

"I already know who you are. Why don't *you* light the fire, as you're nearer to it than me?"

"It's your house and it's only proper that you light it yourself."

"I don't feel like it."

"At least wake up so we can talk, as I have something to tell you."

"Say it."

"I need you."

"I do not need one-eyed types like yourself."

"One-eyed people are people too."

"That might be so, but they are not to my taste."

They continued talking for quite some time, and the more they spoke, the braver he became. He did not sleep with her that night, but later on he persisted until he won her over. I doubted whether I was as strong-willed as he, but the fact that he had met with success encouraged me. I told my warrior friend where to find me should he need me, and then I departed.

When I entered the house of my *esiankiki,* I called for the woman of the house, and as luck would have it, my lady responded. She was waiting for me. I felt better, and I proceeded to talk to her like a professional. After much talking back and forth, I joined her in bed.

The night was calm, tender, and loving, like most nights after initiation ceremonies as big as this one. There must have been a lot of courting and lovemaking.

Maasai women can be very hard to deal with sometimes. They can simply reject a man outright and refuse to change their minds. Some play hard to get, but in reality are testing the man to see whether he is worth their while. Once a friend of mine while still young was powerfully attracted to a woman nearly his mother's age. He put a bold move on her. At first the woman could not believe his intention, or rather was amazed by his courage. The name of the warrior was Ngengeiya, or Drizzle.

"Drizzle, what do you want?"

The warrior stared her right in the eye and said, "You."

"For what?"

"To make love to you."

"I am your mother's age."

"The choice was either her or you."

This remark took the woman by surprise. She had underestimated the saying "There is no such thing as a young warrior." When you are a warrior, you are expected to perform bravely in any situation. Your age and size are immaterial.

"You mean you could really love me like a grown-up man?"

"Try me, woman."

He moved in on her. Soon the woman started moaning with excitement, calling out his name. "Honey Drizzle, Honey Drizzle, you *are* a man." In a breathy, stammering voice, she said, "A real man."

Her attractiveness made Honey Drizzle ignore her relative old age. The Maasai believe that if an older and a younger person have intercourse, it is the older person who stands to gain. For instance, it is believed that an older woman having an affair with a young man starts to appear younger and healthier, while the young man grows older and unhealthy.

The following day when the initiation rites had ended, I decided to return home. I had offended my father by staying away from home without his consent, so I prepared myself for whatever punishment he might inflict on me. I walked home alone.

JOURNAL PROMPT:

Saitoti makes a decision, without his father's permission, to stay in the Highlands. Write about a time when an action you took contributed to your newfound sense of adulthood.

COLLABORATIVE EXERCISE:

Why do you think that Saitoti's seduction of an *esiankiki* is included as part of his initiation into adulthood? Why is it significant? What would be the difference in the tradition if this part of the initiation were eliminated? Include in your discussion whether you feel this inclusion of the seduction resembles sexism in any way.

ESSAY ASSIGNMENT:

1. Consider what young men you know do to prove their bravery. Are women under any pressure to exhibit signs of bravery?
2. The Maasai warrior must agree to begin life all over again. Saitoti explains, "You must put all the sins you have committed during childhood behind and embark as a new person with a different outlook on a new life." How might the media in the United States respond if this were the case for U.S. citizens? How might they respond to the adoption of such a tradition? What impact would the tradition have on their livelihoods?

JUDITH ORTIZ COFER was born in Puerto Rico and lived there until she was eight. She currently teaches at the University of Georgia at Athens. Cofer writes poems, essays, and short fiction that focus on her heritage, as well as the difficulties encountered in blending two cultures. In this poem she speaks in the voice of a young Latina who faces the inevitable journey from adolescence to adulthood in the traditional *quinceañera* ceremony and celebration.

JUDITH ORTIZ COFER

QUINCEAÑERA

My dolls have been put away like dead
children in a chest I will carry
with me when I marry.
I reach under my skirt to feel
a satin slip bought for this day. It is soft
as the inside of my thighs. My hair
has been pulled back with my mother's
black hairpins to my skull. Her hands
stretched my eyes open as she twisted
braids into a tight circle at the nape
of my neck. I am to wash my own clothes
and sheets from this day on, as if
the fluids of my body were poison, as if
the little trickle of blood I believe
travels from my heart to the world were
shameful. Is not the blood of saints and
men in battle beautiful? Do Christ's hands
not bleed into your eyes from His cross?
At night I hear myself growing and wake
to find my hands drifting of their own will
to soothe skin stretched tight
over my bones.
I am wound like the guts of a clock,
Waiting for each hour to release me.

JOURNAL PROMPT:

Were there any celebrations according to your religion or culture to acknowledge your coming-of-age? Explain what they were.

COLLABORATIVE EXERCISE:

In most Latin American cultures, when a fifteen-year-old girl celebrates her *quinceañera*, it is understood that she has become an adult. How do you think

Kay Hymowitz, author of "The Teening of Childhood," might respond to a celebration that places adulthood in the lap of such a young girl? What are the possible advantages and disadvantages of this initiation celebration?

ESSAY ASSIGNMENT:

1. Explain the Latin American tradition of the *quinceañera*. Begin with the origin of the event; explain the details of the preparation, ceremony, and party; and explore any changes the *quinceañera* tradition has undergone.
2. Consider the tone of the poem. How does the poet appear to feel on the eve of her *quinceañera*? How would you describe her mood or attitude about the upcoming celebration? What evidence in the poem supports your assertions? (In particular, note the poet's choice of vocabulary, imagery, and line breaks.)

DORIANNE LAUX was raised in Southern California. She graduated with honors from Mills College with a B.A. in English. Her first book of poetry, *Awake,* was published in 1990 and nominated for the Bay Area Book Reviewers Award. In "Twelve" she asks the reader to "peek in" as an almost classic rite-of-passage scene unfolds. Her choice of words adds a film of subtlety to the moment. The poem is from her collection *What We Carry* (1994).

DORIANNE LAUX

TWELVE

Deep in the canyon, under the red branches
of a manzanita, we turned the pages
slowly, seriously, as if it were a holy text,
just as the summer before we had turned
the dark undersides of rocks to interrupt
the lives of ants, or a black stinkbug
and her hard-backed brood.
And because the boys always came,
even though they weren't invited, we never
said anything, except Brenda who whispered
Turn the page when she thought we'd seen enough.
This went on for weeks one summer, a few of us
meeting at the canyon rim at noon, the glossy

magazine fluttering at the tips of our fingers.
Brenda led the way down, and the others
stumbled after blindly, Martin
always with his little brother
hanging off the pocket of his jeans, a blue
pacifier stuck like candy in his mouth.
Every time he yawned, the wet nipple
fell out into the dirt, and Martin, the good brother,
would pick it up, dust it with the underside
of his shirt, then slip it into his own mouth
and suck it clean. And when the turning
of the pages began, ceremoniously, exposing
thigh after thigh, breast after beautiful,
terrible breast, Martin leaned to one side,
and slid the soft palm of his hand
over his baby brother's eyes.

JOURNAL PROMPT:

What joys and heartaches do you associate with being twelve?

COLLABORATIVE EXERCISE:

How is the presence of Martin's little brother significant to the poem's message? Is the poet's use of repetition of images effective? Explain how this poem reflects a child's initiation into community.

ESSAY ASSIGNMENT:

1. Write an essay about a pivotal moment in your life when you realized you were no longer a child. Who were the other players in your drama? Describe them, and describe the situation, using what you have learned about how details can create a mood. Try to capture a moment in time.
2. What are some of the author's clues that Martin loves his little brother?

CHARLES MUNGOSHI, a Zimbabwean author, received international PEN awards for his work in 1976 and 1981. This piece, which is the title story from a collection published in 1989, is a tale about separation in which the reader is asked to "see" both sides—the pain and disappointment of the father and the eagerness and sensibility of the son.

CHARLES MUNGOSHI

THE SETTING SUN AND THE ROLLING WORLD

Old Musoni raised his dusty eyes from his hoe and the unchanging stony earth he had been tilling and peered into the sky. The white speck whose sound had disturbed his work and thoughts was far out at the edge of the yellow sky, near the horizon. Then it disappeared quickly over the southern rim of the sky and he shook his head. He looked to the west. Soon the sun would go down. He looked over the sunblasted land and saw the shadows creeping east, blearer and taller with every moment that the sun shed each of its rays. Unconsciously wishing for rain and relief, he bent down again to his work and did not see his son, Nhamo, approaching.

Nhamo crouched in the dust near his father and greeted him. The old man half raised his back, leaning against his hoe, and said what had been bothering him all day long.

"You haven't changed your mind?"

"No, father."

There was a moment of silence. Old Musoni scraped earth off his hoe.

"Have you thought about this, son?"

"For weeks, father."

"And you think that's the only way?"

"There is no other way."

The old man felt himself getting angry again. But this would be the last day he would talk to his son. If his son was going away, he must not be angry. It would be equal to a curse. He himself had taken chances before, in his own time, but he felt too much of a father. He had worked and slaved for his family and the land had not betrayed him. He saw nothing now but disaster and death for his son out there in the world. Lions had long since vanished but he knew of worse animals of prey, animals that wore redder claws than the lion's, beasts that would not leave an unprotected homeless boy alone. He thought of the white metal bird and he felt remorse.

"Think again. You will end dead. Think again, of us, of your family. We have a home, poor though it is, but can you think of a day you have gone without?"

"I have thought everything over, father, I am convinced this is the only way out."

"There is no only way out in the world. Except the way of the land, the way of the family."

"The land is overworked and gives nothing now, father. And the family is almost broken up."

The old man got angry. Yes, the land is useless. True, the family tree is uprooted and it dries in the sun. True, many things are happening that haven't happened before, that we did not think would happen, ever. But nothing is more certain to hold you together than the land and a home, a family. And where do you think you are going, a mere beardless kid with the milk not yet dry on your baby nose? What do you think you will do in the great treacherous world where men twice your age have gone and returned with their backs broken—if they returned at all? What do you know of life? What do you know of the false honey bird that leads you the whole day through the forest to a snake's nest? But all he said was: "Look. What have you asked me and I have denied you? What, that I have, have I not given you for the asking?"

"All. You have given me all, father." And here, too, the son felt hampered, patronized and his pent-up fury rolled through him. It showed on his face but stayed under control. You have given me damn all and nothing. You have sent me to school and told me the importance of education, and now you ask me to throw it on the rubbish heap and scrape for a living on this tired cold shell of the moon. You ask me to forget it and muck around in this slow dance of death with you. I have this one chance of making my own life, once in all eternity, and now you are jealous. You are afraid of your own death. It is, after all, your own death. I shall be around a while yet. I will make my way home if a home is what I need. I am armed more than you think and wiser than you can dream of. But all he said, too, was:

"Really, father, have no fear for me. I will be all right. Give me this chance. Release me from all obligations and pray for me."

There was a spark in the old man's eyes at these words of his son. But just as dust quickly settles over a glittering pebble revealed by the hoe, so a murkiness hid the gleam in the old man's eye. Words are handles made to the smith's fancy and are liable to break under stress. They are too much fat on the hard unbreaking sinews of life.

"Do you know what you are doing, son?"

"Yes."

"Do you know what you will be a day after you leave home?"

"Yes, father."

"A homeless, nameless vagabond living on dust and rat's droppings, living on thank-yous, sleeping up a tree or down a ditch, in the rain, in the sun, in the cold, with nobody to see you, nobody to talk to, nobody at all to tell your dreams to. Do you know what it is to see your hopes come crashing down like an old house out of season and your dreams turning to ash and dung without a tang of salt in your skull? Do you know what it is to live without a single hope of ever seeing good in your own lifetime?" And to himself: Do you know, young bright ambitious son of my loins, the ruins of time and the pains of old age? Do you know how to live beyond a dream, a hope, a faith? Have you seen black despair, my son?

"I know it, father. I know enough to start on. The rest I shall learn as I go on. Maybe I shall learn to come back."

The old man looked at him and felt: Come back where? Nobody comes back to ruins. You will go on, son. Something you don't know will drive you on along deserted plains, past ruins and more ruins, on and on until there is only one ruin left: yourself. You will break down, without tears, son. You are human, too. Learn to the *haya*—the rain bird, and heed its warning of coming storm: plough no more, it says. And what happens if the storm catches you far, far out on the treeless plain? What, then, my son?

But he was tired. They had taken over two months discussing all this. Going over the same ground like animals at a drinking place until, like animals, they had driven the water far deep into the stony earth, until they had sapped all the blood out of life and turned it into a grim skeleton, and now they were creating a stampede on the dust, groveling for water. Mere thoughts. Mere words. And what are words? Trying to grow a fruit tree in the wilderness.

"Go son, with my blessings. I give you nothing. And when you remember what I am saying you will come back. The land is still yours. As long as I am alive you will find a home waiting for you."

"Thank you, father."

"Before you go, see Chiremba. You are going out into the world. You need something to strengthen yourself. Tell him I shall pay him. Have a good journey, son."

"Thank you, father."

Nhamo smiled and felt a great love for his father. But there were things that belonged to his old world that were just lots of humbug on the mind, empty load, useless scrap. He would go to Chiremba but he would burn the charms as soon as he was away from home and its sickening environment. A man stands on his feet and guts. Charms were for you—so was God, though much later. But for us now the world is godless, no charms will work. All that is just the opium you take in the dark in the hope of a light. You don't need that now. You strike a match for a light. Nhamo laughed.

He could be so easily light-hearted. Now his brain worked with a fury only known to visionaries. The psychological ties were now broken, only the biological tied him to his father. He was free. He too remembered the aeroplane which his father had seen just before their talk. Space had no bounds and no ties. Floating laws ruled the darkness and he would float with the fiery balls. He was the sun, burning itself out every second and shedding tons of energy which it held in its power, giving it the thrust to drag its brood wherever it wanted to. This was the law that held him. The mystery that his father and ancestors had failed to grasp and which had caused their being wiped off the face of the earth. This thinking reached such a pitch that he began to sing, imitating as intimately as he could Satchmo's voice: "What a wonderful world." It was Satchmo's voice that he turned to when he felt buoyant.

Old Musoni did not look at his son as he left him. Already, his mind was trying to focus at some point in the dark unforeseeable future. Many things could happen and while he still breathed he would see that nothing terribly painful happened to his family, especially to his stubborn last born, Nhamo.

Tomorrow, before sunrise, he would go to see Chiremba and ask him to throw bones over the future of his son. And if there were a couple of ancestors who needed appeasement, he would do it while he was still around.

He noticed that the sun was going down and he scraped the earth off his hoe.

The sun was sinking slowly, bloody red, blunting and blurring all the objects that had looked sharp in the light of day. Soon a chilly wind would blow over the land and the cold cloudless sky would send down beads of frost like white ants over the unprotected land.

JOURNAL PROMPT:

In your opinion, what is the son running *from* or *to,* and what does the father mean about there being "no only way out in the world. Except the way of the land, the way of the family"?

COLLABORATIVE EXERCISE:

Consider an issue about which you care strongly, one for which you would *fight to the death.* Now, elect others from your group to play devil's advocate (defend the other position). Since this works best if you have an equal number of students defending each position, divide your group in half. Spend ten minutes together brainstorming your argument. Try to assume how the other group is going to present its position. (This is your refutation, a logical and fair recognition of the other side's position.) In front of the class, debate your position. Remember that you must rely on factual information, not an emotional response, to create your argument. As you are doing this exercise, think about your role in the group: do you become the leader? Are you the person who tries to make peace at all costs? Do you remain silent and say nothing? How do you function in a group? (You will learn more in this exercise if you take a position *contrary* to the one you wish to defend and then try to convince others of the rightness of that position. A good debater knows both sides of an argument.)

ESSAY ASSIGNMENT:

1. This short story deals with two different ways of looking at the world. While there is no *correct* way to view the situation, both of the characters are convinced that they are *right.* In other words, they are wedded to their convictions, their view of the world. It is the stuff of classic drama; as in the play *Antigone,* both strong characters are right. Think about a time when you viewed a situation as black or white, when there was just one right and one wrong, and someone you cared for viewed it differently. What happened? Did either one of you *give in?* Do you still think that you were *right* and the other person *wrong?*
2. Where does this story take place? What are some of the clues to the setting? Do you think this tale could have been set somewhere else and still have been as effective?

LANGSTON HUGHES was a leading figure in the Harlem Renaissance of the 1920s and was one of the most prominent African American writers of his day. This essay is from his autobiography, *The Big Sea,* published in 1940. Religion, and more specifically, salvation, was a significant event in his community. How Hughes responds to pressure creates a thoughtful and humorous tale.

LANGSTON HUGHES

SALVATION

I was saved from sin when I was going on thirteen. But not really saved. It happened like this. There was a big revival at my Auntie Reed's church. Every night for weeks there had been much preaching, singing, praying, and shouting, and some very hardened sinners had been brought to Christ, and the membership of the church had grown by leaps and bounds. Then just before the revival ended, they held a special meeting for children, "to bring the young lambs to the fold." My aunt spoke of it for days ahead. That night I was escorted to the front row and placed on the mourners' bench with all the other young sinners, who had not yet been brought to Jesus.

My aunt told me that when you were saved you saw a light, and something happened to you inside! And Jesus came into your life! And God was with you from then on! She said you could see and hear and feel Jesus in your soul. I believed her. I had heard a great many old people say the same thing and it seemed to me they ought to know. So I sat there calmly in the hot, crowded church, waiting for Jesus to come to me.

The preacher preached a wonderful rhythmical sermon, all moans and shouts and lonely cries and dire pictures of hell, and then he sang a song about the ninety and nine safe in the fold, but one little lamb was left out in the cold. Then he said: "Won't you come? Won't you come to Jesus? Young lambs, won't you come?" And he held out his arms to all us young sinners there on the mourners' bench. And the little girls cried. And some of them jumped up and went to Jesus right away. But most of us just sat there.

A great many old people came and knelt around us and prayed, old women with jet-black faces and braided hair, old men with work-gnarled hands. And the church sang a song about the lower lights are burning, some poor sinners to be saved. And the whole building rocked with prayer and song.

Still I kept waiting to *see* Jesus.

Finally all the young people had gone to the altar and were saved, but one boy and me. He was a rounder's son named Westley. Westley and I were surrounded by sisters and deacons praying. It was very hot in the church, and getting late now. Finally Westley said to me in a whisper: "God damn! I'm tired o' sitting here. Let's get up and be saved." So he got up and was saved.

Then I was left all alone on the mourners' bench. My aunt came and knelt at my knees and cried, while prayers and songs swirled all around me in the little church. The whole congregation prayed for me alone, in a mighty wail of moans and voices. And I kept waiting serenely for Jesus, waiting, waiting—but he didn't come. I wanted to see him, but nothing happened to me. Nothing! I wanted something to happen to me, but nothing happened.

I heard the songs and the minister saying: "Why don't you come? My dear child, why don't you come to Jesus? Jesus is waiting for you. He wants you. Why don't you come? Sister Reed, what is this child's name?"

"Langston," my aunt sobbed.

"Langston, why don't you come? Why don't you come and be saved? Oh, Lamb of God! Why don't you come?"

Now it was really getting late. I began to be ashamed of myself, holding everything up so long. I began to wonder what God thought about Westley, who certainly hadn't seen Jesus either, but who was now sitting proudly on the platform, swinging his knickerbockered legs and grinning down at me, surrounded by deacons and old women on their knees praying. God had not struck Westley dead for taking his name in vain or for lying in the temple. So I decided that maybe to save further trouble, I'd better lie, too, and say that Jesus had come, and get up and be saved.

So I got up.

Suddenly the whole room broke into a sea of shouting, as they saw me rise. Waves of rejoicing swept the place. Women leaped in the air. My aunt threw her arms around me. The minister took me by the hand and led me to the platform.

When things quieted down, in a hushed silence, punctuated by a few ecstatic "Amens," all the new young lambs were blessed in the name of God. Then joyous singing filled the room.

That night, for the last time in my life but one—for I was a big boy twelve years old—I cried. I cried, in bed alone, and couldn't stop. I buried my head under the quilts, but my aunt heard me. She woke up and told my uncle I was crying because the Holy Ghost had come into my life, and because I had seen Jesus. But I was really crying because I couldn't bear to tell her that I had lied, that I had deceived everybody in the church, that I hadn't seen Jesus, and that now I didn't believe there was a Jesus any more, since he didn't come to help me.

JOURNAL PROMPT:

The narrator's aunt tells him that "when you were saved you saw a light, and something happened to you inside!" Nearly thirteen, Hughes trusts that this will certainly happen for him as well. Write about a time you placed your trust in someone "older and wiser."

COLLABORATIVE EXERCISE:

Hughes uses description to illustrate for the reader the sense of conflict he is experiencing. Locate at least five incidences where the author uses descriptive detail to inform the reader about his inner turmoil and heightened sense of conflict.

ESSAY ASSIGNMENT:

1. Religious or spiritual beliefs are often transmitted from one generation to the next. Select a religion or spiritual belief system with which you are not familiar; then, using outside sources, explore that religion or belief system, arguing how it benefits or detracts from the survival of the culture.
2. In the story "Salvation," Hughes starts to become an adult when he bases his belief system on his own experiences rather than on what others want him to believe. Trace a similar moment in your own life when you came to conclusions perhaps far different from the conclusions of those around you. Did you share these *epiphanies* with others? How were they received?

ANNE TYLER, American novelist and short-story writer, spent most of her younger years in North Carolina. She enrolled at Duke University at age sixteen and settled in Minnesota after graduation. Tyler's best work, including this short story, focuses on eccentric middle-class people living in chaotic, discontented families.

ANNE TYLER

TEENAGE WASTELAND

He used to have very blond hair—almost white—cut shorter than other children's so that on his crown a little cowlick always stood up to catch the light. But this was when he was small. As he grew older, his hair grew darker, and he wore it longer—past his collar even. It hung in lank, taffy-colored ropes around his face, which was still an endearing face, fine-featured, the eyes an unusual aqua blue. But his cheeks, of course, were no longer round, and a sharp new Adam's apple jogged in his throat when he talked.

In October, they called from the private school he attended to request a conference with his parents. Daisy went alone; her husband was at work.

Clutching her purse, she sat on the principal's couch and learned that Donny was noisy, lazy, and disruptive; always fooling around with his friends, and he wouldn't respond in class.

In the past, before her children were born, Daisy had been a fourth-grade teacher. It shamed her now to sit before this principal as a parent, a delinquent parent, a parent who struck Mr. Lanham, no doubt, as unseeing or uncaring. "It isn't that we're not concerned," she said. "Both of us are. And we've done what we could, whatever we could think of. We don't let him watch TV on school nights. We don't let him talk on the phone till he's finished his homework. But he tells us he doesn't *have* any homework or he did it all in study hall. How are we to know what to believe?"

From early October through November, at Mr. Lanham's suggestion, Daisy checked Donny's assignments every day. She sat next to him as he worked, trying to be encouraging, sagging inwardly as she saw the poor quality of everything he did—the sloppy mistakes in math, the illogical leaps in his English themes, the history questions left blank if they required any research.

Daisy was often late starting supper, and she couldn't give as much attention to Donny's younger sister. "You'll never guess what happened at . . ." Amanda would begin, and Daisy would have to tell her, "Not now, honey."

By the time her husband, Matt, came home, she'd be snappish. She would recite the day's hardships—the fuzzy instructions in English, the botched history map, the morass of unsolvable algebra equations. Matt would look surprised and confused, and Daisy would gradually wind down. There was no way, really, to convey how exhausting all this was.

In December, the school called again. This time, they wanted Matt to come as well. She and Matt had to sit on Mr. Lanham's couch like two bad children and listen to the news: Donny had improved only slightly, raising a D in history to a C, and a C in algebra to a B-minus. What was worse, he had developed new problems. He had cut classes on at least three occasions. Smoked in the furnace room. Helped Sonny Barnett break into a freshman's locker. And last week, during athletics, he and three friends had been seen off the school grounds; when they returned, the coach had smelled beer on their breath.

Daisy and Matt sat silent, shocked. Matt rubbed his forehead with his fingertips. Imagine, Daisy thought, how they must look to Mr. Lanham: an overweight housewife in a cotton dress and a too-tall, too-thin insurance agent in a baggy, frayed suit. Failures, both of them—the kind of people who are always hurrying to catch up, missing the point of things that everyone else grasps at once. She wished she'd worn nylons instead of knee socks.

It was arranged that Donny would visit a psychologist for testing. Mr. Lanham knew just the person. He would set this boy straight, he said.

When they stood to leave, Daisy held her stomach in and gave Mr. Lanham a firm, responsible handshake.

Donny said the psychologist was a jackass and the tests were really dumb; but he kept all three of his appointments, and when it was time for the follow-up conference with the psychologist and both parents, Donny combed his hair and seemed unusually sober and subdued. The psychologist said Donny had no serious emotional problems. He was merely going through a difficult period in his life. He required some academic help and a better sense of self-worth. For this reason, he was suggesting a man named Calvin Beadle, a tutor with considerable psychological training.

In the car going home, Donny said he'd be damned if he'd let them drag him to some stupid fairy tutor. His father told him to watch his language in front of his mother.

That night, Daisy lay awake pondering the term "selfworth." She had always been free with her praise. She had always told Donny he had talent, was smart, was good with his hands. She had made a big to-do over every little gift he gave her. In fact, maybe she had gone too far, although, Lord knows, she had meant every word. Was that his trouble?

She remembered when Amanda was born. Donny had acted lost and bewildered. Daisy had been alert to that, of course, but still, a new baby keeps you so busy. Had she really done all she could have? She longed—she ached—for a time machine. Given one more chance, she'd do it perfectly—hug him more, praise him more, or perhaps praise him less. Oh, who can say . . .

The tutor told Donny to call him Cal. All his kids did, he said. Daisy thought for a second that he meant his own children, then realized her mistake. He seemed too young, anyhow, to be a family man. He wore a heavy brown handlebar mustache. His hair was as long and stringy as Donny's, and his jeans as faded. Wire-rimmed spectacles slid down his nose. He lounged in a canvas director's chair with his fingers laced across his chest, and he casually, amiably questioned Donny, who sat upright and glaring in an armchair.

"So they're getting on your back at school," said Cal. "Making a big deal about anything you do wrong."

"Right," said Donny.

"Any idea why that would be?"

"Oh, well, you know, stuff like homework and all," Donny said.

"You don't do your homework?"

"Oh, well, I might do it sometimes but not just exactly like they want it." Donny sat forward and said, "It's like a prison there, you know? You've got to go to every class, you can never step off the school grounds."

"You cut classes sometimes?"

"Sometimes," Donny said, with a glance at his parents.

Cal didn't seem perturbed. "Well," he said, "I'll tell you what. Let's you and me try working together three nights a week. Think you could handle that? We'll see if we can show that school of yours a thing or two. Give it a month; then if you don't like it, we'll stop. If *I* don't like it, we'll stop. I mean, sometimes people just don't get along, right? What do you say to that?"

"Okay," Donny said. He seemed pleased.

"Make it seven o'clock till eight, Monday, Wednesday, and Friday," Cal told Matt and Daisy. They nodded. Cal shambled to his feet, gave them a little salute, and showed them to the door.

This was where he lived as well as worked, evidently. The interview had taken place in the dining room, which had been transformed into a kind of office. Passing the living room, Daisy winced at the rock music she had been hearing, without registering it, ever since she had entered the house. She looked in and saw a boy about Donny's age lying on a sofa with a book. Another boy and a girl were playing Ping-Pong in front of the fireplace. "You have several here together?" Daisy asked Cal.

"Oh, sometimes they stay on after their sessions, just to rap. They're a pretty sociable group, all in all. Plenty of goof-offs like young Donny here."

He cuffed Donny's shoulder playfully. Donny flushed and grinned.

Climbing into the car, Daisy asked Donny, "Well? What did you think?"

But Donny had returned to his old evasive self. He jerked his chin toward the garage. "Look," he said. "He's got a basketball net."

Now on Mondays, Wednesdays, and Fridays, they had supper early—the instant Matt came home. Sometimes, they had to leave before they were really finished. Amanda would still be eating her dessert. "Bye, honey. Sorry," Daisy would tell her.

Cal's first bill sent a flutter of panic through Daisy's chest, but it was worth it, of course. Just look at Donny's face when they picked him up: alight and full of interest. The principal telephoned Daisy to tell her how Donny had improved. "Of course, it hasn't shown up in his grades yet, but several of the teachers have noticed how his attitude's changed. Yes, sir, I think we're onto something here."

At home, Donny didn't act much different. He still seemed to have a low opinion of his parents. But Daisy supposed that was unavoidable—part of being fifteen. He said his parents were too "controlling"—a word that made Daisy give him a sudden look. He said they acted like wardens. On weekends, they enforced a curfew. And any time he went to a party, they always telephoned first to see if adults would be supervising. "For God's sake!" he said. "Don't you trust me?"

"It isn't a matter of trust, honey . . ." But there was no explaining to him.

His tutor called one afternoon. "I get the sense," he said, "that this kid's feeling . . . underestimated, you know? Like you folks expect the worst of him. I'm thinking we ought to give him more rope."

"But see, he's still so suggestible," Daisy said. "When his friends suggest some mischief—smoking or drinking or such—why, he just finds it hard not to go along with them."

"Mrs. Coble," the tutor said, "I think this kid is hurting. You know? Here's a serious, sensitive kid, telling you he'd like to take on some grown-up challenges, and you're giving him the message that he can't be trusted. Don't you understand how that hurts?"

"Oh," said Daisy.

"It undermines his self-esteem—don't you realize that?"

"Well, I guess you're right," said Daisy. She saw Donny suddenly from a whole new angle: his pathetically poor posture, that slouch so forlorn that his shoulders seemed about to meet his chin . . . oh, wasn't it awful being young? She'd had a miserable adolescence herself and had always sworn no child of hers would ever be that unhappy.

They let Donny stay out later, they didn't call ahead to see if the parties were supervised, and they were careful not to grill him about his evening. The tutor had set down so many rules! They were not allowed any questions at all about any aspect of school, nor were they to speak with his teachers. If a teacher had some complaint, she should phone Cal. Only one teacher disobeyed—the history teacher, Miss Evans. She called one morning in February. "I'm a little concerned about Donny, Mrs. Coble."

"Oh, I'm sorry, Miss Evans, but Donny's tutor handles these things now . . ."

"I always deal directly with the parents. You are the parent," Miss Evans said, speaking very slowly and distinctly. "Now, here is the problem. Back when you were helping Donny with his homework, his grades rose from a D to a C, but now they've slipped back, and they're closer to an F."

"They are?"

"I think you should start overseeing his homework again."

"But Donny's tutor says . . ."

"It's nice that Donny has a tutor, but you should still be in charge of his homework. With you, he learned it. Then he passed his tests. With the tutor, well, it seems the tutor is more of a crutch. 'Donny,' I say, 'a quiz is coming up on Friday. Hadn't you better be listening instead of talking?' 'That's okay, Miss Evans,' he says. 'I have a tutor now.' Like a talisman! I really think you ought to take over, Mrs. Coble."

"I see," said Daisy. "Well, I'll think about that. Thank you for calling."

Hanging up, she felt a rush of anger at Donny. A talisman! For a talisman, she'd given up all luxuries, all that time with her daughter, her evenings at home!

She dialed Cal's number. He sounded muzzy. "I'm sorry if I woke you," she told him, "but Donny's history teacher just called. She says he isn't doing well."

"She should have dealt with me."

"She wants me to start supervising his homework again. His grades are slipping."

"Yes," said the tutor, "but you and I both know there's more to it than mere grades, don't we? I care about the *whole* child—his happiness, his self-esteem. The grades will come. Just give them time."

When she hung up, it was Miss Evans she was angry at. What a narrow woman!

It was Cal this, Cal that, Cal says this, Cal and I did that. Cal lent Donny an album by the Who. He took Donny and two other pupils to a rock concert. In March, when Donny began to talk endlessly on the phone with a girl named Miriam, Cal even let Miriam come to one of the tutoring sessions. Daisy was touched that Cal would grow so involved in Donny's life, but she was also a little hurt, because she had offered to have Miriam to dinner and Donny had refused. Now he asked them to drive her to Cal's house without a qualm.

This Miriam was an unappealing girl with blurry lipstick and masses of rough red hair. She wore a short, bulky jacket that would not have been out of place on a motorcycle. During the trip to Cal's she was silent, but coming back, she was more talkative. "What a neat guy, and what a house! All those kids hanging out, like a club. And the stereo playing rock . . . gosh, he's not like a grown-up at all! Married and divorced and everything, but you'd think he was our own age."

"Mr. Beadle was married?" Daisy asked.

"Yeah, to this really controlling lady. She didn't understand him a bit."

"No, I guess not," Daisy said.

Spring came, and the students who hung around at Cal's drifted out to the basketball net above the garage. Sometimes, when Daisy and Matt arrived to pick up Donny, they'd find him there with the others—spiky and excited, jittering on his toes beneath the backboard. It was staying light much longer now, and the neighboring fence cast narrow bars across the bright grass. Loud music would be spilling from Cal's windows. Once it was the Who, which Daisy recognized from the time that Donny had borrowed the album. "*Teenage Wasteland,*" she said aloud, identifying the song, and Matt gave a short, dry laugh. "It certainly is," he said. He'd misunderstood; he thought she was commenting on the scene spread before them. In fact, she might have been. The players looked like hoodlums, even her son. Why, one of Cal's students had recently been knifed in a tavern. One had been shipped off to boarding school in midterm; two had been withdrawn by their parents. On the other hand, Donny had mentioned someone who'd been studying with Cal for five years. "Five years!" said Daisy. "Doesn't anyone ever stop needing him?"

Donny looked at her. Lately, whatever she said about Cal was read as criticism. "You're just feeling competitive," he said. "And controlling."

She bit her lip and said no more.

In April, the principal called to tell her that Donny had been expelled. There had been a locker check, and in Donny's locker they found five cans of beer and half a pack of cigarettes. With Donny's previous record, this offense meant expulsion.

Daisy gripped the receiver tightly and said, "Well, where is he now?"

"We've sent him home," said Mr. Lanham. "He's packed up all his belongings, and he's coming home on foot."

Daisy wondered what she would say to him. She felt him looming closer and closer, bringing this brand-new situation that no one had prepared her to handle. What other place would take him? Could they enter him in public school? What were the rules? She stood at the living room window, waiting for him to show up. Gradually, she realized that he was taking too long. She checked the clock. She stared up the street again.

When an hour had passed, she phoned the school. Mr. Lanham's secretary answered and told her in a grave, sympathetic voice that yes, Donny Coble had most definitely gone home. Daisy called her husband. He was out of the office. She went back to the window and thought awhile, and then she called Donny's tutor.

"Donny's been expelled from school," she said, "and now I don't know where he's gone. I wonder if you've heard from him?"

There was a long silence. "Donny's with me, Mrs. Coble," he finally said.

"With you? How'd he get there?"

"He hailed a cab, and I paid the driver."

"Could I speak to him, please?"

There was another silence. "Maybe it'd be better if we had a conference," Cal said.

"I don't *want* a conference. I've been standing at the window picturing him dead or kidnapped or something, and now you tell me you want a—"

"Donny is very, very upset. Understandably so," said Cal. "Believe me, Mrs. Coble, this is not what it seems. Have you asked Donny's side of the story?"

"Well, of course not, how could I? He went running off to you instead."

"Because he didn't feel he'd be listened to."

"But I haven't even—"

"Why don't you come out and talk? The three of us," said Cal, "will try to get this thing in perspective."

"Well, all right," Daisy said. But she wasn't as reluctant as she sounded. Already, she felt soothed by the calm way Cal was taking this.

Cal answered the doorbell at once. He said, "Hi, there," and led her into the dining room. Donny sat slumped in a chair, chewing the knuckle of one thumb. "Hello, Donny," Daisy said. He flicked his eyes in her direction.

"Sit here, Mrs. Coble," said Cal, placing her opposite Donny. He himself remained standing, restlessly pacing. "So," he said.

Daisy stole a look at Donny. His lips were swollen, as if he'd been crying.

"You know," Cal told Daisy, "I kind of expected something like this. That's a very punitive school you've got him in—you realize that. And any half-decent lawyer will tell you they've violated his civil rights. Locker checks! Where's their search warrant?"

"But if the rule is—" Daisy said.

"Well, anyhow, let him tell you his side."

She looked at Donny. He said, "It wasn't my fault. I promise."

"They said your locker was full of beer."

"It was a put-up job! See, there's this guy that doesn't like me. He put all these beers in my locker and started a rumor going, so Mr. Lanham ordered a locker check."

"What was the boy's name?" Daisy asked.

"Huh?"

"Mrs. Coble, take my word, the situation is not so unusual," Cal said. "You can't imagine how vindictive kids can be sometimes."

"What was the boy's *name*," said Daisy, "so that I can ask Mr. Lanham if that's who suggested he run a locker check."

"You don't believe me," Donny said.

"And how'd this boy get your combination in the first place?"

"Frankly," said Cal, "I wouldn't be surprised to learn the school was in on it. Any kid that marches to a different drummer, why, they'd just love an excuse to get rid of him. The school is where I lay the blame."

"Doesn't *Donny* ever get blamed?"

"Now, Mrs. Coble, you heard what he—"

"Forget it," Donny told Cal. "You can see she doesn't trust me."

Daisy drew in a breath to say that of course she trusted him—a reflex. But she knew that bold-faced, wide-eyed look of Donny's. He had worn that look when he was small, denying some petty misdeed with the evidence plain as day all around him. Still, it was hard for her to accuse him outright. She temporized and said, "The only thing I'm sure of is that they've kicked you out of school, and now I don't know what we're going to do."

"We'll fight it," said Cal.

"We can't. Even you must see we can't."

"I could apply to Brantly," Donny said.

Cal stopped his pacing to beam down at him. "Brantly! Yes. They're really onto where a kid is coming from, at Brantly. Why, *I* could get you into Brantly. I work with a lot of their students."

Daisy had never heard of Brantly, but already she didn't like it. And she didn't like Cal's smile, which struck her now as feverish and avid—a smile of hunger.

On the fifteenth of April, they entered Donny in a public school, and they stopped his tutoring sessions. Donny fought both decisions bitterly. Cal, surprisingly enough, did not object. He admitted he'd made no headway with Donny and said it was because Donny was emotionally disturbed.

Donny went to his new school every morning, plodding off alone with his head down. He did his assignments, and he earned average grades, but he gathered no friends, joined no clubs. There was something exhausted and defeated about him.

The first week in June, during final exams, Donny vanished. He simply didn't come home one afternoon, and no one at school remembered seeing him. The police were reassuring, and for the first few days, they worked hard. They combed Donny's sad, messy room for clues; they visited Miriam and Cal. But then they started talking about the number of kids who ran away every year. Hundreds, just in this city. "He'll show up, if he wants to," they said. "If he doesn't, he won't."

Evidently, Donny didn't want to.

It's been three months now and still no word. Matt and Daisy still look for him in every crowd of awkward, heartbreaking teenage boys. Every time the phone rings, they imagine it might be Donny. Both parents have aged. Donny's sister seems to be staying away from home as much as possible.

At night, Daisy lies awake and goes over Donny's life. She is trying to figure out what went wrong, where they made their first mistake. Often, she finds herself blaming Cal, although she knows he didn't begin it. Then at other times she excuses him, for without him, Donny might have left earlier. Who really knows? In the end, she can only sigh and search for a cooler spot on the pillow. As she falls asleep, she occasionally glimpses something in the corner of her vision. It's something fleet and round, a ball—a basketball. It flies up, it sinks through the hoop, descends, lands in a yard littered with last year's leaves and striped with bars of sunlight as white as bones, bleached and parched and cleanly picked.

JOURNAL PROMPT:

One of the many ironic issues in this short story is that Daisy bemoans the fact she has focused so much on Donny and that Amanda, her younger daughter, is practically ignored. Write about a time when you were so distracted by someone or something that the rest of your life suffered as a result.

COLLABORATIVE EXERCISE:

Working in small groups, think about how Tyler develops her short story. Begin with what you believe Tyler's purpose was in writing this story. Then, identify some of the literary devices she incorporates (i.e., irony, metaphor, personification, imagery, character development strategies).

ESSAY ASSIGNMENT:

1. In the story, the school psychologist recommends that Donny get "some academic help and a better sense of self-worth" from Calvin Beadle, "a tutor with considerable psychological training." Unfortunately, Donny's experience with Calvin is not beneficial. What is *your* impression and/or experience with high school counselors? Under what circumstances might counseling be recommended as the road to travel? In what ways can counseling help an adolescent who might be suffering from depression and a lack of self-esteem or direction?
2. What is the author's tone in this short story? Is the tone consistent throughout? How does the tone relate to the story's message?

BARBARA CAIN wrote this article in 1990 for *The New York Times Magazine*. Most published studies on divorce include commentary and research on the effect of divorce on young children. However, Cain breaks new ground in her careful consideration of the college-age population and the impact of divorce on this group.

BARBARA S. CAIN

Older Children and Divorce

They were more sanguine about Laura. She was, after all, in college and on the far side of growing up. They said she had loosened her tether to the family and was no longer hostage to the twists of their fate. They allowed that she would be shaken for a time by their divorce, but insisted that before long she would find her balance and regain her stride. Her younger brothers, on the other hand, were a constant source of nagging concern. At home and in the eye of the storm, they were in closer range and at higher risk. But Laura, they said, was less vulnerable. Not to worry, Laura would be fine.

So go the prevailing attitudes toward college-age children of a midlife divorce. Moreover, these assumptions appear to be shared by social scientists and cultural tribunes who have rigorously investigated the impact of divorce on younger children but have, nevertheless, overlooked the plight of a college-age population, even though statistics show increased incidence of divorce during midlife, thereby involving greater numbers of young adult offspring.

In an effort to narrow this gap in the literature, a study was launched in 1984 at the University of California at San Diego and the University of Michigan at Ann Arbor—in which 50 college students between the ages of 18 and 26 were interviewed by this writer, who reported the findings in the journal *Psychiatry* in May 1989. There were obvious differences among the students, their families and each individual divorce process, but recurrent themes and threads of discourse wove themselves within and across the interviews with striking regularity.

Perhaps most consistent among them were the students' initial reactions to news of their parents' divorce. All but three in the study recalled an immediate state of shock followed by a lingering sense of disbelief. Even those who grew up amid a turbulent marriage were incredulous when a separation was announced.

"I shouldn't have been surprised," a 20-year-old woman reflected. "I used to hear them argue night after night. I used to hear Mom cry and Dad take off in the car. I used to lie awake until he came back, but he always did come back, so I just assumed they would carry on like that for the rest of their lives."

Others who had observed their parents slowly disengage solaced themselves with the belief that though a marriage of more than two decades might inevitably lose its luster it would not necessarily lose its life. "Sure, I noticed them drift apart," a 21-year-old woman remarked. "But then I surveyed the marriages in our neighborhood, and nobody was exactly hearing violins, so I relaxed and told myself that Mom and Dad were like every other couple who had spent half their lives in one relationship."

An unexpected finding was that more than half the youngsters surveyed had glorified the marriage preceding its breach, claiming theirs was "the all-American family," their parents were "the ideal couple"—and "the envy of everyone they knew."

"I mean I wasn't exactly naïve about divorce," a 19-year-old woman explained. "Half my friends grew up with a single parent, but my Mom and Dad were considered Mr. and Mrs. Perfect Couple. So when they split up, all our friends were just as freaked out as I was."

When the veil of denial began to lift and reality took hold, these young adults experienced a profound sense of loss. They felt bereft of the family of childhood, the one in the photo album, the one whose members shared the same history, the same humor, the same address. Many described in graphic detail the wrenching pain when the family house was sold, when the furniture was divided and delivered to two separate addresses, neither of which "would ever be home."

"Nothing really sank in," explained a 20-year-old man, "until I watched the movers denude the house I lived in for most of my life. And then I sat on the bare floor and stared at the marks on the wall which outlined the places where our furniture used to be. And I cried until I couldn't see those borders anymore." Clearly the dismantling of the family house symbolized in stark relief the final dismantling of the family itself.

As each parent began living with new partners, the young adults surveyed said that they felt estranged from the resented interloper and displaced by the new mate's younger (often live-in) children. Others felt virtually evicted from the parents' new homes, which simply could not accommodate two sets of children during over-lapping visits.

"When neither Mom nor Dad had room for me during spring break," a 19-year-old man recalled, "it finally hit me that I no longer had a home to go back to and, like it or not, I'd better get my act together because it was, 'Welcome to the adult world, kid, you're now completely on your own.'"

Because the divorce represented the first sobering crisis in their young adult lives, many in the study believed it marked the end of an era of trust and ushered in a new apprehension about life's unforeseen calamities. They reported an unprecedented preoccupation with death, disease and crippling disabilities. They became self-described cynics, and began scanning relationships for subterfuge. "I used to believe what people said," a 22-year-old woman recalled. "I used to trust my roommates. I used to trust my boyfriends, and now I know I also used to be certifiably 'judgment impaired.'"

Striking among this age group was the way in which harsh moral opprobrium became the conduit through which anger toward parents was expressed. Pejoratives like irresponsible, self-indulgent and hypocritical punctuated the interviews.

"You accept as an article of faith that your parents will stay together until they die," explained a thoughtful 20-year-old woman, "and then they pull the rug out from under you and you want to scream out" and ask, "How can you break the very rules you yourselves wrote?"

Many described being gripped by an unforgiving fury toward parents who they felt had deprived them of a home, a family and that inseparable parental pair they assumed would always be there, together, at birthdays, holidays and vacations at home. Furthermore, they viewed these losses to have been preventable, hence they deeply resented learning of the decision when it was a fait accompli. And they upbraided their parents for excluding them from a process they might have otherwise reversed.

"Why didn't they tell me they were having trouble?" one young woman asked in barely muted exasperation. "If I had known, I would have helped them find a marriage counselor. If they were unhappy then why didn't they do something about it? My dad spent more time fixing his car than he ever did his marriage."

Most in the study blamed the parent who initiated the break and relentlessly hectored that parent for explanations. "Every day I'd ask my mother 'Why,'" one young woman recalled, "and no answer ever made sense. They all sounded so feeble, and so absolutely wrong."

The young adults surveyed were most staggered by the apparent moral reversals in their parents' behavior. In stunned disbelief, a 20-year-old woman discovered her "buttoned up, Bible-carrying" mother in bed with a man two years older than her son. Another student witnessed his ambitious, seemingly conscience-ridden father walk away from his family and his lucrative law firm for destinations unknown. As though looking through lenses badly out of focus, many gazed upon parents they no longer recognized and struggled over which image was false, which authentic.

"Was the old Mom just hiding under the real one that was coming out now?" a 21-year-old man wondered. "Was that tender, loving person all a lie? Was I just not seeing what I didn't want to see? And if that's true, then how am I supposed to trust what I think I see now?"

Upon observing their mothers' unbridled sexuality, several young women withdrew from romantic relationships, retreated to solitary study, became abstemious and, in Anna Freud's words, declared war on the pursuit of pleasure.

In sharp contrast, others plunged into hedonism, flaunting their indulgences, daring their parents to forbid activity that mirrored their own. A 20-year-old woman launched a series of sexual liaisons with older married men. A 19-year-old moved in with a graduate student after knowing him for 10 days. And a 22-year-old male dropped out of school to deal in drugs.

In response to their parents' apparent moral inversion, a small subgroup temporarily took refuge in a protective nihilism, reasoning that illusions that never form are illusions that never shatter. "Since their breakup I don't pin my hopes on anything anymore," a disenchanted young man declared. "And I no longer have a secret dream. What will be will be. Since I can't change any of that, why even try and why even care?"

At variance with the familiar loyalty conflict observed in younger children of divorce, most young adults considered one parent worthy of blame, the other worthy of compassion. Several openly stated they were sorely tempted to sever ties permanently with the parent who initiated the break. And when asked, "What would you advise someone your age whose parents were divorcing?" many answered, "Do not write one parent off totally, even though you might be tempted to at the time of the split."

Several said they feigned an affectionate tie to the rejected parent simply because of financial need. "Between you and me," a spunky 19-year-old man confessed, "I can't wait till I'm self-supporting, so then I won't have to humor my father with a phony song and dance every time my tuition is due." And a number reported that their overt condemnation of their father cost them a long-enjoyed relationship with paternal grandparents as battle lines between "his" and "her" side of the family were drawn.

Despite their censoriousness and ascriptions of blame, these young adults staunchly insisted that each parent honor their attempted neutrality. "I refused to let my Mom put down my Dad," one 23-year-old man declared emphatically, "and I artfully dodged every invitation to spy on one and report to the other."

Remarks such as these suggest that, whatever else, these college-age youngsters are better able than younger children to remove themselves from the internecine warfare and resist colluding with the parent "spurned" in excoriating the parent blamed.

In sharp contrast to younger children of divorce who frequently hold themselves responsible for the separation, the young adults surveyed did not reveal even the slightest traces of guilt or blame. Though most were certain they had not caused their parents' divorce, several lamented having failed to prevent it. A 19-year-old woman believed that had she managed her mother's domestic chores more effectively, her mother would not have ended her marriage in favor of her career. And a 21-year-old woman chided herself for not noticing her parents' estrangement: "Sometimes I still wonder if I had paid more attention to *them,* maybe we would all still be *us.*"

And because each youngster in the study was living away from home at the time of the separation, many believed that their parents had literally "stayed together for the sake of the children." Indeed, several parents did not disabuse their children of this notion. When a 20-year-old man accused his father of being foolishly head-strong in abruptly ending his 25-year marriage, his father informed him that he had wanted to end his marriage for more than 20 years but had waited until his son was grown and gone.

Three in the study proudly announced that they were responsible for their parents' separations and celebrated the fact that they urged upon their mothers a much overdue separation from chronically abusive alcoholic fathers. "Do I feel responsible for my parents splitting? You bet I do," one 24-year-old man trumpeted. "And my only regret is not pushing for it sooner."

With few exceptions, the young adults surveyed described an unremitting concern for their single parents, particularly the one who opposed the break. They dropped courses, cut classes, extended weekends away from school in an effort to bolster the spirit of the parent at home. "I flew home so often," one young man mused, "I was awarded three free tickets in less than one year."

In striking role reversals, these youngsters disavowed their own wish for support and ministered to their parents instead. They nurtured mothers who cried in their arms, they discouraged fathers from reckless decisions, they variously counseled, succored, reassured and advised. And many reported they were unable to resume the natural rhythms of their lives until their parents were clearly back on track.

"I was nervous most of the time I wasn't with my Mom," a 20-year-old man explained. ". . . I called her constantly and went home as often as I could. . . . Deep down, I was worried she'd take her own life or accidentally smash the car as she was thinking about Dad or money or being too old and too fat to start over again."

These young adults also assumed the role of proxies. "After the split, I felt I was wearing a thousand hats," a 19-year-old woman recalled. "In one day I could be a college student, my mother's therapist, my dad's escort and my brother's mother. Small wonder I was a little ditzy that year."

After their parents had parted, some of those surveyed recalled allowing themselves to return to a recently relinquished parent-child relationship in which they "tolerated" parental overprotection from the "spurned" partner. They no longer balked at queries about eating habits and dating behavior. "If Mom's happier treating me like a kid, I'm willing to be that for her," a 20-year-old man admitted. "She just lost her husband, the least I can do is let her have her kid." Others described a quasi-symbiotic relationship with one or the other parent in which both parent and child were by turns both host and parasite.

Though many felt compelled to rescue their parents, several baldly stated that they deeply resented the "hysterical calls in the middle of the night," the incessant ruminations about "the same old stuff." It is note-worthy, however, that those who were enraged by parental pleas and demands felt, nonetheless, obliged to leave school at times and comfort the beleaguered parent at home. As a young woman stated succinctly, "If I stayed at school, I was worried about my Mom; if I went home I was worried about me."

Perhaps the most uniform finding in this study was the radically altered attitudes toward love and marriage held by many following their parents' divorce.

When a young woman's parents separated soon after their 20th anniversary, she created her own theory of marriage: "People marry in order to have children, and parenthood is what holds a marriage together. When children are grown and gone, marriage no longer has a reason for being and couples will then drift apart and the marriage will slowly die. If couples stay together even after their last child leaves home, then they are truly in love and they are the lucky few."

Several categorically forswore marriage, vowing to spare themselves and their unborn children the pain and dislocation they had recently endured. Others allowed for a long-term live-in relationship but pledged to forestall indefinitely a legally binding commitment. A disenchanted young man spoke for many: "Since their divorce, I'm gun-shy about love and spastic about marriage. To me, getting married is like walking over a minefield, you know it's going to explode . . . you just don't know when!"

Those who were already involved in longstanding romances felt their parents' divorce cast a long shadow on their own relationship. As a 20-year-old woman explained: "You become super alert to everything your boyfriend does. You suddenly notice his wandering eye as you walk together across campus. You start resenting it when he yawns or fidgets or looks at his watch while you're talking. And you spend a whole lot of time holding your breath braced for the moment when he hits you with, 'I mean I really like you, but I really need more space.'"

Some young women withdrew from boyfriends they suddenly suspected as being unfaithful, indifferent or increasingly remote. Others demanded premature commitments or promises thereof. And many abruptly aborted solid relationships in an effort to actively master what they believed they might otherwise helplessly endure.

With rare exception, most in the study feared they were destined to repeat their parents' mistakes, a concern frequently reinforced by the parents themselves. "You're attracted to the same kind of charming Don Juan who did me in," one mother admonished. "Beware of the womanizer just like your father or you'll be dumped in your 40's, just like me." Many of the youngsters deeply resented these apocalyptic, cautionary tales. Others felt burdened by having to wrestle with the ghosts of their parents' past. "Most people meet, fall in love and marry," a 21-year-old lamented, "but I have to find someone who convinces my mother he's not my father and then he has to fit the job description of a saint."

Whereas most felt fated to repeat their parents' past, many were determined to avoid the perils their parents did not. Many pledged never to let feelings fester until "they explode in everybody's face." They planned a "playmate relationship" in order to avoid the pallor of their parents' middle years. In an effort to revise their parents' history, some feared they would submit a potential partner to such dissecting scrutiny no mortal would qualify, and marriage would be forever postponed.

Nevertheless, when asked at the close of their interviews, "Where do you see yourself 10 years from now?" many of those who earlier had denounced marriage stated unhesitatingly that they would in all probability "be married with kids and a house of my own."

Not every divorce was emotionally wrenching. It was least disruptive when the parents' decision was mutual and their initial rancor was relatively short-lived. Youngsters fared best when their attachment to each parent was honored by the other, when their quest for neutrality was respected and when their relationship with each parent remained virtually unmarred. Few were so fortunate, however.

Friendship and religion were great comforts for many, but the majority said that soul-baring marathons with siblings clearly offered the greatest amount of comfort with the least amount of shame.

"I couldn't have made it without my sister," one college junior recalled. "Talking to friends was like going public, but with my sister it was safe, it was private, and a lifeline for us both."

Whether or not the profound sense of loss, the disillusionment, the revised attitudes toward love and marriage remain an enduring legacy of parental divorce for college-age youngsters, only future studies can determine. It should be noted, however, that most of these youngsters unsuccessfully disguised a deep and abiding wish to marry, to have children and to recapture the family of childhood—the one in the picture frame, animated, intertwined and inseparable.

JOURNAL PROMPT:

Write about a time in your life when you experienced a profound sense of loss. What were the circumstances, and how did you react? Do you believe it's true that time heals all wounds?

COLLABORATIVE EXERCISE:

The author writes, "Perhaps the most uniform finding in this study was the radically altered attitudes toward love and marriage held by many following their parents' divorce." Working in small groups, discuss your own attitudes about marriage. If your parents have divorced, does your response parallel the experiences of the young adults discussed in this study?

ESSAY ASSIGNMENT:

1. Barbara Dafoe Whitehead, author of *The Divorce Culture,* claims that "divorce is now part of everyday American life." Write an essay in which you support or refute her assertion. Use your observations of popular American culture, as well as evidence from your own experiences.
2. Write about current healing and therapy techniques used with children of divorce.
3. The author writes that "the dismantling of the family house symbolized in stark relief the final dismantling of the family itself." Think about the many ways a physical house represents the family contained therein.

American poet, novelist, and critic **JAMES DICKEY** became nationally known with the publication of his controversial novel *Deliverance,* in 1970. Much of his work involves combining themes of nature and mysticism. Dickey never strayed far from his Southern roots. He taught at the University of South Carolina for over two decades.

JAMES DICKEY

CHERRYLOG ROAD

Off Highway 106
At Cherrylog Road I entered
The '34 Ford without wheels,
Smothered in kudzu,[1]
With a seat pulled out to run
Corn whiskey down from the hills,

And then from the other side
Crept into an Essex
With a rumble seat of red leather
And then out again, aboard
A blue Chevrolet, releasing
The rust from its other color,

Reared up on three building blocks
None had the same body heat;
I changed with them inward, toward
The weedy heart of the junkyard,
For I knew that Doris Holbrook
Would escape from her father at noon

And would come from the farm
To seek parts owned by the sun
Among the abandoned chassis,
Sitting in each in turn
As I did, leaning forward
As in a wild stock-car race

[1] **kudzu:** prolific Asian vine widespread in the South.

In the parking lot of the dead.
Time after time, I climbed in
And out the other side, like
An envoy or movie star
Met at the station by crickets.
A radiator cap raised its head,

Become a real toad or a kingsnake
As I neared the hub of the yard,
Passing through many states,
Many lives, to reach
Some grandmother's long Pierce-Arrow
Sending platters of blindness forth

From its nickel hubcaps
And spilling its tender upholstery
On sleepy roaches,
The glass panel in between
Lady and colored driver
Not all the way broken out,

The back-seat phone
Still on its hook.
I got in as though to exclaim,
"Let us go to the orphan asylum,
John; I have some old toys
For children who say their prayers."

I popped with sweat as I thought
I heard Doris Holbrook scrape
Like a mouse in the southern-state sun
That was eating the paint in blisters
From a hundred car tops and hoods
She was tapping like code,

Loosening the screws,
Carrying off headlights,
Sparkplugs, bumpers,
Cracked mirrors and gear-knobs,
Getting ready, already,
To go back with something to show

Other than her lips' new trembling
I would hold to me soon, soon,

Where I sat in the ripped back seat
Talking over the interphone,
Praying for Doris Holbrook
To come from her father's farm

And to get back there
With no trace of me on her face
To be seen by her red-haired father
Who would change, in the squalling barn
Her back's pale skin with a strop,
Then lay for me

In a bootlegger's roasting car
With a string-triggered 12-gauge shotgun
To blast the breath from the air.
Not cut by the jagged windshields,
Through the acres of wrecks she came
With a wrench in her hand,

Through dust where the blacksnake dies
Of boredom, and the beetle knows
The compost has no more life.
Someone outside would have seen
The oldest car's door inexplicably
Close from within:

I held her and held her and held her,
Convoyed at terrific speed
By the stalled, dreaming traffic around us,
So the blacksnake, stiff
With inaction, curved back
Into life, and hunted the mouse

With deadly overexcitement,
The beetles reclaimed their field
As we clung, glued together,
With the hooks of the seat springs
Working through to catch us red-handed
Amidst the gray breathless batting

That burst from the seat at our backs.
We left by separate doors
Into the changed, other bodies
Of cars, she down Cherrylog Road

And I to my motorcycle
Parked like the soul of the junkyard

Restored, a bicycle fleshed
With power, and tore off
Up Highway 106, continually
Drunk on the wind in my mouth,
Wringing the handlebar for speed,
Wild to be wreckage forever.

JOURNAL PROMPT:

Write about your first love.

COLLABORATIVE EXERCISE:

What do you think is the significance of the poet's "scene" of young love taking place in an old abandoned car? What might Dickey be suggesting about the cycle of life? About rites of passage? Note lines from the poem that explain or support your analysis.

ESSAY ASSIGNMENT:

1. Consider the three poems in this section: "Quinceañera," "Twelve," and "Cherrylog Road." Each poem examines the fears, anxieties, and expectations of both separation and initiation. Compare and contrast each poet's approach to these two issues.
2. The sentiments expressed in James Dickey's poem in some ways parallel the opinion expressed by Ovid in *Metamorphoses, Book IX.*

   Venus is kind to creatures young as we;
   We know not what we do, and while we're young
   We have the right to live and love like gods.

   Compare the theme(s) of Dickey's poem to this quotation.

TIM O'BRIEN grew up in Minnesota, served as a foot soldier in Vietnam, and now lives north of Boston. This excerpt is from his collection *The Things They Carried,* which consists of fictional episodes that take place in the childhoods of its characters in the forests of Vietnam and back home in America. According to one reviewer, his stories "reflect on the terrible weight of those things people carry through their lives."

TIM O'BRIEN

ON THE RAINY RIVER

This is one story I've never told before. Not to anyone. Not to my parents, not to my brother or sister, not even to my wife. To go into it, I've always thought, would only cause embarrassment for all of us, a sudden need to be elsewhere, which is the natural response to a confession. Even now, I'll admit, the story makes me squirm. For more than twenty years I've had to live with it, feeling the shame, trying to push it away, and so by this act of remembrance, by putting the facts down on paper, I'm hoping to relieve at least some of the pressure on my dreams. Still, it's a hard story to tell. All of us, I suppose, like to believe that in a moral emergency we will behave like the heroes of our youth, bravely and forthrightly, without thought of personal loss or discredit. Certainly that was my conviction back in the summer of 1968. Tim O'Brien: a secret hero. The Lone Ranger. If the stakes ever became high enough—if the evil were evil enough, if the good were good enough—I would simply tap a secret reservoir of courage that had been accumulating inside me over the years. Courage, I seemed to think, comes to us in finite quantities, like an inheritance, and by being frugal and stashing it away and letting it earn interest, we steadily increase our moral capital in preparation for that day when the account must be drawn down. It was a comforting theory. It dispensed with all those bothersome little acts of daily courage; it offered hope and grace to the repetitive coward; it justified the past while amortizing the future.

In June of 1968, a month after graduating from Macalester College, I was drafted to fight a war I hated. I was twenty-one years old. Young, yes, and politically naive, but even so the American war in Vietnam seemed to me wrong. Certain blood was being shed for uncertain reasons. I saw no unity of purpose, no consensus on matters of philosophy or history or law. The very facts were shrouded in uncertainty: Was it a civil war? A war of national liberation or simple aggression? Who started it, and when, and why? What really happened to the USS *Maddox* on that dark night in the Gulf of Tonkin? Was Ho Chi Minh a Communist stooge, or a nationalist savior, or both, or neither? What about the Geneva Accords? What about SEATO and the Cold War? What about dominoes? America was divided on these and a thousand other issues, and the debate had spilled out across the floor of the United States Senate and into the streets, and smart men in pinstripes could not agree on even the most fundamental matters of public policy. The only certainty that summer was moral confusion. It was my view then, and still is, that you don't make war without knowing why. Knowledge, of course, is always imperfect, but it seemed to me that when a nation goes to war it must have reasonable confidence in the justice and imperative of its cause. You can't fix your mistakes. Once people are dead, you can't make them undead.

In any case those were my convictions, and back in college I had taken a modest stand against the war. Nothing radical, no hothead stuff, just ringing a few doorbells for Gene McCarthy, composing a few tedious, uninspired editorials for the campus newspaper. Oddly, though, it was almost entirely an intellectual activity. I brought some energy to it, of course, but it was the energy that accompanies almost any abstract endeavor; I felt no personal danger; I felt no sense of an impending crisis in my life. Stupidly, with a kind of smug removal that I can't begin to fathom, I assumed that the problems of killing and dying did not fall within my special province.

The draft notice arrived on June 17, 1968. It was a humid afternoon, I remember, cloudy and very quiet, and I'd just come in from a round of golf. My mother and father were having lunch out in the kitchen. I remember opening up the letter, scanning the first few lines, feeling the blood go thick behind my eyes. I remember a sound in my head. It wasn't thinking, it was just a silent howl. A million things all at once—I was too *good* for this war. Too smart, too compassionate, too everything. It couldn't happen. I was above it. I had the world dicked—Phi Beta Kappa and summa cum laude and president of the student body and a full-ride scholarship for grad studies at Harvard. A mistake, maybe—a foul-up in the paperwork. I was no soldier. I hated Boy Scouts. I hated camping out. I hated dirt and tents and mosquitoes. The sight of blood made me queasy, and I couldn't tolerate authority, and I didn't know a rifle from a slingshot. I was a *liberal,* for Christ sake: If they needed fresh bodies, why not draft some back-to-the-stone-age hawk? Or some dumb jingo in his hard hat and Bomb Hanoi button? Or one of LBJ's pretty daughters? Or Westmoreland's whole family—nephews and nieces and baby grandson? There should be a law, I thought. If you support a war, if you think it's worth the price, that's fine, but you have to put your own life on the line. You have to head for the front and hook up with an infantry unit and help spill the blood. And you have to bring along your wife, or your kids, or your lover. A *law,* I thought.

I remember the rage in my stomach. Later it burned down to a smoldering self-pity, then to numbness. At dinner that night my father asked what my plans were.

"Nothing," I said. "Wait."

I spent the summer of 1968 working in an Armour meatpacking plant in my hometown of Worthington, Minnesota. The plant specialized in pork products, and for eight hours a day I stood on a quarter-mile assembly line—more properly, a disassembly line—removing blood clots from the necks of dead pigs. My job title, I believe, was Declotter. After slaughter, the hogs were decapitated, split down the length of the belly, pried open, eviscerated, and strung up by the hind hocks on a high conveyer belt. Then gravity took over. By the time a carcass reached my spot on the line, the fluids had mostly drained out, everything except for thick clots of blood in the neck and upper chest cavity. To remove the stuff, I used a kind of water gun. The machine was heavy, maybe eighty pounds, and was suspended from the ceiling by a heavy rubber cord. There was some bounce to it, an elastic up-and-down give, and the trick was to maneuver the gun with your whole body, not lifting with the arms, just letting the rubber cord do the work for you. At one end was a trigger; at the muzzle end was a small nozzle and a steel roller brush. As a carcass passed by, you'd lean forward and swing the gun up against the clots and squeeze the trigger, all in one motion, and the brush would whirl and water would come shooting out and you'd hear a quick splattering sound as the clots dissolved into a fine red mist. It was not pleasant work. Goggles were a necessity, and a rubber apron, but even so it was like standing for eight hours a day under a lukewarm blood-shower. At night I'd go home smelling of pig. I couldn't wash it out. Even after a hot bath, scrubbing hard, the stink was always there—like old bacon, or sausage, a dense greasy pig-stink that soaked deep into my skin and hair. Among other things, I remember, it was tough getting dates that summer. I felt isolated; I spent a lot of time alone. And there was also that draft notice tucked away in my wallet.

In the evenings I'd sometimes borrow my father's car and drive aimlessly around town, feeling sorry for myself, thinking about the war and the pig factory and how my life seemed to be collapsing toward slaughter. I felt paralyzed. All around me the options seemed to be narrowing, as if I were hurtling down a huge black funnel, the whole world squeezing in tight. There was no happy way out. The government had ended most graduate school deferments; the waiting lists for the National Guard and Reserves were impossibly long; my health was solid; I didn't qualify for CO status—no religious grounds, no history as a pacifist. Moreover, I could not claim to be opposed to war as a matter of general principle. There were occasions, I believed, when a nation was justified in using military force to achieve its ends, to stop a Hitler or some comparable evil, and I told myself that in such circumstances I would've willingly marched off to the battle. The problem, though, was that a draft board did not let you choose your war.

Beyond all this, or at the very center, was the raw fact of terror. I did not want to die. Not ever. But certainly not then, not there, not in a wrong war. Driving up Main Street, past the courthouse and the Ben Franklin store, I sometimes felt the fear spreading inside me like weeds. I imagined myself dead. I imagined myself doing things I could not do—charging an enemy position, taking aim at another human being.

At some point in mid-July I began thinking seriously about Canada. The border lay a few hundred miles north, an eight-hour drive. Both my conscience and my instincts were telling me to make a break for it, just take off and run like hell and never stop. In the beginning the idea seemed purely abstract, the word Canada printing itself out in my head; but after a time I could see particular shapes and images, the sorry details of my own future—a hotel room in Winnipeg, a battered old suitcase, my father's eyes as I tried to explain myself over the telephone. I could almost hear his voice, and my mother's. Run, I'd think. Then I'd think, Impossible. Then a second later I'd think, *Run.*

It was a kind of schizophrenia. A moral split. I couldn't make up my mind. I feared the war, yes, but I also feared exile. I was afraid of walking away from my own life, my friends and my family, my whole history, everything that mattered to me. I feared losing the respect of my parents. I feared the law. I feared ridicule and censure. My hometown was a conservative little spot on the prairie, a place where tradition counted, and it was easy to imagine people sitting around a table down at the old Gobbler Café on Main Street, coffee cups poised, the conversation slowly zeroing in on the young O'Brien kid, how the damned sissy had taken off for Canada. At night, when I couldn't sleep, I'd sometimes carry on fierce arguments with those people. I'd be screaming at them, telling them how much I detested their blind, thoughtless, automatic acquiescence to it all, their simple-minded patriotism, their prideful ignorance, their love-it-or-leave-it platitudes, how they were sending me off to fight a war they didn't understand and didn't want to understand. I held them responsible. By God, yes, I *did.* All of them—I held them personally and individually responsible—the polyestered Kiwanis boys, the merchants and farmers, the pious churchgoers, the chatty housewives, the PTA and the Lions club and the Veterans of Foreign Wars and the fine upstanding gentry out at the country club. They didn't know Bao Dai from the man in the moon. They didn't know history. They didn't know the first thing about Diem's tyranny, or the nature of Vietnamese nationalism, or the long colonialism of the French—this was all too damned complicated, it required some reading—but no matter, it was a war to stop the Communists, plain and simple, which was how they liked things, and you were a treasonous pussy if you had second thoughts about killing or dying for plain and simple reasons.

I was bitter, sure. But it was so much more than that. The emotions went from outrage to terror to bewilderment to guilt to sorrow and then back again to outrage. I felt a sickness inside me. Real disease.

Most of this I've told before, or at least hinted at, but what I have never told is the full truth. How I cracked. How at work one morning, standing on the pig line, I felt something break open in my chest. I don't know what it was. I'll never know. But it was real, I know that much, it was a physical rupture—a cracking-leaking-popping feeling. I remember dropping my water gun. Quickly, almost without thought, I took off my apron and walked out of the plant and drove home. It was midmorning, I remember, and the house was empty. Down in my chest there was still that leaking sensation, something very warm and precious spilling out, and I was covered with blood and hog-stink, and for a long while I just concentrated on holding myself together. I remember taking a hot shower. I remember packing a suitcase and carrying it out to the kitchen, standing very still for a few minutes, looking carefully at the familiar objects all around me. The old chrome toaster, the telephone, the pink and white Formica on the kitchen counters. The room was full of bright sunshine. Everything sparkled. My house, I thought. My life. I'm not sure how long I stood there, but later I scribbled out a short note to my parents.

What it said, exactly, I don't recall now. Something vague. Taking off, will call, love Tim.

I drove north.

It's a blur now, as it was then, and all I remember is a sense of high velocity and the feel of the steering wheel in my hands. I was riding on adrenaline. A giddy feeling, in a way, except there was the dreamy edge of impossibility to it—like running a dead-end maze—no way out—it couldn't come to a happy conclusion and yet I was doing it anyway because it was all I could think of to do. It was pure flight, fast and mindless. I had no plan. Just hit the border at high speed and crash through and keep on running. Near dusk I passed through Bemidji, then turned northeast toward International Falls. I spent the night in the car behind a closed-down gas station a half mile from the border. In the morning, after gassing up, I headed straight west along the Rainy River, which separates Minnesota from Canada, and which for me separated one life from another. The land was mostly wilderness. Here and there I passed a motel or bait shop, but otherwise the country unfolded in great sweeps of pine and birch and sumac. Though it was still August, the air already had the smell of October, football season, piles of yellow-red leaves, everything crisp and clean. I remember a huge blue sky. Off to my right was the Rainy River, wide as a lake in places, and beyond the Rainy River was Canada.

For a while I just drove, not aiming at anything, then in the late morning I began looking for a place to lie low for a day or two. I was exhausted, and scared sick, and around noon I pulled into an old fishing resort called the Tip Top Lodge. Actually it was not a lodge at all, just eight or nine tiny yellow cabins clustered on a peninsula that jutted northward into the Rainy River. The place was in sorry shape. There was a dangerous wooden dock, an old minnow tank, a flimsy tar paper boathouse along the shore. The main building, which stood in a cluster of pines on high ground, seemed to lean heavily to one side, like a cripple, the roof sagging toward Canada. Briefly, I thought about turning around, just giving up, but then I got out of the car and walked up to the front porch.

The man who opened the door that day is the hero of my life. How do I say this without sounding sappy? Blurt it out—the man saved me. He offered exactly what I needed, without questions, without any words at all. He took me in. He was there at the critical time—a silent, watchful presence. Six days later, when it ended, I was unable to find a proper way to thank him, and I never have, and so, if nothing else, this story represents a small gesture of gratitude twenty years overdue.

Even after two decades I can close my eyes and return to that porch at the Tip Top Lodge. I can see the old guy staring at me. Elroy Berdahl: eighty-one years old, skinny and shrunken and mostly bald. He wore a flannel shirt and brown work pants. In one hand, I remember, he carried a green apple, a small paring knife in the other. His eyes had the bluish gray color of a razor blade, the same polished shine, and as he peered up at me I felt a strange sharpness, almost painful, a cutting sensation, as if his gaze were somehow slicing me open. In part, no doubt, it was my own sense of guilt, but even so I'm absolutely certain that the old man took one look and went right to the heart of things—a kid in trouble. When I asked for a room, Elroy made a little clicking sound with his tongue. He nodded, led me out to one of the cabins, and dropped a key in my hand. I remember smiling at him. I also remember wishing I hadn't. The old man shook his head as if to tell me it wasn't worth the bother.

"Dinner at five-thirty," he said. "You eat fish?"

"Anything," I said.

Elroy grunted and said, "I'll bet."

We spent six days together at the Tip Top Lodge. Just the two of us. Tourist season was over, and there were no boats on the river, and the wilderness seemed to withdraw into a great permanent stillness. Over those six days Elroy Berdahl and I took most of our meals together. In the mornings we sometimes went out on long hikes into the woods, and at night we played Scrabble or listened to records or sat reading in front of his big stone fireplace. At times I felt the awkwardness of an intruder, but Elroy accepted me into his quiet routine without fuss or ceremony. He took my presence for granted, the same way he might've sheltered a stray cat—no wasted sighs or pity—and there was never any talk about it. Just the opposite. What I remember more than anything is the man's willful, almost ferocious silence. In all that time together, all those hours, he never asked the obvious questions: Why was I there? Why alone? Why so preoccupied? If Elroy was curious about any of this, he was careful never to put it into words.

My hunch, though, is that he already knew. At least the basics. After all, it was 1968, and guys were burning draft cards, and Canada was just a boat ride away. Elroy Berdahl was no hick. His bedroom, I remember, was cluttered with books and newspapers. He killed me at the Scrabble board, barely concentrating, and on those occasions when speech was necessary he had a way of compressing large thoughts into small, cryptic packets of language. One evening, just at sunset, he pointed up at an owl circling over the violet-lighted forest to the west.

"Hey, O'Brien," he said. "There's Jesus."

The man was sharp—he didn't miss much. Those razor eyes. Now and then he'd catch me staring out at the river, at the far shore, and I could almost hear the tumblers clicking in his head. Maybe I'm wrong, but I doubt it.

One thing for certain, he knew I was in desperate trouble. And he knew I couldn't talk about it. The wrong word—or even the right word—and I would've disappeared. I was wired and jittery. My skin felt too tight. After supper one evening I vomited and went back to my cabin and lay down for a few moments and then vomited again; another time, in the middle of the afternoon,

I began sweating and couldn't shut it off. I went through whole days feeling dizzy with sorrow. I couldn't sleep; I couldn't lie still. At night I'd toss around in bed, half awake, half dreaming, imagining how I'd sneak down to the beach and quietly push one of the old man's boats out into the river and start paddling my way toward Canada. There were times when I thought I'd gone off the psychic edge. I couldn't tell up from down, I was just falling, and late in the night I'd lie there watching weird pictures spin through my head. Getting chased by the Border Patrol—helicopters and searchlights and barking dogs—I'd be crashing through the woods, I'd be down on my hands and knees—people shouting out my name—the law closing in on all sides—my hometown draft board and the FBI and the Royal Canadian Mounted Police. It all seemed crazy and impossible. Twenty-one years old, an ordinary kid with all the ordinary dreams and ambitions, and all I wanted was to live the life I was born to—a mainstream life—I loved baseball and hamburgers and cherry Cokes—and now I was off on the margins of exile, leaving my country forever, and it seemed so impossible and terrible and sad.

I'm not sure how I made it through those six days. Most of it I can't remember. On two or three afternoons, to pass some time, I helped Elroy get the place ready for winter, sweeping down the cabins and hauling in the boats, little chores that kept my body moving. The days were cool and bright. The nights were very dark. One morning the old man showed me how to split and stack firewood, and for several hours we just worked in silence out behind his house. At one point, I remember, Elroy put down his maul and looked at me for a long time, his lips drawn as if framing a difficult question, but then he shook his head and went back to work. The man's self-control was amazing. He never pried. He never put me in a position that required lies or denials. To an extent, I suppose, his reticence was typical of that part of Minnesota, where privacy still held value, and even if I'd been walking around with some horrible deformity—four arms and three heads—I'm sure the old man would've talked about everything except those extra arms and heads. Simple politeness was part of it. But even more than that, I think, the man understood that words were insufficient. The problem had gone beyond discussion. During that long summer I'd been over and over the various arguments, all the pros and cons, and it was no longer a question that could be decided by an act of pure reason. Intellect had come up against emotion. My conscience told me to run, but some irrational and powerful force was resisting, like a weight pushing me toward the war. What it came down to, stupidly, was a sense of shame. Hot, stupid shame. I did not want people to think badly of me. Not my parents, not my brother and sister, not even the folks down at the Gobbler Café. I was ashamed to be there at the Tip Top Lodge. I was ashamed of my conscience, ashamed to be doing the right thing.

Some of this Elroy must've understood. Not the details, of course, but the plain fact of crisis.

Although the old man never confronted me about it, there was one occasion when he came close to forcing the whole thing out into the open. It was early evening, and we'd just finished supper, and over coffee and dessert I asked him about my bill, how much I owed so far. For a long while the old man squinted down at the tablecloth.

"Well, the basic rate," he said, "is fifty bucks a night. Not counting meals. This makes four nights, right?"

I nodded. I had three hundred and twelve dollars in my wallet.

Elroy kept his eyes on the tablecloth. "Now that's an on season price. To be fair, I suppose we should knock it down a peg or two." He leaned back in his chair. "What's a reasonable number, you figure?"

"I don't know," I said. "Forty?"

"Forty's good. Forty a night. Then we tack on food—say another hundred? Two hundred sixty total?"

"I guess."

He raised his eyebrows. "Too much?"

"No, that's fair. It's fair. Tomorrow, though . . . I think I'd better take off tomorrow."

Elroy shrugged and began clearing the table. For a time he fussed with the dishes, whistling to himself as if the subject had been settled. After a second he slapped his hands together.

"You know what we forgot?" he said. "We forgot wages. Those odd jobs you done. What we have to do, we have to figure out what your time's worth. Your last job—how much did you pull in an hour?"

"Not enough," I said.

"A bad one?"

"Yes. Pretty bad."

Slowly then, without intending any long sermon, I told him about my days at the pig plant. It began as a straight recitation of the facts, but before I could stop myself I was talking about the blood clots and the water gun and how the smell had soaked into my skin and how I couldn't wash it away. I went on for a long time. I told him about wild hogs squealing in my dreams, the sounds of butchery, slaughterhouse sounds, and how I'd sometimes wake up with that greasy pig-stink in my throat.

When I was finished, Elroy nodded at me.

"Well, to be honest," he said, "when you first showed up here, I wondered about all that. The aroma, I mean. Smelled like you was awful damned fond of pork chops." The old man almost smiled. He made a snuffling sound, then sat down with a pencil and a piece of paper. "So what'd this crud job pay? Ten bucks an hour? Fifteen?"

"Less."

Elroy shook his head. "Let's make it fifteen. You put in twenty-five hours here, easy. That's three hundred seventy-five bucks total wages. We subtract the two hundred sixty for food and lodging, I still owe you a hundred and fifteen."

He took four fifties out of his shirt pocket and laid them on the table.

"Call it even," he said.

"No."

"Pick it up. Get yourself a haircut."

The money lay on the table for the rest of the evening. It was still there when I went back to my cabin. In the morning, though, I found an envelope tacked to my door. Inside were the four fifties and a two-word note that said EMERGENCY FUND.

The man knew.

Looking back after twenty years, I sometimes wonder if the events of that summer didn't happen in some other dimension, a place where your life exists before you've lived it, and where it goes afterward. None of it ever seemed real. During my time at the Tip Top Lodge I had the feeling that I'd slipped out of my own skin, hovering a few feet away while some poor yo-yo with my name and face tried to make his way toward a future he didn't understand and didn't want. Even now I can see myself as I was then. It's like watching an old home movie: I'm young and tan and fit. I've got hair—lots of it. I don't smoke or drink. I'm wearing faded blue jeans and a white polo shirt. I can see myself sitting on Elroy Berdahl's dock near dusk one evening, the sky a bright shimmering pink, and I'm finishing up a letter to my parents that tells what I'm about to do and why I'm doing it and how sorry I am that I'd never found the courage to talk to them about it. I ask them not to be angry. I try to explain some of my feelings, but there aren't enough words, and so I just say that it's a thing that has to be done. At the end of the letter I talk about the vacations we used to take up in this north country, at a place called Whitefish Lake, and how the scenery here reminds me of those good times. I tell them I'm fine. I tell them I'll write again from Winnipeg or Montreal or wherever I end up.

On my last full day, the sixth day, the old man took me out fishing on the Rainy River. The afternoon was sunny and cold. A still breeze came in from the north, and I remember how the little fourteen-foot boat made sharp rocking motions as we pushed off from the dock. The current was fast. All around us, I remember, there was a vastness to the world, an unpeopled rawness, just the trees and the sky and the water reaching out toward nowhere. The air had the brittle scent of October.

For ten or fifteen minutes Elroy held a course upstream, the river choppy and silver-gray, then he turned straight north and put the engine on full throttle. I felt the bow lift beneath me. I remember the wind in my ears, the sound of the old outboard Evinrude. For a time I didn't pay attention to anything, just feeling the cold spray against my face, but then it occurred to me that at some point we must've passed into Canadian waters, across that dotted line between two different worlds, and I remember a sudden tightness in my chest as I looked up and watched the far shore come at me. This wasn't a daydream. It was tangible and real. As we came in toward land, Elroy cut the engine, letting the boat fishtail lightly about twenty yards off shore. The old man didn't look at me or speak. Bending down, he opened up his tackle box and busied himself with a bobber and a piece of wire leader, humming to himself, his eyes down.

It struck me then that he must've planned it. I'll never be certain, of course, but I think he meant to bring me up against the realities, to guide me across the river and to take me to the edge and to stand a kind of vigil as I chose a life for myself.

I remember staring at the old man, then at my hands, then at Canada. The shoreline was dense with brush and timber. I could see tiny red berries on the bushes. I could see a squirrel up in one of the birch trees, a big crow looking at me from a boulder along the river. That close—twenty yards—and I could see the delicate latticework of the leaves, the texture of the soil, the browned needles beneath the pines, the configurations of geology and human history. Twenty yards. I could've done it. I could've jumped and started swimming for my life. Inside me, in my chest, I felt a terrible squeezing pressure. Even now, as I write this, I can still feel that tightness. And I want you to feel it—the wind coming off the river, the waves, the silence, the wooded frontier. You're at the bow of a boat on the Rainy River. You're twenty-one years old, you're scared, and there's a hard squeezing pressure in your chest.

What would you do?

Would you jump? Would you feel pity for yourself? Would you think about your family and your childhood and your dreams and all you're leaving behind? Would it hurt? Would it feel like dying? Would you cry, as I did?

I tried to swallow it back. I tried to smile, except I was crying.

Now, perhaps, you can understand why I've never told this story before. It's not just the embarrassment of tears. That's part of it, no doubt, but what embarrasses me much more, and always will, is the paralysis that took my heart. A moral freeze: I couldn't decide, I couldn't act, I couldn't comport myself with even a pretense of modest human dignity.

All I could do was cry. Quietly, not bawling, just the chest-chokes.

At the rear of the boat Elroy Berdahl pretended not to notice. He held a fishing rod in his hands, his head bowed to hide his eyes. He kept humming a soft, monotonous little tune. Everywhere, it seemed, in the trees and water and sky, a great worldwide sadness came pressing down on me, a crushing sorrow, sorrow like I had never known it before. And what was so sad, I realized, was that Canada had become a pitiful fantasy. Silly and hopeless. It was no longer a possibility. Right then, with the shore so close, I understood that I would not do what I should do. I would not swim away from my hometown and my country and my life. I would not be brave. That old image of myself as a hero, as a man of conscience and courage, all that was just a threadbare pipe dream. Bobbing there on the Rainy River, looking back at the Minnesota shore, I felt a sudden swell of helplessness come over me, a drowning sensation, as if I had toppled overboard and was being swept away by the silver waves. Chunks of my own history flashed by. I saw a seven-year-old boy in a white cowboy hat and a Lone Ranger mask and a pair of holstered six-shooters; I saw a twelve-year-old Little League shortstop pivoting to turn a double play; I saw a sixteen-year-old kid decked out for his first prom, looking spiffy in a white tux and a black bow tie, his hair cut short and flat, his shoes freshly polished. My whole life seemed to spill out into the river, swirling away from me, everything I had ever been or ever wanted to be. I couldn't get my breath; I couldn't stay afloat; I couldn't tell which way to swim. A hallucination, I suppose, but it was as real as anything I would ever feel. I saw my parents calling to me from the far shoreline. I saw my brother and sister, all the townsfolk, the mayor and the entire Chamber of Commerce and all my old teachers and girlfriends and high school buddies. Like some weird sporting event: everybody screaming from the sidelines, rooting me on—a loud stadium roar. Hotdogs and popcorn—stadium smells, stadium heat. A squad of cheerleaders did cartwheels along the banks of the Rainy River; they had megaphones and pompoms and smooth brown thighs. The crowd swayed left and right. A marching band played fight songs. All my aunts and uncles were there, and Abraham Lincoln, and Saint George, and a nine-year-old girl named Linda who had died of a brain tumor back in fifth grade, and several members of the United States Senate, and a blind poet scribbling notes, and LBJ, and Huck Finn, and Abbie Hoffman, and all the dead soldiers back from the grave, and the many thousands who were later to die—villagers with terrible burns, little kids without arms or legs—yes, and the Joint Chiefs of Staff were there, and a couple of popes, and a first lieutenant named Jimmy Cross, and the last surviving veteran of the American Civil War, and Jane Fonda dressed up as Barbarella, and an old man sprawled beside a pigpen, and my grandfather, and Gary Cooper, and a kind-faced woman carrying an umbrella and a copy of Plato's *Republic,* and a million ferocious citizens waving flags of all shapes and colors—people in hard hats, people in headbands—they were all whooping and chanting and urging me toward one shore or the other. I saw faces from my distant past and distant future. My wife was there. My unborn daughter waved at me, and my two sons hopped up and down, and a drill sergeant named Blyton sneered and shot up a finger and shook his head. There was a choir in bright purple robes. There was a cabbie from the Bronx. There was a slim young man I would one day kill with a hand grenade along a red clay trail outside the village of My Khe.

The little aluminum boat rocked softly beneath me. There was the wind and the sky.

I tried to will myself overboard.

I gripped the edge of the boat and leaned forward and thought, *Now.*

I did try. It just wasn't possible.

All those eyes on me—the town, the whole universe—and I couldn't risk the embarrassment. It was as if there were an audience to my life, that swirl of faces along the river, and in my head I could hear people screaming at me. Traitor! they yelled. Turncoat! Pussy! I felt myself blush. I couldn't tolerate it. I couldn't endure the mockery, or the disgrace, or the patriotic ridicule. Even in my imagination, the shore just twenty yards away, I couldn't make myself be brave. It had nothing to do with morality. Embarrassment, that's all it was.

And right then I submitted.

I would go to the war—I would kill and maybe die—because I was embarrassed not to.

That was the sad thing. And so I sat in the bow of the boat and cried.

It was loud now. Loud, hard crying.

Elroy Berdahl remained quiet. He kept fishing. He worked his line with the tips of his fingers, patiently, squinting out at his red and white bobber on the Rainy River. His eyes were flat and impassive. He didn't speak. He was simply there, like the river and the late-summer sun. And yet by his presence, his mute watchfulness, he made it real. He was the true audience. He was a witness, like God, or like the gods, who look on in absolute silence as we live our lives, as we make our choices or fail to make them.

"Ain't biting," he said.

Then after a time the old man pulled in his line and turned the boat back toward Minnesota.

I don't remember saying goodbye. That last night we had dinner together, and I went to bed early, and in the morning Elroy fixed breakfast for me. When I told him I'd be leaving, the old man nodded as if he already knew. He looked down at the table and smiled.

At some point later in the morning it's possible that we shook hands—I just don't remember—but I do know that by the time I'd finished packing the old man had disappeared. Around noon, when I took my suitcase out to the car, I noticed that his old black pickup truck was no longer parked in front of the house. I went inside and waited for a while, but I felt a bone certainty that he wouldn't be back. In a way, I thought, it was appropriate. I washed up the breakfast dishes, left his two hundred dollars on the kitchen counter, got into the car, and drove south toward home.

The day was cloudy. I passed through towns with familiar names, through the pine forests and down to the prairie, and then to Vietnam, where I was a soldier, and then home again. I survived, but it's not a happy ending. I was a coward. I went to the war.

JOURNAL PROMPT:

What frightens you? In general, how do you handle fear?

COLLABORATIVE EXERCISE:

Working in small groups, discuss the significance of Elroy Berdahl, the old man at the Tip Top Lodge. What is his purpose in the story? How would the story have been different without him?

ESSAY ASSIGNMENT:

1. Using outside sources, write a research paper exploring the draft situation during the time of the O'Brien story.

2. Consider O'Brien's decision. Do you think he made the best choice, considering his desire not to fight in a war he did not support? Explain your answer fully and logically.
3. At times, fear may paralyze us and prevent us from moving forward or making a life-changing decision. (In the study of myth, this is a situation involving issues of separation.) O'Brien feels frozen with fear ("a moral freeze") as he tries to come to grips with his life-changing decision of whether to go to war. Write about a time when you had a monumental decision to make. What were some of the fears you felt? How did you get past the fears, or did you?

T. Coraghessan Boyle was born in Peekskill, New York; earned a doctorate at the University of Iowa; and has taught at the University of Southern California. He is the recipient of several literary awards, including a National Endowment for the Arts Creative Writing Fellowship and the PEN/Faulkner Award for fiction. This story was originally published in his collection *Greasy Lake and Other Stories* (1985).

T. C. BOYLE

Greasy Lake

It's about a mile down on the dark side of Route 8.
—Bruce Springsteen

There was a time when courtesy and winning ways went out of style, when it was good to be bad, when you cultivated decadence like a taste. We were all dangerous characters then. We wore torn-up leather jackets, slouched around with toothpicks in our mouths, sniffed glue and ether and what somebody claimed was cocaine. When we wheeled our parents' whining station wagons out onto the street we left a patch of rubber half a block long. We drank gin and grape juice, Tango, Thunderbird, and Bali Hai. We were nineteen. We were bad. We read André Gide[1] and struck elaborate poses to show that we didn't give a shit about anything. At night, we went up to Greasy Lake.

[1] *André Gide:* controversial French writer (1869–1951) whose novels, including *The Counterfeiters* and *Lafcadio's Adventures,* often show individuals in conflict with accepted morality.

Through the center of town, up the strip, past the housing developments and shopping malls, street lights giving way to the thin streaming illumination of the headlights, trees crowding the asphalt in a black unbroken wall: that was the way out to Greasy Lake. The Indians had called it Wakan, a reference to the clarity of its waters. Now it was fetid and murky, the mud banks glittering with broken glass and strewn with beer cans and the charred remains of bonfires. There was a single ravaged island a hundred yards from shore, so stripped of vegetation it looked as if the air force had strafed it. We went up to the lake because everyone went there, because we wanted to snuff the rich scent of possibility on the breeze, watch a girl take off her clothes and plunge into the festering murk, drink beer, smoke pot, howl at the stars, savor the incongruous full-throated roar of rock and roll against the primeval susurrus of frogs and crickets. This was nature.

I was there one night, late, in the company of two dangerous characters. Digby wore a gold star in his right ear and allowed his father to pay his tuition at Cornell; Jeff was thinking of quitting school to become a painter/musician/head-shop proprietor. They were both expert in the social graces, quick with a sneer, able to manage a Ford with lousy shocks over a rutted and gutted blacktop road at eighty-five while rolling a joint as compact as a Tootsie Roll Pop stick. They could lounge against a bank of booming speakers and trade "man"s with the best of them or roll out across the dance floor as if their joints worked on bearings. They were slick and quick and they wore their mirror shades at breakfast and dinner, in the shower, in closets and caves. In short, they were bad.

I drove. Digby pounded the dashboard and shouted along with Toots & the Maytals while Jeff hung his head out the window and streaked the side of my mother's Bel Air with vomit. It was early June, the air soft as a hand on your cheek, the third night of summer vacation. The first two nights we'd been out till dawn, looking for something we never found. On this, the third night, we'd cruised the strip sixty-seven times, been in and out of every bar and club we could think of in a twenty-mile radius, stopped twice for bucket chicken and forty-cent hamburgers, debated going to a party at the house of a girl Jeff's sister knew, and chucked two dozen raw eggs at mailboxes and hitchhikers. It was 2:00 A.M.; the bars were closing. There was nothing to do but take a bottle of lemon-flavored gin up to Greasy Lake.

The taillights of a single car winked at us as we swung into the dirt lot with its tufts of weed and washboard corrugations; '57 Chevy, mint, metallic blue. On the far side of the lot, like the exoskeleton of some gaunt chrome insect, a chopper leaned against its kickstand. And that was it for excitement: some junkie halfwit biker and a car freak pumping his girlfriend. Whatever it was we were looking for, we weren't about to find it at Greasy Lake. Not that night.

But then all of a sudden Digby was fighting for the wheel. "Hey, that's Tony Lovett's car! Hey!" he shouted, while I stabbed at the brake pedal and the Bel Air nosed up to the gleaming bumper of the parked Chevy. Digby leaned on the horn, laughing, and instructed me to put my brights on. I flicked on the brights. This was hilarious. A joke. Tony would experience premature withdrawal and expect to be confronted by grim-looking state troopers with flashlights. We hit the horn, strobed the lights, and then jumped out of the car to press our witty faces to Tony's windows; for all we knew we might even catch a glimpse of some little fox's tit, and then we could slap backs with red-faced Tony, roughhouse a little, and go on to new heights of adventure and daring.

The first mistake, the one that opened the whole floodgate, was losing my grip on the keys. In the excitement, leaping from the car with the gin in one hand and a roach clip in the other, I spilled them in the grass—in the dark, rank, mysterious nighttime grass of Greasy Lake. This was a tactical error, as damaging and irreversible in its way as Westmoreland's decision to dig in at Khe Sanh.[2] I felt it like a jab of intuition, and I stopped there by the open door, peering vaguely into the night that puddled up round my feet.

The second mistake—and this was inextricably bound up with the first—was identifying the car as Tony Lovett's. Even before the very bad character in greasy jeans and engineer boots ripped out of the driver's door, I began to realize that this chrome blue was much lighter than the robin's-egg of Tony's car, and that Tony's car didn't have rear-mounted speakers. Judging from their expressions, Digby and Jeff were privately groping toward the same inevitable and unsettling conclusion as I was.

In any case, there was no reasoning with this bad greasy character—clearly he was a man of action. The first lusty Rockette[3] kick of his steel-toed boot caught me under the chin, chipped my favorite tooth, and left me sprawled in the dirt. Like a fool, I'd gone down on one knee to comb the stiff hacked grass for the keys, my mind making connections in the most dragged-out, testudineous way, knowing that things had gone wrong, that I was in a lot of trouble, and that the lost ignition key was my grail and my salvation. The three or four succeeding blows were mainly absorbed by my right buttock and the tough piece of bone at the base of my spine.

Meanwhile, Digby vaulted the kissing bumpers and delivered a savage kungfu blow to the greasy character's collarbone. Digby had just finished a course in martial arts for phys-ed credit and had spent the better part of the past two nights telling us apocryphal tales of Bruce Lee types and of the raw power invested in lightning blows shot from coiled wrists, ankles, and elbows. The greasy character was unimpressed. He merely backed off a step, his face like a Toltec mask, and laid Digby out with a single whistling roundhouse blow . . . but by now Jeff had got into the act, and I was beginning to extricate myself from the dirt, a tinny compound of shock, rage, and impotence wadded in my throat.

---

[2] *Westmoreland's decision . . . Khe Sanh:* General William C. Westmoreland commanded United States troops in Vietnam (1964–68). In late 1967 the North Vietnamese and Viet Cong forces attacked Khe Sanh (or Khesanh) with a show of strength, causing Westmoreland to expend great effort to defend a plateau of relatively little tactical importance.

[3] *Rockette:* member of a dancing troupe in the stage show at Radio City Music Hall, New York, famous for the ability to kick fast and high with wonderful coordination.

Jeff was on the guy's back, biting at his ear. Digby was on the ground, cursing. I went for the tire iron I kept under the driver's seat. I kept it there because bad characters always keep tire irons under the driver's seat, for just such an occasion at this. Never mind that I hadn't been involved in a fight since sixth grade, when a kid with a sleepy eye and two streams of mucus depending from his nostrils hit me in the knee with a Louisville slugger,[4] never mind that I'd touched the tire iron exactly twice before, to change tires: it was there. And I went for it.

I was terrified. Blood was beating in my ears, my hands were shaking, my heart turning over like a dirtbike in the wrong gear. My antagonist was shirtless, and a single cord of muscle flashed across his chest as he bent forward to peel Jeff from his back like a wet overcoat. "Motherfucker," he spat, over and over, and I was aware in that instant that all four of us—Digby, Jeff, and myself included—were chanting "motherfucker, motherfucker," as if it were a battle cry. (What happened next? the detective asks the murderer from beneath the turned-down brim of his porkpie hat. I don't know, the murderer says, something came over me. Exactly.)

Digby poked the flat of his hand in the bad character's face and I came at him like a kamikaze, mindless, raging, stung with humiliation—the whole thing, from the initial boot in the chin to this murderous primal instant involving no more than sixty hyperventilating, gland-flooding seconds—I came at him and brought the tire iron down across his ear. The effect was instantaneous, astonishing. He was a stunt man and this was Hollywood, he was a big grimacing toothy balloon and I was a man with a straight pin. He collapsed. Wet his pants. Went loose in his boots.

A single second, big as a zeppelin, floated by. We were standing over him in a circle, gritting our teeth, jerking our necks, our limbs and hands and feet twitching with glandular discharges. No one said anything. We just stared down at the guy, the car freak, the lover, the bad greasy character laid low. Digby looked at me; so did Jeff. I was still holding the tire iron, a tuft of hair clinging to the crook like dandelion fluff, like down. Rattled, I dropped it in the dirt, already envisioning the headlines, the pitted faces of the police inquisitors, the gleam of handcuffs, clank of bars, the big black shadows rising from the back of the cell . . . when suddenly a raw torn shriek cut through me like all the juice in all the electric chairs in the country.

It was the fox. She was short, barefoot, dressed in panties and a man's shirt. "Animals!" she screamed, running at us with her fists clenched and wisps of blow-dried hair in her face. There was a silver chain round her ankle, and her toenails flashed in the glare of the headlights. I think it was the toenails that did it. Sure, the gin and the cannabis and even the Kentucky Fried may have had a hand in it, but it was the sight of those flaming toes that set us off—the toad

---

[4] *Louisville slugger:* a brand of baseball bat.

emerging from the loaf in *Virgin Spring,*[5] lipstick smeared on a child; she was already tainted. We were on her like Bergman's deranged brothers—see no evil, hear none, speak none—panting, wheezing, tearing at her clothes, grabbing for flesh. We were bad characters, and we were scared and hot and three steps over the line—anything could have happened.

It didn't.

Before we could pin her to the hood of the car, our eyes masked with lust and greed and the purest primal badness, a pair of headlights swung into the lot. There we were, dirty, bloody, guilty, dissociated from humanity and civilization, the first of the Ur-crimes behind us, the second in progress, shreds of nylon panty and spandex brassiere dangling from our fingers, our flies open, lips licked—there we were, caught in the spotlight. Nailed.

We bolted. First for the car, and then, realizing we had no way of starting it, for the woods. I thought nothing. I thought escape. The headlights came at me like accusing fingers. I was gone.

Ram-bam-bam, across the parking lot, past the chopper and into the feculent undergrowth at the lake's edge, insects flying up in my face, weeds whipping, frogs and snakes and red-eyed turtles splashing off into the night: I was already ankle-deep in muck and tepid water and still going strong. Behind me, the girl's screams rose in intensity, disconsolate, incriminating, the screams of the Sabine women,[6] the Christian martyrs, Anne Frank[7] dragged from the garret. I kept going, pursued by those cries, imagining cops and bloodhounds. The water was up to my knees when I realized what I was doing: I was going to swim for it. Swim the breadth of Greasy Lake and hide myself in the thick clot of woods on the far side. They'd never find me there.

I was breathing in sobs, in gasps. The water lapped at my waist as I looked out over the moon-burnished ripples, the mats of algae that clung to the surface like scabs. Digby and Jeff had vanished. I paused. Listened. The girl was quieter now, screams tapering to sobs, but there were male voices, angry, excited, and the high-pitched ticking of the second car's engine. I waded deeper, stealthy, hunted, the ooze sucking at my sneakers. As I was about to take the plunge—at the very instant I dropped my shoulder for the first slashing stroke—I blundered into something. Something unspeakable, obscene, something soft, wet, moss-grown. A patch of weed? A log? When I reached out to touch it, it gave like a rubber duck, it gave like flesh.

---

[5] *Virgin Spring:* film by Swedish director Ingmar Bergman.

[6] *Sabine women:* members of an ancient tribe in Italy, according to legend, forcibly carried off by the early Romans under Romulus to be their wives. The incident is depicted in a famous painting, "The Rape of the Sabine Women," by seventeenth-century French artist Nicolas Poussin.

[7] *Anne Frank:* German Jewish girl (1929–1945) whose diary written during the Nazi occupation of the Netherlands later became world famous. She hid with her family in a secret attic in Amsterdam, but was caught by storm troopers and sent to the concentration camp at Belsen, where she died.

In one of those nasty little epiphanies for which we are prepared by films and TV and childhood visits to the funeral home to ponder the shrunken painted forms of dead grandparents, I understood what it was that bobbed there so inadmissibly in the dark. Understood, and stumbled back in horror and revulsion, my mind yanked in six different directions (I was nineteen, a mere child, an infant, and here in the space of five minutes I'd struck down one greasy character and blundered into the waterlogged carcass of a second), thinking, The keys, the keys, why did I have to go and lose the keys? I stumbled back, but the muck took hold of my feet—a sneaker snagged, balance lost—and suddenly I was pitching face forward into the buoyant black mass, throwing out my hands in desperation while simultaneously conjuring the image of reeking frogs and muskrats revolving in slicks of their own deliquescing juices. AAAAArrrgh! I shot from the water like a torpedo, the dead man rotating to expose a mossy beard and eyes cold as the moon. I must have shouted out, thrashing around in the weeds, because the voices behind me suddenly became animated.

"What was that?"

"It's them, it's them: they tried to, tried to . . . *rape* me!" Sobs.

A man's voice, flat Midwestern accent. "You sons a bitches, we'll kill you!"

Frogs, crickets.

Then another voice, harsh, *r*-less, Lower East Side: "Motherfucker!" I recognized the verbal virtuosity of the bad greasy character in the engineer boots. Tooth chipped, sneakers gone, coated in mud and slime and worse, crouching breathless in the weeds waiting to have my ass thoroughly and definitively kicked and fresh from the hideous stinking embrace of a three-days-dead-corpse, I suddenly felt a rush of joy and vindication: the son of a bitch was alive! Just as quickly, my bowels turned to ice. "Come on out of there, you pansy mothers!" the bad greasy character was screaming. He shouted curses till he was out of breath.

The crickets started up again, then the frogs. I held my breath. All at once was a sound in the reeds, a swishing, a splash: thunk-a-thunk. They were throwing rocks. The frogs fell silent. I cradled my head. Swish, swish, thunk-a-thunk. A wedge of feldspar the size of a cue ball glanced off my knee. I bit my finger.

It was then that they turned to the car. I heard a door slam, a curse, and then the sound of the headlights shattering—almost a good-natured sound, celebratory, like corks popping from the necks of bottles. This was succeeded by the dull booming of the fenders, metal on metal, and then the icy crash of the windshield. I inched forward, elbows and knees, my belly pressed to the muck, thinking of guerrillas and commandos and *The Naked and the Dead*.[8] I parted the weeds and squinted the length of the parking lot.

---

[8] *The Naked and the Dead:* novel (1948) by Norman Mailer, of U.S. Army life in World War II.

The second car—it was a Trans-Am—was still running, its high beams washing the scene in a lurid stagy light. Tire iron flailing, the greasy bad character was laying into the side of my mother's Bel Air like an avenging demon, his shadow riding up the trunks of the trees. Whomp. Whomp. Whomp-whomp. The other two guys—blond types, in fraternity jackets—were helping out with tree branches and skull-sized boulders. One of them was gathering up bottles, rocks, muck, candy wrappers, used condoms, poptops, and other refuse and pitching it through the window on the driver's side. I could see the fox, a white bulb behind the windshield of the '57 Chevy. "Bobbie," she whined over the thumping, "come on." The greasy character paused a moment, took one good swipe at the left taillight, and then heaved the tire iron halfway across the lake. Then he fired up the '57 and was gone.

Blond head nodded at blond head. One said something to the other, too low for me to catch. They were no doubt thinking that in helping to annihilate my mother's car they'd committed a fairly rash act, and thinking too that there were three bad characters connected with that very car watching them from the woods. Perhaps other possibilities occurred to them as well—police, jail cells, justices of the peace, reparations, lawyers, irate parents, fraternal censure. Whatever they were thinking, they suddenly dropped branches, bottles, and rocks and sprang for their car in unison, as if they'd choreographed it. Five seconds. That's all it took. The engine shrieked, the tires squealed, a cloud of dust rose from the rutted lot and then settled back on darkness.

I don't know how long I lay there, the bad breath of decay all around me, my jacket heavy as a bear, the primordial ooze subtly reconstituting itself to accommodate my upper thighs and testicles. My jaws ached, my knee throbbed, my coccyx was on fire. I contemplated suicide, wondered if I'd need bridgework, scraped the recesses of my brain for some sort of excuse to give my parents—a tree had fallen on the car, I was blinded by a bread truck, hit and run, vandals had got to it while we were playing chess at Digby's. Then I thought of the dead man. He was probably the only person on the planet worse off than I was. I thought about him, fog on the lake, insects chirring eerily, and felt the tug of fear, felt the darkness opening up inside me like a set of jaws. Who was he, I wondered, this victim of time and circumstance bobbing sorrowfully in the lake at my back. The owner of the chopper, no doubt, a bad older character come to this. Shot during a murky drug deal, drowned while drunkenly frolicking in the lake. Another headline. My car was wrecked; he was dead.

When the eastern half of the sky went from black to cobalt and the trees began to separate themselves from the shadows, I pushed myself up from the mud and stepped out into the open. By now the birds had begun to take over for the crickets, and dew lay slick on the leaves. There was a smell in the air, raw and sweet at the same time, the smell of the sun firing buds and opening blossoms. I contemplated the car. It lay there like a wreck along the highway, like a steel sculpture left over from a vanished civilization. Everything was still. This was nature.

I was circling the car, as dazed and bedraggled as the sole survivor of an air blitz, when Digby and Jeff emerged from the trees behind me. Digby's face was crosshatched with smears of dirt; Jeff's jacket was gone and his shirt was torn across the shoulder. They slouched across the lot, looking sheepish, and silently came up beside me to gape at the ravaged automobile. No one said a word. After a while Jeff swung open the driver's door and began to scoop the broken glass and garbage off the seat. I looked at Digby. He shrugged. "At least they didn't slash the tires," he said.

It was true: the tires were intact. There was no windshield, the headlights were staved in, and the body looked as if it had been sledge-hammered for a quarter a shot at the county fair, but the tires were inflated to regulation pressure. The car was drivable. In silence, all three of us bent to scrape the mud and shattered glass from the interior. I said nothing about the biker. When we were finished, I reached in my pocket for the keys, experienced a nasty stab of recollection, cursed myself, and turned to search the grass. I spotted them almost immediately, no more than five feet from the open door, glinting like jewels in the first tapering shaft of sunlight. There was no reason to get philosophical about it: I eased into the seat and turned the engine over.

It was at that precise moment that the silver Mustang with the flame decals rumbled into the lot. All three of us froze; then Digby and Jeff slid into the car and slammed the door. We watched as the Mustang rocked and bobbed across the ruts and finally jerked to a halt beside the forlorn chopper at the far end of the lot. "Let's go," Digby said. I hesitated, the Bel Air wheezing beneath me.

Two girls emerged from the Mustang. Tight jeans, stiletto heels, hair like frozen fur. They bent over the motorcycle, paced back and forth aimlessly, glanced once or twice at us, and then ambled over to where the reeds sprang up in a green fence round the perimeter of the lake. One of them cupped her hands to her mouth. "Al," she called. "Hey, Al!"

"Come on," Digby hissed. "Let's get out of here."

But it was too late. The second girl was picking her way across the lot, unsteady on her heels, looking up at us and then away. She was older—twenty-five or -six—and as she came closer we could see there was something wrong with her: she was stoned or drunk, lurching now and waving her arms for balance. I gripped the steering wheel as if it were the ejection lever of a flaming jet, and Digby spat out my name, twice, terse and impatient.

"Hi," the girl said.

We looked at her like zombies, like war veterans, like deaf-and-dumb pencil peddlers.

She smiled, her lips cracked and dry. "Listen," she said, bending from the waist to look in the window, "you guys seen Al?" Her pupils were pinpoints, her eyes glass. She jerked her neck. "That's his bike over there—Al's. You seen him?"

Al. I didn't know what to say. I wanted to get out of the car and retch, I wanted to go home to my parents' house and crawl into bed. Digby poked me in the ribs. "We haven't seen anybody," I said.

The girl seemed to consider this, reaching out a slim veiny arm to brace herself against the car. "No matter," she said, slurring the *t*'s, "he'll turn up." And then, as if she'd just taken stock of the whole scene—the ravaged car and our battered faces, the desolation of the place—she said: "Hey, you guys look like some pretty bad characters—been fightin', huh?" We stared straight ahead, rigid as catatonics. She was fumbling in her pocket and muttering something. Finally she held out a handful of tablets in glassine wrappers: "Hey, you want to party, you want to do some of these with me and Sarah?"

I just looked at her. I thought I was going to cry. Digby broke the silence. "No, thanks," he said, leaning over me. "Some other time."

I put the car in gear and it inched forward with a groan, shaking off pellets of glass like an old dog shedding water after a bath, heaving over the ruts on its worn springs, creeping toward the highway. There was a sheen of sun on the lake. I looked back. The girl was still standing there, watching us, her shoulders slumped, hand outstretched.

JOURNAL PROMPT:

Is there a special place from your childhood or adolescence that draws you back in memory? Write about that place. Can you identify what it is that resonates with you when you think of your special spot? Is it the relationships you shared there or the comfort of nature?

COLLABORATIVE EXERCISE:

Certain symbols appear time and again in literature, art, and music because of the emotional power they convey. What is the power of the body of water in Boyle's story?

ESSAY ASSIGNMENT:

1. The opening paragraph is filled with very specific details that take the reader back to a particular time period. This opening would probably read with very *different* details now. Rewrite the opening paragraph, inserting new details that better "match" the current times. Then, analyze how Boyle's details play a role in the purpose of this story.
2. Trace the main character's transformation in this story.

STEVEN STARK is a graduate of Yale Law School and worked as an aide to Jimmy Carter before becoming a journalist. He is a regular commentator on National Public Radio, speaking about popular culture. Stark is the author of *Glued to the Set: The 60 Television Shows That Made Us Who We Are Today*. In addition to this article, which originally appeared in *The Atlantic Monthly* (1994), Stark has had articles in *The New York Times* and the *Los Angeles Times*.

STEVEN STARK

WHERE THE BOYS ARE

Over the past several years American pop culture has spawned a wide range of wildly popular offerings that appear remarkably similar in sensibility. Although at first glance little appears to link the infamous syndicated-radio talk-meisters Howard Stern and Don Imus with the movies *Jurassic Park* and *Field of Dreams,* the comedy of David Letterman and Jerry Seinfeld, the cartoon series *Beavis and Butt-head* and *The Simpsons,* and journalism's *The McLaughlin Group,* they in fact share a motif: though for the most part aimed at adults, these are all offerings that strongly echo the world of boys in early adolescence, ages eleven to fifteen. The unspoken premise of much of American pop culture today is that a large group of men would like nothing better than to go back to their junior high school locker rooms and stay there.

There is nothing new, of course, about men acting like boys, as anyone who has read the *The Odyssey* or *Don Quixote* knows. But something different is going on today: never before have so many seemed to produce so much that is so popular to evoke what is, after all, a brief and awkward stage of life. What's more, the trend spans the range of popular culture. Take talk radio: One of its most popular approaches today is to offer the listener a world of close-knit boyish pals. The style of Stern and Imus is that of the narcissistic class cutup in seventh grade: both sit in a playhouse-like radio studio with a bunch of guys and horse around for hours talking about sex or sports, along with political and show-biz gossip, all the while laughing at the gang's consciously loutish, subversive jokes. To the extent that women participate, they are often treated to a barrage of sexual and scatological humor. It's no wonder the audience for both shows is predominantly male.

Late Show With David Letterman and *Seinfeld* similarly echo the ethos of young teenage boys. Late-night television has always been a chiefly male world, but until recently it wasn't a boy's world. One of Letterman's contributions to late-night entertainment has been to take its humor out of the nightclub-act tradition—replete with all of Johnny Carson's jokes about drinking or adult sex—and place it firmly in that prankish, subversive, back-of-the-classroom seventh-grade realm that has become so culturally prominent. Although Letterman rarely greets women guests with filthy jokes (you can't do that on network television), he often treats them with the exaggerated deference and shyness typical of fourteen-year-old boys.

Like a group of fourteen-year-olds, the men on *Seinfeld* seem not to hold regular jobs, the better to devote time to "the gang." One woman, Elaine, is allowed to tag along with the boys, much like those younger sisters who are permitted to hang out with their brothers. It's not simply that everyone in Seinfeld's gang is unmarried and pushing fortysomething. It's that given their personas, it's difficult to imagine any of them having a real relationship with any woman but his mother. (Note how much more often parents of adult children appear here than on other shows.) Compare this situation comedy with the one that was roughly its cultural predecessor, *Cheers,* which appeared in the same time slot. On that show, too, the men didn't spend much time at work, but they did hang out in a traditional domain of adults (the tavern), and the hero, Sam Malone, spent many of his waking hours chasing women. Seinfeld is better known for sitting in a diner eating french fries with his pals. One of the show's most celebrated "risqué" episodes was about—what else?—masturbation.

And so it goes in various ways, as the early-teen male sensibility is celebrated in everything from *Wayne's World* (the adventures of two adolescent goofballs) to *The Simpsons* (starring the proud underachiever Bart) to *Beavis and Butt-head* (MTV's notorious early-adolescent icons). The heavy-metal sound of bands with names like Danzig, Gwar, and Genitorturers is in vogue now, and with its constant evocation of sexism, violence, and hostility for hostility's sake, that rock genre has always reeked of the adolescent experience more than others have.

Like many recent cinema hits, ranging from the Indiana Jones series to most Arnold Schwarzenegger offerings, last year's blockbuster film *Jurassic Park* was largely a traditional teenage "boys' movie"—heavy on adventure and violence, light on romance and relationships. Psychologists have observed that the culture-wide trend toward "pumped-up" male heroes—Schwarzenegger, Sylvester Stallone, and half the guys at your local health club—is a pre-teen male fantasy brought to life. Even popular "adult movies," such as *City Slickers* and *Big,* often revolve around the premise that once a man has passed through puberty, it's pretty much all downhill.

The cult of baseball can be seen as an intensely nostalgic return to early adolescence for many Americans. The rite of Rotisserie League baseball—an activity in which men spend hours every week poring over sheets of statistics, as they did when they were young—is part of this phenomenon, as are the wearing of baseball hats and the collecting of autographs and baseball cards by men of all ages. So, too, are baseball-movie parables like the quasi-religious *Field of Dreams,* in which male adolescence, the pastoral life, and baseball are linked in a way that would make both Jean Jacques Rousseau and Casey Stengel proud. In these visions of utopia, of course, women are again peripheral—except, perhaps, when baking cookies or waving in maternal fashion from the front porch as Dad and Son play catch. In the 1955 America that is usually the baseball lover's Paradise Lost, there are no Astroturf, no new stadiums, and no western teams to challenge the prominence of New York and the eastern urban society it represents. That America is not only a man's world but also, by and large, a white man's world.

Today's early-adolescent attitude is certainly on display throughout the news media. It's not simply that in a tabloid age many publications have adopted a kind of sneering, sophomoric attitude toward public affairs, or that shows such as *Crossfire* and *The McLaughlin Group*—with their mostly male screaming casts—resemble nothing so much as a junior high social-studies debate (in which the girls were always shouted down by the boys regardless of what they had to say). It's that today's journalism is obsessed with the kinds of things that tend to preoccupy thirteen-year-old boys: sports, sex, crime, and narcissism—that is, itself. Also in journalism as currently practiced, reporters often set themselves up as passive observers of events and then spend much of their time identifying with those who exercise real power—a point of view that is reminiscent of the way a young teenager views his parents. Moreover, if today's journalism has a driving principle, that principle centers on an obsession with hypocrisy. Journalism is about many things, but these days it is often about revealing that public figures are phonies. Covering Bill Clinton, or Prince Charles, or Michael Jackson, reporters frame their stories by saying implicitly, "These people aren't what they say they are. Look, they lied to you." Although there is a cultural role for balloon deflators, journalism has brought this characteristic attitude of the early adolescent to the adult world and elevated it to the status of cultural religion. That's why much of journalism today is really a form of institutionalized early adolescence.

Because the press tends to set the agenda for our culture, these sentiments have enormous ramifications. Whether in the form of the media's obsession with violence or its preoccupation with polls and popularity, the fantasy life of the adolescent male ends up defining much of our political reality. Political coverage tends to focus on gaffes, girlfriends, and youthful indiscretions while far more important, "adult" issues go underreported.

The press has also seen to it that the cardinal sin in American politics today is not to run up a deficit or lose an important court case but to change one's mind: like a fourteen-year-old, the press always takes a switch as evidence of hypocrisy. Thus George Bush was skewered by the media in 1990 for flip-flopping on the issue of taxes, and Bill Clinton was attacked unmercifully last year for going back on his promise of a tax cut for the middle class. Maybe both men had misled the voters during their campaigns, but a less iconoclastic press corps might have concluded that both men changed their minds for unselfish policy reasons. While an adolescent often looks at a change in direction and sees deceit, an adult realizes that life is usually more complex than that. Mature leaders recognize their mistakes and often adjust accordingly—though not without peril in today's climate.

Admittedly, too much can be made of all this. Entertainment has always evoked certain stages of life in ways that appeal to the masses: think of *The Wizard of Oz* and *Rebel Without a Cause*. The fourteen-year-old sensibility is certainly not the only one celebrated in a culture that includes *The Golden Girls, Murphy Brown,* and Barney the dinosaur. And it's true that other eras in America have celebrated youth in various forms, from Shirley Temple to the Brady Bunch. But it's hard to make the case that the male early-adolescent mind-set was as pervasive or influential in those eras as it is in this one.

There are, of course, antecedents in our cultural life for this veneration of male early adolescence. The western often celebrated the young cowboy or outlaw like Billy the Kid, who, surrounded by his loyal gang in a world without commitment to women, broke the rules. In his recent book, *American Manhood,* E. Anthony Rotundo shows how American culture came to celebrate the misbehavior of boys as a way of idolizing the traits of childishness without idolizing children. In *Love and Death in the American Novel* (1960) Leslie Fiedler traces the evolution of the "bad boy" in American fiction from its roots in late-nineteenth-century bestsellers like *Peck's Bad Boy* and *The Story of a Bad Boy.* He also describes American fiction's traditional preoccupation with "The Good Bad Boy"—from Huckleberry Finn to Holden Caulfield to the characters in Jack Kerouac's *On the Road.* Fiedler wrote, "The Good Bad Boy is, of course, America's vision of itself, crude and unruly in his beginnings, but endowed by his creator with an instinctive sense of what is right."

Thirty-four years ago Fiedler wrote that from the Puritan-influenced Hawthorne and Melville on, Americans had been drawn to tales of boys and neutered women as a way of avoiding the subject of sex. In a tabloid era of penis-mutilation trials, prime-time network nudity, condom ads, and endless talk-show discussions of sexual fetishes, however, it's hard to continue to make his case. Still, if early-adolescent boys are notable for their inclinations to look at dirty pictures and talk about sex, they aren't quite ready to do something about it responsibly with a woman. That propensity to be in the world of sex but not really of it is certainly a sign of the times.

What's more, even if men aren't trying to avoid sex today, a retreat into teenhood may be a convenient way to avoid the opposite sex. As Susan Faludi and other writers have noted, the women's movement—perhaps the greatest social change of our time—has triggered something of a well-documented backlash. One result may be the creation of this boyish countermovement that looks with nostalgic longing on perhaps the last period in life when it's socially acceptable for males to exclude women, if not deride them.

The reasons for the cultural ubiquity of male early adolescence have little to do with puritanism. Many psychologists consider that stage of life, when one is acutely aware of being powerless, to be the time when individuals are most subversive of the society at large. That idea also fits a wider cultural mood, always somewhat prevalent in America, that exalts the outsider. Such an anti-establishment mood, rooted in powerlessness, is particularly strong today, and the proof is not simply in the Ross Perot phenomenon. Whether the subject is how the tabloid press now eagerly tears down public figures or the pervasiveness of gossip masquerading as news (to demonstrate how the famous are no better than anyone else) or the rise of anti-establishment talk radio and comedy clubs where the humor grows more derisive by the day, America is full of the defiant, oppositional anger that often characterizes the early adolescent.

That anger is also an asset for TV programmers in the cable era. Television, of course, tends to encourage a kind of passivity that isn't ultimately much different from the angry powerlessness early teens tend to feel: Beavis and Butthead have become cultural symbols precisely because a nation of couch potatoes feels like a nation of fifteen-year-olds. Moreover, in an age of multiple offerings and channel surfing, what tends to draw these passive audiences is the irately outrageous and exhibitionistic—the Howard Sterns, not the Arthur Godfreys. It also doesn't hurt that adolescents tend to be what advertisers call "good consumers"—narcissistic, with a fair amount of disposable income, and with no one but themselves to spend it on. A culture that is obsessed with this stage of life is arguably in a better frame of mind to buy—to run up the limit on Dad's (or Uncle Sam's) credit card—than one that worships, say, thrifty middle age.

In a country whose citizens have always had tendencies that remind observers of those of a fourteen-year-old boy, it would be wrong to lay all the blame for society's vulgarity and violence, its exhibitionist inclinations, its fear of powerful women, its failure to grow up and take care of its real children, and its ambivalence about paternal authority at the feet of Howard Stern, John McLaughlin, and Jerry Seinfeld. But they have helped, and many of us have willingly obliged. After all, as Fiedler reminded us, boys will be boys.

JOURNAL PROMPT:

Steven Stark makes the statement that "America is full of the defiant, oppositional anger that often characterizes the early adolescent." Write about an experience where you might have been seen as defiant or acting from a place of anger.

COLLABORATIVE EXERCISE:

The author writes, "Entertainment has always evoked certain stages of life in ways that appeal to the masses." In fact, studio demographic records reveal which shows appeal to particular age groups. Working in small groups, think of five television shows that are currently popular, and then rate them according to your understanding of who you assume their target audience to be. (First, rate them individually, and then see if your group agrees about audience appeal.) Finally, discuss how you made your determinations and what factors played a part in your decision making.

ESSAY ASSIGNMENT:

1. The author claims that "'adult' issues go underreported" today because of our preoccupation with the fantasy life of the adolescent male, a preoccupation, he claims, that defines our political reality. Do you agree with the author's assessment of modern journalism? Use examples from a newspaper to validate your position.
2. Look at some television programs, advertisements, and movies from an earlier time period: the fifties or the sixties. Can you characterize an earlier era based on what you've studied, as has the author of "Where the Boys Are" in his examination of the nineties?

ADDITIONAL ESSAY PROMPTS

1. Did you move frequently from place to place as an adolescent? Explain the impact moving had on your life at the time.
2. Consider the activities practiced by some adolescents that might be construed as ritual: getting a tattoo, eating at the same fast-food restaurant, etc. From what you have learned of the role of ritualistic practices, explore how the activity you choose does or does not conform to the purpose of a ritual.
3. What was one of the most unusual ceremonial events you have witnessed? Describe the event, including your role (either as participant or observer). What was the religious, social, or cultural importance of this event?
4. Compare the narrators in "Salvation" and in "On the Rainy River." How were they each influenced by older, seemingly wiser people during their rite of passage into adulthood?
5. Psychologist Mary Pipher in her book *Reviving Ophelia* claims that our "junk culture" is the source of many of the difficulties girls must face. What are some of the difficulties adolescent girls encounter?
6. How does the male experience of growing up differ from the female experience? Do boys face the same social pressures?
7. As an adolescent, did you feel that you "fit in," or did you feel like an outsider? Explain.
8. Do you think having a job while still in high school is a valuable experience? Explain.
9. Do you see yourself as caught up in a desire for material possessions? Are your "wants" similar to those of your friends? Have those "wants" changed over the years? Explain.
10. The author of "Where the Boys Are" claims that many activities in Western society can be read as a nostalgic return to adolescence. The author of "Promiscuities" feels that teenage girls are being asked to grow up too fast. Write about whether or not you believe adolescents are receiving mixed messages.

ADDITIONAL RESEARCH QUESTIONS

1. In the early 1900's, the average age at which a girl reached puberty was sixteen or seventeen. Today that age has dropped to below twelve. What are some of the factors that account for this drop? What are some of the possible consequences of this change?

2. Read about the Vietnam War. (You may want to interview friends or relatives who were participants in that war.) What was the conflict here at home?

3. Both T. C. Boyle and E. B. White ("Once More to the Lake," chapter 8) write about bodies of water that play an important role in their lives. Research what Joseph Campbell and Carl Jung have to say about water as an archetype. Why do they say it has the power to transform? Why is it used in so many different religious ceremonies?

4. In the world of a Maasai warrior, one painful act of circumcision is believed to immediately transform a young boy into a man, "a responsible person." Research and locate at least two other cultures practicing a rite of passage for young boys. How are their traditions similar and/or different from that of the Maasai?

5. Research the effects of divorce on young children, and compare it with research reported in Barbara Cain's essay. What are the similarities and differences?

5

Adulthood

It is ironic that while growing up we often attempt to prove we are adults in ways that reinforce rather than obliterate childhood fears. Without an appropriate context to help affirm adulthood (i.e., rites of passage), many strive to achieve false goals and through competitive struggles find themselves lusting for bigger houses and bigger cars, only to discover the thrill of such acquisitions is short-lived and limiting rather than growth enhancing.

The writers in this unit focus on what it means to be an adult, on what social, psychological, and cultural dynamics aid or interfere with the process of becoming fully actualized in the Western world. Robert Bly claims we have a lot of work to do to counter the commercial pressures that push us backward toward adolescence. Anne Morrow Lindbergh and Joan Didion give us tools for mastering our often cruel, fast-paced world. Nathan McCall in "Makes Me Wanna Holler" explores what happens when we give in to impulse and the subsequent trial of life in prison.

Writer, journalist, and editor **Gail Sheehy** is best known for her work *Pathfinders: Predictable Crises of Adult Life.* In 1958 she earned a B.S. from the University of Vermont, and was a fellow in Columbia University's Journalism School in 1970. This essay comes from the second chapter of her book *Passages,* where she explores adult development from the perspective of a journalist rather than a scholar. In an interview, Sheehy offered this bit of wisdom: "With each passage from one stage of human growth to the next we, too, must shed a protective structure [like a hardy crustacean]. . . . We are left exposed and vulnerable—but also yeasty and embryonic again, capable of stretching in ways we hadn't known before."

GAIL SHEEHY

PREDICTABLE CRISES OF ADULTHOOD

We are not unlike a particularly hardy crustacean. The lobster grows by developing and shedding a series of hard, protective shells. Each time it expands from within, the confining shell must be sloughed off. It is left exposed and vulnerable until, in time, a new covering grows to replace the old.

With each passage from one stage of human growth to the next we, too, must shed a protective structure. We are left exposed and vulnerable—but also yeasty and embryonic again, capable of stretching in ways we hadn't known before. These sheddings may take several years or more. Coming out of each passage, though, we enter a longer and more stable period in which we can expect relative tranquility and a sense of equilibrium regained. . . .

As we shall see, each person engages the steps of development in his or her own characteristic *step-style.* Some people never complete the whole sequence. And none of us "solves" with one step—by jumping out of the parental home into a job or marriage, for example—the problems in separating from the caregivers of childhood. Nor do we "achieve" autonomy once and for all by converting our dreams into concrete goals, even when we attain those goals. The central issues or tasks of one period are never fully completed, tied up, and cast aside. But when they lose their primacy and the current life structure has served its purpose, we are ready to move on to the next period.

Can one catch up? What might look to others like listlessness, contrariness, a maddening refusal to face up to an obvious task may be a person's own unique detour that will bring him out later on the other side. Developmental gains won can later be lost—and rewon. It's plausible, though it can't be proven, that the mastery of one set of tasks fortifies us for the next period and the next set of challenges. But it's important not to think too mechanistically. Machines work by units. The bureaucracy (supposedly) works step by step. Human beings, thank God, have an individual inner dynamic that can never be precisely coded.

Although I have indicated the ages when Americans are likely to go through each stage, and the differences between men and women where they are striking, do not take the ages too seriously. The stages are the thing, and most particularly the sequence.

Here is the briefest outline of the developmental ladder.

Pulling Up Roots

Before 18, the motto is loud and clear: "I have to get away from my parents." But the words are seldom connected to action. Generally still safely part of our families, even if away at school, we feel our autonomy to be subject to erosion from moment to moment.

After 18, we begin Pulling Up Roots in earnest. College, military service, and short-term travels are all customary vehicles our society provides for the first round trips between family and a base of one's own. In the attempt to separate our view of the world from our family's view, despite vigorous protestations to the contrary—"I know exactly what I want!"—we cast about for any beliefs we can call our own. And in the process of testing those beliefs we are often drawn to fads, preferably those most mysterious and inaccessible to our parents.

Whatever tentative memberships we try out in the world, the fear haunts us that we are really kids who cannot take care of ourselves. We cover that fear with acts of defiance and mimicked confidence. For allies to replace our parents, we turn to our contemporaries. They become conspirators. So long as their perspective meshes with our own, they are able to substitute for the sanctuary of the family. But that doesn't last very long. And the instant they diverge from the shaky ideals of "our group," they are seen as betrayers. Rebounds to the family are common between the ages of 18 and 22.

The tasks of this passage are to locate ourselves in a peer group role, a sex role, an anticipated occupation, an ideology or world view. As a result, we gather the impetus to leave home physically and the identity to *begin* leaving home emotionally.

Even as one part of us seeks to be an individual, another part longs to restore the safety and comfort of merging with another. Thus one of the most popular myths of this passage is: We can piggyback our development by attaching to a Stronger One. But people who marry during this time often prolong financial and emotional ties to the family and relatives that impede them from becoming self-sufficient.

A stormy passage through the Pulling Up Roots years will probably facilitate the normal progression of the adult life cycle. If one doesn't have an identity crisis at this point, it will erupt during a later transition, when the penalties may be harder to bear.

The Trying Twenties

The Trying Twenties confront us with the question of how to take hold in the adult world. Our focus shifts from the interior turmoils of late adolescence—"Who am I?" "What is truth?"—and we become almost totally preoccupied with working out the externals. "How do I put my aspirations into effect?" "What is the best way to start?" "Where do I go?" "Who can help me?" "How did *you* do it?"

In this period, which is longer and more stable compared with the passage that leads to it, the tasks are as enormous as they are exhilarating: To shape a Dream, that vision of ourselves which will generate energy, aliveness, and hope. To prepare for a lifework. To find a mentor if possible. And to form the capacity for intimacy, without losing in the process whatever consistency of self we have thus far mustered. The first test structure must be erected around the life we choose to try.

Doing what we "should" is the most pervasive theme of the twenties. The "shoulds" are largely defined by family models, the press of the culture, or the prejudices of our peers. If the prevailing cultural instructions are that one should get married and settle down behind one's own door, a nuclear family is born. If instead the peers insist that one should do one's own thing, the 25-year-old is likely to harness himself onto a Harley-Davidson and burn up Route 66 in the commitment to have no commitments.

One of the terrifying aspects of the twenties is the inner conviction that the choices we make are irrevocable. It is largely a false fear. Change is quite possible, and some alteration of our original choices is probably inevitable.

Two impulses, as always, are at work. One is to build a firm, safe structure for the future by making strong commitments, to "be set." Yet people who slip into a ready-made form without much self-examination are likely to find themselves *locked in.*

The other urge is to explore and experiment, keeping any structure tentative and therefore easily reversible. Taken to the extreme, these are people who skip from one trial job and one limited personal encounter to another, spending their twenties in the *transient* state.

Although the choices of our twenties are not irrevocable, they do set in motion a Life Pattern. Some of us follow the lock-in pattern, others the transient pattern, the wunderkind pattern, the caregiver pattern, and there are a number of others. Such patterns strongly influence the particular questions raised for each person during each passage. . . .

Buoyed by powerful illusions and belief in the power of the will, we commonly insist in our twenties that what we have chosen to do is the one true course in life. Our backs go up at the merest hint that we are like our parents, that two decades of parental training might be reflected in our current actions and attitudes.

"Not me," is the motto, "I'm different."

Catch-30

Impatient with devoting ourselves to the "shoulds," a new vitality springs from within as we approach 30. Men and women alike speak of feeling too narrow and restricted. They blame all sorts of things, but what the restrictions boil down to are the outgrowth of career and personal choices of the twenties. They may have been choices perfectly suited to that stage. But now the fit feels different. Some inner aspect that was left out is striving to be taken into account. Important new choices must be made, and commitments altered or deepened. The work involves great change, turmoil, and often crisis—a simultaneous feeling of rock bottom and the urge to bust out.

One common response is the tearing up of the life we spent most of our twenties putting together. It may mean striking out on a secondary road toward a new vision or converting a dream of "running for president" into a more realistic goal. The single person feels a push to find a partner. The woman who was previously content at home with children chafes to venture into the world. The childless couple reconsiders children. And almost everyone who is married, especially those married for seven years, feels a discontent.

If the discontent doesn't lead to a divorce, it will, or should, call for a serious review of the marriage and of each partner's aspirations in their Catch-30 condition. The gist of that condition was expressed by a 29-year-old associate with a Wall Street law firm:

"I'm considering leaving the firm. I've been there four years now; I'm getting good feedback, but I have no clients of my own. I feel weak. If I wait much longer, it will be too late, too close to that fateful time of decision on whether or not to become a partner. I'm success-oriented. But the concept of being 55 years old and stuck in a monotonous job drives me wild. It drives me crazy now, just a little bit. I'd say that 85 percent of the time I thoroughly enjoy my work. But when I get a screwball case, I come away from court saying, 'What am I doing here?' It's a *visceral* reaction that I'm wasting my time. I'm trying to find some way to make a social contribution or a slot in city government. I keep saying, 'There's something more.'"

Besides the push to broaden himself professionally, there is a wish to expand his personal life. He wants two or three more children. "The concept of a home has become very meaningful to me, a place to get away from troubles and relax. I love my son in a way I could not have anticipated. I never could live alone."

Consumed with the work of making his own critical life-steering decisions, he demonstrates the essential shift at this age: an absolute requirement to be more self-concerned. The self has new value now that his competency has been proved.

His wife is struggling with her own age-30 priorities. She wants to go to law school, but he wants more children. If she is going to stay home, she wants him to make more time for the family instead of taking on even wider professional commitments. His view of the bind, of what he would most like from his wife, is this:

"I'd like not to be bothered. It sounds cruel, but I'd like not to have to worry about what she's going to do next week. Which is why I've told her several times that I think she should do something. Go back to school and get a degree in social work or geography or whatever. Hopefully that would fulfill her, and then I wouldn't have to worry about her line of problems. I want her to be decisive about herself."

The trouble with his advice to his wife is that it comes out of concern with *his* convenience, rather than with *her* development. She quickly picks up on this lack of goodwill: He is trying to dispose of her. At the same time, he refuses her the same latitude to be "selfish" in making an independent decision to broaden her horizons. Both perceive a lack of mutuality. And that is what Catch-30 is all about for the couple.

Rooting and Extending

Life becomes less provisional, more rational and orderly in the early thirties. We begin to settle down in the full sense. Most of us begin putting down roots and sending out new shoots. People buy houses and become very earnest about climbing career ladders. Men in particular concern themselves with "making it." Satisfaction with marriage generally goes downhill in the thirties (for those who have remained together) compared with the highly valued, vision-supporting marriage of the twenties. This coincides with the couple's reduced social life outside the family and the inturned focus on raising their children.

The Deadline Decade

In the middle of the thirties we come upon a crossroads. We have reached the halfway mark. Yet even as we are reaching our prime, we begin to see there is a place where it finishes. Time starts to squeeze.

The loss of youth, the faltering of physical powers we have always taken for granted, the fading purpose of stereotyped roles by which we have thus far identified ourselves, the spiritual dilemma of having no absolute answers—any or all of these shocks can give this passage the character of crisis. Such thoughts usher in a decade between 35 and 45 that can be called the Deadline Decade. It is a time of both danger and opportunity. All of us have the chance to rework the narrow identity by which we defined ourselves in the first half of life. And those of us who make the most of the opportunity will have a full-out authenticity crisis.

To come through this authenticity crisis, we must reexamine our purposes and reevaluate how to spend our resources from now on. "Why am I doing all this? What do I really believe in?" No matter what we have been doing, there will be parts of ourselves that have been suppressed and now need to find expression. "Bad" feelings will demand acknowledgment along with the good.

It is frightening to step off onto the treacherous footbridge leading to the second half of life. We can't take everything with us on this journey through uncertainty. Along the way, we discover that we are alone. We no longer have to ask permission because we are the providers of our own safety. We must learn to give ourselves permission. We stumble upon feminine or masculine aspects of our natures that up to this time have usually been masked. There is grieving to be done because an old self is dying. By taking in our suppressed and even our unwanted parts, we prepare at the gut level for the reintegration of an identity that is ours and ours alone—not some artificial form put together to please the culture or our mates. It is a hard passage at the beginning. But by disassembling ourselves, we can glimpse the light and gather our parts into a renewal.

Women sense this inner crossroads earlier than men do. The time pinch often prompts a woman to stop and take an all-points survey at age 35. Whatever options she has already played out, she feels a "my last chance" urgency to review those options she has set aside and those that aging and biology will close off in the *now foreseeable* future. For all her qualms and confusion about where to start looking for a new future, she usually enjoys an exhilaration of release. Assertiveness begins rising. There are so many firsts ahead.

Men, too, feel the time push in the mid-thirties. Most men respond by pressing down harder on the career accelerator. It's "my last chance" to pull away from the pack. It is no longer enough to be the loyal junior executive, the promising young novelist, the lawyer who does a little *pro bono* work on the side. He wants now to become part of top management, to be recognized as an established writer, or an active politician with his own legislative program. With some chagrin, he discovers that he has been too anxious to please and too vulnerable to criticism. He wants to put together his own ship.

During this period of intense concentration on external advancement, it is common for men to be unaware of the more difficult, gut issues that are propelling them forward. The survey that was neglected at 35 becomes a crucible at 40. Whatever rung of achievement he has reached, the man of 40 usually feels stale, restless, burdened, and unappreciated. He worries about his health. He wonders, "Is this all there is?" He may make a series of departures from well-established lifelong base lines, including marriage. More and more men are seeking second careers in midlife. Some become self-destructive. And many men in their forties experience a major shift of emphasis away from pouring all their energies into their own advancement. A more tender, feeling side comes into play. They become interested in developing an ethical self.

Renewal or Resignation

Somewhere in the mid-forties, equilibrium is regained. A new stability is achieved, which may be more or less satisfying.

If one has refused to budge through the midlife transition, the sense of staleness will calcify into resignation. One by one, the safety and supports will be withdrawn from the person who is standing still. Parents will become children; children will become strangers; a mate will grow away or go away; the career will become just a job—and each of these events will be felt as an abandonment. The crisis will probably emerge again around 50. And although its wallop will be greater, the jolt may be just what is needed to prod the resigned middle-ager toward seeking revitalization.

On the other hand . . .

If we have confronted ourselves in the middle passage and found a renewal of purpose around which we are eager to build a more authentic life structure, these may well be the best years. Personal happiness takes a sharp turn upward for partners who can now accept the fact: "I cannot expect *anyone* to fully understand me." Parents can be forgiven for the burdens of our childhood. Children can be let go without leaving us in collapsed silence. At 50, there is a new warmth and mellowing. Friends become more important than ever, but so does privacy. Since it is so often proclaimed by people past midlife, the motto of this stage might be "No more bullshit."

JOURNAL PROMPT:

Without referring back to Sheehy's essay, which of her developmental stages do you most remember? What specific details do you recall?

COLLABORATIVE EXERCISE:

Why do you suppose the author stops her classification at age fifty? In doing so, do you think the author has made some assumptions about older people?

ESSAY ASSIGNMENT:

1. Compare Sheehy's essay with Shakespeare's passage in this chapter, "The Seven Ages of Man." Do you note any similarities?
2. Sheehy claims that adults who fail to experience a "stage" at the usual time have difficulties later on. How closely does your life experience parallel the patterns described by the author?
3. Select one of Sheehy's stages, and interview at least five people you know who are in or have lived through this particular stage. How do your interviewees' experiences reflect or contradict Sheehy's assertions?

Born in Madison, Minnesota, **ROBERT BLY** is an award-winning poet, storyteller, translator, and lecturer. He has traveled around the country presenting poetry in the form of song and story. Bly was a central figure in the men's liberation movement and held workshops to help men get beyond the stereotypes of our culture. He was the 1967 recipient of the National Book Award for his second collection of poetry, *The Light around the Body*. The following essay is taken from "The Sibling Society," which was originally published in the *Utne Reader* (May/June 1996).

ROBERT BLY

A WORLD OF HALF-ADULTS

It's the worst of times; it's the best of times. That's how we feel as we navigate from a paternal society, now discredited, to a society in which impulse is given its way. People don't bother to grow up, and we are all fish swimming in a tank of half-adults. The rule is: Where repression was before, fantasy will now be; we human beings limp along, running after our own fantasy. We can never catch up, and so we defeat ourselves by the simplest possible means: speed. Everywhere we go there's a crowd, and the people all look alike.

We begin to live a lateral life, catch glimpses out of the corners of our eyes, keep the TV set at eye level, watch the scores move horizontally across the screen.

We see what's coming out the sideview mirror. It seems like intimacy; maybe not intimacy as much as proximity; maybe not proximity as much as sameness. Americans who are 20 years old see others who look like them in Bosnia, Greece, China, France, Brazil, Germany, and Russia, wearing the same jeans, listening to the same music, speaking a universal language that computer literacy demands. Sometimes they feel more vitally connected to siblings elsewhere than to family members in the next room.

When we see the millions like ourselves all over the world, our eyes meet uniformity, resemblance, likeness, rather than distinction and differences. Hope rises immediately for the long-desired possibility of community. And yet it would be foolish to overlook the serious implications of this glance to the side, this tilt of the head. "Mass society, with its demand for work without responsibility, creates a gigantic army of rival siblings," in German psychoanalyst Alexander Mitscherlich's words.

Commercial pressures push us backward, toward adolescence, toward childhood. With no effective rituals of initiation, and no real way to know when our slow progress toward adulthood has reached its goal, young men and women in our culture go around in circles. Those who should be adults find it difficult or impossible to offer help to those behind. That pressure seems even more intense than it was in the 1960s, when the cry "Turn on, tune in, drop out" was so popular. Observers describe many contemporaries as "children with children of their own."

"People look younger all the time." Photographs of men and women a hundred years ago—immigrants, for example—show a certain set of the mouth and jaws that says, "We're adults. There's nothing we can do about it."

By contrast, the face of Marilyn Monroe, of Kevin Costner, or of the ordinary person we see on the street says, "I'm a child. There's nothing I can do about it."

People watching Ken Burns' *History of Baseball* remarked that faces of fans even in the 1920s looked more mature than faces of fans now. Looking at those old photos, one sees men and women who knew how to have fun, but they had one foot in Necessity. Walk down a European street these days and you will see that American faces stand out for their youthful and naive look. Some who are 50 look 30. Part of this phenomenon is good nutrition and exercise, but part of it is that we are losing our ability to mature.

Perhaps one-third of our society has developed these new sibling qualities. The rest of us are walking in that direction. When we all arrive there may be no public schools at all, nor past paradigms, because only people one's own age will be worth listening to.

We know that the paternal society had an elaborate and internally consistent form with authoritative father reflected upward to the strong community leader and beyond him to the father god up among the stars, which were also arranged in hierarchical levels, called "the seven heavens." Children imitated adults and were often far too respectful for their own good to authorities of all kinds. However, they learned in school the adult ways of talking, writing, and thinking. For some, the home was safe, and the two-parent balance gave them maximum possibility for growth; for others, the home was a horror of beatings, humiliation, and sexual abuse, and school was the only safe place. The teaching at home and in school encouraged religion, memorization, ethics, and discipline, but resolutely kept hidden the historical brutalities of the system.

Our succeeding sibling society, in a relatively brief time, has taught itself to be internally consistent in a fairly thorough way. The teaching is that no one is superior to anyone else: high culture is to be destroyed, and business leaders look sideways to the other business leaders. The sibling society prizes a state of half-adulthood in which repression, discipline, and the Indo-European, Islamic, Hebraic impulse-control system are jettisoned. The parents regress to become more like children, and the children, through abandonment, are forced to become adults too soon, and never quite make it. There's an impulse to set children adrift on their own. The old (in the form of crones, elders, ancestors, grandmothers and grandfathers) are thrown away and the young (in the form of street children in South America, or latchkey children in the suburbs of this country, or poor children in the inner city) are thrown away.

When I first began to write about this subject, I found it hard to understand why a society run by adolescents should show so much disregard for children who are, in the mass, worse off under Bill Clinton than they were under Theodore Roosevelt or Warren Harding. And yet, in an actual family, adolescents do not pay much attention to the little ones or to the very old. Newt Gingrich's Contract with America is adolescent.

The deepening rage of the unparented is becoming a mark of the sibling society. Of course, some children in our society feel well parented, and there is much adequate parenting; but there is also a new rage. A man said to me, "Having made it to the one-parent family, we are now on our way toward the zero-parent family." The actual wages of working-class and middle-class parents have fallen significantly since 1972, so that often both parents work, one parent the day shift, another at night; family meals, talks, reading together no longer take place.

What the young need—stability, presence, attention, advice, good psychic food, unpolluted stories—is exactly what the sibling society won't give them. As we look at the crumbling schools, the failure to protect students from guns, the cutting of funds for Head Start and breakfasts for poor children, cutting of music and art lessons, the enormous increase in numbers of children living in poverty, the poor prenatal care for some, we have to wonder whether there might not be a genuine anger against children in the sibling society.

If we think of catching these changes in story form, "Jack and the Beanstalk" immediately comes to mind. There a fatherless boy, Jack, living alone with his mother, climbs the stalk and finds himself in danger of being eaten by a cruel and enormous giant. Jack, from his hiding place in the kitchen, "was astonished to see how much the giant devoured, and thought he would never have done eating and drinking." That's the way the rest of the world thinks of the United States.

More specifically, the boy, as helpless and vulnerable as the young ones are today, finds himself faced with an enemy much stronger than he is. We could say that the giant represents the current emphasis on greed, violent movies, and pornographic advertising. The giant is television. It eats up more and more of childhood each year. In the original story Jack learns to steal back some of his family treasures—the gold and silver coins, the divine hen, the golden harp—from the giant. But we have not gotten to that part of the story in our time. We have no idea how to steal back "gold" from the giant. Rather than keeping the children hidden, the adults in the sibling society call the giant over to the cabinet where the children are hidden, open the door and say, "Here they are!" In the sibling society Jack gets eaten alive.

Television is the thalidomide of the 1990s. In 1995 American children spent about one-third of their waking hours out of school watching television. The National Assessment of Educational Progress reported that only 5 percent of high school graduates could make their way through college-level literature. A recent 1,200-subject study, supported by the National Institute of Mental Health and guided by Mihaly Csikszentmihalyi and Robert Kuby, found that more skill and concentration were needed to eat a meal than to watch television, and the watching left people passive, yet tense, and it left them unable to concentrate.

Television provides a garbage dump of obsessive sexual material inappropriate to the child's age, minute description of brutalities, wars, and tortures all over the world: an avalanche of specialized information that stuns the brain. Even lyrics of songs come too fast for the brain to hear.

Grade school teachers report that in recent years they have had to repeat instructions over and over, or look each child in the face and give instructions separately, which interrupts class work. We know that the sort of music children hear much of—characterized by a heavy beat—is processed mainly by the right brain, which hears the tune as a whole and doesn't see its parts or question it. The brain goes into an alpha state, which rules out active thinking or learning.

American movies in the late 1950s vividly brought forward an old theme of adolescence: the impulse not to defend common projects, common stories, common values. James Dean and Marlon Brando played the roles of young men who demonstrated this rebellion, and the theme began to have an edge on it. "What are you rebelling against?" a Brando character is asked. "What do you have?" is the witty reply.

Human beings often struggle to preserve a given cultural group through the stories it holds in common, its remembered history of fragments of it, and certain agreed-on values and courtesies. A gathering of novels, plays, poems, and songs—these days wrongly called "the canon," more properly "the common stories"—held middle-aged people, elders, and the very young together.

That most adolescents these days reject the common stories is no surprise. More often than not, they reject them without having read or heard them. When adolescence lasted only three or four years, the youths' refusal to support the commonly agreed on novels and poems did not affect the long-range commitment of the group to the reservoir; but now, as American adolescence stretches from age 15 or so all the way to 35, those 20 years of sullen silence or active rejection of any commonality, in literature or otherwise, can have devastating results. One can say that colleges and universities are precisely where the gifts of the past are meant to be studied and absorbed, yet those very places are where the current damage to the common reservoir is taking place. Men and women in their 20s take teaching jobs, and if they are still adolescent in their 30s, their hostility to the group's literature and to the group itself becomes palpable.

We know it is essential to open the cabinet of common stories to include literature from other cultures besides the European, and to include much more women's literature than the old reservoir held. That is long overdue. But inclusion, one could say, is a job for adults. When the adolescent gets hold of it, a deep-lying impulse comes into play, and it says, "I'm taking care of people my age, and that's it! My needs are important, and if the group doesn't survive, it doesn't deserve to."

What is asked of adults now is that they stop going *forward,* to retirement, to Costa Rica, to fortune, and turn to face the young siblings and the adolescents—the thousands of young siblings we see around us. Many of these siblings are remarkable and seem to have a kind of emotional knowledge that is far older than they are. Some have sharper intuitions into human motives and people's relationships with each other than any of us had at that age. Some who expect to die early—as many do—see with a brilliant clarity into the dramas taking place all around them.

One can imagine a field with the adolescents on one side of a line drawn on the earth and adults on the other side looking into their eyes. The adult in our time is asked to reach his or her hand across the line and pull the youth into adulthood. That means of course that the adults will have to decide what genuine adulthood is. If the adults do not turn and walk up to this line and help pull the adolescents over, the adolescents will stay exactly where they are for another 20 or 30 years. If we don't turn to face the young ones, their detachment machines, which are louder and more persistent than ours, will say, "I am not a part of this family," and they will kill any relationship with their parents. The parents have to know that.

During the paternal society, there were "representatives" of the adult community: highly respected grade school and high school teachers, strong personalities of novels and epics, admired presidents and senators, Eleanor Roosevelts and Madame Curies, priests untouched by scandal, older men and women in each community, both visible and capable of renunciation, who drew young people over the line by their very example. But envy and the habit of ingratitude have ended all that.

The hope lies in the longing we have to be adults. If we take an interest in younger ones by helping them find a mentor, by bringing them along to adult activities, by giving attention to young ones who aren't in our family at all, then our own feeling of being adult will be augmented, and adulthood might again appear to be a desirable state for many young ones.

In the sibling society, as a result of the enormous power of the leveling process, few adults remain publicly visible as models. Because they are invisible, the very idea of the adult has fallen into confusion. As ordinary adults, we have to ask ourselves, in a way that people 200 years ago did not, what an adult is. I have to ask myself what I have found out in my intermittent, poem-ridden attempts to become an adult. Someone who has succeeded better than I could name more qualities of the adult than I will, but I will list a few.

I would say that an adult is a person not governed by what we have called pre-Oedipal wishes, the demands for immediate pleasure, comfort, and excitement. The adult quality that has been hardest to understand for me, as a greedy person, is renunciation. Moreover, an adult is able to organize the random emotions and events of his or her life into a memory, a rough meaning, a story.

It is an adult perception to understand that the world belongs primarily to the dead, and we only rent it from them for a little while. The idea that each of us has the right to change everything is a deep insult to them.

The true adult is the one who has been able to preserve his or her intensities, including those intensities proper to his or her generation and creativity, so that he or she has something with which to meet the intensities of the adolescent. We could say that an adult becomes an elder when he not only preserves his intensities but adds more. In the words of the Persian poet Ansari, an adult is a person who goes out into the world and "gathers jewels of feeling for others."

The hope lies in our longing to be adults, and the longing for the young ones, if they knew what an honorable adulthood is, to become adults as well. It's as if all this has to be newly invented, and the adults then have to imagine as well what an elder is, what the elder's responsibilities are, what it takes for an adult to become a genuine elder.

I will end with a Norwegian story. A man walking through the forest and in danger of dying from cold sees at last a house with smoke rising from the chimney. He sees a 30-year-old man chopping wood and says to him, "Pardon me, but I am a traveler who has been walking all day. Would it be possible for me to stay overnight in your house?" The man says, "It's all right with me, but I am not the father of the house. You'll have to ask my father." He sees a 70-year-old man standing just inside the door, and the man says, "Pardon me, but I am a traveler and have been walking all day. Would it be possible to stay overnight in your house?" The old man says, "It's all right with me, but I am not the father of this house. You'll have to ask my father, who is sitting at the table." He says to this man, who looks about a hundred years old, "Pardon me, but I am a traveler who has been walking all day. Would it be possible for me to stay overnight in your house?" The hundred-year-old says, "It's all right with me, but I am not the father of this house. You'll have to ask my father." And he gestures toward the fireplace. He sees a very old man sitting in a chair near the fire. He goes up to him and says, "I am a traveler, and I have been walking all day. Would it be possible for me to stay overnight in your house?" In a hoarse voice this old man says, "It's all right with me, but I am not the father of the house. You'll have to ask my father." The traveler glances at the boxed-in bed, and he sees a very, very old man who seems no more than four feet tall lying in the bed. He raises his voice and says to him, "Pardon me, I am a traveler, and I have been walking all day. Would it be possible for me to stay overnight in your house?" The little man in the bed says in a weak voice, "It's all right with me, but I am not the father of this house. You'll have to ask my father." Suddenly the traveler sees a cradle standing at the foot of the bed. In it, there is a very, very little man, hardly the size of a baby, lying curled in the cradle. The man says, "Pardon me, but I am a traveler. I have been walking all day. Would it be possible for me to stay at your house tonight?" In a voice so faint it can hardly be heard, the man in the cradle says, "It's all right with me, but I am not the father of this house. You'll have to ask my father." As the traveler lifts his eyes, he sees an old hunting horn hanging on the wall, made from a sheep's horn, curved like the new moon. He stands and walks over to it, and there he sees a tiny old man no more than six inches long with his head on a tiny pillow and a tiny wisp of white hair. The traveler says, "Pardon me, I am a traveler, and I have been walking all day. Would it be possible for me to stay overnight in your house?" He puts his ear down close to the hunting horn, and the oldest man says, "Yes."

We know there is a Seventh Mother of the House, who is also very small. Perhaps she is far inside the womb, or sitting in the innermost cell of our body, and she gives us permission to live, to be born, to have joy. Her contribution is life. The contribution of the Seventh Father is a house. Together they grant permission from the universe for civilization.

JOURNAL PROMPT:

Define the term "adulthood," based on your own experiences and observations.

COLLABORATIVE EXERCISE:

The author relates a Norwegian tale in which a traveler, wishing to find shelter for the night, journeys to a house and asks seven times, "Would it be possible for me to stay overnight in your house?" What is the meaning of this story? How does it relate to Bly's title, "A World of Half-Adults"?

ESSAY ASSIGNMENT:

1. Bly retells the "Jack and the Beanstalk" story and makes a metaphorical connection with what he claims is happening in our "sibling society." Write an essay in which you discuss some fairy tales that might better serve as models for a healthy society.
2. Bly suggests that in modern Western culture, adolescence is unduly prolonged. Do you agree with his assessment? Why or why not? Refer to your own experience with friends and family.
3. In his essay, Bly suggests that commercialism keeps adults from growing up: "Commercial pressures push us backward, toward adolescence, toward childhood." How do you interpret this assertion? To what specific commercial pressures could Bly be referring? Finally, how do you suggest we can lessen the influence of these pressures?

Linda Pastan was poet laureate of Maryland from 1991 through 1994 and has received fellowships from the National Endowment for the Arts and from the Maryland Arts Council. She has won the Dylan Thomas Award, the Virginia Faulkner Award from *Prairie Schooner,* and a Pushcart Prize. In this poem, Pastan offers a metaphor of sorts to capture the sometimes difficult moments in adulthood when one is confronted with ethical issues. Pastan lives in Potomac, Maryland.

LINDA PASTAN

Ethics

In ethics class so many years ago
our teacher asked this question every fall:
if there were a fire in a museum
which would you save, a Rembrandt painting
or an old woman who hadn't many

years left anyhow? Restless on hard chairs
caring little for pictures or old age
we'd opt one year for life, the next for art
and always half-heartedly. Sometimes
the woman borrowed my grandmother's face
leaving her usual kitchen to wander
some drafty, half imagined museum.
One year, feeling clever, I replied
why not let the woman decide herself?
Linda, the teacher would report, eschews
the burdens of responsibility.
This fall in a real museum I stand
before a real Rembrandt, old woman,
or nearly so, myself. The colors
within the frame are darker than autumn,
darker even than winter—the browns of earth,
though earth's most radiant elements burn
through the canvas. I know now that woman
and painting and season are almost one
and all beyond saving by children.

JOURNAL PROMPT:

Write about a time when you were impatient or perhaps even disrespectful toward an older adult. What were the circumstances? Did you experience any feelings of regret or guilt afterward? Explain.

COLLABORATIVE EXERCISE:

Working in small groups, consider how Pastan's last lines in her poem might be interpreted: "I know now that woman / and painting and season are almost one / and all beyond saving by children." While you discuss possible meanings, consider the *tone* of the poem as well as the *setting,* which carries the reader back to a childhood experience.

ESSAY ASSIGNMENT:

1. Consider the ethical situation presented in Pastan's poem: the value of a human life versus the value of a very prized painting. Imagine that you are faced with this same question. How would you respond? On what is your answer based? What personal beliefs, attitudes, understandings, and commitments help you come to your conclusion?
2. Both the author of this poem and Louise Erdrich, author of "*Z:* The Movie That Changed my Life" (also in this chapter), consider how an artistic endeavor has affected their lives. Compare the two. How is the

Rembrandt painting important in Pastan's memory, and likewise, how is the film significant to Erdrich? Be specific.

3. Assume the role of the classroom teacher in the poem, and explain the lesson and its purpose to your audience (the parents of these children).

American writer **ANNE MORROW LINDBERGH** is best known for her five collections of diaries and letters that offer readers a record of her life during the intense period of the celebrity of her husband, American aviator Charles Lindbergh. In her books she uses metaphors of flight to define her search for an inner balance in life to counter the forces that can pull one off center. In addition to her series of diaries and letters, her best-known work is a meditative work titled *Gift from the Sea* (1955), from which this essay is taken.

ANNE MORROW LINDBERGH

CHANNELLED WHELK

The shell in my hand is deserted. It once housed a whelk, a snail-like creature, and then temporarily, after the death of the first occupant, a little hermit crab, who has run away, leaving his tracks behind him like a delicate vine on the sand. He ran away, and left me his shell. It was once a protection to him. I turn the shell in my hand, gazing into the wide open door from which he made his exit. Had it become an encumbrance? Why did he run away? Did he hope to find a better home, a better mode of living? I too have run away, I realize, I have shed the shell of my life, for these few weeks of vacation.

But his shell—it is simple; it is bare, it is beautiful. Small, only the size of my thumb, its architecture is perfect, down to the finest detail. Its shape, swelling like a pear in the center, winds in a gentle spiral to the pointed apex. Its color, dull gold, is whitened by a wash of salt from the sea. Each whorl, each faint knob, each criss-cross vein in its egg-shell texture, is as clearly defined as on the day of creation. My eye follows with delight the outer circumference of that diminutive winding staircase up which this tenant used to travel.

My shell is not like this, I think. How untidy it has become! Blurred with moss, knobby with barnacles, its shape is hardly recognizable any more. Surely, it had a shape once. It has a shape still in my mind. What is the shape of my life?

The shape of my life today starts with a family. I have a husband, five children and a home just beyond the suburbs of New York. I have also a craft, writing, and therefore work I want to pursue. The shape of my life is, of course, determined by many other things; my background and childhood, my mind and its education, my conscience and its pressures, my heart and its desires. I want to give and take from my children and husband, to share with friends and community, to carry out my obligations to man and to the world, as a woman, as an artist, as a citizen.

But I want first of all—in fact, as an end to these other desires—to be at peace with myself. I want a singleness of eye, a purity of intention, a central core to my life that will enable me to carry out these obligations and activities as well as I can. I want, in fact—to borrow from the language of the saints—to live "in grace" as much of the time as possible. I am not using this term in a strictly theological sense. By grace I mean an inner harmony, essentially spiritual, which can be translated into outward harmony. I am seeking perhaps what Socrates asked for in the prayer from the *Phaedrus* when he said, "May the outward and inward man be at one." I would like to achieve a state of inner spiritual grace from which I could function and give as I was meant to in the eye of God.

Vague as this definition may be, I believe most people are aware of periods in their lives when they seem to be "in grace" and other periods when they feel "out of grace," even though they may use different words to describe these states. In the first happy condition, one seems to carry all one's tasks before one lightly, as if borne along on a great tide; and in the opposite state one can hardly tie a shoe-string. It is true that a large part of life consists in learning a technique of tying the shoe-string, whether one is in grace or not. But there are techniques of living too; there are even techniques in the search for grace. And techniques can be cultivated. I have learned by some experience, by many examples, and by the writings of countless others before me, also occupied in the search, that certain environments, certain modes of life, certain rules of conduct are more conducive to inner and outer harmony than others. There are, in fact, certain roads that one may follow. Simplification of life is one of them.

I mean to lead a simple life, to choose a simple shell I can carry easily—like a hermit crab. But I do not. I find that my frame of life does not foster simplicity. My husband and five children must make their way in the world. The life I have chosen as wife and mother entrains a whole caravan of complications. It involves a house in the suburbs and either household drudgery or household help which wavers between scarcity and non-existence for most of us. It involves food and shelter; meals, planning, marketing, bills, and making the ends meet in a thousand ways. It involves not only the butcher, the baker, the candlestickmaker, but countless other experts to keep my modern house with its modern "simplifications" (electricity, plumbing, refrigerator, gas-stove, oil-burner, dish-washer, radios, car, and numerous other labor-saving devices) functioning properly. It involves health; doctors, dentists, appointments, medicine, cod-liver oil, vitamins, trips to the drugstore. It involves education, spiritual, intellectual, physical; schools, school conferences, car-pools, extra trips for basket-ball or orchestra practice; tutoring; camps, camp equipment and transportation. It involves clothes, shopping, laundry, cleaning, mending, letting skirts down and sewing buttons on, or finding someone else to do it. It involves friends, my husband's, my children's, my own, and endless arrangements to get together; letters, invitations, telephone calls and transportation hither and yon.

For life today in America is based on the premise of ever-widening circles of contact and communication. It involves not only family demands, but community demands, national demands, international demands on the good citizen, through social and cultural pressures, through newspapers, magazines, radio programs, political drives, charitable appeals, and so on. My mind reels with it. What a circus act we women perform every day of our lives. It puts the trapeze artist to shame. Look at us. We run a tight rope daily, balancing a pile of books on the head. Baby-carriage, parasol, kitchen chair, still under control. Steady now!

This is not the life of simplicity but the life of multiplicity that the wise men warn us of. . . . Plotinus was preaching the dangers of multiplicity of the world back in the third century. Yet, the problem is particularly and essentially woman's. Distraction is, always has been, and probably always will be, inherent in woman's life.

For to be a woman is to have interests and duties, raying out in all directions from the central mother-core, like spokes from the hub of a wheel. The pattern of our lives is essentially circular. We must be open to all points of the compass; husband, children, friends, home, community; stretched out, exposed, sensitive like a spider's web to each breeze that blows, to each call that comes. How difficult for us, then, to achieve a balance in the midst of these contradictory tensions, and yet how necessary for the proper functioning of our lives. How much we need, and how arduous of attainment is that steadiness preached in all rules for holy living. How desirable and how distant is the ideal of the contemplative, artist, or saint—the inner inviolable core, the single eye.

With a new awareness, both painful and humorous, I begin to understand why the saints were rarely married women. I am convinced it has nothing inherently to do, as I once supposed, with chastity or children. It has to do primarily with distractions. The bearing, rearing, feeding and educating of children; the running of a house with its thousand details; human relationships with their myriad pulls—woman's normal occupations in general run counter to creative life, or contemplative life, or saintly life. The problem is not merely one of *Woman and Career, Woman and the Home, Woman and Independence.* It is more basically: how to remain whole in the midst of the distractions of life; how to remain balanced, no matter what centrifugal forces tend to pull one off center; how to remain strong, no matter what shocks come in at the periphery and tend to crack the hub of the wheel.

What is the answer? There is no easy answer, no complete answer. I have only clues, shells from the sea. The bare beauty of the channelled whelk tells me that one answer, and perhaps a first step, is in simplification of life, in cutting out some of the distractions. But how? Total retirement is not possible. I cannot shed my responsibilities. I cannot permanently inhabit a desert island. I cannot be a nun in the midst of family life. I would not want to be. The solution for me, surely, is neither in total renunciation of the world, nor in total acceptance of it. I must find a balance somewhere, or an alternating rhythm between these two extremes; a swinging of the pendulum between solitude and communion, between retreat and return. In my periods of retreat, perhaps I can learn something to carry back into my worldly life. I can at least practice for these two weeks the simplification of outward life, as a beginning. I can follow this superficial clue, and see where it leads. Here, in beach living, I can try.

One learns first of all in beach living the art of shedding; how little one can get along with, not how much. Physical shedding to begin with, which then mysteriously spreads into other fields. Clothes, first. Of course, one needs less in the sun. But one needs less anyway, one finds suddenly. One does not need a closet-full, only a small suitcase-full. And what a relief it is! Less taking up and down of hems, less mending, and—best of all—less worry about what to wear. One finds one is shedding not only clothes—but vanity.

Next, shelter. One does not need the airtight shelter one has in winter in the North. Here I live in a bare sea-shell of a cottage. No heat, no telephone, no plumbing to speak of, no hot water, a two-burner oil stove, no gadgets to go wrong. No rugs. There were some, but I rolled them up the first day; it is easier to sweep the sand off a bare floor. But I find I don't bustle about with unnecessary sweeping and cleaning here. I am no longer aware of the dust. I have shed my Puritan conscience about absolute tidiness and cleanliness. Is it possible that, too, is a material burden? No curtains. I do not need them for privacy; the pines around my house are enough protection. I want the windows open all the time, and I don't want to worry about rain. I begin to shed my Martha-like anxiety about many things. Washable slipcovers, faded and old—I hardly see them; I don't worry about the impression they make on other people. I am shedding pride. As little furniture as possible; I shall not need much. I shall ask into my shell only those friends with whom I can be completely honest. I find I am shedding hypocrisy in human relationships. What a rest that will be! The most exhausting thing in life, I have discovered, is being insincere. That is why so much of social life is exhausting; one is wearing a mask. I have shed my mask.

I find I live quite happily without those things I think necessary in winter in the North. And as I write these words, I remember, with some shock at the disparity in our lives, a similar statement made by a friend of mine in France who spent three years in a German prison camp. Of course, he said, qualifying his remark, they did not get enough to eat, they were sometimes atrociously treated, they had little physical freedom. And yet, prison life taught him how little one can get along with, and what extraordinary spiritual freedom and peace such simplification can bring. I remember again, ironically, that today more of us in America than anywhere else in the world have the luxury of choice between simplicity and complication of life. And for the most part, we, who could choose simplicity, choose complication. War, prison, survival periods, enforce a form of simplicity on man. The monk and the nun choose it of their own free will. But if one accidentally finds it, as I have for a few days, one finds also the serenity it brings.

Is it not rather ugly, one may ask? One collects material possessions not only for security, comfort or vanity, but for beauty as well. Is your sea-shell house not ugly and bare? No, it is beautiful, my house. It is bare, of course, but the wind, the sun, the smell of the pines blow through its bareness. The unfinished beams in the roof are veiled by cobwebs. They are lovely, I think, gazing up at them with new eyes; they soften the hard lines of the rafters as grey hairs soften the lines on a middle-aged face. I no longer pull out grey hairs or sweep down cobwebs. As for the walls, it is true they looked forbidding at first. I felt cramped and enclosed by their blank faces. I wanted to knock holes in them, to give them another dimension with pictures or windows. So I dragged home from the beach grey arms of driftwood, worn satin-smooth by wind and sand. I gathered trailing green vines with floppy red-tipped leaves. I picked up the whitened skeletons of conchshells, their curious hollowed-out shapes faintly reminiscent of abstract sculpture. With these tacked to walls and propped up in corners, I am satisfied. I have a periscope out to the world. I have a window, a view, a point of flight from my sedentary base.

I am content. I sit down at my desk, a bare kitchen table with a blotter, a bottle of ink, a sand dollar to weight down one corner, a clam shell for a pen tray, the broken tip of a conch, pink-tinged, to finger, and a row of shells to set my thoughts spinning.

I love my sea-shell of a house. I wish I could live in it always. I wish I could transport it home. But I cannot. It will not hold a husband, five children and the necessities and trappings of daily life. I can only carry back my little channelled whelk. It will sit on my desk in Connecticut, to remind me of the ideal of a simplified life, to encourage me in the game I played on the beach. To ask how little, not how much, can I get along with. To say—is it necessary?—when I am tempted to add one more accumulation to my life, when I am pulled toward one more centrifugal activity.

Simplification of outward life is not enough. It is merely the outside. But I am starting with the outside. I am looking at the outside of a shell, the outside of my life—the shell. The complete answer is not to be found on the outside, in an outward mode of living. This is only a technique, a road to grace. The final answer, I know, is always inside. But the outside can give a clue, can help one to find the inside answer. One is free, like the hermit crab, to change one's shell.

Channelled whelk, I put you down again, but you have set my mind on a journey, up an inwardly winding spiral staircase of thought.

JOURNAL PROMPT:

Write about what sort of response Robert Bly, author of "A World of Half-Adults," might have to this reading. Why might Bly be supportive or not supportive of Lindbergh's sensibilities?

COLLABORATIVE EXERCISE:

Although Lindbergh's essay was first published in 1955, it continues to be very popular and often read. Why do you think this is so?

ESSAY ASSIGNMENT:

1. Read Lindbergh's entire book *Gift from the Sea,* and write an essay in which you either recommend this book as required reading for every adult because of its helpfulness in maintaining a focused, stress-free life, or argue against this book as required reading for every adult. Be sure to include a short but concise summary of the book, as well as the highlights of each chapter. Follow strategies for an argumentative essay.
2. In the preface of her book in which this essay is found, Lindbergh explains that she wrote *Gift from the Sea* to explore her own "individual balance of life, work and human relationships." How do you maintain a balance in your life (family and friend relationships, work and school demands, etc.) What do you do when you realize your life is out of balance?
3. Write an essay in which you discuss what lessons in life Lindbergh learns about living in the world as an adult. What answers does she have for how to retain a sense of self despite the adult responsibilities pulling us all directions?

English poet, dramatist, and actor **WILLIAM SHAKESPEARE** is frequently called the English national poet and considered by many to be the greatest dramatist of all time. This excerpt is from his comedy *As You Like It.* In this soliloquy, the character Jaques suggests that surviving the various stages of our lives is the ultimate human achievement.

WILLIAM SHAKESPEARE

THE SEVEN AGES OF MAN

All the world's a stage,
And all the men and women merely players:
They have their exits and their entrances;
And one man in his time plays many parts,
His acts being seven ages. At first the infant,
Mewling and puking in the nurse's arms.

And then the whining school-boy, with his satchel
And shining morning face, creeping like snail
Unwillingly to school. And then the lover,
Sighing like furnace, with a woeful ballad
Made to his mistress' eyebrow. Then a soldier,
Full of strange oaths and bearded like the pard,
Jealous in honor, sudden and quick in quarrel,
Seeking the bubble reputation
Even in the cannon's mouth. And then the justice,
In fair round belly with good capon lined,
With eyes severe and beard of formal cut,
Full of wise saws and modern instances;
And so he plays his part. The sixth age shifts
Into the lean and slipper'd pantaloon,
With spectacles on nose and pouch on side,
His youthful hose, well saved, a world too wide
For his shrunk shank; and his big manly voice,
Turning again toward childish treble, pipes
And whistles in his sound. Last scene of all,
That ends this strange eventful history,
Is second childishness and mere oblivion,
Sans teeth, sans eyes, sans taste, sans everything.

JOURNAL PROMPT:

This excerpt from Shakespeare's play *As You Like It* suggests that the speaker views life as a series of stages. Do you think the speaker is accurate in his descriptions? Why or why not?

COLLABORATIVE EXERCISE:

Shakespeare gives equal attention to each of his seven stages. Working in small groups, imagine that each of you must take on the task of revising this poem. Would you place more importance on some ages over others? Why? Create a list of suggestions to consider. Provide specific reasons for each suggestion. If no one in the group feels the need for revision, provide reasons why each of you is satisfied with how Shakespeare presented these seven stages.

ESSAY ASSIGNMENT:

1. Consider issues currently associated with aging in America (i.e., homelessness, health care, housing). How do these concerns compare and/or contrast with Shakespeare's seven-part division of the aging

process? Write an essay in which you compare current issues of aging with Shakespeare's thoughts on aging.

2. Analyze the tone implied in this speech, line by line. Consider word choice, line breaks, imagery, and use of punctuation.

Poet and writer **JUDITH ORTIZ COFER** was born in Puerto Rico. She teaches literature and writing at the University of Georgia in Athens. Her works include *The Latin Deli: Prose and Poetry* and many other poems, stories, and novels. Her story "*Nada*" won the O. Henry Short Story Prize.

JUDITH ORTIZ COFER

ADVANCED BIOLOGY

As I lay out clothes for the trip to Miami to do a reading from my recently published novel, then on to Puerto Rico to see my mother, I take a close look at my travel wardrobe—the tailored skirts in basic colors easily coordinated with my silk blouses—I have to smile to myself remembering what my mother had said about my conservative outfits when I visited her the last time—that I looked like the Jehovah's Witnesses who went from door to door in her pueblo trying to sell tickets to heaven to the die-hard Catholics. I would scare people she said. They would bolt their doors if they saw me approaching with my briefcase. As for her, she dresses in tropical colors—a red skirt and parakeet-yellow blouse look good on her tan skin, and she still has a good enough figure that she can wear a tight, black cocktail dress to go dancing at her favorite club, *El Palacio,* on Saturday nights. And, she emphasizes, still make it to the 10 o'clock mass on Sunday. Catholics can have fun and still be saved, she has often pointed out to me, but only if you pay your respects to God and all His Court with the necessary rituals. She has never accepted my gradual slipping out of the faith in which I was so strictly brought up.

As I pack my clothes into the suitcase, I recall our early days in Paterson, New Jersey, where we lived for most of my adolescence while my father was alive and stationed in Brooklyn Yard in New York. At that time, my mother's views on everything from clothing to (the for bidden subject) sex were ruled by the religious fervor that she had developed as a shield against the cold foreign city. These days we have traded places in a couple of areas since she has "gone home" after my father's death, and "gone native." I chose to attend college in the United States and make a living as an English teacher and, lately, on the lecture circuit as a novelist and poet. But, though our lives are on the surface radically different, my mother and I have affected each other reciprocally over the past twenty years; she has managed to liberate herself from the rituals, mores, and traditions that "cramp" her style, while retaining her femininity and "Puertoricanness," while I struggle daily to consolidate my opposing cultural identities. In my adolescence, divided into my New Jersey years and my Georgia years, I received an education in the art of cultural compromise.

In Paterson in the 1960s I attended a public school in our neighborhood. Still predominantly white and Jewish, it was rated very well academically in a city where the educational system was in chaos, deteriorating rapidly as the best teachers moved on to suburban schools following the black and Puerto Rican migration into, and the white exodus from, the city proper.

The Jewish community had too much at stake to make a fast retreat; many of the small businesses and apartment buildings in the city's core were owned by Jewish families of the World War II generation. They had seen worse things happen than the influx of black and brown people that was scaring away the Italians and the Irish. But they too would gradually move their families out of the best apartments in their buildings and into houses in East Paterson, Fairlawn, and other places with *lawns*. It was how I saw the world then; either you lived without your square of grass or you bought a house to go with it. But for most of my adolescence, I lived among the Jewish people of Paterson. We rented an apartment owned by the Milsteins, proprietors also of the deli on the bottom floor. I went to school with their children. My father took his business to the Jewish establishments, perhaps because these men symbolized "dignified survival" to him. He was obsessed with privacy, and could not stand the personal turns conversations almost always took when two or more Puerto Ricans met casually over a store counter. The Jewish men talked too, but they concentrated on externals. They asked my father about his job, politics, his opinion on Vietnam, Lyndon Johnson. And my father, in his quiet voice, answered their questions knowledgeably. Sometimes before we entered a store, the cleaners, or a shoe-repair shop, he would tell me to look for the blue-inked numbers on the owner's left forearm.[1] I would stare at these numbers, now usually faded enough to look like veins in the wrong place. I would try to make them out. They were a telegram from the past, I later decided, informing the future of the deaths of millions. My father discussed the Holocaust with me in the same hushed tones my mother used to talk about God's Mysterious Ways. I could not reconcile both in my mind. This conflict eventually led to my first serious clash with my mother over irreconcilable differences between the "real world" and religious doctrine.

It had to do with the Virgin Birth.

---

[1] Jews held in German concentration camps during World War II were tattooed on their forearms with identity numbers.—EDS.

And it had to do with my best friend and study partner, Ira Nathan, the acknowledged scientific genius at school. In junior high school it was almost a requirement to be "in love" with an older boy. I was an eighth grader and Ira was in the ninth grade that year and preparing to be sent away to some prep school in New England. I chose him as my boyfriend (in the eyes of my classmates, if a girl spent time with a boy that meant they were "going together") because I needed tutoring in biology—one of his best subjects. I ended up having a crush on him after our first Saturday morning meeting at the library. Ira was my first exposure to the wonders of an analytical mind.

The problem was the subject. Biology is a dangerous topic for young teenagers who are themselves walking laboratories, experimenting with interesting combinations of chemicals every time they make a choice. In my basic biology class, we were looking at single-cell organisms under the microscope, and watching them reproduce in slow-motion films in a darkened classroom. Though the process was as unexciting as watching a little kid blow bubbles, we were aroused by the concept itself. Ira's advanced class was dissecting fetal pigs. He brought me a photograph of his project, inner organs labeled neatly on the paper the picture had been glued to. My eyes refused to budge from the line drawn from "genitals" to a part of the pig it pertained to. I felt a wave of heat rising from my chest to my scalp. Ira must have seen my discomfort, though I tried to keep my face behind the black curtain of my hair, but as the boy-scientist, he was relentless. He actually traced the line from label to pig with his pencil.

"All mammals reproduce sexually," he said in a teacherly monotone.

The librarian, far off on the other side of the room, looked up at us and frowned. Logically, it was not possible that she could have heard Ira's pronouncement, but I was convinced that the mention of sex enhanced the hearing capabilities of parents, teachers and librarians by one hundred percent. I blushed more intensely, and peeked through my hair at Ira.

He was holding the eraser of his pencil on the pig's blurry sexual parts and smiling at me. His features were distinctly Eastern European. I had recently seen the young singer Barbra Streisand on the Red Skelton show and had been amazed at how much similarity there was in their appearances. She could have been his sister. I was particularly attracted to the wide mouth and strong nose. No one that I knew in school thought that Ira was attractive, but his brains had long ago overshadowed his looks as his most impressive attribute. Like Ira, I was also a straight A student and also considered odd because I was one of the few Puerto Ricans on the honor roll. So it didn't surprise anyone that Ira and I had drifted toward each other. Though I could not have articulated it then, Ira was seducing me with his No. 2 pencil and the laboratory photograph of his fetal pig. The following Saturday, Ira brought in his advanced biology book and showed me the transparencies of the human anatomy in full color that I was not meant to see for a couple more years. I was shocked. The cosmic jump between paramecium and the human body was almost too much for me to take in. These were the first grown people I had ever seen naked and they revealed too much.

"Human sexual reproduction can only take place when the male's sperm is introduced into the female womb and fertilization of the egg takes place," Ira stated flatly.

The book was open to the page labeled "The Human Reproductive System." Feeling that my maturity was being tested, as well as my intelligence, I found my voice long enough to contradict Ira.

"There has been one exception to this, Ira." I was feeling a little smug about knowing something that Ira obviously did not.

"Judith, there are no exceptions in biology, only mutations, and adaptations through evolution." He was smiling in a superior way.

"The Virgin Mary had a baby without . . ." I couldn't say *having sex* in the same breath as the name of the Mother of God. I was totally unprepared for the explosion of laughter that followed my timid statement. Ira had crumped in his chair and was laughing so hard that his thin shoulders shook. I could hear the librarian approaching. Feeling humiliated, I started to put my books together. Ira grabbed my arm.

"Wait, don't go," he was still giggling uncontrollably, "I'm sorry. Let's talk a little more. Wait, give me a chance to explain."

Reluctantly, I sat down again mainly because the librarian was already at our table, hands on hips, whispering angrily: "If you *children* cannot behave in this *study area,* I will have to ask you to leave." Ira and I both apologized, though she gave him a nasty look because his mouth was still stretched from ear to ear in a hysterical grin.

"Listen, listen. I'm sorry that I laughed like that. I know you're Catholic and you believe in the Virgin Birth (he bit his lower lip trying to regain his composure), but it's just not biologically possible to have a baby without . . . (he struggled for control) . . . losing your virginity."

I sank down on my hard chair. "Virginity." He had said another of the forbidden words. I glanced back at the librarian who was keeping her eye on us. I was both offended and excited by Ira's blasphemy. How could he deny a doctrine that people had believed in for 2,000 years? It was part of my prayers every night. My mother talked about *La Virgen* as if she were our most important relative.

Recovering from his fit of laughter, Ira kept his hand discreetly on my elbow as he explained in the seductive language of the scientific laboratory how babies were made, and how it was impossible to violate certain natural laws.

"Unless God will it," I argued feebly.

"There is no God," said Ira, and the last shred of my innocence fell away as I listened to his arguments backed up by irrefutable scientific evidence.

Our meetings continued all that year, becoming more exciting with every chapter in his biology book. My grades improved dramatically since one-celled organisms were no mystery to a student of advanced biology. Ira's warm, moist hand often brushed against mine under the table at the library, and walking home one bitter cold day, he asked me if I would wear his Beta Club pin. I nodded and when we stepped inside the hallway of my building where he removed his thick mittens which his mother had knitted, he pinned the blue enamel B to my collar. And to the hissing of the steam heaters, I received a serious kiss from Ira. We separated abruptly when we heard Mrs. Milstein's door open.

"Hello, Ira."

"Hello, Mrs. Milstein."

"And how is your mother? I haven't seen Fritzie all week. She's not sick, is she?"

"She's had a mild cold, Mrs. Milstein. But she is steadily improving." Ira's diction became extremely precise and formal when he was in the presence of adults. As an only child and a prodigy, he had to live up to very high standards.

"I'll call her today," Mrs. Milstein said, finally looking over at me. Her eyes fixed on the collar of my blouse which was, I later saw in our hall mirror, sticking straight up with Ira's pin attached crookedly to the edge.

"Good-bye, Mrs. Milstein."

"Nice to see you, Ira."

Ira waved awkwardly to me as he left. Mrs. Milstein stood in the humid hallway of her building watching me run up the stairs.

Our "romance" lasted only a week; long enough for Mrs. Milstein to call Ira's mother, and for Mrs. Nathan to call my mother. I was subjected to a lecture on moral behavior by my mother, who, carried away by her anger and embarrassed that I had been seen kissing a boy (understood: a boy who was not even Catholic), had begun a chain of metaphors for the loss of virtue that was on the verge of the tragi/comical:

"A *perdida,* a cheap item," she said trembling before me as I sat on the edge of my bed, facing her accusations, "a girl begins to look like one when she allows herself to be *handled* by men."

"Mother . . ." I wanted her to lower her voice so that my father, sitting at the kitchen table reading, would not hear. I had already promised her that I would confess my sin that Saturday and take communion with a sparkling clean soul. I had not been successful at keeping the sarcasm out of my voice. Her fury was fueled by her own bitter litany.

"A dirty joke, a burden to her family . . ." She was rolling with her Spanish now; soon the Holy Mother would enter into the picture for good measure. "It's not as if I had not taught you better. Don't you know that those people do not have the example of the Holy Virgin Mary and her Son to follow and that is why they do things for the wrong reasons. Mrs. Nathan said she did not want her son messing around with you—not because of the wrongness of it—but because it would interfere with his studies!" She was yelling now. "She's afraid that he will (she crossed herself at the horror of the thought) make you pregnant!"

"We could say an angel came down and put a baby in my stomach, Mother." She had succeeded in dragging me into her field of hysteria. She grabbed my arm and pulled me to my feet.

"I do not want you associating any more than necessary with people who do not have God, do you hear me?"

"They have a god!" I was screaming now too, trying to get away from her suffocating grasp: "They have an intelligent god who doesn't ask you to believe that a woman can get pregnant without having sex!" That's when she slapped me. She looked horrified at what she had instinctively done.

"Nazi," I hissed, out of control by then too, "I bet you'd like to send Ira and his family to a concentration camp!" At that time I thought that was the harshest thing I could have said to anyone. I was certain that I had sentenced my soul to eternal damnation the minute the words came out of my mouth; but my cheek was burning from the slap and I wanted to hurt her. Father walked into my room at that moment looking shocked at the sight of the two of us entangled in mortal combat.

"Please, please," his voice sounded agonized. I ran to him and he held me in his arms while I cried my heart out on his starched white shirt. My mother, also weeping quietly, tried to walk past us, but he bulled her into the circle. After a few moments, she put her trembling hand on my head.

"We are a family," my father said, "there is only the three of us against the world. Please, please . . ." But he did not follow the "please" with any suggestions as to what we could do to make things right in a world that was as confusing to my mother as it was to me.

I finished the eighth grade in Paterson, but Ira and I never got together to study again. I sent his Beta Club pin back to him via a mutual friend. Once in a while I saw him in the hall or the playground. But he seemed to be in the clouds, where he belonged. In the fall, I was enrolled at St. Joseph's Catholic High School where everyone believed in the Virgin Birth, and I never had to take a test on the human reproductive system. It was a chapter that was not emphasized.

In 1968, the year Paterson, like many U.S. cities, exploded in racial violence, my father moved us to Augusta, Georgia, where two of his brothers had retired from the army at Fort Gordon. They had convinced him that it was a healthier place to rear teenagers. For me it was a shock to the senses, like moving from one planet to another: where Paterson had concrete to walk on and gray skies, bitter winters, and a smorgasbord of an ethnic population, Georgia was red like Mars, and Augusta was green—exploding in colors in more gardens of azaleas and dogwood and magnolia trees—more vegetation than I imagined was possible anywhere not tropical like Puerto Rico. People seemed to come in two basic colors: black and blond. And I could barely understand my teachers when they talked in a slowed-down version of English like one of those old 78-speed recordings played at 33. But I was placed in all advanced classes and one of them was biology. This is where I got to see my first real fetal pig which my assigned lab partner had chosen. She picked it up gingerly by the ends of the plastic bag in which it was stored: "Ain't he cute?" she asked. I nodded, nearly fainting from the overwhelming combination of the smell of formaldehyde and my sudden flashback to my brief but intense romance with Ira Nathan.

"What you want to call him?" My partner unwrapped our specimen on the table, and I surprised myself by my instant recall of Ira's chart. I knew all the parts. In my mind's eye I saw the pencil lines, the labeled photograph. I had had an excellent teacher.

"Let's call him Ira."

"That's a funny name, but OK." My lab partner, a smart girl destined to become my mentor in things Southern, then gave me a conspiratorial wink and pulled out a little perfume atomizer from her purse. She sprayed Ira from snout to tail with it. I noticed this operation was taking place at other tables too. The teacher had conveniently left the room a few minutes before. I was once again stunned—almost literally knocked out by a fist of smell: "What is it?"

"*Intimate,*" my advanced biology partner replied smiling.

And by the time our instructor came back to the room, we were ready to delve into this mystery of muscle and bone; eager to discover the secrets that lie just beyond fear a little past loathing; of acknowledging the corruptibility of the flesh, and our own fascination with the subject.

As I finish packing, the telephone rings and it's my mother. She is reminding me to be ready to visit relatives, to go to a dance with her, and, of course, to attend a couple of the services at the church. It is the feast of the Black Virgin, revered patron saint of our home town in Puerto Rico. I agree to everything, and find myself anticipating the eclectic itinerary. Why not allow Evolution and Eve, Biology and the Virgin Birth? Why not take a vacation from logic? I will not be away for too long, I will not let myself be tempted to remain in the sealed garden of blind faith; I'll stay just long enough to rest myself from the exhausting enterprise of leading the examined life.

JOURNAL PROMPT:

Write about the role, if any, religion played in your early years.

COLLABORATIVE EXERCISE:

Irony is a literary device that adds richness to a story, revealing the complexities of our lives. The author's mother returns to her native land—Puerto Rico—after the death of her husband. Here she dons the colorful costumes of the island and dances until dawn. What is ironic about the mother's behavior? Can you find other examples of irony in this essay?

ESSAY ASSIGNMENT:

1. Write an essay about a time when a belief of yours contrasted starkly with your family's way of looking at the world. What happened? Did the issue finally resolve itself, or is the matter something that still holds the power to erupt into family squabbles?
2. Compare Cofer and her mother. In what ways are they alike? Different? Explain your assertions, using specific incidents from the essay.

3. Cofer relates the story of her first romance with a boy whose background differed significantly from hers. What are the positive and negative aspects of cross-cultural, cross-racial, and/or cross-religious relationships?

This excerpt is from NATHAN MCCALL'S autobiography, *Makes Me Wanna Holler: A Young Black Man in America.* In this painful yet hopeful memoir, McCall, street hood turned *Washington Post* reporter, describes the passages and experiences of his life growing up an African American male in the latter half of the twentieth century.

NATHAN MCCALL

MAKES ME WANNA HOLLER

There were moments in that jail when the confinement and heat nearly drove me mad. At those times, I desperately needed to take my thoughts beyond the concrete and steel. When I felt restless tension rising, I'd try anything to calm it. I'd slap-box with other inmates until I got exhausted, or play chess until my mind shut down. When all else failed. I'd pace the cellblock perimeter like a caged lion. Sometimes, other inmates fighting the temptation to give in to madness joined me, and we'd pace together, round and round, and talk for hours about anything that got our minds off our misery.

I eventually found a better way to relieve the boredom. I noticed that some inmates broke the monotony by volunteering for certain jobs in the jail. Some mopped the halls, and others worked in the dispensary or the kitchen. When the inmate librarian was released from jail, I asked for and was given his job. I began distributing books on the sixth floor as part of a service provided by the Norfolk Public Library. A couple of times a week, I pushed a cart to each cellblock and let inmates choose books and place orders for literature not on the cart. I enjoyed the library work. It gave me a chance to get out into the halls and walk around, and to stick my face to the screens on the floor windows and inhale fresh air.

Beyond the short stories I'd read in high school, I hadn't done much reading. Naturally, while working for the library, I leafed through more books than I normally would have. One day, shortly after starting the job, I picked up a book featuring a black man's picture on the cover. It was titled *Native Son,* and the author was Richard Wright.[1] I leafed through a few pages in the front of the

[1] Wright's classic protest novel was published in 1940.

book, and couldn't put it down. The story was about a confused, angry young black man named Bigger Thomas, whose racial fears lead him to accidentally suffocate a white woman. In doing so, he delivers himself into the hands of the very people he despises and fears.

I identified strongly with Bigger and the book's narrative. He was twenty, the same age as me. He felt the things I felt, and, like me, he wound up in prison. The book's portrait of Bigger captured all those conflicting feelings—restless anger, hopelessness, a tough facade among blacks and a deep-seated fear of whites—that I'd sensed in myself but was unable to express. Often, during my teenage years, I'd felt like Bigger—headed down a road toward a destruction I couldn't ward off, beaten by forces so large and amorphous that I had no idea how to fight back. I was surprised that somebody had written a book that so closely reflected my experiences and feelings.

I read that book every day, and continued reading by the dim light of the hall lamps at night, while everyone slept. On that early morning when I finished reading *Native Son,* which ends with Bigger waiting to go to the electric chair, I broke down and sobbed like a baby. There is one passage that so closely described how I felt that it stunned me. It is a passage where a lawyer is talking to Bigger, who has given up hope and is waiting to die:

> You're trying to believe in yourself. And every time you try to find a way to live, your own mind stands in the way. You know why that is? It's because others have said you were bad and they made you live in bad conditions. When a man hears that over and over and looks about him and sees that life is bad, he begins to doubt his own mind. His feelings drag him forward and his mind, full of what others say about him, tells him to go back. The job in getting people to fight and have faith is in making them believe in what life has made them feel, making them feel that their feelings are as good as others'.

After reading that, I sat up in my bunk, buried my face in my hands, and wept uncontrollably. I cried so much that I felt relieved. It was like I had been carrying those feelings and holding in my pain for years, keeping it pushed into the back of my mind somewhere.

I was unaccustomed to dealing with such deep feelings. Occasionally, I'd opened up to Liz,[2] but not a lot. I was messed up inside, empty and afraid, just like Bigger. *Native Son* confirmed for me that my fears *weren't* imagined and that there were rational reasons why I'd been hurting inside.

I developed through my encounter with Richard Wright a fascination with the power of words. It blew my mind to think that somebody could take words that described exactly how I felt and put them together in a story like that. Most of the books I'd been given in school were about white folks' experiences and feelings. I spent all that time learning about damned white folks, like my

---

[2] Liz: McCall's ex-fiancée and the mother of his son.

reality didn't exist and wasn't valid to the rest of the world. In school, the only time we'd really focused on the lives of black people was during Black History Week, which they set aside for us to learn the same old tired stories about Booker T. Washington and a few other noteworthy, dead black folks I couldn't relate to. But in *Native Son* I found a book written about a plain, everyday brother like myself. That turned me on in a big way and inspired me to look for more books like that.

Before long, I was reading every chance I got, trying to more fully understand why my life and the lives of friends had been so contained and predictable, and why prison—literally—had become a rite of passage for so many of us. I found books that took me places I'd never dreamed I could travel to and exposed me to a range of realities that seemed as vast as the universe itself.

Once, after reading a book of poems by Gwendolyn Brooks,[3] I wrote to her, not really expecting to receive a reply. She wrote me back and sent me an inspirational paperback of hers titled *Aloneness*. I was thrilled that a well-known black writer like her had taken the time to respond to me.

I was most attracted to black classics, such as Malcolm X's autobiography. Malcolm's tale helped me understand the devastating effects of self-hatred and introduced me to a universal principle: that if you change your self-perception, you can change your behavior. I concluded that if Malcolm X, who had also gone to prison, could pull his life out of the toilet, then maybe I could, too.

Up to that point, I'd often wanted to think of myself as a baad nigger, and as a result, I'd tried to act like one. After reading about Malcolm X, I worked to get rid of that notion and replace it with a positive image of what I wanted to become. I walked around silently repeating to myself, "You are an intelligent-thinking human being; you are an intelligent-thinking human being . . . ," hoping that it would sink in and help me begin to change the way I viewed myself.

Malcolm X made his conversion through Islam. I'd seen Muslims selling newspapers and bean pies on the streets, but I didn't know anything about their religion. I was drawn to Christianity, mostly because it was familiar. I hadn't spent much time in church. It seemed that all they did in churches I'd been to was learn how to justify suffering at the hands of white folks. But now there were Christian ministers active at the jail, and I became interested. They came around about once a week and talked to inmates through the bars, prayed with them and read Scripture. I started talking with them about God and about life in general.

It wasn't hard to accept the possibility that there was a higher force watching over me. When I looked back at my life, I concluded that there had been far too many close calls—times when I could have offed somebody or gotten killed myself—for me to believe I had survived solely on luck. I wondered, *Why didn't*

---

[3] Pulitzer Prize–winning poet and novelist Gwendolyn Brooks (1917–2000) published *Aloneness* in 1971.

that bullet strike Plaz in the heart when I shot him? Why didn't I pull the trigger on that McDonald's manager when he tried to get away? And why wasn't I on the corner the night my stick partners were shot? Unable to come up with rational answers to those questions, I reasoned that God must have been pulling for me.

My interest in spiritual things also came from a need to reach out at my most powerless point and tap into a higher power, something beyond me and, at the same time, within me. I longed for a sense of wholeness that I had never known but sensed I was entitled to. I set out to learn more about my spiritual self, and I began exploring the Bible with other inmates who held Bible studies some nights in the cellblock.

At some point, I also got a library copy of the book—*As a Man Thinketh*[4]—that Reverend Ellis had given me in college. I immediately understood what he had been trying to get across: that thinking should be an *active* process that, when cultivated, can change a person's behavior, circumstances, and, ultimately, his fate.

When I first started reading, studying, and reflecting on the information I got from books, I had no idea where it all might lead. Really, it didn't matter. I was hungry for change and so excited by the sense of awakening I glimpsed on the horizon that the only thing that mattered was that I had made a start. I often recited the Scripture that Reverend Ellis had given me to read before I was sentenced: "Everything works together for the good of those that love God, for those who are called according to His purpose."[5] *If that's true,* I thought, *maybe I can get something positive out of this time in prison.* It sure didn't seem like it. But it made me feel better just thinking it might be possible.

In a way, Jim[6] was also similar to Mo Battle, my mentor in the Norfolk jail. When he saw young guys with potential come out of the Receiving Unit, he'd take the time to school them about anything he could. He'd pull them aside and tell them the dos and don'ts of prison life so the wolves couldn't get to them. The wolves resented Jim because of that, but none made a move to do anything about it.

It amazed me to see how much the so-called tough cats respected Jim. Whenever he was around, they cursed less and toned down their macho posturing, as if he were an authority figure or a revered elder. Initially, that kind of deference, which bordered on fear, puzzled me, because Jim didn't carry himself like a knockout artist or anything. Brown-skinned and medium-built, he

---

[4] *As a Man Thinketh* was written by James Allen (1864–1912).

[5] "Everything . . . purpose": Romans 8:28.

[6] Jim was an inmate at Southampton prison, to which McCall was transferred after serving time in Norfolk prison.

always dressed neat and spoke softly. He was clean-shaven, and he constantly carried books and newspapers tucked under his arms.

Eventually, I figured out that the characteristics that made him so widely respected had little to do with how he looked; instead, it was his manly demeanor. Ever since I could recall, I and everybody else I knew had associated manhood with physical dominance and conquest of someone else. Watching Jim, I realized we'd gone about it all wrong. Jim didn't have to make a rep for himself as a thumper. He could whip a man with his sharp mind and choice words far more thoroughly than with his fists. The wolves feared his kind of ass-whipping much more than a physical beating, so they kept their distance.

I decided that this was the kind of respect I wanted to command, and I noticed other guys who without being fully aware wanted to be like Jim, too. They strutted on the yard, looking super-macho, like killers, but acted differently in private. In those moments when they weren't profiling with their buddies, some of my tough-acting homies would stop by my perch on the yard or in my cell and ask, "What you reading?" I sensed they wanted to improve themselves but didn't want their other homies to see them, because self-improvement wasn't a macho thing. Pearly Blue was one of them. He sometimes tried to draw me into deep private discussions about God and reality while sticking to the tough street vernacular that helped him maintain his macho facade.

As I learned more about misguided ideas about manhood, I experimented with some of those macho dudes: Whenever I passed them, I looked into their eyes to see what was there. A few had that cold-blooded, killer look about them, but in the eyes of most of them I saw something I hadn't noticed before: fear.

Even in Big Earl. Big Earl was one of the brawniest, most outwardly fearless cats in the place. He was tall and jet-black, his muscles rippled through his T-shirt, and his thighs were so massive that all his pants fit too tight. Big Earl, who was thirtyish, was from a small, off-brand town in rural Virginia, but he didn't need homies to back him up. He walked around the yard, talking loud and intimidating other inmates like he owned the place.

One day, while walking down the long sidewalk on my way to the cafeteria, I spotted Big Earl pimping toward me. (He never said anything to me, Jim, or some of the others who were part of our progressive group.) As he approached, I fixed my eyes on his and kept them locked there. When we got closer. I kept my eyes fastened to his, not in a hostile gaze, but in an expression of serene self-assurance. Initially, he tried to meet my gaze. Then he turned his eyes away and looked toward the ground. I smiled to myself. I would have never been able to back down Big Earl in a rumble, but I had certainly backed him down with my mind.

Several times after that brief, silent encounter, I caught Big Earl watching me curiously. He never said anything. He just watched and turned away whenever he realized I'd caught him staring. I sensed he knew I'd figured that he wasn't as confident of his manhood as he pretended to be, and he felt naked, exposed.

I practiced the piercing eye contact with other guys like Earl and realized that few of the seriously baad cats could meet my gaze. That helped me see my homies and the other toughs at Southampton as they were (and as I had been): streetwise, pseudo baad-asses who were really frightened boys, bluffing, trying to mask their fear of the world behind muscular frames.

On the day I went before the parole board, I was so nervous I was nearly paralyzed. I was scared that I'd get in there, get asked a question, and choke. I was scared that when it was time for me to speak, all my suffering would come to the surface and all my emotions would bum-rush my throat, and nothing would come out. So I did deep-breathing exercises and prayed for the best.

I waited in a hallway with about six other dudes who were going before the board that day. All of us looked alike. We looked like choirboys sitting out there. We were spit-shined and scrubbed and lotioned down to the max. We all had our hair cut short. We had our shirts buttoned to the very top, and we were so quiet you could hear the roaches walking across the shiny floor.

But appearances didn't seem to sway the board. When dudes came out after meeting with the board, they were red-eyed and withdrawn. I asked one guy how he thought things had gone for him. He looked at me, shook his head slowly, and said, "It looks bad for the home team."

When my name was called, I went in and took a seat before the board members—several white men and a black woman—who sat behind a long table. It was a stern-faced, tight-butt bunch. No-nonsense all the way. They asked a few questions about my crime, my family, that sort of thing. Then, after several other minor questions, came the biggie: "So, Mr. McCall, what do you plan to do to better yourself if you get out, and what arrangements have you made to carry out those plans?"

If a cat hasn't given serious consideration to his future, really thought it out, that's the question that cold-cocks him. That's the one that renews his lease for another year. If he's wasted his time and neglected to improve himself, he can't answer that question convincingly. He's down for the count. TKO.[7] With the parole board, you've got to come strong or not at all, because they've heard all the bullshit they care to hear, and they can smell it a mile away.

I knew all that going in. I knew I couldn't go in there half-stepping. I was prepared. My future? Shit, I had thought about it, prayed about it, and dreamed about it the entire time I was down. I had thought a helluva lot about my future—enough to know that I might not *have* a future if I didn't get sprung that first time up. When they hit me with the question, they hit the right person that time, because I was ready.

I rapped. I rapped *hard.* I rapped harder than I'd ever rapped in my life. I took all the skills I'd picked up rapping with those penitentiary philosophers

---

[7] TKO: technical knockout, a boxing term.

out on the yard and threw the whole handful at the parole board. I told them all I'd done to improve myself in the nearly three years that I'd been locked up, and shared my plans to go home to my family and to enroll at Norfolk State. I told them that robbing that hamburger joint was the stupidest thing I could have done, and that I'd spent a lot of time thinking about that and other mistakes I'd made in my life. The bottom line was, I came straight from the heart. I came from so deep within the heart that I surprised myself. But I meant every word I said. I was changed. I knew it, and I wanted to make sure they knew it.

I'll bet those white folks on that parole board were glad when I finally finished talking. I'll bet they thought I'd never shut up. I'll bet that when I finished and left that room, they burst out laughing and said, "Damn! We need to hurry up and let this nigger out. This dude wants *badly* to get out of here."

But they didn't come off like that. They were very professional. When I finished talking, one of the parole board members said, "Thank you, Mr. McCall. The board will take into consideration all that you have said. You will be notified within the next month of our decision." They sent me on my way without a hint of the verdict.

Waiting for an answer was like waiting to be sentenced all over again. Those few weeks were as hard on me as the entire three years had been. I nagged my institutional counselor constantly to see if a response had come. He got mad at me for nagging him, and I got mad at him for getting mad at me. If he had been an inmate and not a counselor, we would have come to blows, because I was uptight as hell and I already had a full head of steam.

When my letter from the board finally arrived, I took it to my bunk and sat down alone. I looked at the letter in the sealed envelope a long time before even attempting to open it. I needed a drink, but since there were no bars open in the penitentiary, I had to face it straight. I gave myself a long talking-to before opening it: *Keep cool. You've done the best you could do. You've given it your best shot and programmed hard. Stay strong, no matter what happens.*

Then I opened the letter and I could hardly believe it. For a long while, I just sat there, staring at the words, reading the letter over and over, making sure I'd gotten it right. I thought, *I made parole. I made it. I'm getting out. They're gonna let me go. I can go home. Soon. I made it. I can't believe it. I made it. I made parole!*

I remember clearly that snowy February day in 1978 when I was released from the joint. My homies gathered on the sidewalk that morning and watched me leave. As I climbed into the car and my mother drove off, I cast a long, hard look at the prison, and tears began streaming uncontrollably down my face. I felt a strange mixture of pain and pride. I was mostly proud that I had survived, and I told myself, then and there, *I can do ANYTHING.*

Although it had been the most tragic event in my life, prison—with all its sickness and suffering—had also been my most instructional challenge. It forced me to go deep, real deep, within and tap a well I didn't even know I had. Through that painful trip, I'd found meaning. No longer was life a thing of bewilderment. No longer did I feel like a cosmic freak, a black intruder in a world not created for me and my people. No longer were my angry feelings about the vast white world simply vague, invalid impulses dangling on the edge of my mind. I knew the reasons for those feelings now. I understood them better, and, most important, I could express them precisely as they arose. I knew that there was purpose and design in creation and that my life was somehow part of that grand scheme. I had just as much right to be alive and happy as anybody else, and I wasn't going to let anybody, especially not white folks, make me feel otherwise.

JOURNAL PROMPT:

What do you think the author means when he says that "prison . . . had become a rite of passage"?

COLLABORATIVE EXERCISE:

Imagine that you are like Nathan McCall, incarcerated for a crime. Working in small groups, devise a meaningful ritual to be performed to mark your release.

ESSAY ASSIGNMENT:

1. McCall includes a discussion of *Native Son,* a book that affected him greatly, both emotionally and spiritually. Write about something you have read, either recently or in your past, that seemed to speak to you. Perhaps it even changed your way of thinking or your attitude about a previously held belief. Write a short summary of the work, and explain how and why it made such an impact.
2. In the last paragraph, McCall shares with the reader that his experience in prison was the "most tragic event" in his life but also was the most "instructional challenge." Write about a tragic event that taught you something.

Some believe America's welfare system to be ill-conceived. Originally published in *The New York Times* magazine, this essay by ROSEMARY BRAY tells the tale of how the author got off welfare and went on to become a very successful, focused, independent woman. Bray is at work on a book titled *Unafraid of the Dark,* which centers on issues of African American identity and attitudes.

ROSEMARY L. BRAY

So How Did I Get Here?

Growing up on welfare was a story I had planned to tell a long time from now, when I had children of my own. My childhood on Aid to Families with Dependent Children (A.F.D.C.) was going to be one of those stories I would tell my kids about the bad old days, an urban legend equivalent to Abe Lincoln studying by firelight. But I know now I cannot wait, because in spite of a wealth of evidence about the true nature of welfare and poverty in America, the debate has turned ugly, vicious, and racist. The "welfare question" has become the race question and the woman question in disguise, and so far the answers bode well for no one.

In both blunt and coded terms, comfortable Americans more and more often bemoan the waste of their tax money on lazy black women with a love of copulation, a horror of birth control and a lack of interest in marriage. Were it not for the experiences of half my life, were I not black and female and of a certain age, perhaps I would be like so many people who blindly accept the lies and distortions, half-truths and wrongheaded notions about welfare. But for better or worse, I do know better. I know more than I want to know about being poor. I know that the welfare system is designed to be inadequate, to leave its constituents on the edge of survival. I know because I've been there.

And finally, I know that perhaps even more dependent on welfare than its recipients are the large number of Americans who would rather accept this patchwork of economic horrors than fully address the real needs of real people.

My mother came to Chicago in 1947 with a fourth-grade education, cut short by working in the Mississippi fields. She pressed shirts in a laundry for a while and later waited tables in a restaurant, where she met my father. Mercurial and independent, with a sixth-grade education, my Arkansas-born father worked at whatever came to hand. He owned a lunch wagon for a time and prepared food for hours in our kitchen on the nights before he took the wagon out. Sometimes he hauled junk and sold it in the open-air markets of Maxwell Street on Sunday mornings. Eight years after they met—seven years after they married—I was born. My father made her quit her job; her work, he told her, was taking care of me. By the time I was 4, I had a sister, a brother and another brother on the way. My parents, like most other American couples of the 1950s, had their own American dream—a husband who worked, a wife who stayed home, a family of smiling children. But as was true for so many African-American couples, their American dream was an illusion.

The house on the corner of Berkeley Avenue and 45th Street is long gone. The other houses still stand, but today the neighborhood is an emptier, bleaker place. When we moved there, it was a street of old limestones with beveled glass windows, all falling into vague disrepair. Home was a four-room apartment on the first floor, in what must have been the public rooms of a formerly grand house. The rent was $110 a month. All of us kids slept in the big front room. Because I was the oldest, I had a bed of my own, near a big plate-glass window.

My mother and father had been married for several years before she realized he was a gambler who would never stay away from the track. By the time we moved to Berkeley Avenue, Daddy was spending more time gambling, and bringing home less and less money and more and more anger. Mama's simplest requests were met with rage. They fought once for hours when she asked for money to buy a tube of lipstick. It didn't help that I always seemed to need a doctor. I had allergies and bronchitis so severe that I nearly died one Sunday after church when I was about 3.

It was around this time that my mother decided to sign up for A.F.D.C. She explained to the caseworker that Daddy wasn't home much, and when he was he didn't have any money. Daddy was furious; Mama was adamant. "There were times when we hardly had a loaf of bread in here," she told me years later. "It was close. I wasn't going to let you all go hungry."

Going on welfare closed a door between my parents that never reopened. She joined the ranks of unskilled women who were forced to turn to the state for the security their men could not provide. In the sterile relationship between herself and the State of Illinois, Mama found an autonomy denied her by my father. It was she who could decide, at last, some part of her own fate and ours. A.F.D.C. relegated marginally productive men like my father to the ranks of failed patriarchs who no longer controlled the destiny of their families. Like so many of his peers, he could no longer afford the luxury of a woman who did as she was told because her economic life depended on it. Daddy became one of the shadow men who walked out back doors as caseworkers came in through the front. Why did he acquiesce? For all his anger, for all his frightening brutality, he loved us, so much that he swallowed his pride and periodically ceased to exist so that we might survive.

In 1960, the year my mother went on public aid, the poverty threshold for a family of five in the United States was $3,560 and the monthly payment to a family of five from the State of Illinois was $182.56, a total of $2,190.72 a year. Once the $110 rent was paid, Mama was left with $72.56 a month to take care of all the other expenses. By any standard, we were poor. All our lives were proscribed by the narrow line between not quite and just enough.

What did it take to live?

It took the kindness of friends as well as strangers, the charity of churches, low expectations, deprivation and patience. I can't begin to count the hours spent in long lines, long waits, long walks in pursuit of basic things. A visit to a local clinic (one housing doctors, a dentist and pharmacy in an incredibly crowded series of rooms) invariably took the better part of a day. I never saw the same doctor twice.

It took, as well, a turning of our collective backs on the letter of a law that required reporting even a small and important miracle like a present of $5. All families have their secrets, but I remember the weight of an extra burden. In a world where caseworkers were empowered to probe into every nook and cranny of our lives, silence became defense. Even now, there are things I will not publicly discuss because I cannot shake the fear that we might be hounded by the state, eager to prosecute us for the crime of survival.

All my memories of our years on A.F.D.C. are seasoned with unease. It's painful to remember how much every penny counted, how even a gap of 25 cents could make a difference in any given week. Few people understand how precarious life is from welfare check to welfare check, how the word "extra" had no meaning. Late mail, a bureaucratic mix-up . . . and a carefully planned method of survival lies in tatters.

What made our lives work as well as they did was my mother's genius at making do—worn into her by a childhood of rural poverty—along with her vivid imagination. She worked at home endlessly, shopped ruthlessly, bargained, cajoled, charmed. Her food store of choice was the one that stocked pork and beans, creamed corn, sardines, Vienna sausages and potted meat all at 10 cents a can. Clothing was the stuff of rummage sales, trips to Goodwill and bargain basements, where thin cotton and polyester reigned supreme. Our shoes came from a discount store that sold two pairs for $5.

It was an uphill climb, but there was no time for reflection; we were too busy with our everyday lives. Yet I remember how much it pained me to know that Mama, who recruited a neighbor to help her teach me how to read when I was 3, found herself left behind by her eldest daughter, then by each of us in turn. Her biggest worry was that we would grow up uneducated, so Mama enrolled us in parochial school.

When one caseworker angrily questioned how she could afford to send four children to St. Ambrose School, my mother, who emphatically declared "My kids need an education," told her it was none of her business. (In fact, the school had a volume discount of sorts; the price of tuition dropped with each child you sent. I still don't know quite how she managed it.) She organized our lives around church and school, including Mass every morning at 7:45. My brother was an altar boy; I laid out the vestments each afternoon for the next day's Mass. She volunteered as a chaperone for every class trip, sat with us as we did homework she did not understand herself. She and my father reminded us again and again and again that every book, every test, every page of homework was in fact a ticket out and away from the life we lived.

My life on welfare ended on June 4, 1976—a month after my 21st birthday, two weeks after I graduated from Yale. My father, eaten up with cancer and rage, lived just long enough to know the oldest two of us had graduated from college and were on our own. Before the decade ended, all of us had left the welfare rolls. The eldest of my brothers worked at the post office, assumed support of my mother (who also went to work, as a companion to an elderly woman) and earned his master's degree at night. My sister married and got a job at a bank. My baby brother parked cars and found a wife. Mama's biggest job was done at last; the investment made in our lives by the State of Illinois had come to fruition. Five people on welfare for 18 years had become five working, taxpaying adults. Three of us went to college, two of us finished; one of us has an advanced degree, all of us can take care of ourselves.

Ours was a best-case phenomenon, based on the synergy of church and state, the government and the private sector and the thousand points of light that we called friends and neighbors. But there was something more: What fueled our dreams and fired our belief that our lives could change for the better was the promise of the civil rights movement and the war on poverty—for millions of African-Americans the defining events of the 1960s. Caught up in the heady atmosphere of imminent change, our world was filled not only with issues and ideas but with amazing images of black people engaged in the struggle for long-denied rights and freedoms. We knew other people lived differently than we did, we knew we didn't have much, but we didn't mind, because we knew it wouldn't be long. My mother borrowed a phrase I had read to her once from Dick Gregory's autobiography. Not poor, just broke. She would repeat it often, as often as she sang hymns in the kitchen. She loved to sing a spiritual Mahalia Jackson had made famous: "Move On Up a Little Higher." Like so many others, Mama was singing about earth as well as heaven.

These are the things I remember every time I read another article outlining America's welfare crisis. The rage I feel about the welfare debate comes from listening to a host of lies, distortions and exaggerations—and taking them personally.

I am no fool. I know of few women—on welfare or off—with my mother's grace and courage and stamina. I know not all women on welfare are cut from the same cloth. Some are lazy; some are ground down. Some are too young; many are without husbands. A few have made welfare fraud a lucrative career; a great many more have pushed the rules on outside income to their very limits.

I also know that none of these things justify our making welfare a test of character and worthiness, rather than an acknowledgment of need. Near-sainthood should not be a requirement for financial and medical assistance.

But all manner of sociologists and policy gurus continue to equate issues that simply aren't equivalent—welfare, race, rates of poverty, crime, marriage and childbirth—and to reach conclusions that serve to demonize the poor. More than one social arbiter would have us believe that we have all been mistaken for the last 30 years—that the efforts to relieve the most severe effects of poverty have not only failed but have served instead to increase and expand the ranks of the poor. In keeping women, children and men from starvation, we are told, we have also kept them from self-sufficiency. In our zeal to do good, we have undermined the work ethic, the family and thus, by association, the country itself.

So how did I get here?

JOURNAL PROMPT:

Do you know anyone on welfare, or have you been on welfare yourself? Write about what you have seen and heard from a friend's experience, or write about your own experiences.

COLLABORATIVE EXERCISE:

The welfare system in America was created for the purpose of offering help to those who needed it, not as "a test of character and worthiness." Working in small groups, discuss reasons why you think the attitude toward people on welfare is often so negative. How did these feelings and attitudes evolve?

ESSAY ASSIGNMENT:

1. Before you read this essay, what were your feelings about people living on welfare? What were these feelings based on (personal experience, observation, news reports, etc.)? After reading about Bray's experience, have your feelings changed at all? Explain.
2. Write an essay in which you explain why and how Bray's essay is or is not effective in presenting a positive view of the welfare system. Make a note of specific places in the essay that support your opinion about the success or failure of this essay.
3. Explore what the effects of going on welfare might have on a family—the role of the mother, the role of the father, or effects on marriage, self-esteem, living conditions, financial issues, etc.

Writer LOUISE ERDRICH was born in 1954 in Little Falls, Minnesota. Her work often centers around the Chippewa Indians in the northern Midwest. Erdrich grew up in Wahpeton, North Dakota, where her German father and Chippewa mother taught at a Bureau of Indian Affairs boarding school. She earned a B.A. from Dartmouth College and an M.A. from Johns Hopkins University. Although she also writes poetry, she is best known for her novels. Her first novel, *Love Medicine* (1984), began a tetralogy that includes *The Beet Queen* (1986), *Tracks* (1988), and *The Bingo Palace* (1994).

LOUISE ERDRICH

Z: THE MOVIE THAT CHANGED MY LIFE

Next to writing full-time, the best job I ever had combined two passions—popcorn and narrative. At fourteen, I was hired as a concessioner at the Gilles

Theater in Wahpeton, North Dakota. Behind a counter of black marbleized glass, I sold Dots, Red Hot Tamales, Jujubes, Orange Crush, and, of course, hot buttered popcorn. My little stand was surrounded by art deco mirrors, and my post, next to the machine itself, was bathed in an aura of salt and butter. All of my sophomore year, I exuded a light nutty fragrance that turned, on my coats and dresses, to the stale odor of mouse nests. The best thing about the job was that, once I had wiped the counters, dismantled the machines, washed the stainless steel parts, totaled up the take and refilled the syrup canisters and wiped off the soft drink machine, I could watch the show, free.

I saw everything that came to Wahpeton in 1969—watched every movie seven times, in fact, since each one played a full week. I saw Zeffirelli's *Romeo and Juliet,* and did not weep. I sighed over Charlton Heston in *Planet of the Apes,* and ground my teeth at the irony of the ending shot. But the one that really got to me was Costa-Gavras's *Z*.

Nobody in Wahpeton walked into the Gilles knowing that the film was about the assassination in Greece of a leftist peace leader by a secret right-wing organization and the subsequent investigation that ended in a bloody coup. The ad in the paper said only "Love Thriller" and listed Yves Montand and Irene Papas as the stars.

"Dear Diary," I wrote the morning after I'd seen *Z* for the first time. "The hypocrites are exposed. He is alive! Just saw the best movie of my life. Must remember to dye my bra and underwear to match my cheerleading outfit."

I forgot to rinse out the extra color, so during the week that *Z* was playing, I had purple breasts. The school color of my schizophrenic adolescence. My parents strictly opposed my career as a wrestling cheerleader, on the grounds that it would change me into someone they wouldn't recognize. Now, they were right, though of course I had never let anyone know my secret.

I had changed in other ways, too. Until I was fourteen, my dad and I would go hunting on weekends or skating in the winter. Now I practiced screaming S-U-C-C-E-S-S and K-I-L-L for hours, and then, of course, had to run to work during the matinee. Not that I was utterly socialized. Over my cheerleading outfit I wore Dad's army jacket, and on my ankle, a bracelet made of twisted blasting-wire given to me by a guitar-playing Teen Corps volunteer, Kurt, who hailed from The Valley of the Jolly Green Giant, a real town in eastern Minnesota.

No, I was not yet completely subsumed into small-town femalehood. I knew there was more to life than the stag leap, or the flying T, but it wasn't until I saw *Z* that I learned language for what that "more" was.

After the third viewing, phrases began to whirl in my head. "The forces of greed and hatred cannot tolerate us"; "There are not enough hospitals, not enough doctors, yet one half of the budget goes to the military"; "Peace at all costs"; and, of course, the final words, "He is alive!" But there was more to it than the language. It was the first *real* movie I had ever seen—one with a cynical, unromantic, deflating ending.

At the fourth viewing of the movie, I had a terrible argument with Vincent, the Gilles's pale, sad ticket taker, who was also responsible for changing the wooden letters on the marquee. At the beginning of the week, he had been pleased. It was he who thought of the ad copy, "Love Thriller." By the middle of the run, he was unhappy, for he sided with the generals, just as he sided with our boss.

Vincent always wore a suit and stood erect. He was officious, a tiger with gatecrashers and tough with those who had misplaced their stubs while going to the bathroom. I, on the other hand, waved people in free when I was left in charge, and regarded our boss with absolute and burning hatred, for he was a piddling authority, a man who enjoyed setting meaningless tasks. I hated being made to rewash the butter dispenser. Vincent liked being scolded for not tearing the tickets exactly in half. Ours was an argument of more than foreign ideologies.

Vincent insisted that the boss was a fair man who made lots of money. I maintained that we were exploited. Vincent said the film was lies, while I insisted it was based on fact. Neither of us checked for the truth in the library. Neither of us knew the first thing about modern Greece, yet I began comparing the generals to our boss. Their pompous egotism, the way they bumbled and puffed when they were accused of duplicity, their self-righteous hatred of "long-haired hippies and dope addicts of indefinite sex."

When I talked behind the boss's back, Vincent was worse than horrified; he was incensed.

"Put what's-his-name in a uniform and he'd be the head of the security police," I told Vincent, who looked like he wanted to pound my head.

But I knew what he knew. I had my reasons. Afraid that I might eat him out of Junior Mints, the boss kept a running tab of how many boxes of each type of candy reposed in the bright glass case. Every day, I had to count the boxes and officially request more to fill the spaces. I couldn't be off by so much as a nickel at closing.

One night, made bold by *Z*, I opened each candy box and ate one Jujube, one Jordan Almond, one Black Crow, and so on, out of each box, just to accomplish something subversive. When I bragged, Vincent cruelly pointed out that I had just cheated all my proletarian customers. I allowed that he was right, and stuck to popcorn after that, eating handfuls directly out of the machine. I had to count the boxes, and the buckets, too, and empty out the ones unsold and fold them flat again and mark them. There was an awful lot of paperwork involved in being a concessioner.

As I watched *Z* again and again, the generals took on aspects of other authorities. I memorized the beginning, where the military officers, in a secret meeting, speak of the left as "political mildew" and deplored "the dry rot of subversive ideologies." It sounded just like the morning farm report on our local radio, with all the dire warnings of cow brucellosis and exhortations to mobilize against the invasion of wild oats. I knew nothing about metaphor, nothing, in fact, of communism or what a dictatorship was, but the language grabbed me and would not let go. Without consciously intending it, I had taken sides.

Then, halfway into Christmas vacation, Vincent told on me. The boss took me down into his neat little office in the basement and confronted me with the denouncement that I had eaten one piece of candy from every box in the glass case. I denied it.

"Vincent does it all the time," I lied with a clear conscience.

So there we were, a nest of informers and counterinformers, each waiting to betray the other over a Red Hot Tamale. It was sad. I accused Vincent of snitching; he accused me of the same. We no longer had any pretense of solidarity. He didn't help me when I had a line of customers, and I didn't give him free pop.

Before watching *Z* again the other night, I took a straw poll of people I knew to have been conscientious in 1969, asking them what they remembered about the movie. It was almost unanimous. People running, darkness, a little blue truck, and Irene Papas. Michael and I sat down and put the rented tape of *Z* into the video recorder. Between us we shared a bowl of air-popped corn. No salt. No butter anymore. Back in 1969, Michael had purchased the soundtrack to the movie and reviewed it for his school newspaper. It had obviously had an effect on both of us, and yet we recalled no more about it than the viewers in our poll. My memories were more intense because of the argument that almost got me fired from my first indoor job, but all was very blurred except for Irene Papas. As the credits rolled I looked forward to seeing the star. Moment after moment went by, and she did not appear. The leftist organizer went to the airport to pick up the peace leader, and somehow I expected Irene to get off the plane and stun everyone with her tragic, moral gaze.

Of course, Yves was the big star, the peace leader. We watched. I waited for Irene, and then, when it became clear she was only a prop for Yves, I began to watch for *any* woman with a speaking role.

The first one who appeared spoke into a phone. The second woman was a maid, the third a secretary, then a stewardess, then finally, briefly, Irene, looking grim, and then a woman in a pink suit handing out leaflets. Finally, a woman appeared in a demonstration, only to get kicked in the rear end.

Not only that, the man who kicked her was gay, and much was made of his seduction of a pinball-playing boy, his evil fey grin, his monstrosity. To the Costa-Gavras of 1969, at least, the lone gay man was a vicious goon, immoral and perverted.

Once Yves was killed, Irene was called in to mourn, on cue. Her main contribution to the rest of the movie was to stare inscrutably, to weep uncomfortably, and to smell her deceased husband's after-shave. How had I gotten the movie so wrong?

By the end, I knew I hadn't gotten it so wrong after all. In spite of all that is lacking from the perspective of twenty years, *Z* is still a good political film. It still holds evil to the light and makes hypocrisy transparent. The witnesses who come forward to expose the assassination are bravely credible, and their loss at the end is terrible and stunning. *Z* remains a moral tale, a story of justice done and vengeance sought. It deals with stupidity and avarice, with hidden motives and the impact that one human being can have on others' lives. I still got a thrill when the last line was spoken, telling us that *Z*, in the language of the ancient Greeks, means "He is alive." I remember feeling that the first time I saw the movie, and now I recalled one other thing. The second evening the movie showed, I watched Vincent, who hadn't even waited for the end, unhook the red velvet rope from its silver post.

Our argument was just starting in earnest. Normally, after everyone was gone and the outside lights were doused, he spent an hour, maybe two if a Disney had played, cleaning up after the crowd. He took his time. After eleven o'-clock, the place was his. He had the keys and the boss was gone. Those nights, Vincent walked down each aisle with a bag, a mop, and a bucket filled with the same pink soapy solution I used on the butter machine. He went after the spilled Coke, the mashed chocolate, the Jujubes pressed flat. He scraped the gum off the chairs before it hardened. And there were things people left, things so inconsequential that the movie goers rarely bothered to claim them—handkerchiefs, lipsticks, buttons, pens, and small change. One of the things I knew Vincent liked best about his job was that he always got to keep what he found.

There was nothing to find that night, however, not a chewed pencil or a hairpin. No one had come. We'd have only a few stragglers the next few nights, then the boss canceled the film. Vincent and I locked the theater and stood for a moment beneath the dark marquee, arguing. Dumb as it was, it was the first time I'd disagreed with anyone over anything but hurt feelings and boyfriends. It was intoxicating. It seemed like we were the only people in the town.

There have been many revolutions, but never one that so thoroughly changed the way women are perceived and depicted as the movement of the last twenty years. In Costa-Gavra's *Missing, Betrayed,* and *Music Box,* strong women are the protagonists, the jugglers of complicated moral dilemmas. These are not women who dye their underwear to lead cheers, and neither am I anymore, metaphorically I mean, but it is hard to escape from expectations. The impulse never stops. Watching *Z* in an empty North Dakota theater was one of those small, incremental experiences that fed into personal doubt, the necessary seed of any change or growth. The country in *Z* seemed terribly foreign, exotic, a large and threatened place—deceptive, dangerous, passionate. As it turned out, it was my first view of the world.

JOURNAL PROMPT:

The movie *Z* is one that Erdrich tells us no one came to see; nevertheless, it had an enormous impact on her. Write about a movie you have seen that is not well known but that you liked and wished more people would have viewed.

COLLABORATIVE EXERCISE:

Working in small groups, make a list of ten movies that individual group members rate as the most memorable they have ever viewed. Be sure each group member contributes at least one movie title. Then, make a list of reasons why these movies "stayed" with you. What qualities of a film help commit it to your memory in such a vivid way?

ESSAY ASSIGNMENT:

1. Spend some time reflecting on the movies you have viewed, and select one that had a very powerful and lasting effect—one that offered you, as *Z* did for Erdrich, a different view of the world. Discuss how and why it changed you, encouraged a new way of thinking, and/or offered a sobering reflection on life. Approach the essay as though the readers have never seen the film you are writing about and convince them that they must!
2. Write about one movie you saw during your childhood or early adolescence and viewed again in adulthood. Explain both experiences. Were they the same or different? How? Why or why not?
3. Write an essay in which you borrow the following line from Erdrich's essay and use it as your first sentence: "The best job I ever had combined two passions: ______________."

Joan Didion, American novelist and essayist, is best known for her perspectives on human behavior and psychological disorder found in our society. Didion graduated from the University of California at Berkeley in 1956 and then worked for three years at *Vogue* magazine. Her first collection of writings, *Slouching towards Bethlehem* (1968), established her reputation as a formidable essayist. Other works by Didion include *Play It As It Lays* (1970), *A Book of Common Prayer* (1977), *Democracy* (1984), *The Last Thing He Wanted* (1996), and the extended essays *Salvador* (1983) and *Miami* (1987). Didion also wrote several screenplays with her husband, writer John Gregory Dunne, including *A Star Is Born* (1976, with others), *True Confessions* (1981), and *Up Close and Personal* (1996).

JOAN DIDION

On Self-Respect

Once, in a dry season, I wrote in large letters across two pages of a notebook that innocence ends when one is stripped of the delusion that one likes oneself. Although now, some years later, I marvel that a mind on the outs with itself should have nonetheless made painstaking record of its every tremor, I recall with embarrassing clarity the flavor of those particular ashes. It was a matter of misplaced self-respect.

I had not been elected to Phi Beta Kappa. This failure could scarcely have been more predictable or less ambiguous (I simply did not have the grades), but I was unnerved by it; I had somehow thought myself a kind of academic Raskolnikov, curiously exempt from the cause-effect relationships which hampered others. Although even the humorless nineteen-year-old that I was must have recognized that the situation lacked real tragic stature, the day that I did not make Phi Beta Kappa nonetheless marked the end of something, and innocence may well be the word for it. I lost the conviction that lights would always turn green for me, the pleasant certainty that those rather passive virtues which had won me approval as a child automatically guaranteed me not only Phi Beta Kappa keys but happiness, honor, and the love of a good man; lost a certain touching faith in the totem power of good manners, clean hair, and proven competence on the Stanford-Binet scale. To such doubtful amulets had my self-respect been pinned, and I faced myself that day with the nonplused apprehension of someone who has come across a vampire and has no crucifix at hand.

Although to be driven back upon oneself is an uneasy affair at best, rather like trying to cross a border with borrowed credentials, it seems to me now the one condition necessary to the beginnings of real self-respect. Most of our platitudes notwithstanding, self-deception remains the most difficult deception. The tricks that work on others count for nothing in that very well-lit back alley where one keeps assignations with oneself; no winning smiles will do here, no prettily drawn lists of good intentions. One shuffles flashily but in vain through one's marked cards—the kindness done for the wrong reason, the apparent triumph which involved no real effort, the seemingly heroic act into which one had been shamed. The dismal fact is that self-respect has nothing to do with the approval of others—who are, after all, deceived easily enough; has nothing to do with reputation, which, as Rhett Butler told Scarlett O'Hara, is something people with courage can do without.

To do without self-respect, on the other hand, is to be an unwilling audience of one to an interminable documentary that details one's failings, both real and imagined, with fresh footage spliced in for every screening. *There's the glass you broke in anger, there's the hurt on X's face; watch now, this next scene, the night Y came back from Houston, see how you muff this one.* To live without self-respect is to lie awake some night, beyond the reach of warm milk, phenobarbital, and the sleeping hand on the coverlet, counting up the sins of commission and omission, the trusts betrayed, the promises subtly broken, the gifts irrevocably wasted through sloth or cowardice or carelessness. However long we postpone it, we eventually lie down alone in that notoriously uncomfortable bed, the one we make ourselves. Whether or not we sleep in it depends, of course, on whether or not we respect ourselves.

To protest that some fairly improbable people, some people who *could not possibly respect themselves,* seem to sleep easily enough is to miss the point entirely, as surely as those people miss it who think that self-respect has necessarily to do with not having safety pins in one's underwear. There is a common superstition that "self-respect" is a kind of charm against snakes, something that keeps those who have it locked in some unblighted Eden, out of strange beds, ambivalent conversations, and trouble in general. It does not at all. It has nothing to do with the face of things, but concerns instead a separate peace, a private reconciliation. Although the careless, suicidal Julian English in *Appointment in Samarra* and the careless, incurably dishonest Jordan Baker in *The Great Gatsby* seem equally improbable candidates for self-respect, Jordan Baker had it, Julian English did not. With that genius for accommodation more often seen in women than in men, Jordan took her own measure, made her own peace, avoided threats to that peace: "I hate careless people," she told Nick Carraway. "It takes two to make an accident."

Like Jordan Baker, people with self-respect have the courage of their mistakes. They know the price of things. If they choose to commit adultery, they do not then go running, in an access of bad conscience, to receive absolution from the wronged parties; nor do they complain unduly of the unfairness, the undeserved embarrassment, of being named corespondent. In brief, people with self-respect exhibit a certain toughness, a kind of moral nerve; they display what was once called *character,* a quality which, although approved in the abstract, sometimes loses ground to other, more instantly negotiable virtues. The measure of its slipping prestige is that one tends to think of it only in connection with homely children and United States senators who have been defeated, preferably in the primary, for reelection. Nonetheless, character—the willingness to accept responsibility for one's own life—is the source from which self-respect springs.

Self-respect is something that our grandparents, whether or not they had it, knew all about. They had instilled in them, young, a certain discipline, the sense that one lives by doing things one does not particularly want to do, by putting fears and doubts to one side, by weighing immediate comforts against the possibility of larger, even intangible, comforts. It seemed to the nineteenth century admirable, but not remarkable, that Chinese Gordon put on a clean white suit and held Khartoum against the Mahdi; it did not seem unjust that the way to free land in California involved death and difficulty and dirt. In a diary kept during the winter of 1846, an emigrating twelve-year-old named Narcissa Cornwall noted coolly: "Father was busy reading and did not notice that the house was being filled with strange Indians until Mother spoke about it." Even lacking any clue as to what Mother said, one can scarcely fail to be impressed by the entire incident: the father reading, the Indians filing in, the mother choosing the words that would not alarm, the child duly recording the event and noting further that those particular Indians were not, "fortunately for us," hostile. Indians were simply part of the *donnée.*

In one guise or another, Indians always are. Again, it is a question of recognizing that anything worth having has its price. People who respect themselves are willing to accept the risk that the Indians will be hostile, that the venture will go bankrupt, that the liaison may not turn out to be one in which *every day is a holiday because you're married to me.* They are willing to invest something of themselves; they may not play at all, but when they do play, they know the odds.

That kind of self-respect is a discipline, a habit of mind that can never be faked but can be developed, trained, coaxed forth. It was once suggested to me that, as an antidote to crying, I put my head in a paper bag. As it happens, there is a sound physiological reason, something to do with oxygen, for doing exactly that, but the psychological effect alone is incalculable: it is difficult in the extreme to continue fancying oneself Cathy in *Wuthering Heights* with one's head in a Food Fair bag. There is a similar case for all the small disciplines, unimportant in themselves; imagine maintaining any kind of swoon, commiserative or carnal, in a cold shower.

But those small disciplines are available only insofar as they represent larger ones. To say that Waterloo was won on the playing fields of Eton is not to say that Napoleon might have been saved by a crash program in cricket; to give formal dinners in the rain forest would be pointless did not the candlelight flickering on the liana call forth deeper, stronger disciplines, values instilled long before. It is a kind of ritual, helping us to remember who and what we are. In order to remember it, one must have known it.

To have that sense of one's intrinsic worth which constitutes self-respect is potentially to have everything: the ability to discriminate, to love and to remain indifferent. To lack it is to be locked within oneself, paradoxically incapable of either love or indifference. If we do not respect ourselves, we are on the one hand forced to despise those who have so few resources as to consort with us, so little perception as to remain blind to our fatal weaknesses. On the other, we are peculiarly in thrall to everyone we see, curiously determined to live out—since our self-image is untenable—their false notions of us. We flatter ourselves by thinking this compulsion to please others an attractive trait: a gist for imaginative empathy, evidence of our willingness to give. *Of course* I will play Francesca to your Paolo, Helen Keller to anyone's Annie Sullivan: no expectation is too misplaced, no role too ludicrous. At the mercy of those we cannot but hold in contempt, we play roles doomed to failure before they are begun, each defeat generating fresh despair at the urgency of divining and meeting the next demand made upon us.

It is the phenomenon sometimes called "alienation from self." In its advanced stages, we no longer answer the telephone, because someone might want something; that we could say *no* without drowning in self-reproach is an idea alien to this game. Every encounter demands too much, tears the nerves, drains the will, and the specter of something as small as an unanswered letter arouses such disproportionate guilt that answering it becomes out of the question. To assign unanswered letters their proper weight, to free us from the expectations of others, to give us back to ourselves—there lies the great, the singular power of self-respect. Without it, one eventually discovers the final turn of the screw: one runs away to find oneself, and finds no one at home.

JOURNAL PROMPT:

Write about a time in your life when you were disappointed about something: not making the team, not receiving the grade you thought you earned, not winning the election, or not being chosen for the lead in the play, etc.

COLLABORATIVE EXERCISE:

List the allusions (both literary and historical) that Didion makes in this essay. Does sharing the author's frame of reference aid in understanding the material?

ESSAY ASSIGNMENT:

1. Think of a concept other than self-respect, one that has importance in your life today (for example, loyalty, courage, honor). Using the same techniques that Didion would, create an extended definition of the concept for your readers.
2. The author gives examples throughout this work to help define her position. Find the examples she uses. Do you believe this method to be an effective way of presenting material? Why or why not?

Probably more changes in women's roles occurred in the 1960's than at any other time in history. American novelist and journalist **SARA DAVIDSON** asks readers to consider an Arthurian legend in the context of a modern tale. This selection is taken from her book *Real Property* (1980).

SARA DAVIDSON

WHAT DO WOMEN WANT?

Danielle Laurent was about to be married, at the age of thirty-three. "Is this your first marriage?" people asked, as she drove around Jerusalem on her motor scooter, ordering flowers and cakes.

"Yes."

"*Mazel tov!*"

Danielle was a French Jew, raised in Paris, but for seven years she had been living in Jerusalem, teaching literature at the Hebrew University. Her fiancé was a professor of physics, thirty-six, also new to marriage. A week before the wedding, Danielle invited friends to come to the home of her aunt, Simone, to spend the evening sewing the wedding dress.

I happened to be visiting Jerusalem and was invited. "Please, make an effort," Danielle had said. "I need you."

Simone's small house in Abu Tor, overlooking King David's Tower, was filled with women, professional women, ranging from twenty-six to thirty-five. Four were American, one was Spanish, one was Romanian, two were French and three were native Israelis. None was legally married at the time, except Simone.

At seventy, Simone is still a beauty, tall and erect, wearing her gray hair in a chignon. Simone has had two lengthy marriages, raised four children and enjoyed a career as a concert violinist. She lived in a villa outside Paris until her first husband died, at forty-two. Her children were away at school by then, so Simone, long a Zionist, immigrated to Israel, where she fell in love with her current husband, Moshe.

"I am someone who has lived by love, in love, all my life," she told me as she sat on the couch, her feet propped on pillows. "I have to be an example to the girls."

It had been Simone's idea to have the young women sew Danielle's dress by hand, from fabric Simone had bought in India: white silk, with delicate gold embroidery. As we came in, she made us wash our hands and cover our laps with sheets, so the fabric would not be soiled.

It was peaceful, sewing together, keeping a watchful circle around Danielle. But there was also a feeling of irony and self-mocking: we were not girls of sixteen, believing in the dress as a passport to the golden land.

Simone asked that we go around the circle and take turns telling stories and legends. Danielle, who was first, shook her head no. Her long dark hair covered her eyes as she bent over her sewing. For years, Danielle had been telling herself that what she wanted more than anything was to have a partner, a "permanent ally," and a house full of children. All through her twenties, she had given priority to her work, and assumed she would never have the patience to care for infants. But around the time she turned thirty, it became painful to walk past a children's store. She began to long, to ache for someone to share life with. For thirteen years she had been a waif, fending for herself and traveling across three continents; now that was to change. But could she adjust? Would the love she felt abide?

"Sara, you must provide us with a story," Simone said. For a moment, I could think of nothing that seemed appropriate; then I remembered an Arthurian legend I had heard from a friend, Winifred Rosen, who was adapting the tale for a children's book.

I began to relate the story, as best I could, from memory. "In the time of King Arthur and the Round Table, the King was out riding in the forest when he was surprised by a strange knight in full battle dress. The knight drew his sword, but the King said, 'Wait. I'm not armed, you can't do this, it would violate our honor code.' So the knight, whose name was Sir Gromer Somer Joure, had to relent. He made the King promise that he would return to the same spot, alone and unarmed, one year later. The King's life would be spared only if he brought back the answer to this riddle: What do women want, more than anything?"

Danielle interrupted the story. "That's what Freud is supposed to have asked. 'What do women want, dear God?'" Simone laughed. "The question did not originate with Freud. It recurs through the ages." She turned to me. "What did King Arthur do?"

"He rode back to the palace and met his nephew, Sir Gawain, who was, you know, the most beautiful and perfect knight in all the kingdom. He told Sir Gawain his plight, and Sir Gawain said, 'Don't worry, I'll ride in one direction, you'll ride in the other, and we'll ask every man and woman we meet, what do women want?'

"So the two of them rode off, and for a year, they asked every person, high and low, wise and simple, what do women want? They were given hundreds of answers."

I stopped to ask the women in Simone's sitting room, "How would you answer if you had to, 'What do women want more than anything?'"

They paused in their stitching.

"Love."

"A child."

"Respect."

"To be worshiped."

The Romanian lady said, "I think women want to be men."

Simone smiled, as if she knew none of the above would have saved the King.

I continued: "At the end of the year, Sir Gawain and the King each had a book full of answers. But King Arthur knew he did not have the right answer, and he was prepared to meet his fate, when he saw a woman approaching. This woman was the ugliest hag in creation. She was fat and wrinkled; she had a big nose with snot dripping and hairs sprouting from her face. She gave off a terrible odor. Her teeth were like tusks. She had warts and pus oozing from her eyes. Her name was Dame Ragnell. She rode straight up to the King and said, 'Sir, I alone have the answer that will save you. I'll tell you on one condition: that you give me Sir Gawain as my husband.'

"The King was horrified. 'I can't give you Sir Gawain.' He would rather have died than commit his nephew to such a fate. But Sir Gawain insisted he would marry the hag, gladly, if it would save the King's life.

"So King Arthur accepted the terms. 'Now, tell me, what do women want more than anything?'

"Dame Ragnell said, 'Sovereignty.'"

I paused in my story. We looked at each other, silently, covered with yards of white silk. Everyone seemed to sense instantly how satisfying the answer was.

"When King Arthur returned to meet Sir Gromer Somer Joure, he told him the answer, and his life *was* spared. Overjoyed, he rode back to the palace, but he found Dame Ragnell waiting to be married. And she wanted a grand wedding, with all the royal court. After the ceremony, Dame Ragnell gave a little tug at

Sir Gawain's sleeve and croaked, 'My lord, I'm your wife now, you have certain duties . . .'"

There were groans in the room.

"Sir Gawain could barely bring himself to look at her hairy snout, but he was bound by honor. He screwed up his courage, shut his eyes and turned to kiss her, and as he did, she was transformed into the most beautiful, delicate, sensuous creature he had ever dreamed of seeing. They spent the night making love, and as the sun was rising, Dame Ragnell said, 'My beauty will not hold all the time, so you must make a choice. Either have me beautiful by day, when the world can see, and ugly at night; or ugly by day and beautiful in your bed.'"

I said to the women, "Which would you choose, if you were Gawain?"

The Spanish woman said, "Beautiful by day." But she was quickly outvoted. Danielle said, "If he was a wise man, he would have her beautiful for him alone." Simone abstained, and asked me to continue.

"What Sir Gawain said was this: 'My lady, I leave it up to you.' And at that, she became beautiful all the time."

Cheers broke out; cakes were passed around. Danielle clapped her hands. "He was a very wise man." Simone, quieting the group, said, "You know, sovereignty is not a problem when you rule alone in your kingdom, but when two sovereign people want to merge their domains . . ." She looked pointedly at her niece. "Ah, that is the riddle you have yet to answer."

JOURNAL PROMPT:

Do you agree with the author's assessment of what it is women want?

COLLABORATIVE EXERCISE:

Working in small groups, discuss the structure of Davidson's essay—the blending of an Arthurian tale with a modern story of a woman preparing for her wedding. What do you think the author's purpose was for merging these two stories? Is her technique successful? Why or why not? Be specific. Consider how effective the essay might be if the story of King Arthur had not been included.

ESSAY ASSIGNMENT:

1. Write a definition/analysis essay in which you define *sovereignty* in your own words. Also, include definitions from at least ten other people whom you interview. Then, based on these descriptions of *sovereignty,* explain why you agree or disagree with the idea that women want sovereignty above anything else in life.
2. If you had to answer the question Davidson poses in the title of her essay, how would you respond? What is your response based upon (observation, firsthand knowledge, intuition, etc.)?
3. Write an essay in which you explain what it is you think *men* want.

JUDIE RAE is the author of four novels for young readers and has published poetry in numerous publications, including *Yankee* and *The Anthology of Magazine Verse & Yearbook of American Poetry.* She lives and teaches in Northern California.

JUDIE RAE

ENCOUNTER AT DAYBREAK

We consider the other.
Your flanks bellowed with
morning air,
ready for flight.
Your eyes wide,
appraising.
I dare imagine
your warm breath
on my hand.

Your fine head turns.

It is
almost
enough,
this reach.

To be glad for
only this:
One doe,
one woman,
patient through thicket, ancient
shrub,
acknowledging
this visage,
this holy presence.

JOURNAL PROMPT:

Would this poem have been as effective if an animal other than a doe had been spotted? What are the connotations of the word *doe*?

COLLABORATIVE EXERCISE:

As readers, we can interpret this poem as an incident that apparently changed the poet in a very profound way. Working in small groups, discuss the following: What rite of passage is the poet writing about? Explain your opinion in detail. Also, what is the significance of the title? Finally, how do you interpret the stanza: "It is almost enough, this reach."

ESSAY ASSIGNMENT:

1. Consider this poem in relationship to one of two other works, either "*Z*: The Movie That Changed My Life" or "Standing Together" (found in the next chapter, "Love, Marriage, and Birth"). In both of these selections the authors learn something profound through their encounters—one with a movie, the other with another person. Choose one of these works and compare the author's experience with "Encounter at Daybreak." How are the experiences similar and how are they different?
2. Write about a time when you experienced a very satisfying, perhaps even enlightening, moment that centered on the natural world. Describe the setting in detail, and explain the impact of the experience at the time. As you look back on the experience, has it had a lasting effect on your life? If so, explain why.

JOHN A. RUSH, PH.D., N.D., is a professor of anthropology at Sierra College, Rocklin, California, teaching physical anthropology and myth, ritual, and religion. His research interests include myth and ritual, as well as health and curing processes from a cross-cultural perspective. Dr. Rush's publications include *Witchcraft and Sorcery: An Anthropological Perspective of the Occult* (1974), *The Way We Communicate* (1976), *Clinical Anthropology: An Application of Anthropological Concepts within Clinical Settings* (1996), and *Stress and Emotional Health: Applications of Clinical Anthropology* (1999). Dr. Rush is also a naturopathic physician in private practice.

JOHN A. RUSH

RITES, RITUAL AND RESPONSIBILITY: DILEMMA IN AMERICAN CULTURE

Living and participating in any group—a family, an organization within a community, a community, or a society—requires that the individual learn a set of rules and engage in what is considered by other group members as "responsible behavior." Moreover, responsible behavior in all cultures is not expected at birth but is revealed during a process called *enculturation.* For example, the responsibilities of a two-year-old are different from that of a six-year-old, and the responsibilities of a twelve-year-old differ from those of an eighteen- or twenty-one-year-old. In our culture we expect a baby at age two to be dependent, to have his or her needs looked after by parents and others. When a child is six years old, we have a different set of expectations. The individual should no longer wear a diaper, should have the basic rules of etiquette, and should be able to perform many tasks without total supervision. At age twelve, the individual should be deciding his or her future, be involved in peer group activity, and be moving into a more "adult" status. At eighteen, in theory, a person should be exhibiting the behavior of a mature adult, and by age twenty-five the adult, self-responsible status should be complete.

Conformity to rules leads to expectations on the part of others, allowing for cooperative behavior, a sense of security, and group survival. Humans are a small-group animal and adhering to rules (and negotiating new rules when necessary) is extremely important in terms of group survival over time.

Symbols

How then do we enculturate and install the rules and roles necessary for social continuance? We use language, and more specifically, *symbols.* It is through symbols that we learn about and organize our lives. Symbols stand for events, ideas, behaviors, and things. For example, the word *dog* is not the dog. The word can represent a mammal we refer to as a dog or a specific animal of this class, Fluffy; or it could also represent the behavior of a person, a male, for example, who uses women sexually or is simply insensitive and inconsiderate; or it could represent a female of unattractive features.

Symbols come in two general varieties: 1) those that are highly compressed, that is, they can have many reference points; and 2) those that have very special meanings. For example, and in a similar fashion to the word *dog,* if I say "bridge," what comes to mind? The reference could be a structure that allows one to cross a stream, gully, or river; but there are many types of bridges. A bridge could also be a card game, dental work, a connection between two or more ideas, and so on. Therefore, *bridge* is highly compressed data and can have many meanings depending on the social context in which it occurs.

The second category has more restricted meaning and is referred to as a sign. For example, a stop sign is red and is octagonal in shape, and no matter where you travel in the United States, all stop signs are essentially the same. When you see a stop sign, the message is "stop at the intersection"; it does not mean stop talking to a friend, turn off the radio, or cease thinking.

Social Symbols and Meanings

Some of the many symbols to which we are exposed tell us who we are and what society expects regarding behavior. Such symbols include *child, boy, girl, male, female, husband, wife,* and so on. The last two are more specifically called *kinship* terms, but all are representative of *roles.* All of us during the course of the average day assume many roles, which can include student, friend, sister, brother, and employee. After assigning a role, society then gives instructions as to appropriate behavior. In North American culture, however, many extremely important roles are no longer clearly defined. This creates a dilemma in the enculturation process of learning a set of expected behavioral patterns for social living. As an example, if someone assigned you the role of airplane pilot, and you had no instruction for dealing with the technology, to actually take on the role would end in disaster. Piloting airplanes, as important as this might be, is only a minor consideration when it comes to defining roles employed on a day-to-day basis by all of us.

Roles, Rituals, and Expectations

There are several roles clearly defined by most cultures. The reason for clear definitions is to create *expectations* about "proper" behavior. Improper behavior upsets social, and often cosmic, balance. In short, group survival is dependent on rules and roles, without which a system devolves into anarchy. Rules attached to roles represent behavioral sets, actions, and reactions that are highly ritualized or stereotyped. Expectations create a sense of security, that is, of knowing what will generally occur during social interaction. In general, and occurring in all cultures, there is a set of instructions for ritual initiation (making contact and communicating with an individual or group) and ritual termination (the ending of the interaction). In between there is small talk and perhaps content, or the reason for the social contact in the first place. Most of us know how to say "Hello" and "Good-bye," as we frequently engage strangers, especially in the marketplace. However, if certain basic roles are not clearly defined in terms of behavioral expectations, the meanings attached to these greeting and ending rituals become unclear. The basic roles to which I am referring are those of male, female, husband, wife, and adult. What are the behaviors associated with these basic roles?

Aside from biology, the social concepts that applied to male and female prior to the WWII are politically incorrect or do not fit the prevailing social climate. Males are no longer dominant over females; females are no longer expected to be submissive to men. Neither are males the primary breadwinners, nor do women necessarily stay home and take care of the children. The lack of clarity in these roles has led to friction and hostility between men and women and a great deal of sexual confusion. Because there is no clear definition of *adult,* men have great difficulty growing up and assuming a sense of commitment and responsibility in the institution of marriage. If we do not have a clear definition of *male* and *female,* how then do we define *husband* and *wife?*

Male, female, and *adult* are the building blocks of the rest of the roles we play, and if society does not define and condition a set of rules or expected behaviors, stress is the obvious result. This can be seen in the increasing rates of divorce, sexual harassment suits, and confusion as to sexual identity, as well as rates of depression and numerous other physical ailments.

Rites of Passage in Current North American Cultural Context

Rites of passage for males in many cultures, especially those centered on the equator (Australia, New Guinea), are usually seen as harsh by North American standards. The circumcision and subincision rites of the Arunda of south central Australia, or the scarification practices in New Guinea, serve to move the individual from child to adult and to anchor him in the identity of male through actually altering the physical body. In this fashion the male always knows his role and expected behaviors; the scars serve as a reminder. However, these extreme rites, although effective in defining and anchoring rules and roles, are not appropriate in a culture such as ours. The reason is that they do not lend themselves to the flexibility necessary in a philosophy centered around change. Each year, for example, new clothing styles are directed at the identity of the *individual* rather than the group. Until recent times, a person's clothing represented rank, status, and membership in a specific group. Only in special, specific groups (the white coat and stethoscope of a medical doctor or the collar of a priest or habit of a nun) does clothing serve to accentuate status and group belonging. Art forms, such as music, are no longer specifically associated with a culture but instead are marketed to fit the diverse needs of individuals within our culture, the males and females who make up the populace. When you accentuate individualism, male and female identities merge, and we hear about "unisex" and see attachments, like clothing, recreational activities, sexual identity blur into an unidentifiable mist. What is pushed aside are specific biological differences, especially hormonal, which a culturally constructed "unisex" label cannot ignore.

The dilemma, then, is both to connect appropriate behaviors to the roles of male, female, and adult, and yet allow flexibility that is necessary in a rapidly changing society. How do we accomplish this?

Relationships and Roles: Moving out of the Shadow of the Past

It is doubtful, and probably unwise, to return to the harsh, physical processes of installing the specific role definitions utilized by our ancestors. What becomes important, then, is to accentuate *rules of relationship* regardless of social role. In a culture that worships individualism and equality (although we may not always live up to the latter), all social roles have come under attack. The misdeeds of senators, representatives, and presidents, medical doctors, ministers, priests, and teachers, are aired in public. The message, loud and clear, is that *your dominant social role is less important than your relationship with others.* Therefore, our basic and necessary rite of passage in our time period is the learning and utilizing of communication skills that accentuate equality and allow information to be exchanged in a "low-risk" manner; you do not need to be scarified to know who you are and how to relate to others.

First, you are responsible for the information that you send and how you translate the messages from others. Quite simply, if you want to be respected with equality from others, then *be* respectful of those others. When you use sarcasms, order, warn, threaten, ignore, and make trivial the actions of others, you are being disrespectful. Such communication strategies, common on the situation comedies (*Frasier, Seinfeld,* etc.), alienate, and if you want to be included, avoid these techniques.

Likewise, you are also responsible for how you receive information. When people are disrespectful of you, what do they really mean? If I tell you to "Go to hell," it does not mean get on the next bus. Learning how to send and receive information in a respectful manner has been neglected in our schools, churches, and certainly in the mass media. By learning how to communicate, to avoid high-risk messages, *you* initiate your own rite of passage leading to responsible adulthood. You have to be willing to examine the way you communicate and the communication patterns of others.

Second, your emotions are your own; no one can give you a feeling. Yes, people can set up situations where there is a high probability that you will get angry, frustrated, happy, and so on, but if you want equality, if you want individual freedom, you have to take charge. You generate your feelings as you interpret the world around you. That is why not everyone likes chocolate ice cream, cool summer evenings, cats, dogs, the color green, or Arnold Schwarzenegger movies. It is your interpretation, your preference. No one can make you angry, happy, sad, or content, and realizing this puts you on the road to self-responsible adulthood.

Third, you need to *listen* to others. You need to be able to stay external, regardless of whether you are being insulted, flattered, or sold a new idea. It is only through listening and interpreting symbols that humankind has been able to socially and technologically move to our present condition.

Fourth, sending *positives* is absolutely necessary. We are apparently programmed to pick up negatives because there is survival value in this. We have to override this tendency and, in the process, send out positives. When you positively reward the behaviors or ideas of others, those behaviors and ideas are likely to continue.

Fifth, we also need to be able to *shut off unwanted behavior* in others without creating resentment and war. This will take some work as most of us have learned to order, warn, threaten, name-call, withdraw, and so on.

Sixth, it is important to have a process of *negotiation,* one that points toward negotiating *needs,* not the individual wants of the participants.

Conclusion

Becoming a responsible adult can no longer be left to society, your tribe, or your family. You have to do it, and *you have to do it willingly.* Our ancient ancestors told stories that would help to secure our identities. Logic, too, often does not penetrate our current beliefs about ourselves and who we are with respect to the group. When our parents, for example, attempt logically to tell us what is best, such messages are often ignored. Stories, because they are "just stories," secure our attention and can speak to ideas, concerns, and behaviors. Our ancestors realized early on that values are more likely to be internalized in story form because they are not personal, at least at the conscious level, and appeal to universal ideals or issues: cooperation, growing up and contributing to the group, and so on. Such story telling avoids defensive reactions.

Our current artists, however, rely on sensationalistic renditions of the individual, which usually negate sensitivity toward others and accentuate full participation in one's self at the exclusion of others. The news media accentuates this ignorance and insensitivity toward others. Our government officials present images of disrespect and immaturity; our schools are not concerned with communication tools for intimate social living.

Moreover, our ancient ancestors, including contemporary preliterate cultures, subjected males to extreme rites of passage that involved scarification and other types of body mutilation. The goal was to kill the child symbolically and bring the individual to adult status. In Western culture, we no longer purposely engage in extreme rites of passage. In fact, it is up to the individual to enact his or her own rites of passage, which often spontaneously evolve out of social circumstances. A car accident, or pulling someone from a house fire, being lost in the woods, an unwanted pregnancy, or a near-death experience from a drug overdose are all spontaneous and serve as rites of passage for moving the individual to another life stage.

Specific literary forms can likewise emotionally and symbolically serve as rites of passage without physical participation. A suggestion, and as emphasized by Joseph Campbell, read (and analyze) the Arthurian legends, especially those of Perceval, Lancelot, and Erec. All of the youthful urges, spontaneous adventures and quests, spiritual striving, growing up, living one's own path, and relationship ideals (honor, loyalty, and integrity) are right there. Relationship ideals, unfortunately, have been corrupted by an economic philosophy of personal gain at the expense of others. Look in a mirror and you see yourself as an image separate from those surrounding you. Now think of a wave in an ocean. Is that ocean really separate from that wave? No; it is not. So who are you? Are you the wave, the ocean, or both?

Suggested Readings

Bettelheim, B. 1962. *Symbolic Wounds: Puberty Rites and the Envious Male.* New York: Collier Books.

Campbell, J. 1990. *Transformation of Myth through Time.* New York: Harper & Row.

Lutkehaus, N., and R. Roscoe, 1995. *Gender Rituals: Female Initiation in Melanesia.* New York: Routledge.

Mahdi, L., S. Foster, and M. Little, 1988. *Betwixt & Between: Patterns of Masculine and Feminine Initiation.* La Salle, IL.: Open Court.

Raphael, R. 1988. *The Men from the Boys: Rites of Passage in Male America.* Lincoln: University of Nebraska Press.

Rush, J. 1996. *Clinical Anthropology: An Application of Anthropological Concepts within Clinical Settings.* Westport, CT: Preager Publications.

———. 1999. *Stress and Emotional Health: Application of Clinical Anthropology.* Westport, CT: Auburn House.

Schlegel, A., and H. Barry, 1979. "Adolescent Initiation Ceremonies: A Cross-Cultural Code." *Ethnology* 18 (2) 199–210.

Spencer, B., and F. Gillen, 1899. *The Native Tribes of Central Australia.* London: MacMillan.

Van Gennep, A. 1909. *The Rites of Passage.* Chicago: University of Chicago Press, 1960.

JOURNAL PROMPT:

In his second paragraph, Rush writes that as the individual grows into society, "conformity to rules leads to expectations on the part of others, allowing for cooperative behavior . . ." Write about a time as an adult when you had to conform to rules that you did not agree with or feel comfortable about.

COLLABORATIVE EXERCISE:

The author claims that we tend to focus on the negative because there is survival value in this. What do you think he means by this statement? Does his background as an anthropologist perhaps color this assertion? How? Explain. (Think about early man's struggle for survival when formulating your answer.)

ESSAY ASSIGNMENT:

1. Write your own story that traces your unique journey to adulthood. Who is the wisdom figure in your tale? (Remember: A metaphor is an implied comparison, a nonlinear way of viewing the world. Try to incorporate symbolic imagery in your story.)
2. Elaborate on the author's claim that sarcasm alienates. Investigate the difference between sarcasm and satire.

ADDITIONAL ESSAY PROMPTS

1. Other authors in earlier chapters used classification techniques similar to those used by Gail Sheehy in "Predictable Crises of Adulthood." How does Sheehy's work compare to Egan's "The Mythic Stage" or John Holt's "Three Kinds of Discipline"?

2. How do you define the "American Dream"? Is it different from how your parents or grandparents viewed it? Write an essay in which you explain what role the "American Dream" plays in your life, either directly or indirectly.

3. Prioritize the following accomplishments, usually associated with adulthood, in order of personal importance, and then explain your order:

   - raising a family
   - being financially successful at your work
   - working at a job that is enjoyable and purposeful
   - enjoying a lot of leisure time
   - having a dependable, supportive circle of friends

4. When you were a child, what were the occupations of your parents? Write about how you felt about your parents' work life. How did it affect you?

5. Imagine that you have the opportunity to teach an English class. What selections from this chapter would you use to illustrate what it means to be an adult? Why did you pick these particular works?

6. By the time one becomes an adult, many of life's lessons have already been learned. These lessons are learned through experience and classroom encounters, as well as through advice given by friends and family. For you, which has been the best instructor of your "life" lessons?

7. To be an adult means acting out certain roles: the role of student, the role of worker, the role of mate, the role of parent. What roles have you learned to play? Which, if any, of these roles would you at times like to discard? Explain fully.

8. Using the book review "Spare the Chores, Spoil the Child," found in chapter 2, as reference, write an essay in which you analyze how a person approaching adulthood might benefit from the "chores" he or she was expected to do as a child.

9. At some point in your life as an adult and as a student, you may have noticed some books on your shelves that have remained unread. What are the titles of these books? What do these books say about you and your desires, goals, or fears? Write an essay explaining how these unread books might define who you are or the type of person you wish to become.

10. Reread your favorite selections from this chapter. Many of them demonstrate through example and illustration what it means to be an adult. Others make use of narrative, or storytelling, to reveal a theme. Which method do you find the most effective? Why do you suppose you prefer one approach to another?

Additional Research Questions

1. The trips to the moon enhanced our scientific, as well as our spiritual, knowledge; they gave us a new perspective on the earth as a finite planet swirling in a very large universe. Research some of the technological advances that are part of our lives today that resulted from those voyages into outer space.

2. Linguistics professor Deborah Tannen asserts that men and women have very different ways of communicating with their friends; in fact, she claims that male-female communication is cross-cultural communication. Write a paper in which you examine how men and women use language differently.

3. Nathan McCall, in his essay "Makes Me Wanna Holler," paraphrases Reverend Ellis by stating "that thinking should be an *active* process that, when cultivated, can change a person's behavior, circumstances, and ultimately, his fate." Investigate the latest research on how we think. How do early influences and experiences impact how we think?

4. According to Rosemary L. Bray, author of "So How Did I Get Here?" there are many "lies and distortions, half-truths and wrongheaded notions about welfare." Research the pros and cons of the welfare system. Then, in your concluding remarks, consider the future of welfare and make a prediction of what you believe might be the fate of the welfare system.

5. Many people believe that being a responsible adult necessitates participating in the political process. Research how a particular decision made in Washington affects you. (You might want to explore a recent environmental or tax law change.) Does your research lead you to take a more active role in the public debate on this issue?

6

Love, Marriage, and Birth

No emotion has so many symbolic associations as romantic love. No rite marks the passage from adolescence to adulthood as clearly as the marriage ceremony, for it is here that we are told to leave behind once and for all our infantile pursuits and put first the welfare of another.

In many myths, the soul of the beloved is featured as a butterfly. The butterfly goes through a metamorphosis, and love is the catalyst. According to author J. F. Bierlein in his book, *Living Myths,* "The power of love to transform reminds us that our existence is in, with, and through others." When we become parents, love is the catalyst for this continuing process of becoming. Both romantic love and parental love are shared struggles for existence and meaning.

The selections in this unit take very different looks at love, marriage, and the birth experience. Bobbie Ann Mason explores love gone awry, while Judith Wallerstein and Sandra Blakeslee describe what makes a good marriage.

After exposure to this material, the reader may choose to explore his or her own love relationships.

In this cause-and-effect essay, author **Anne Roiphe** explores why approximately 50 percent of modern marriages fail. Roiphe, a novelist, is the author of *Up the Sandbox,* another work that examines relationships.

ANNE ROIPHE

Why Marriages Fail

These days so many marriages end in divorce that our most sacred vows no longer ring with truth. "Happily ever after" and "Till death do us part" are expressions that seem on the way to becoming obsolete. Why has it become so hard for couples to stay together? What goes wrong? What has happened to us that close to one-half of all marriages are destined for the divorce courts? How could we have created a society in which 42 percent of our children will grow up in single-parent homes? If statistics could only measure loneliness, regret, pain, loss of self-confidence and fear of the future, the numbers would be beyond quantifying.

Even though each broken marriage is unique, we can still find the common perils, the common causes for marital despair. Each marriage has crisis points and each marriage tests endurance, the capacity for both intimacy and change. Outside pressures such as job loss, illness, infertility, trouble with a child, care of aging parents and all the other plagues of life hit marriage the way hurricanes blast our shores. Some marriages survive these storms and others don't. Marriages fail, however, not simply because of the outside weather but because the inner climate becomes too hot or too cold, too turbulent or too stupefying.

When we look at how we choose our partners and what expectations exist at the tender beginnings of romance, some of the reasons for disaster become quite clear. We all select with unconscious accuracy a mate who will recreate with us the emotional patterns of our first homes. Dr. Carl A. Whitaker, a marital therapist and emeritus professor of psychiatry at the University of Wisconsin, explains, "From early childhood on, each of us carried models for marriage, femininity, masculinity, motherhood, fatherhood and all the other family roles." Each of us falls in love with a mate who has qualities of our parents, who will help us rediscover both the psychological happiness and miseries of our past lives. We may think we have found a man unlike Dad, but then he turns to drink or drugs, or loses his job over and over again or sits silently in front of the T.V. just the way Dad did. A man may choose a woman who doesn't like kids just like his mother or who gambles away the family savings just like his mother. Or he may choose a slender wife who seems unlike his obese mother but then turns out to have other addictions that destroy their mutual happiness.

A man and a woman bring to their marriage bed a blended concoction of conscious and unconscious memories of their parents' lives together. The human way is to compulsively repeat and recreate the patterns of the past. Sigmund Freud so well described the unhappy design that many of us get trapped in: the unmet needs of childhood, the angry feelings left over from frustrations of long ago, the limits of trust and the recurrence of old fears. Once an individual senses this entrapment, there may follow a yearning to escape, and the result could be a broken, splintered marriage.

Of course people can overcome the habits and attitudes that developed in childhood. We all have hidden strengths and amazing capacities for growth and creative change. Change, however, requires work—observing your part in a rotten pattern, bringing difficulties out into the open—and work runs counter to the basic myth of marriage: "When I wed this person all my problems will be over. I will have achieved success and I will become the center of life for this other person and this person will be my center, and we will mean everything to each other forever." This myth, which every marriage relies on, is soon exposed. The coming of children, the pulls and tugs of their demands on affection and time, place a considerable strain on that basic myth of meaning everything to each other, of merging together and solving all of life's problems.

Concern and tension about money take each partner away from the other. Obligations to demanding parents or still-depended-upon parents create further strain. Couples today must also deal with all the cultural changes brought on in recent years by the women's movement and the sexual revolution. The altering of roles and the shifting of responsibilities have been extremely trying for many marriages.

These and other realities of life erode the visions of marital bliss the way sandstorms eat at rock and the ocean nibbles away at the dunes. Those euphoric, grand feelings that accompany romantic love are really self-delusions, self-hypnotic dreams that enable us to forge a relationship. Real life, failure at work, disappointments, exhaustion, bad smells, bad colds and hard times all puncture the dream and leave us stranded with our mate, with our childhood patterns pushing us this way and that, with our unfulfilled expectations.

The struggle to survive in marriage requires adaptability, flexibility, genuine love and kindness and an imagination strong enough to feel what the other is feeling. Many marriages fall apart because either partner cannot imagine what the other wants or cannot communicate what he or she needs or feels. Anger builds until it erupts into a volcanic burst that buries the marriage in ash.

It is not hard to see, therefore, how essential communication is for a good marriage. A man and a woman must be able to tell each other how they feel and why they feel the way they do; otherwise they will impose on each other roles and actions that lead to further unhappiness. In some cases, the communication patterns of childhood—of not talking, of talking too much, of not listening, of distrust and anger, of withdrawal—spill into the marriage and prevent a healthy exchange of thoughts and feelings. The answer is to set up new patterns of communication and intimacy.

At the same time, however, we must see each other as individuals. "To achieve a balance between separateness and closeness is one of the major psychological tasks of all human beings at every stage of life," says Dr. Stuart Bartle, a psychiatrist at the New York University Medical Center.

If we sense from our mate a need for too much intimacy, we tend to push him or her away, fearing that we may lose our identities in the merging of marriage. One partner may suffocate the other partner in a childlike dependency.

A good marriage means growing as a couple but also growing as individuals. This isn't easy. Richard gives up his interest in carpentry because his wife, Helen, is jealous of the time he spends away from her. Karen quits her choir group because her husband dislikes the friends she makes there. Each pair clings to each other and are angry with each other as life closes in on them. This kind of marital balance is easily thrown as one or the other pulls away and divorce follows.

Sometimes people pretend that a new partner will solve the old problems. Most often extramarital sex destroys a marriage because it allows an artificial split between the good and the bad—the good is projected on the new partner and the bad is dumped on the head of the old. Dishonesty, hiding and cheating create walls between men and women. Infidelity is just a symptom of trouble. It is a symbolic complaint, a weapon of revenge, as well as an unraveler of closeness. Infidelity is often that proverbial last straw that sinks the camel to the ground.

All right—marriage has always been difficult. Why then are we seeing so many divorces at this time? Yes, our modern social fabric is thin, and yes the permissiveness of society has created unrealistic expectations and thrown the family into chaos. But divorce is so common because people today are unwilling to exercise the self-discipline that marriage requires. They expect easy joy, like the entertainment on TV, the thrill of a good party.

Marriage takes some kind of sacrifice, not dreadful self-sacrifice of the soul, but some level of compromise. Some of one's fantasies, some of one's legitimate desires have to be given up for the value of the marriage itself. "While all marital partners feel shackled at times, it is they who really choose to make the marital ties into confining chains or supporting bonds," says Dr. Whitaker. Marriage requires sexual, financial and emotional discipline. A man and a woman cannot follow every impulse, cannot allow themselves to stop growing or changing.

Divorce is not an evil act. Sometimes it provides salvation for people who have grown hopelessly apart or were frozen in patterns of pain or mutual unhappiness. Divorce can be, despite its initial devastation, like the first cut of the surgeon's knife, a step toward new health and a good life. On the other hand, if the partners can stay past the breaking up of the romantic myths into the development of real love and intimacy, they have achieved a work as amazing as the greatest cathedrals of the world. Marriages that do not fail but improve, that persist despite imperfections, are not only rare these days but offer a wondrous shelter in which the face of our mutual humanity can safely show itself.

JOURNAL PROMPT:

If you could offer one gem of advice to a couple planning to marry, what would it be? Why?

COLLABORATIVE EXERCISE:

Roiphe asserts that marriage is hard work and requires "some kind of sacrifice . . . some level of compromise." Working in small groups, use personal observations and experiences as resources to address the following question: What specific sacrifices and compromises must be made in a marriage for a couple to stay together happily *and* continue to grow and change as individuals?

ESSAY ASSIGNMENT:

1. Roiphe believes that the habits and attitudes acquired in childhood strongly influence one's choice for a life partner. She maintains that parental behavior can be especially influential. Using a combination of personal interviews and outside research, refute or agree with Roiphe's assertions. Suggest ways in which people might overcome the attitudes developed in childhood.
2. In your opinion, is divorce ever a good and logical choice? If so, when is it an "acceptable" decision? Be specific. If you believe divorce is never a good choice, explain your answer. Utilize examples of couples you may know who have divorced.
3. According to J. Donald Walters, author of *Expansive Marriage,* "People are conditioned from early childhood to look upon marriage as Nature's solution to the search for happiness. Such a view of marriage is two-dimensional. It suggests no road disappearing gradually into the distant future, and therefore no future challenges." Write an essay in which you agree or disagree with Walters's opinion that the search for happiness as a reason to get married may create a problem in maintaining a marriage.

In this piece, JILL TWEEDIE describes her failed attempts at marriage and offers some suggestions about why so many relationships fail. The author was married three times and was a regular columnist for the *Guardian,* a well-known London newspaper. She is best known for her work *Letters from a Faint-Hearted Feminist* (1982). Jill Tweedie died in 1993.

JILL TWEEDIE

THE EXPERIENCE

'Some day my prince will come . . .'

I have no particular qualifications to write about love but then, who has? There are no courses of higher learning offered in the subject except at the University of Life, as they say, and there I have put in a fair amount of work. So I offer my own thoughts, experiences and researches into love in the only spirit possible to such an enterprise—a combination of absolute humility and utter arrogance that will cause the reader either to deride my wrong-headedness or, with luck, to recognise some of the same lessons.

I am a white, Anglo-Saxon, heterosexual, happily married, middle-income female whose experience of what is called love spans forty years of the mid-twentieth century in one of the most fortunate parts of the globe. I mention this because I am profoundly aware of the limits these facts give to my vision; also because, in spite of such advantages, my experience of love has hardly been uplifting and yet, because of them to, I have at least been vouchsafed a glimpse of what love might be, some day.

I took my first steps in what I was told was love when the idea of high romance and living happily ever after still held sway. They said that whatever poisoned apple I might bite would surely be dislodged by a Prince's kiss and I would then rise from all the murderous banalities of living and, enfolded in a strong man's arms, gallop away on a white charger to the better land called love. The way it turned out, this dream of love did not do much to irradiate my life. The ride was nice enough but 'twas better to travel than to arrive and—oh, shame—there was more than one Prince. Of two previous marriages and a variety of other lovings, very little remains and that mostly ugly. However sweet love's initial presence, when it goes it leaves horrid scars. Unlike friendship and other forms of love, the tide of male/female sex love does not ebb imperceptibly, leaving the stones it reveals gleaming and covetable. No. It only shows that what was taken to be precious is simply a bare, dull pebble like any other.

Loving, lovers fill each other's lives, Siamese twins joined at the heart, bees that suck honey from each other's blossoms. When love ebbs, nothing remains. Ex-lovers rarely meet again or write or offer each other even those small kindnesses and comforts that strangers would not withhold. Birthdays, high days and holidays pass unmarked where once they were entered in New Year diaries and planned for months ahead. Photographs of the beloved are discarded or curl up, yellowing, in some dusty drawer. What was once the world becomes a no-man's-land, fenced with barbed wire, where trespassers are prosecuted and even the civilities given a passing acquaintance are forbidden. What was most intimate—private thoughts, dreams, nightmares and childhood panics soothed in warm arms—are now merely coinage for a pub joke, a hostess flippancy, worth a line or two in the local paper or the old school magazine. Divorced. Separated. Split.

For the first man I thought I loved, and therefore married, I bear, at most, a distant anger for injuries received. For the second I carefully suppress the good times, burying them with the bad. All those hours, weeks, months, years passed in the same bed have vanished, leaving only the traces of an old wound, an ache where a growth was removed.

Was either a part of love, ever? Of a kind. The best we could manage at the time, a deformed seedling planted in infertile ground. The three of us, each of them and me, carried loads on our backs when we met, all the clobber of past generations. This I must do, that you must be, this is good, that is bad, you must, I must, we must. By the time we met, we were already proficient puppeteers, hands stuck up our stage dolls, our real selves well concealed behind the striped canvas. You Punch, me Judy. Me Jane, you Tarzan.

I had a conventional 1940s and 1950s childhood, cut to the pattern of time. I adored and admired my father and my father did not adore or admire me. My mother was there like the curtains and the carpets were there, taken for loving granted in early childhood and then ruthlessly discarded, the living symbol of everything my world did not regard and that I, therefore, did not wish to become. Rejecting her caused a very slight wreckage inside, nothing you'd notice, though transfusions would later be necessary. Powerful unloving father, powerless loving mother. Cliché.

So I did what I could to make my way and married an older man. Love and marriage go together like a horse and carriage. This act imposed certain conditions. First of all, you cannot grow up if you marry a father figure because this is no part of the contract, and besides, growing up is a disagreeable occupation. Then, of course, a continuing virginity of mind, if not of body, is essential because Daddy's girl has never known other men and any evidence of sexual curiosity or, worse, a touch of ribaldry might cause him to withdraw his protection. Indeed, a daughter must not know much of anything at all because Daddy must teach and daughter learn, for ever. Competence, independence, self-sufficiency, talent in anything but the most girlish endeavours, toughness of any kind, is against the rules. Light-heartedness, giggling, little tantrums and a soupçon of mischief are permitted because Daddy is a Daddy, after all, and likes to be amused after a long day or even smack a naughty bum, in his wisdom. My first marriage was a romper room and each day I laid plans to negotiate the next, with my thumb stuck endearingly in my mouth.

To begin with, we both enjoyed the game we didn't know we were playing. He was a proper husband in the eyes of the outside world, protective and admonitory, and I was a proper wife, that is to say, a child; charming and irresponsible. But quite soon these playful rituals began to harden into concrete, so that we could no longer move, even if we wished, as long as we were together. For a few years I was satisfied enough, the drama of my life absorbed me, it was a stage and I was the star. First a house to play with and later, in case the audience began to cough and fidget, a pregnancy to hold them riveted. Later, like Alice in Wonderland, I came across the cake labelled 'eat me' and whenever my husband was away at work, I ate and I grew. My legs stuck out of the windows, my arms snaked round the doors, my head above an endless neck loomed through the chimney and my heartbeat rocked the room. Each day, just before 5 p.m., I nibbled the other side of Alice's cake and, in the nick of time, shrank to being a little woman again. Hullo, darling, how was your day? Me? Oh, nothing happened. Terrified, I knew that one day I wouldn't make it down again and my husband, returning from work, would fall back in horror at the monster who had taken over his home and push me out into the big wide world.

Writing this now perhaps suggests that I was aware of a pretence and set up my false self knowingly, for reward. Not so. The boundaries given me in girlhood were strictly defined, allowing only minimum growth and that mainly physical. To sprout the titivating secondary sexual characteristics was expected, but woe betide the *enfant terrible* who tried to burst that tight cocoon and emerge as a full-grown adult in mind as well as body. The penalty was ill-defined but all-pervasive, like those sci-fi novels of a post-nuclear generation bred to fear the radioactive world above their subterranean tunnels that threatens isolation, mutilation and death. The reward for my self-restraint (in the most literal sense) was a negative one—be good and tractable and you will be looked after—but it was none the less powerful for that. So my real self, or hints of it, was as frightening to me as I feared it would be to my husband, a dark shadow given to emerging at less and less acceptable times. I was Mr Rochester secure in his mansion but I was also his mad wife in the attic. I had to conceal her existence to preserve my way of life but all the time she was setting matches to the bedding, starting a flame at the hem of the curtains, hoping to burn the mansion down.

Things became more and more schizoid. The demure façade of a prim girl hid a raucous fishwife who folded her massive arms against her chest and cursed. She horrified me, so much so—threatening, as she did, my exile from society—that in spite of increasing marital quarrels and even spurts of pure hatred, never once did I let that fishwife out to hurl the oaths she could have hurled or yelled the truths she knew. How could I, without revealing what I really was, to him and to myself?

The inner split opened wider. When my husband said he loved me, I knew he meant he loved the doll I had created and I accepted his love smugly enough, on her behalf. She was worth it. She wore the right clothes, she said the right things, the span of her waist would bring tears to your eyes and the tiny staccato of her heels across a floor would melt the sternest heart. She turned her head upon its graceful stem just so and her camellia hands, laced on her lap, could make a stone bleed. She smiled just enough to give a man the wildest expectations and frowned just enough to make him feel safe. This doll is a good doll. This doll is a marriageable doll. This doll is a real doll.

I knew, of course, that my doll self was only a front but it was the one I had deliberately created in response to popular demand. My real self knew all the things the doll did not wish to know. She was human and therefore hopelessly unfeminine, she had no pretty ways. Her voice was harsh, pumped from the guts instead of issuing sweetly from the throat, and every now and then she howled and the doll was forced to look at her face, bare as a picked bone. No wonder the poor dolly gathered up her ruffled skirts and ran shrieking down corridors to find reassurance in a man's eyes. See my soft red lips, my white skin, feel how smooth the shaven legs, smell the scented underarms, tell me you love me, dolly me.

There were, of course, other ways to accommodate the spectre within and other ways became more necessary as the spectre grew stronger and rattled the bars of the cage. My husband was a man of uncertain temper. I was quite aware of this before we married. He came from a country ravaged by war, his home had been destroyed, his brother killed, his family made refugees and he, corralled off the streets of his town, had spent two years starving in the polar wastes of a Russian prison camp. Understandably, he was outside the conventional pale. I was afraid of him.

The fear was seductive. The dolly shook with it at times, was martyred by it. Hit, punched, she fell to the floor and lay, a poor pale victim, her lashes fanned against an appealingly white cheek stained, briefly, dull red. Later, kindly, she accepted the remorse of her attacker, grovelling before her. Yes, I forgive you, she said. And well she might forgive, because down in the dungeon beneath, her other self was quiet for the time being, gorged to quiescence on the thick hot adrenalin provided by the man. A small price to pay.

I do not know how many people stand at the altar repeating the marriage vows and knowing, however unclearly, that what they say is false and what they do calamitous. My doll stood stiffly in her stiff dress, the groom beside her, and there was not a hope for them. Upbringing had set us against each other from the start and each was busily preparing to hammer the other into an appropriate frame. After the service well-wishers launched our raft with champagne; lashed together, not far out, we sank.

Next time, I chose more carefully. The doll, anyway, was aware that her days were numbered. Winning ways must be adjusted if they are to go on being useful and a good actress acknowledges that she has aged out of *ingénue* roles before the casting director says don't call us. Besides, I was no longer enamoured of my puppet and did not want to extend her life much further. She had become more obstacle than defence, the way a wall, originally built to keep enemies out, can come to be a prison keeping you in.

So I let my real self out on probation, to be called in only now and then for discipline. And now I needed a male with all the right worldly appurtenances, whom I could use as a hermit crab uses a shell, to reach full growth without exposing vulnerable flesh. Using him, I could flex my own muscles in safety until they were strong enough to risk exposure.

So I fell in love with my second husband. This time, the emotion was much more powerful because I knew he had seen something of my real before he took me on. I thought him beautiful, a golden man, flamboyant and seductively hollow, like a rocket into which I could squeeze myself and guide the flight, using his engines. He was so large he filled a room, his laugh set it shaking, his shining head topped everyone, he drew all eyes. In the turmoil of his wake I found breathing space, I could advance or retreat as I chose. He had another desirable asset and that was his lack of self-restraint. He never talked if he could shout, he never saved if he could spend, he was full of tall stories and the drinks were always on him. All of which combined to make him a natural force and natural forces can be harnessed for other ends. By his noisy, infuriating, unpredictable, ebullient and blustering existence he made me look, in comparison, a good, calm, reasonable and deeply feminine woman and thus I was able, over the years with him, to allow my real self out for airings in the sure knowledge that though

I might not be as adorable as the doll, I was bound to appear more acceptable than I actually was.

There were drawbacks, of course. Originally, the space within our relationship was almost entirely taken up with the volume of his ego and I made do in a little left-over corner. He breathed deeply, his lungs fully expanded, and I breathed lightly, in short thin gasps, and there was air enough for both of us. But then things changed. I learned a trade, began to work, worked hard and earned money. Hey, he said, getting a little stuffy in here, isn't it? Sorry, darling, I said. I breathed more deeply and new ideas rushed in. The voices of American women reached me, ideas on women's rights that linked me to the clamour of the outside world. For the first time I saw myself face to face, recognised myself, realised that I was not my own creation, uniquely formed in special circumstances, but much of a muchness with other women, a fairly standard female product made by a conveyor-belt society. Inner battles, to be fought for myself alone, became outer battles, to be fought alongside the whole female sex. Release, euphoria. Look, said my husband, I haven't enough room. Neither have I, I said. I would not placate, I would not apologise, I would not give ground any more because I was connected now to a larger army that waged a bigger war, and rescue was at hand. The slaves had revolted and even the most abject gained strength for their individual skirmishes from the growing awareness that they were not personally slavish but merely enslaved. My poor man had his problems, too, but I felt no pity, then. The walls of our relationship were closing in, we fought each other as the oxygen gave out and finally I made it into the cold, invigorating fresh air. The dolly died of double pneumonia but I was still alive.

That is a brief sketch of two marriages, founded on something we all called love because we lived in the romantic West and what other reason is allowed for marriage, if not love? On the surface, of course, the upheavals were not so apparent, being thought of as private quarrels, and I have anyway condensed them greatly—they were actually spread over seven years each, the seven years they say it takes a human to replace every cell of body skin. In the lulls between there were good times, when we laughed together and shared quite a deal of tenderness and celebrated the birth of children, and just ordinary times when we went about the business of marriage, the paying of bills, the buying of goods, the cooking and the cleaning and the entertainment of friends, as every couple does. I make very little of them because the world made so much, crowding round the happy wife, the successful husband, and abruptly turning away, turning a blind and embarrassed eye to the sobbing wife and the angry, frustrated husband. Besides, the violence was endemic and perhaps because of that, ignored as much as possible. Each of us thought we were building new houses, especially designed for us, but we didn't know about the quicksand beneath or the death-watch beetles munching the timbers. An all-pervading dishonesty hung over our enterprise. I was not what I pretended and neither were they. I sold my soul for a mess of sacrificial femininity, sugar and spice and all things nice. They built a prison with their own masculinity, so constricting it made them red in the face, choleric. And the impulsion to act out our roles, the sheer effort it took, left little time or energy to investigate small sounds of protest within. What reward, anyway, would there be for such investigation? In fact, only penalties would be paid. Loss of social approval, isolation from friends and family, accusations of bizarre behaviour and, for the woman, selfishness, that sin forbidden to any female unless she be extraordinarily rich, beautiful or old. To let the human being show behind the mask of gender was to risk even madness. They might come and take us away to the funny farm, make arrangements for derangement.

Much safer to be what they wanted, what was considered respectable. Much better to lean heavily upon each other for support and set up a quarrel, some drama, whenever the inner voices grew querulous and needed to be drowned. *Men,* said my mother, wiping my tears away. *Women,* said my father, soothing a husband. They sounded calm and quite pleased. Well, it was all very natural, wasn't it?

Long before all this, in my very first close encounter with the opposite sex, the pattern was laid down. I was ten at the time and jaunted daily back and forth to school on a bus. Every morning a boy was also waiting at the stop, he with his mates and I with mine. I liked the way he looked, I laughed a little louder when he was about. One afternoon, on the way home, it happened. I was sitting right at the front of the bus and he was two rows behind. There came a rustle, sounds of suppressed mirth, a hand stuck itself over my shoulder and thrust a small piece of paper at me. I unfolded it. There upon the graph-lined page were fat letters in pencil. 'Dear Girl,' said the letters, 'I love you.'

I read the message and stared out of the window and watched the grass that lined the road grow as green as emeralds, as if a light had been lit under every leaf. An ache started at my chest and spread through every vein until I was heavy, drugged with glucose, banjaxed by that most potent of love-surrogates—thick undiluted narcissism. A boy, a stranger, a member of the male sex, encased in his own unknown life, lying on his unknown bed, had thought of me and, by doing so, given me surreality. Until that moment 'I' was who I thought I was. From then on for a very long time, 'I' was whoever a man thought I was. That pencilled note signalled the end of an autonomy I was not to experience again for many years. As I turned towards that boy, tilting my chin, narrowing my eyes, pulling down my underlip to show my pearly teeth, giving him my first consciously manufactured, all synthetic skin-deep smile, I entered into my flawed inheritance.

Looking back on all this and other episodes of lust and affection, encounters that lasted a week or a year, the picture seems at first glance chaotic and a gloomy sort of chaos at that. Love and failure. By the standards of my time, success in love is measured in bronze and gold and diamonds, anniversaries of the day when love was firstly publicly seen to be there, at the altar. Thus I am found wanting, like any other whose marriage and relationships have ended in separation, and to be found wanting is meant to induce a sense of failure because those who do not conform must be rendered impotent.

In fact, people of my generation, like all the generations before, have had little chance of success in love of any kind. Many of those who offer the longevity of their marriage as proof of enduring love are often only revealing their own endurance in the face of ravaging compromises and a resulting anaesthesia that has left them half-way dead. In the name of that love they have jettisoned every grace considered admirable in any other part or act of life: honesty, dignity, self-respect, courtesy, kindness, integrity, steadfastness of principle. They have said those things to each other that are unsayable and done those things that are undoable and there is no health in them. They have not been true to themselves and therefore they are false to everyone else, including their children. The man has become and been allowed to become an autocrat, a tin-pot dictator in love's police state. The woman has lowered herself upon the floor to lick his jackboots. Or, sometimes, vice versa. What would never have been permitted strangers is given a free licence under love—abuse, insults, petty denigration, physical attack, intrusions on personal privacy, destruction of personal beliefs, destruction of any other friendships, destruction of sex itself. In order to enter the kingdom of love they have shrunk themselves to the space of less than one and, atrophied in every part, they claim love's crown. Two individuals who could have reached some stature have settled for being pygmies whose life's work, now, is the similar distortion of their offspring.

If love takes any other form than this tight, monogamous, heterosexual, lifelong reproductive unit, blessed by the law, the State, the priests and sanctified by gods, it is dismissed as an aberration, hounded as a perversion, insulted as a failure and refused the label 'love'. The incredible shrinking couple is presented to the world as the central aim and reward of life, a holy grail for which it is never too early to begin searching. Worst of all, we are given to believe that these dwarfish twosomes form the rock upon which all the rest of life is built, from the mental health of children to whole political systems and to remain outside it is to opt out of a cosmic responsibility and threaten the very roots of the human community. Love is all, they say. Love makes the world go round, they say. And you know it's true love, they say, when two people remain together from youth to death.

But you don't and it doesn't and you can't. The truth is that we have not yet created upon this earth the conditions in which true love can exist. Most of us are quite aware that most of mankind's other developments, emotional or technological, have been dependent upon certain prerequisites. Fire had to be discovered before we could develop a taste for cooked food and a pot to cook it in. Mass literacy was only possible after the invention of printing and printing itself depended on the much earlier Chinese discovery of paper-making. The geodesic dome was an absolute impossibility before the computer age. The emotions are based on something of the same rules. Men's lives were not overshadowed by the certainty of death (and this is still so in some primitive tribes) until life itself was safer and death could be seen inevitably to arrive without sudden injury or accident. Unlike his fellow Greeks, Xenophanes was a monotheist, largely because he guessed that the physical characteristics of the earth changed with time and belief in one universal god is dependent upon belief in universal rules. And man can only be said to have become truly self-conscious after Freud's delineation of the unconscious. Just so has love its necessary prerequisites, its birth-time in history, its most favourable climatic conditions.

So for all that we lay claim to an eternal heritage of love, man's bosom companion since the dawn of time, we have got it wrong. We have called other emotions love and they do not smell as sweet. Love itself has been very nearly impossible for most of us most of our history and is only just becoming possible today. I failed in love, like many others, because given the tools I had to hand the work could not be done. More hopelessly still, the very blueprint was flawed, a rough sketch of the eventual edifice without a single practical instruction, without a brick or a nail, without a vital part or principle. Dreams are not enough.

JOURNAL PROMPT:

From your readings to date and from your life experience, do you think young women today still believe that "some day my prince will come"?

COLLABORATIVE EXERCISE:

Tweedie believes that "we have not yet created upon this earth the conditions in which true love can exist." Do you agree or disagree? As a group, define the qualities of "true love." Has your perception of "true love" changed through the years?

ESSAY ASSIGNMENT:

1. The author of this piece relies heavily on figurative language to enhance her essay. In describing herself, she makes several allusions to literary works. What are these allusions? Do you think they contribute to the overall effectiveness of this piece? Why or why not?
2. What is your favorite film that deals with romantic love, and why is it a favorite? Explore the attitude toward love that the film reveals, both explicitly and implicitly.
3. Discuss some of the myths Tweedie refers to that surround the subject of marriage. Where do you think they originated? Do you believe these myths hold any intrinsic value? Do you believe they are potentially dangerous for a marriage? Explain.

LINDA GREGG is the author of *The Sacraments of Desire, Too Bright to See, Things and Flesh,* and *Alma.* In this poem the author describes the conditions necessary for love to bloom, although these conditions, according to her, are not rational, linear ones.

LINDA GREGG

THE CONDITIONS

You will have to stand in the clearing and see
your arms glow near ferns and roots. Hear things
moving in the branches heavy with black green.
You will be silvery, knowing death could capture
you in that condition of yielding. You will be alarmed
by everything real, even moisture. She will not
tell you there is nothing to fear. You will come
to see her and she will blaze upon you, stun you
with the radiance of a feral world. But she cannot
take you up into herself whenever you desire,
as the world can. She is the other nature,
and sexual in a way that makes the intervening flesh
thin as paper. You will feel your bones getting
lighter. You will feel more and more at risk.
You will think her shining drains you of meaning,
but it is a journey you must take. And when the sun
returns, when you walk from the forest to your world,
you will have known the land where your spirit lives.
Will have diagrams drawn by creases on your body,
and maps on your palms that were also there. Now
you will recognize them as geography. You will know
an unkempt singing you will never hear without her.

JOURNAL PROMPT:

Write the conditions—in a poem if you can—under which you give yourself to a love relationship.

COLLABORATIVE EXERCISE:

Poet Linda Gregg asks a great deal of her lover. Working in small groups, discuss what she expects of the other person. Are her requests reasonable and rational or impossible? Why or why not?

ESSAY ASSIGNMENT:

1. Write a line-by-line explication of "The Conditions."
2. What is Gregg implying about romantic love? How does her attitude compare to Jill Tweedie's attitude in "The Experience"?

This selection comes from a text on human sexuality. Here, **Susan M. Garfield** traces the history of love's role in marriage from the time of the ancient Greeks.

SUSAN M. GARFIELD

Love's Role in Marriage

The joining of love and marriage has not been a constant in human history. An overview of love's role in marriage beginning with the ancient Greeks and concluding with modern times reveals that the notion of love as a prerequisite for marriage has been a relatively recent phenomenon. The ancient Greeks perceived a schism between sexual and spiritual love. They distinguished between *eros,* carnal love associated with the sensual, physical and sexual aspects of love, and *agapé,* spiritual love which is associated with protective and altruistic feelings. *Agapé* is the non-demanding side of love, which is demonstrated, for example, in parents' love for their children and in the genuine concern that we have for the life and growth of those whom we love.

Although *eros* and *agapé* may have occurred in the ancient Greek marriage, a man married primarily in order to increase his estate and to insure its continuity by producing children. According to the Greek philosopher Demosthenes, the appropriate age for marriage was eighteen for a woman and thirty-seven for a man; the appropriate role for a wife was "to provide . . . legitimate children and to grow old faithfully in the interior of the house." Greeks regarded heterosexual domestic relations as a normal part of a man's life cycle, but they did not assume that the major love of a man's life would be his wife.

Greek culture considered women to be inferior to men; conversely, it celebrated what it perceived to be the greater physical beauty of young boys and the intellect of mature men. Apparently, the male homosexual relationship—and we do not know how prevalent such relationships were—was that of an older man and a youth. It was believed that the unity of *eros* and *agapé* might be realized in such relationships. The underlying assumption was that the young boy would himself grow up, in time, marry, continue his family line, and engage in normal masculine activities. Then, at sometime in his life, he might, in turn, have a relationship with a younger man or boy. A man's liaisons with boys and with *heterae,* the educated and independent entertainer women of Athenian society, were not considered threats to marriage.

Christianity, following Jewish tradition, condemned homosexuality and drew a distinction between love and sex. Under the influence of the church, sexuality was suppressed and women were idealized as nonsexual beings. The idealization of women reached its zenith in Mariolatry, the adoration of the Virgin Mother.

In the eleventh century courtly love, a new male-female relationship, emerged, which combined the idealization of women with chivalry, the knights' code of honor. Love became a novel and fashionable subject of discussion among aristocrats, who, in their formal "courts of love," argued its merits, described its characteristics and even devised rules to regulate lovers' behavior. Love came to mean a romantic relationship with someone other than one's spouse. It was synonymous with desire, yearning for what one could never entirely possess.

A liaison was formed between a knight and a lady, a woman whose husband, more than likely, was away for many years fighting a crusade. The knight pledged unselfish service to the lady. She was his source of inspiration. He fought tournaments in her honor and praised her goodness and beauty in song and poetry. In keeping with the Christian contempt for sex, chastity was observed in these affairs. Occasionally, the "purity" of the love was put to the test, when a couple slept together nude but refrained from sexual intercourse.

The courtly love relationship developed out of the social conditions of medieval life. Marriage in the Middle Ages had several clearly defined functions: financial benefits, personal protection, procreation, but love was not among them. Romantic love and marriage were two separate entities that fulfilled separate needs. If marriage entailed obligation, love, on the contrary, was freely extended and returned. It enabled men and women to experience feelings of tenderness for one another; it introduced gentleness and restraint into the male-female relationship, and it ensured sexual fidelity in marriage. As knighthood declined, however, so did the sexual inhibitions of romantic lovers, and love and sex began to merge, at least, outside of marriage.

The Renaissance period continued to deny the existence of love in marriage. A European nobleman may have had as many as three women in his life: a wife for representative purposes, a mistress for aesthetic conversation and a woman to fulfill his sexual needs. Yet, sometime during the Renaissance the idea that sex and romantic love could exist in marriage and that romantic love was a prelude to marriage began taking hold. Romantic love assumes that it is not necessary to have a separation between spiritual love and marital sex relations and that the latter is sanctified by the former.

Surprisingly, the Puritans of the seventeenth century, whom we regard in a very different light, were, in fact, appreciative of physical closeness coupled with emotional warmth. It is true that they put people in the stocks for committing what we consider minor social transgressions such as gossiping, but they also engaged in *bundling,* where sweethearts spent long cold winter nights together in bed fully clothed. A New England custom for two centuries, *bundling* afforded several practical benefits: warmth, privacy, the avoidance of a return journey in treacherous darkness. Moreover, the Puritans apparently considered sex a good and natural part of marriage. Pastor Daniel Rogers preached to his congregation, "Married love is a sweet compound of spiritual affection and carnal affection, and this blend of the two is the vital spirit and heartblood of wedlock."

In the eighteenth and nineteenth centuries, politics, economics and technology combined to underscore the need for stable monogamous family life. Revolutions tumbled monarchs and leveled aristocratic regimes; common folk, citizens of new democracies, could not afford various companions to meet various needs. Moreover, the industrial revolution fostered the idea that the family was a refuge, a safe harbor, from the isolation and alienation of a rapidly industrializing society. Kindness, altruism, self-sacrifice, peace, harmony: all were to be found in the ideal nineteenth-century Victorian family.

What happened to sex? The Victorians had large families, but sexual desire was regarded as an exclusively male phenomenon; women were supposed to be passionless, actually devoid of sexual feeling. Men sought sexual fulfillment outside of marriage, and prostitution flourished on a grand scale. A double standard of behavior was recognized: Men had far more sexual freedom than women and women were categorized as "good" and "bad." Men married the former; they had sexual relations with the latter.

In the twentieth century, in Western countries particularly, romantic love has become a pre- and co-requisite for marriage. However, soaring divorce rates in recent decades may indicate that the romance requirement is having a disruptive effect on the institution of marriage itself. In explanation, psychologists suggest that we often seek in our mates those qualities which we, ourselves, lack, with a resulting personality clash that can destroy even the strongest romantic attraction. Moreover, the changing self-image of women is reflected in modern marriage. Unwilling to play traditional nurturing roles, eager to achieve career goals, outspoken about their own sexual needs, many women have concluded that marriage with or without romance is not as important a factor in their lives as it was for their mother and grandmothers.

In despair, modern romantics are experimenting with various forms of marriage: open marriage; marriage by contract; homosexual marriage; group marriage; childless marriage; celibate marriage; and no marriage (living together without benefit of ceremony). The search for *eros* and *agapé,* together forever, continues.

JOURNAL PROMPT:

In your opinion, is there a difference between *loving* someone and *being in love?* Explain.

COLLABORATIVE EXERCISE:

Working in small groups, discuss the idea of a marriage grounded in love vs. a marriage of convenience and sexual fulfillment only.

ESSAY ASSIGNMENT:

1. Examine the advantages and disadvantages of arranged marriage vs. modern Western marriage.
2. The author claims that "the romance requirement is having a disruptive effect on the institution of marriage itself." Respond to this assertion.
3. What is the origin of the honeymoon? Has the tradition of the honeymoon changed over time?

JOY HARJO is a Native American who writes about the Native American experience. She is the author of poetry, screenplays, and essays. Harjo lives in Albuquerque, New Mexico, and received an American Book Award for *In Mad Love and War* (1990). Her most recent work is *A Map to the Next World: Poems.*

JOY HARJO

THREE GENERATIONS OF NATIVE AMERICAN WOMEN'S BIRTH EXPERIENCE

It was still dark when I awakened in the stuffed back room of my mother-in-law's small rented house with what felt like hard cramps. At 17 years of age I had read everything I could from the Tahlequah Public Library about pregnancy and giving birth. But nothing prepared me for what was coming. I awakened my child's father and then ironed him a shirt before we walked the four blocks to the Indian hospital because we had no car and no money for a taxi. He had been working with another Cherokee artist silk-screening signs for specials at the supermarket and making $5 a day, and had to leave me alone at the hospital because he had to go to work. We didn't awaken his mother. She had to get up soon enough to fix breakfast for her daughter and granddaughter before leaving for her job at the nursing home. I knew my life was balanced at the edge of great, precarious change and I felt alone and cheated. Where was the circle of women to acknowledge and honor this birth?

It was still dark as we walked through the cold morning, under oaks that symbolized the stubbornness and endurance of the Cherokee people who had made Tahlequah their capital in the new lands. I looked for handholds in the misty gray sky, for a voice announcing this impending miracle. I wanted to change everything; I wanted to go back to a place before childhood, before our tribe's removal to Oklahoma. What kind of life was I bringing this child into? I was a poor, mixed-blood woman heavy with a child who would suffer the struggle of poverty, the legacy of loss. For the second time in my life I felt the sharp tug of my own birth cord, still connected to my mother. I believe it never pulls away, until death, and even then it becomes a streak in the sky symbolizing that most important warrior road. In my teens I had fought my mother's weaknesses with all my might, and here I was at 17, becoming as my mother, who was in Tulsa, cooking breakfasts and preparing for the lunch shift at a factory cafeteria as I walked to the hospital to give birth. I should be with her; instead, I was far from her house, in the house of a mother-in-law who later would try to use witchcraft to destroy me.

After my son's father left me I was prepped for birth. This meant my pubic area was shaved completely and then I endured the humiliation of an enema, all at the hands of strangers. I was left alone in a room painted government green. An overwhelming antiseptic smell emphasized the sterility of the hospital, a hospital built because of the U.S. government's treaty and responsibility to provide health care to Indian people.

I intellectually understood the stages of labor, the place of transition, of birth—but it was difficult to bear the actuality of it, and to bear it alone. Yet in some ways I wasn't alone, for history surrounded me. It is with the birth of children that history is given form and voice. Birth is one of the most sacred acts we take part in and witness in our lives. But sacredness seemed to be far from my lonely labor room in the Indian hospital. I heard a woman screaming in the next room with her pain, and I wanted to comfort her. The nurse used her as a bad example to the rest of us who were struggling to keep our suffering silent.

The doctor was a military man who had signed on this watch not for the love of healing or out of awe at the miracle of birth, but to fulfill a contract for medical school payments. I was another statistic to him; he touched me as if he were moving equipment from one place to another. During my last visit I was given the option of being sterilized. He explained to me that the moment of birth was the best time to do it. I was handed the form but chose not to sign it, and am amazed now that I didn't think too much of it at the time. Later I would learn that many Indian women who weren't fluent in English signed, thinking it was a form giving consent for the doctor to deliver their babies. Others were sterilized without even the formality of signing. My light skin had probably saved me from such a fate. It wouldn't be the first time in my life.

When my son was finally born I had been deadened with a needle in my spine. He was shown to me—the incredible miracle nothing prepared me for—then taken from me in the name of medical progress. I fell asleep with the weight of chemicals and awoke yearning for the child I had suffered for, had anticipated in the months proceeding from this unexpected genesis when I was still 16 and a student at Indian school. I was not allowed to sit up or walk because of the possibility of paralysis (one of the drug's side effects), and when I finally got to hold him, the nurse stood guard as if I would hurt him. I felt enmeshed in a system in which the wisdom that had carried my people from generation to generation was ignored. In that place I felt ashamed I was an Indian woman. But I was also proud of what my body had accomplished despite the rape by the bureaucracy's machinery, and I got us out of there as soon as possible. My son would flourish on beans and fry bread, and on the dreams and stories we fed him.

My daughter was born four years later, while I was an art student at the University of New Mexico. Since my son's birth I had waitressed, cleaned hospital rooms, filled cars with gas (while wearing a miniskirt), worked as a nursing assistant, and led dance classes at a health spa. I knew I didn't want to cook and waitress all my life, as my mother had done. I had watched the varicose veins grow branches on her legs, and as they grew, her zest for dancing and sports dissolved into utter tiredness. She had been born with a caul over her face, the sign of a gifted visionary.

My earliest memories are of my mother writing songs on an ancient Underwood typewriter after she had washed and waxed the kitchen floor on her hands and knees. She too had wanted something different for her life. She had left an impoverished existence at age 17, bound for the big city of Tulsa. She was shamed in a time in which to be even part Indian was to be an outcast in the great U.S. system. Half her relatives were Cherokee full-bloods from near Jay, Oklahoma, who for the most part had nothing to do with white people. The other half were musically inclined "white trash" addicted to country-western music and Holy Roller fervor. She thought she could disappear in the city; no one would know her family, where she came from. She had dreams of singing and had once been offered a job singing on the radio but turned it down because she was shy. Later one of her songs would be stolen before she could copyright it and would make someone else rich. She would quit writing songs. She and my father would divorce and she would be forced to work for money to feed and clothe four children, all born within two years of each other.

As a child growing up in Oklahoma, I liked to be told the story of my birth. I would beg for it while my mother cleaned and ironed. "You almost killed me," she would say. "We almost died." That I could kill my mother filled me with remorse and shame. And I imagined the push-pull of my life, which is a legacy I deal with even now when I am twice as old as my mother was at my birth. I loved to hear the story of my warrior fight for my breath. The way it was told, it had been my decision to live. When I got older, I realized we were both nearly casualties of the system, the same system flourishing in the Indian hospital where later my son Phil would be born.

My parents felt lucky to have insurance, to be able to have their children in the hospital. My father came from a fairly prominent Muscogee Creek family. *His* mother was a full-blood who in the early 1920s got her degree in art. She was a painter. She gave birth to him in a private hospital in Oklahoma City; at least that's what I think he told me before he died at age 53. It was something of which they were proud.

This experience was much different from my mother's own birth. She and five of her six brothers were born at home, with no medical assistance. The only time a doctor was called was when someone was dying. When she was born her mother named her Wynema, a Cherokee name my mother says means beautiful woman, and Jewell, for a can of shortening stored in the room where she was born.

I wanted something different for my life, for my son, and for my daughter, who later was born in a university hospital in Albuquerque. It was a bright summer morning when she was ready to begin her journey. I still had no car, but I had enough money saved for a taxi for a ride to the hospital. She was born "naturally," without drugs. I could look out of the hospital window while I was in labor at the bluest sky in the world. Her father was present in the delivery room—though after her birth he disappeared on a drinking binge. I understood his despair, but did not agree with the painful means to describe it. A few days later Rainy Dawn was presented to the sun at her father's pueblo and given a name so that she will always be recognized as a part of the people, as a child of the sun.

That's not to say that my experience in the hospital reached perfection. The clang of metal against metal in the delivery room had the effect of a tuning fork reverberating fear in my pelvis. After giving birth I held my daughter, but they took her from me for "processing." I refused to lie down to be wheeled to my room after giving birth: I wanted to walk out of there to find my daughter. We reached a compromise and I rode in a wheelchair. When we reached the room I stood up and walked to the nursery and demanded my daughter. I knew she needed me. That began my war with the nursery staff, who deemed me unknowledgeable because I was Indian and poor. Once again I felt the brushfire of shame, but I'd learned to put it out much more quickly, and I demanded early release so I could take care of my baby without the judgment of strangers.

I wanted something different for Rainy, and as she grew up I worked hard to prove that I could make "something" of my life. I obtained two degrees as a single mother. I wrote poetry, screenplays, became a professor, and tried to live a life that would be a positive influence for both of my children. My work in this life has to do with reclaiming the memory stolen from our peoples when we were dispossessed from our lands east of the Mississippi; it has to do with restoring us. I am proud of our history, a history so powerful that it both destroyed my father and guarded him. It's a history that claims my mother as she lives not far from the place her mother was born, names her as she cooks in the cafeteria of a small college in Oklahoma.

When my daughter told me she was pregnant, I wasn't surprised. I had known it before she did, or at least before she would admit it to me. I felt despair, as if nothing had changed or ever would. She had run away from Indian school with her boyfriend and they had been living in the streets of Gallup, a border town notorious for the suicides and deaths of Indian peoples. I brought her and her boyfriend with me because it was the only way I could bring her home. At age 16, she was fighting me just as I had so fiercely fought my mother. She was making the same mistakes. I felt as if everything I had accomplished had been in vain. Yet I felt strangely empowered, too, at this repetition of history, this continuance, by a new possibility of life and love, and I steadfastly stood by my daughter.

I had a university job, so I had insurance that covered my daughter. She saw an obstetrician in town who was reputed to be one of the best. She had the choice of a birthing room. She had the finest care. Despite this, I once again battled with a system in which physicians are taught the art of healing by dissecting cadavers. My daughter went into labor a month early. We both knew intuitively the baby was ready, but how to explain that to a system in which numbers and statistics provide the base of understanding? My daughter would have her labor interrupted: her blood pressure would rise because of the drug given to her to stop the labor. She would be given an unneeded amniocentesis and would have her labor induced—after having it artificially stopped! I was warned that if I took her out of the hospital so her labor could occur naturally my insurance would cover nothing.

My daughter's induced labor was unnatural and difficult, monitored by machines, not by touch. I was shocked. I felt as if I'd come full circle, as if I were watching my mother's labor and the struggle of my own birth. But I was there in the hospital room with her, as neither my mother had been for me, nor her mother for her. My daughter and I went through the labor and birth together.

And when Krista Rae was born she was born to her family. Her father was there for her, as were both her grandmothers and my friend who had flown in to be with us. Her paternal great-grandparents and aunts and uncles had also arrived from the Navajo Reservation to honor her. Something *had* changed.

Four days later, I took my granddaughter to the Saguaro forest before dawn and gave her the name I had dreamed for her just before her birth. Her name looks like clouds of mist settling around a sacred mountain as it begins to speak. A female ancestor approaches on a horse. We are all together.

JOURNAL PROMPT:

Do you consider this essay hopeful or discouraging? Explain.

COLLABORATIVE EXERCISE:

Harjo relates some very humiliating, painful moments connected with birth. She admits, "I wanted to go back to a place before childhood, before our tribe's removal to Oklahoma. What kind of life was I bringing this child into?" Consider the responsibilities—physical, emotional, and ethical—involved in deciding to have a child.

ESSAY ASSIGNMENT:

1. The story of birth holds the possibilities of repeating history within a family, of creating a "continuance." If possible, trace three other generations of birth experience from your own family. Compare the experiences to Harjo's. How are they the same? How are they different?
2. There are several views concerning the best time in a couple's life to begin a family. Do you think there is an ideal time and age to have children? Interview parents who had their children in their twenties and other parents who decided to wait until their thirties or forties. Discuss the advantages and disadvantages of both.
3. Harjo relies a lot on memory to tell her story. She writes: "I liked to be told the story of my birth. I would beg for it while my mother cleaned and ironed." Do you know any stories passed down to you about your birth, your first days of life? Are you also aware of any other birth stories of family members? Why do you think someone would desire to know his or her birth story?

BOBBIE ANN MASON is a PEN/Hemingway Award winner for her book *Shiloh and Other Stories,* from which this selection is taken. Her novel *Feather Crowns* was nominated for the National Book Critics Circle Award and has won the Southern Book Award. Mason lives in Kentucky.

BOBBIE ANN MASON

SHILOH

Leroy Moffitt's wife, Norma Jean, is working on her pectorals. She lifts three-pound dumbbells to warm up, then progresses to a twenty-pound barbell. Standing with her legs apart, she reminds Leroy of Wonder Woman.

"I'd give anything if I could just get these muscles to where they're real hard," says Norma Jean. "Feel this arm. It's not as hard as the other one."

"That's 'cause you're right-handed," says Leroy, dodging as she swings the barbell in an arc.

"Do you think so?"

"Sure."

Leroy is a truckdriver. He injured his leg in a highway accident four months ago, and his physical therapy, which involves weights and a pulley, prompted Norma Jean to try building herself up. Now she is attending a body-building class. Leroy has been collecting temporary disability since his tractor-trailer jackknifed in Missouri, badly twisting his left leg in its socket. He has a steel pin in his hip. He will probably not be able to drive his rig again. It sits in the backyard, like a gigantic bird that has flown home to roost. Leroy has been home in Kentucky for three months, and his leg is almost healed, but the accident frightened him and he does not want to drive any more long hauls. He is not sure what to do next. In the meantime, he makes things from craft kits. He started by building a miniature log cabin from notched Popsicle sticks. He varnished it and placed it on the TV set, where it remains. It reminds him of a rustic Nativity scene. Then he tried string art (sailing ships on black velvet), a macramé owl kit, a snap-together B-17 Flying Fortress, and a lamp made out of a model truck, with a light fixture screwed on the top of the cab. At first the kits were diversions, something to kill time, but now he is thinking about building a full-scale log house from a kit. It would be considerably cheaper than building a regular house, and besides, Leroy has grown to appreciate how things are put together. He has begun to realize that in all the years he was on the road he never took time to examine anything. He was always flying past scenery.

"They won't let you build a log cabin in any of the new subdivisions," Norma Jean tells him.

"They will if I tell them it's for you," he says, teasing her. Ever since they were married, he has promised Norma Jean he would build her a new home one day. They have always rented, and the house they live in is small and nondescript. It does not even feel like a home, Leroy realizes now.

Norma Jean works at the Rexall drugstore, and she has acquired an amazing amount of information about cosmetics. When she explains to Leroy the three stages of complexion care, involving creams, toners, and moisturizers, he thinks happily of other petroleum products—axle grease, diesel fuel. This is a connection between him and Norma Jean. Since he has been home, he has felt unusually tender about his wife and guilty over his long absences. But he can't tell what she feels about him. Norma Jean has never complained about his traveling; she has never made hurt remarks, like calling his truck a "widowmaker." He is reasonably certain she has been faithful to him, but he wishes she would celebrate his permanent homecoming more happily. Norma Jean is often startled to find Leroy at home, and he thinks she seems a little disappointed about it. Perhaps he reminds her too much of the early days of their marriage, before he went on the road. They had a child who died as an infant, years ago. They never speak about their memories of Randy, which have almost faded, but now that Leroy is home all the time, they sometimes feel awkward around each other, and Leroy wonders if one of them should mention the child. He has the feeling that they are waking up out of a dream together—that they must create a new marriage, start afresh. They are lucky they are still married. Leroy has read that for most people losing a child destroys the marriage—or else he heard this on *Donahue*. He can't always remember where he learns things anymore.

At Christmas, Leroy bought an electric organ for Norma Jean. She used to play the piano when she was in high school. "It don't leave you," she told him once. "It's like riding a bicycle."

The new instrument had so many keys and buttons that she was bewildered by it at first. She touched the keys tentatively, pushed some buttons, then pecked out "Chopsticks." It came out in an amplified fox-trot rhythm, with marimba sounds.

"It's an orchestra!" she cried.

The organ had a pecan-look finish and eighteen preset chords, with optional flute, violin, trumpet, clarinet, and banjo accompaniments. Norma Jean mastered the organ almost immediately. At first she played Christmas songs. Then she bought *The Sixties Songbook* and learned every tune in it, adding variations to each with the rows of brightly colored buttons.

"I didn't like these old songs back then," she said. "But I have this crazy feeling I missed something."

"You didn't miss a thing," said Leroy.

Leroy likes to lie on the couch and smoke a joint and listen to Norma Jean play "Can't Take My Eyes Off You" and "I'll Be Back." He is back again. After fifteen years on the road, he is finally settling down with the woman he loves. She is still pretty. Her skin is flawless. Her frosted curls resemble pencil trimmings.

Now that Leroy has come home to stay, he notices how much the town has changed. Subdivisions are spreading across western Kentucky like an oil slick. The sign at the edge of town says "Pop: 11,500"—only seven hundred more than it said twenty years before. Leroy can't figure out who is living in all the new houses. The farmers who used to gather around the courthouse square on Saturday afternoons to play checkers and spit tobacco juice have gone. It has been years since Leroy has thought about the farmers, and they have disappeared without his noticing.

Leroy meets a kid named Stevie Hamilton in the parking lot at the new shopping center. While they pretend to be strangers meeting over a stalled car, Stevie tosses an ounce of marijuana under the front seat of Leroy's car. Stevie is wearing orange jogging shoes and a T-shirt that says CHATTAHOOCHEE SUPER-RAT. His father is a prominent doctor who lives in one of the expensive subdivisions in a new white-columned brick house that looks like a funeral parlor. In the phone book under his name there is a separate number, with the listing "Teenagers."

"Where do you get this stuff?" asks Leroy. "From your pappy?"

"That's for me to know and you to find out," Stevie says. He is slit-eyed and skinny.

"What else you got?"

"What you interested in?"

"Nothing special. Just wondered."

Leroy used to take speed on the road. Now he has to go slowly. He needs to be mellow. He leans back against the car and says, "I'm aiming to build me a log house, soon as I get time. My wife, though, I don't think she likes the idea."

"Well, let me know when you want me again," Stevie says. He has a cigarette in his cupped palm, as though sheltering it from the wind. He takes a long drag, then stomps it on the asphalt and slouches away.

Stevie's father was two years ahead of Leroy in high school. Leroy is thirty-four. He married Norma Jean when they were both eighteen, and their child Randy was born a few months later, but he died at the age of four months and three days. He would be about Stevie's age now. Norma Jean and Leroy were at the drive-in, watching a double feature (*Dr. Strangelove* and *Lover Come Back*), and the baby was sleeping in the back seat. When the first movie ended, the baby was dead. It was the sudden infant death syndrome. Leroy remembers handing Randy to a nurse at the emergency room, as though he were offering her a large doll as a present. A dead baby feels like a sack of flour. "It just happens sometimes," said the doctor, in what Leroy always recalls as a nonchalant tone. Leroy can hardly remember the child anymore, but he still sees vividly a scene from *Dr. Strangelove* in which the President of the United States was talking in a folksy voice on the hot line to the Soviet premier about the bomber accidentally headed toward Russia. He was in the War Room, and the world map was lit up. Leroy remembers Norma Jean standing catatonically beside him in the hospital and himself thinking: Who is this strange girl? He had forgotten who she was. Now scientists are saying that crib death is caused by a virus. Nobody knows anything, Leroy thinks. The answers are always changing.

When Leroy gets home from the shopping center, Norma Jean's mother, Mabel Beasley, is there. Until this year, Leroy has not realized how much time she spends with Norma Jean. When she visits, she inspects the closets and then the plants, informing Norma Jean when a plant is droopy or yellow. Mabel calls the plants "flowers," although there are never any blooms. She always notices if Norma Jean's laundry is piling up. Mabel is a short, overweight woman whose tight, brown-dyed curls look more like a wig than the actual wig she sometimes wears. Today she has brought Norma Jean an off-white dust ruffle she made for the bed; Mabel works in a custom-upholstery shop.

"This is the tenth one I made this year," Mabel says. "I got started and couldn't stop."

"It's real pretty," says Norma Jean.

"Now we can hide things under the bed," says Leroy, who gets along with his mother-in-law primarily by joking with her. Mabel has never really forgiven him for disgracing her by getting Norma Jean pregnant. When the baby died, she said that fate was mocking her.

"What's that thing?" Mabel says to Leroy in a loud voice, pointing to a tangle of yarn on a piece of canvas.

Leroy holds it up for Mabel to see. "It's my needlepoint," he explains. "This is a *Star Trek* pillow cover."

"That's what a woman would do," says Mabel. "Great day in the morning!"

"All the big football players on TV do it," he says.

"Why, Leroy, you're always trying to fool me. I don't believe you for one minute. You don't know what to do with yourself—that's the whole trouble. Sewing!"

"I'm aiming to build us a log house," says Leroy. "Soon as my plans come."

"Like *heck* you are," says Norma Jean. She takes Leroy's needlepoint and shoves it into a drawer. "You have to find a job first. Nobody can afford to build now anyway."

Mabel straightens her girdle and says, "I still think before you get tied down y'all ought to take a little run to Shiloh."

"One of these days, Mama," Norma Jean says impatiently.

Mabel is talking about Shiloh, Tennessee. For the past few years, she has been urging Leroy and Norma Jean to visit the Civil War battleground there. Mabel went there on her honeymoon—the only real trip she ever took. Her husband died of a perforated ulcer when Norma Jean was ten, but Mabel, who was accepted into the United Daughters of the Confederacy in 1975, is still preoccupied with going back to Shiloh.

"I've been to kingdom come and back in that truck out yonder," Leroy says to Mabel, "but we never yet set foot in that battleground. Ain't that something? How did I miss it?"

"It's not even that far," Mabel says.

After Mabel leaves, Norma Jean reads to Leroy from a list she has made. "Things you could do," she announces. "You could get a job as a guard at Union Carbide, where they'd let you set on a stool. You could get on at the lumberyard. You could do a little carpenter work, if you want to build so bad. You could—"

"I can't do something where I'd have to stand up all day."

"You ought to try standing up all day behind a cosmetics counter. It's amazing that I have strong feet, coming from two parents that never had strong feet at all." At the moment Norma Jean is holding on to the kitchen counter, raising her knees one at a time as she talks. She is wearing two-pound ankle weights.

"Don't worry," says Leroy. "I'll do something."

"You could truck calves to slaughter for somebody. You wouldn't have to drive any big old truck for that."

"I'm going to build you this house," says Leroy. "I want to make you a real home."

"I don't want to live in any log cabin."

"It's not a cabin. It's a house."

"I don't care. It looks like a cabin."

"You and me together could lift those logs. It's just like lifting weights."

Norma Jean doesn't answer. Under her breath, she is counting. Now she is marching through the kitchen. She is doing goose steps.

Before his accident, when Leroy came home he used to stay in the house with Norma Jean, watching TV in bed and playing cards. She would cook fried chicken, picnic ham, chocolate pie—all his favorites. Now he is home alone much of the time. In the mornings, Norma Jean disappears, leaving a cooling place in the bed. She eats a cereal called Body Buddies, and she leaves the bowl on the table, with the soggy tan balls floating in a milk puddle. He sees things about Norma Jean that he never realized before. When she chops onions, she stares off into a corner, as if she can't bear to look. She puts on her house slippers almost precisely at nine o'clock every evening and nudges her jogging shoes under the couch. She saves bread heels for the birds. Leroy watches the birds at the feeder. He notices the peculiar way goldfinches fly past the window. They close their wings, then fall, then spread their wings to catch and lift themselves. He wonders if they close their eyes when they fall. Norma Jean closes her eyes when they are in bed. She wants the lights turned out. Even then, he is sure she closes her eyes.

He goes for long drives around town. He tends to drive a car rather carelessly. Power steering and an automatic shift make a car feel so small and inconsequential that his body is hardly involved in the driving process. His injured leg stretches out comfortably. Once or twice he has almost hit something, but even the prospect of an accident seems minor in a car. He cruises the new subdivisions, feeling like a criminal rehearsing for a robbery. Norma Jean is probably right about a log house being inappropriate here in the new subdivisions. All the houses look grand and complicated. They depress him.

One day when Leroy comes home from a drive he finds Norma Jean in tears. She is in the kitchen making a potato and mushroom-soup casserole, with grated-cheese topping. She is crying because her mother caught her smoking.

"I didn't hear her coming. I was standing here puffing away pretty as you please," Norma Jean says, wiping her eyes.

"I knew it would happen sooner or later," says Leroy, putting his arm around her.

"She don't know the meaning of the word 'knock,'" says Norma Jean. "It's a wonder she hadn't caught me years ago."

"Think of it this way," Leroy says. "What if she caught me with a joint?"

"You better not let her!" Norma Jean shrieks. "I'm warning you, Leroy Moffitt!"

"I'm just kidding. Here, play me a tune. That'll help you relax."

Norma Jean puts the casserole in the oven and sets the timer. Then she plays a ragtime tune, with horns and banjo, as Leroy lights up a joint and lies on the couch, laughing to himself about Mabel's catching him at it. He thinks of Stevie Hamilton—a doctor's son pushing grass. Everything is funny. The whole town seems crazy and small. He is reminded of Virgil Mathis, a boastful policeman Leroy used to shoot pool with. Virgil recently led a drug bust in a back room at a bowling alley, where he seized ten thousand dollars' worth of marijuana. The newspaper had a picture of him holding up the bags of grass and grinning widely. Right now, Leroy can imagine Virgil breaking down the door and arresting him with a lungful of smoke. Virgil would probably have been alerted to the scene because of all the racket Norma Jean is making. Now she sounds like a hard-rock band. Norma Jean is terrific. When she switches to a Latin-rhythm version of "Sunshine Superman," Leroy hums along. Norma Jean's foot goes up and down, up and down.

"Well, what do you think?" Leroy says, when Norma Jean pauses to search through her music.

"What do I think about what?"

His mind had gone blank. Then he says, "I'll sell my rig and build us a house." That wasn't what he wanted to say. He wanted to know what she thought—what she *really* thought—about them.

"Don't start in on that again," says Norma Jean. She begins playing "Who'll Be the Next in Line?"

Leroy used to tell hitchhikers his whole life story—about his travels, his hometown, the baby. He would end with a question: "Well, what do you think?" It was just a rhetorical question. In time, he had the feeling that he'd been telling the same story over and over to the same hitchhikers. He quit talking to hitchhikers when he realized how his voice sounded—whining and self-pitying, like some teenage-tragedy song. Now Leroy has the sudden impulse to tell Norma Jean about himself, as if he had just met her. They have known each other so long they have forgotten a lot about each other. They could become reacquainted. But when the oven timer goes off and she runs to the kitchen, he forgets why he wants to do this.

The next day, Mabel drops by. It is Saturday and Norma Jean is cleaning. Leroy is studying the plans for his log house, which have finally come in the mail. He has them spread out on the table—big sheets of stiff blue paper, with diagrams and numbers printed in white. While Norma Jean runs the vacuum, Mabel drinks coffee. She sets her coffee cup on a blueprint.

"I'm just waiting for time to pass," she says to Leroy, drumming her fingers on the table.

As soon as Norma Jean switches off the vacuum, Mabel says in a loud voice, "Did you hear about the datsun dog that killed the baby?"

Norma Jean says, "The word is 'dachshund.'"

Mabel goes on. "I just hoped y'all could see it once before I die, so you could tell me about it." Later, she whispers to Leroy, "You do what I said. A little change is what she needs."

"Your name means 'the king,'" Norma Jean says to Leroy that evening. He is trying to get her to go to Shiloh, and she is reading a book about another century.

"Well, I reckon I ought to be right proud."

"I guess so."

"Am I still king around here?"

Norma Jean flexes her biceps and feels them for hardness. "I'm not fooling around with anybody, if that's what you mean," she says.

"Would you tell me if you were?"

"I don't know."

"What does *your* name mean?"

"It was Marilyn Monroe's real name."

"No kidding!"

"Norma comes from the Normans. They were invaders," she says. She closes her book and looks hard at Leroy. "I'll go to Shiloh with you if you'll stop staring at me."

On Sunday, Norma Jean packs a picnic and they go to Shiloh. To Leroy's relief, Mabel says she does not want to come with them. Norma Jean drives, and Leroy, sitting beside her, feels like some boring hitchhiker she has picked up. He tries some conversation, but she answers him in monosyllables. At Shiloh, she drives aimlessly through the park, past bluffs and trails and steep ravines. Shiloh is an immense place, and Leroy cannot see it as a battleground. It is not what he expected. He thought it would look like a golf course. Monuments are everywhere, showing through the thick clusters of trees. Norma Jean passes the log cabin Mabel mentioned. It is surrounded by tourists looking for bullet holes.

"That's not the kind of log house I've got in mind," says Leroy apologetically.

"I know *that.*"

"This is a pretty place. Your mama was right."

"It's O.K.," says Norma Jean. "Well, we've seen it. I hope she's satisfied."

They burst out laughing together.

At the park museum, a movie on Shiloh is shown every half hour, but they decide that they don't want to see it. They buy a souvenir Confederate flag for Mabel, and then they find a picnic spot near the cemetery. Norma Jean has brought a picnic cooler, with pimiento sandwiches, soft drinks, and Yodels. Leroy eats a sandwich and then smokes a joint, hiding it behind the picnic cooler. Norma Jean has quit smoking altogether. She is picking cake crumbs from the cellophane wrapper, like a fussy bird.

Leroy says, "So the boys in gray ended up in Corinth. The Union soldiers zapped 'em finally. April 7, 1862."

They both know that he doesn't know any history. He is just talking about some of the historical plaques they have read. He feels awkward, like a boy on a date with an older girl. They are still just making conversation.

"Corinth is where Mama eloped to," says Norma Jean.

They sit in silence and stare at the cemetery for the Union dead and, beyond, at a tall cluster of trees. Campers are parked nearby, bumper to bumper, and small children in bright clothing are cavorting and squealing. Norma Jean wads up the cake wrapper and squeezes it tightly in her hand. Without looking at Leroy, she says, "I want to leave you."

Leroy takes a bottle of Coke out of the cooler and flips off the cap. He holds the bottle poised near his mouth but cannot remember to take a drink. Finally he says, "No, you don't."

"Yes, I do."

"I won't let you."

"You can't stop me."

"Don't do me that way."

Leroy knows Norma Jean will have her own way. "Didn't I promise to be home from now on?" he says.

"In some ways, a woman prefers a man who wanders," says Norma Jean. "That sounds crazy, I know."

"You're not crazy."

Leroy remembers to drink from his Coke. Then he says, "Yes, you *are* crazy. You and me could start all over again. Right back at the beginning."

"We *have* started all over again," says Norma Jean. "And this is how it turned out."

"What did I do wrong?"

"Nothing."

"Is this one of those women's lib things?" Leroy asks.

"Don't be funny."

The cemetery, a green slope dotted with white markers, looks like a subdivision site. Leroy is trying to comprehend that his marriage is breaking up, but for some reason he is wondering about white slabs in a graveyard.

"Everything was fine till Mama caught me smoking," says Norma Jean, standing up. "That set something off."

"What are you talking about?"

"She won't leave me alone—*you* won't leave me alone." Norma Jean seems to be crying, but she is looking away from him. "I feel eighteen again. I can't face that all over again." She starts walking away. "No, it *wasn't* fine. I don't know what I'm saying. Forget it."

Leroy takes a lungful of smoke and closes his eyes as Norma Jean's words sink in. He tries to focus on the fact that thirty-five hundred soldiers died on the grounds around him. He can only think of that war as a board game with plastic soldiers. Leroy almost smiles, as he compares the Confederates' daring attack on the Union camps and Virgil Mathis's raid on the bowling alley. General Grant, drunk and furious, shoved the southerners back to Corinth, where Mabel and Jet Beasley were married years later, when Mabel was still thin and good-looking. The next day, Mabel and Jet visited the battleground, and then Norma Jean was born, and then she married Leroy and they had a baby, which they lost, and now Leroy and Norma Jean are here at the same battleground.

Leroy knows he is leaving out a lot. He is leaving out the insides of history. History was always just names and dates to him. It occurs to him that building a house out of logs is similarly empty—too simple. And the real inner workings of a marriage, like most of history, have escaped him. Now he sees that building a log house is the dumbest idea he could have had. It was clumsy of him to think Norma Jean would want a log house. It was a crazy idea. He'll have to think of something else, quickly. He will wad the blueprints into tight balls and fling them into the lake. Then he'll get moving again. He opens his eyes. Norma Jean has moved away and is walking through the cemetery, following a serpentine brick path.

Leroy gets up to follow his wife, but his good leg is asleep and his bad leg still hurts him. Norma Jean is far away, walking rapidly toward the bluff by the river, and he tries to hobble toward her. Some children run past him, screaming noisily. Norma Jean has reached the bluff, and she is looking out over the Tennessee River. Now she turns toward Leroy and waves her arms. Is she beckoning to him? She seems to be doing an exercise for her chest muscles. The sky is unusually pale—the color of the dust ruffle Mabel made for their bed.

JOURNAL PROMPT:

What do you think about the familiar adage, "opposites attract"?

COLLABORATIVE EXERCISE:

Working in small groups, compare the Moffitts' marital situation with the issues discussed in the essay, "Why Marriages Fail." How does the Moffitts' marriage mirror the danger zones discussed in Roiphe's piece? (To begin your discussion, remember that Roiphe refers to adaptability, flexibility, and kindness as a few of the requirements for a successful marriage.) How would the Moffitts' marriage rank on these issues?

ESSAY ASSIGNMENT:

1. Using your knowledge of metaphor and irony, write an essay in which you analyze Mason's choice of titles. Then, go on to examine how and why the trip to Shiloh represents the failure of the Moffitts' marriage.
2. Both Norma Jean and Leroy have lost touch with the past and face the task of trying to piece together their present lives. Specifically, how do both Norma Jean and Leroy contribute to their crumbling marriage?
3. How do you feel about couples taking separate vacations? Is this ever a wise choice? Does it have potential to enhance the marriage? Write an essay in which you explore the pros and cons of couples spending periods of time apart from each other.

ERNEST HEMINGWAY, American novelist and short-story writer, began his writing career as a journalist. During the 1920s, he lived in Paris with a community of writers that included Ezra Pound and Gertrude Stein. Hemingway received the Nobel Prize for Literature in 1954.

ERNEST HEMINGWAY

HILLS LIKE WHITE ELEPHANTS

The hills across the valley of the Ebro were long and white. On this side there was no shade and no trees and the station was between two lines of rails in the sun. Close against the side of the station there was the warm shadow of the building and a curtain, made of strings of bamboo beads, hung across the open door into the bar, to keep out flies. The American and the girl with him sat at a table in the shade, outside the building. It was very hot and the express from Barcelona would come in forty minutes. It stopped at this junction for two minutes and went on to Madrid.

"What should we drink?" the girl asked. She had taken off her hat and put it on the table.

"It's pretty hot," the man said.

"Let's drink beer."

"*Dos cervezas,*" the man said into the curtain.

"Big ones?" a woman asked from the doorway.

"Yes. Two big ones."

The woman brought two glasses of beer and two felt pads. She put the felt pads and the beer glasses on the table and looked at the man and the girl. The girl was looking off at the line of hills. They were white in the sun and the country was brown and dry.

"They look like white elephants," she said.

"I've never seen one," the man drank his beer.

"No, you wouldn't have."

"I might have," the man said. "Just because you say I wouldn't have doesn't prove anything."

The girl looked at the bead curtain. "They've painted something on it," she said. "What does it say?"

"Anis del Toro. It's a drink."

"Could we try it?"

The man called "Listen" through the curtain. The woman came out from the bar.

"Four reales."

"We want two Anis del Toro."

"With water?"

"Do you want it with water?"

"I don't know," the girl said. "Is it good with water?"

"It's all right."

"You want them with water?" asked the woman.

"Yes, with water."

"It tastes like licorice," the girl said and put the glass down.

"That's the way with everything."

"Yes," said the girl. "Everything tastes of licorice. Especially all the things you've waited so long for, like absinthe."

"Oh, cut it out."

"You started it," the girl said. "I was being amused. I was having a fine time."

"Well, let's try and have a fine time."

"All right. I was trying. I said the mountains looked like white elephants. Wasn't that bright?"

"That was bright."

"I wanted to try this new drink: That's all we do, isn't it—look at things and try new drinks?"

"I guess so."

The girl looked across at the hills.

"They're lovely hills," she said. "They don't really look like white elephants. I just meant the coloring of their skin through the trees."

"Should we have another drink?"

"All right."

The warm wind blew the bead curtain against the table.

"The beer's nice and cool," the man said.

"It's lovely," the girl said.

"It's really an awfully simple operation, Jig," the man said. "It's not really an operation at all."

The girl looked at the ground the table legs rested on.

"I know you wouldn't mind it, Jig. It's really not anything. It's just to let the air in."

The girl did not say anything.

"I'll go with you and I'll stay with you all the time. They just let the air in and then it's all perfectly natural."

"Then what will we do afterward?"

"We'll be fine afterward. Just like we were before."

"What makes you think so?"

"That's the only thing that bothers us. It's the only thing that's made us unhappy."

The girl looked at the bead curtain, put her hand out, and took hold of two of the strings of beads.

"And you think then we'll be all right and be happy."

"I know we will. You don't have to be afraid. I've known lots of people that have done it."

"So have I," said the girl. "And afterward they were all so happy."

"Well," the man said, "if you don't want to you don't have to. I wouldn't have you do it if you didn't want to. But I know it's perfectly simple."

"And you really want to?"

"I think it's the best thing to do. But I don't want you to do it if you don't really want to."

"And if I do it you'll be happy and things will be like they were and you'll love me?"

"I love you now. You know I love you."

"I know. But if I do it, then it will be nice again if I say things are like white elephants, and you'll like it?"

"I'll love it. I love it now but I just can't think about it. You know how I get when I worry."

"If I do it you won't ever worry?"

"I won't worry about that because it's perfectly simple."

"Then I'll do it. Because I don't care about me."

"What do you mean?"

"I don't care about me."

"Well, I care about you."

"Oh, yes. But I don't care about me. And I'll do it and then everything will be fine."

"I don't want you to do it if you feel that way."

The girl stood up and walked to the end of the station. Across, on the other side, were fields of grain and trees along the banks of the Ebro. Far away, beyond the river, were mountains. The shadow of a cloud moved across the field of grain and she saw the river through the trees.

"And we could have all this," she said. "And we could have everything and every day we make it more impossible."

"What did you say?"

"I said we could have everything."

"We can have everything."

"No, we can't."

"We can have the whole world."

"No, we can't."

"We can go everywhere."

"No, we can't. It isn't ours any more."

"It's ours."

"No, it isn't. And once they take it away, you never get it back."

"But they haven't taken it away."

"We'll wait and see."

"Come on back in the shade," he said. "You mustn't feel that way."

"I don't feel any way," the girl said. "I just know things."

"I don't want you to do anything that you don't want to do ——"

"Nor that isn't good for me," she said. "I know. Could we have another beer?"

"All right. But you've got to realize ——"

"I realize," the girl said. "Can't we maybe stop talking?"

They sat down at the table and the girl looked across at the hills on the dry side of the valley and the man looked at her and at the table.

"You've got to realize," he said, "that I don't want you to do it if you don't want to. I'm perfectly willing to go through with it if it means anything to you."

"Doesn't it mean anything to you? We could get along."

"Of course it does. But I don't want anybody but you. I don't want any one else. And I know it's perfectly simple."

"Yes, you know it's perfectly simple."

"It's all right for you to say that, but I do know it."

"Would you do something for me now?"

"I'd do anything for you."

"Would you please please please please please please please stop talking?"

He did not say anything but looked at the bags against the wall of the station. There were labels on them from all the hotels where they had spent nights.

"But I don't want you to," he said, "I don't care anything about it."

"I'll scream," the girl said.

The woman came out through the curtains with two glasses of beer and put them down on the damp felt pads. "The train comes in five minutes," she said.

"What did she say?" asked the girl.

"That the train is coming in five minutes."

The girl smiled brightly at the woman, to thank her.

"I'd better take the bags over to the other side of the station," the man said. She smiled at him.

"All right. Then come back and we'll finish the beer."

He picked up the two heavy bags and carried them around the station to the other tracks. He looked up the tracks but could not see the train. Coming back, he walked through the barroom, where people waiting for the train were drinking. He drank an Anis at the bar and looked at the people. They were all waiting reasonably for the train. He went out through the bead curtain. She was sitting at the table and smiled at him.

"Do you feel better?" he asked.

"I feel fine," she said. "There's nothing wrong with me. I feel fine."

JOURNAL PROMPT:

Write about a time you when you were in a public place with someone, yet had to discuss something fairly private. Describe the setting and how you felt.

COLLABORATIVE EXERCISE:

With a partner, point to the lines that reveal Jig's nature. How would you describe her way of looking at the world? Then, find the lines that reveal the man's response. Do you believe these two people belong together? Why or why not?

ESSAY ASSIGNMENT:

1. Authors often purposely choose the setting of their stories to create a feeling; in other words, the setting has metaphoric importance. Write an essay in which you discuss the significance of the setting Hemingway chose for "Hills like White Elephants."
2. If you were in the position of marriage counselor, what would be your response to Jig and the man?
3. Write an essay in which you assert that Hemingway favors one of the characters over the other, or that his telling is neutral, and he appears to have no opinion one way or the other about either of the two.

CATHERINE FRAGA's poems have been published in several literary magazines, including *South Coast Poetry Journal* and *Sonoma Mandala*. Her poem "Braided Lives" earned a Pushcart nomination.

CATHERINE FRAGA

STANDING TOGETHER

In the tenuous half-light of dusk
outside Coffee World
two women talk
they are one voice
words crash into each other
echo the sameness in their lives
old scenes played over and over and
it is only after
they drive away
under a starless sky
that they both understand

at once
that marriage is a
precarious stretch of
tight rope
approached with abandon and now
they ache from the act of
keeping balance
head back
shoulders strong
sure footed
hearts that cannot break while
the laundry hangs like sorrow
in the yard.

JOURNAL PROMPT:

Imagine that you are one of the women in the poem. What do you say to the other woman standing with you outside Coffee World? How does your friend answer?

COLLABORATIVE EXERCISE:

Working in small groups, consider the elements of male/male friendships vs. female/female friendships. From your experiences and observations, what are the most important requirements for each of the types of friendship? What are the similarities and differences between the two?

ESSAY ASSIGNMENT:

1. How does gender influence this poem? Can you imagine two men engaged in the same way discussing the same subject? Why or why not?
2. What are some counterarguments to the statement that poetry transcends gender?

Judith Wallerstein and **Sandra Blakeslee** have coauthored not only the book from which this selection was taken, *The Good Marriage: How and Why Love Lasts,* but also *Second Chances: Men, Women, and Children a Decade after Divorce.* Wallerstein is the founder of the Center for the Family in Transition; Blakeslee is a science writer for *The New York Times.* In this selection the authors interviewed fifty couples in an attempt to answer the question of how we can make love last.

JUDITH WALLERSTEIN AND
SANDRA BLAKESLEE

THE GOOD MARRIAGE

We have been so preoccupied with divorce and crisis in the American family that we have failed to notice the good marriages that are all around us and from which we can learn. In today's world it's easy to become overwhelmed by problems that seem to have no solution. But we *can* shape our lives at home, including our relationships with our children and marriage itself. The home is the one place where we have the potential to create a world that is to our own liking; it is the last place where we should feel despair. As never before in history, men and women today are free to design the kind of marriage they want, with their own rules and expectations.

Fortunately, many young people have not yet become cynical and are still able to speak directly from the heart. After spending some wonderful hours talking to college students about their views of marriage, I received the next day a letter from Randolph Johnson, a twenty-one-year-old senior at the University of California in Santa Cruz. He wrote: "What I want in a wife is someone whom I know so well that she is a part of who I am and I of her. Someone to fill all that I am not but aspire to be. My wife is someone not just to share a life with but to build a life with. This is what marriage is to me, the sharing of two lives to complete each other. It is true that people change, but if people can change together then they need not grow apart."

Randolph speaks for a new generation that is still capable of optimism about love and marriage and "the sharing of two lives to complete each other." He also speaks for a society that is tired to death of the war on marriage, escalating divorce rates, and the search for new partners in middle age. All of us want a different world for our children. When we're honest, we want it for ourselves.

It is absurd, in fact, to suggest that the need for enduring love and intimacy in marriage is passé. The men and women I've seen in twenty-five years of studying divorce begin actively searching for a new relationship even before the divorce is final. In every study in which Americans are asked what they value most in assessing the quality of their lives, marriage comes first—ahead of friends, jobs, and money. In our fast-paced world men and women need each other more, not less. We want and need erotic love, sympathetic love, passionate love, tender, nurturing love all of our adult lives. We desire friendship, compassion, encouragement, a sense of being understood and appreciated, not only for what we do but for what we try to do and fail at. We want a relationship in which we can test our half-baked ideas without shame or pretense and give voice to our deepest fears. We want a partner who sees us as unique and irreplaceable.

In the past twenty years, marriage in America has undergone a profound, irrevocable transformation, driven by changes in women's roles and the heightened expectations of both men and women. Without realizing it, we have crossed a marital Rubicon. For the first time in our history, the decision to stay married is purely voluntary. Anyone can choose to leave at any time—and everyone knows it, including the children. There used to be only two legal routes out of marriage—adultery and abandonment. Today one partner simply has to say, for whatever reason, "I want out." Divorce is as simple as a trip to the nearest courthouse.

Each year two million adults and a million children in this country are newly affected by divorce. One in two American marriages ends in divorce, and one in three children can expect to experience their parents' divorce. This situation has powerful ripple effects that touch us all. The sense that relationships are unstable affects the family next door, the people down the block, the other children in the classroom. Feelings of intense anxiety about marriage permeate the consciousness of all young men and women on the threshold of adulthood. At every wedding the guests wonder, privately, will this marriage last? The bride and groom themselves may question why they should marry, since it's likely to break up.

To understand how our social fabric has been transformed, think of marriage as an institution acted upon by centripetal forces pulling inward and centrifugal forces pulling outward. In times past the centripetal forces—law, tradition, religion, parental influence—exceeded those that could pull a marriage apart, such as infidelity, abuse, financial disaster, failed expectations, or the lure of the frontier. Nowadays the balance has changed. The weakened centripetal forces no longer exceed those that tug marriages apart.

In today's marriages, in which people work long hours, travel extensively, and juggle careers with family, more forces tug at the relationship than ever before. Modern marriages are battered by the demands of her workplace as well as his, by changing community values, by anxiety about making ends meet each month, by geographical moves, by unemployment and recession, by the vicissitudes of child care, and by a host of other issues.

Marriage counselors like to tell their clients that there are at least six people in every marital bed—the couple and both sets of parents. I'm here to say that a crazy quilt of conflicting personal values and shifting social attitudes is also in that bed. The confusion over roles and the indifference of the community to long-term conjugal relationships are there, as are the legacies of a self-absorbed, me-first, feminist-do-or-die, male-backlash society. The ease of divorce and changing attitudes about the permanence of marriage have themselves become centrifugal forces.

Our great unacknowledged fear is that these potent outside forces will overwhelm the human commitment that marriage demands and that marriage as a lasting institution will cease for most people. We are left with a crushing anxiety about the future of marriage and about the men and women within it.

My study of divorce has inevitably led me to think deeply about marriage. Just as people who work with the dying worry about death, those of us who work with troubled marriages are constantly forced to look at our own relationships. So I have carefully taken note of my marriage and those of my three grown children. As our fiftieth wedding anniversary approaches, I have thought long and hard about what my husband and I have done to protect our marriage. Why have we been able to love each other for so many years? Did we begin differently from those who divorced? Did we handle crises differently? Or were we just lucky? What have I learned that I can pass on to my children and my grandchildren?

I certainly have not been happy all through each year of my marriage. There have been good times and bad, angry and joyful moments, times of ecstasy and times of quiet contentment. But I would never trade my husband, Robert, for another man. I would not swap my marriage for any other. This does not mean that I find other men unattractive, but there is all the difference in the world between a passing fancy and a life plan. For me, there has always been only one life plan, the one I have lived with my husband. But why is this so? What makes some marriages work while others fail?

An acquaintance of mine—a highly regarded psychologist who has done extensive marriage counseling—called me when she became engaged. She said, "I want to spend several hours with you, drawing on your experience. My fiancé is several years older than I am and has been through one divorce. He's afraid of another failure. I'm thirty-eight years old and have for many years been frightened of marriage. What wisdom do you have for me based on your own marriage, which has always looked so ideal to me, and also based on your many years of work with divorce? Help me anticipate what lies ahead for Jim and me, so I can be prepared." Her request intrigued me. What wisdom did she seek? She did not want shortcuts or hints but a realistic vision that could guide their efforts in building a successful marriage.

Not long after her call I decided to design a qualitative study of fifty couples who had built lasting, happy marriages, couples who had confronted the same obstacles, crises, and temptations as everyone else and had overcome them. As I began setting up the study, I drew up a list of questions that would guide my inquiry. Are the people in good marriages different from the men and women whose marriages fall apart? Are there common ideas, ways of dealing with the inevitable crises? What can we learn about selecting a partner, about sex, the stresses of the workplace, infidelity, the arrival of a baby or of adolescence, coping with midlife, aging, and retirement? What is happy in a marriage when people are in their twenties, thirties, forties, or fifties, or when they reach retirement? What are the central themes at each life stage? What makes men happy?

What makes women happy? What does each spouse value in one another? What do they regard as the glue of the marriage?

A good marriage is a process of continual change as it reflects new issues, deals with problems that arise, and uses the resources available at each stage of life. All long-lasting marriages change, if simply because we all change as we grow older. People's needs, expectations, and wishes change during the life cycle; biological aging is intertwined with psychological change in every domain, including work, health, sex, parenting, and friends. The social milieu and external circumstances change as well. Thus the individuals change, the marriage changes, and the world outside changes—and not necessarily in sync with one another. As one woman said, "John and I have had at least six different marriages."

Many men and women are still becoming adults as they work on the first chapter of their lives together—getting to know each other sexually, emotionally, and psychologically. This time of absorbing exploration is critically important for defining the couple's core relationship. Sadly, many couples find they cannot navigate this difficult first leg of the course. But if they do succeed, they will have a sturdy foundation for the structure of their marriage.

The birth of a child entirely revamps the internal landscape of marriage. Becoming a father or mother is a major step in the life course, a step that requires inner psychological growth as well as changes in every part of the marital relationship and in the extended family. It is also usually a time when one or both partners have made career commitments; the tough road of the workplace stretches ahead, and its stresses are high.

For many people the years when the children are growing up is the busiest time of their lives. A central issue is balancing the demands of work and of home. Children's needs for parental time and attention multiply along with the continuing demands of the workplace and often of school. Many couples cannot find enough time to be together even to exchange greetings, let alone make love.

The course of marriage changes again when children become adolescents, when parents dealing with midlife issues and presentiments of aging are suddenly faced with sexually active youngsters. The growing dependency, illness, or death of the spouses' own aging parents adds further turbulence to this period. When the children leave home, the couple must find each other again and rebuild their relationship. This new stage provides an opportunity to re-create the marriage in a different mold, perhaps with time to travel and play together. If a husband and wife have not succeeded in building a good marriage by now, they may find themselves merely sharing a household.

A later part of the journey is retirement, when issues of dependency and illness, as well as the opportunity to pursue new hobbies and interests and the continuing need for sexuality, take center stage. Once again the marriage is redefined, as the couple face life's final chapters and inevitably consider the loss of the partner and their own deaths.

All through adulthood our internal lives change as we create new images of ourselves and call up old images from the past. At each stage we draw on different memories and wishes, pulling them out like cards from a deck held close to the heart. The birth of a child draws on the memories and unconscious images of each parent's own infancy and childhood. That child's adolescence evokes the memories and conflicts of one's own teen years. Parents, watching their teenagers assert their independence, remember their own risk-taking behavior and realize that they were often saved from disaster by the skin of their teeth. And as old age approaches, every person draws on the experiences of prior losses in the family.

We have for many years told our children that marriage requires hard and continuing work, but since we could not tell them where or how to begin this work, we soon lost their attention. How could we tell them what we did not know?

What then are the secrets? How do a man and a woman who meet as strangers create a relationship that will satisfy them both throughout their lives?

First, the answer to the question I started with—what do people define as happy in their marriage?—turned out to be straightforward. For everyone, happiness in marriage meant feeling respected and cherished. Without exception, these couples mentioned the importance of liking and respecting each other and the pleasure and comfort they took in each other's company. Some spoke of the passionate love that began their relationship, but for a surprising number love grew in the rich soil of the marriage, nourished by emotional and physical intimacy, appreciation, and fond memories. Some spoke of feeling well cared for, others of feeling safe, and still others of friendship and trust. Many talked about the family they had created together. But all felt that they were central to their partner's world and believed that creating the marriage and the family was the major commitment of their adult life. For most, marriage and children were the achievements in which they took the greatest pride.

For these couples, respect was based on integrity; a partner was admired and loved for his or her honesty, compassion, generosity of spirit, decency, loyalty to the family, and fairness. An important aspect of respect was admiration of the partner as a sensitive, conscientious parent. The value these couples placed on the partner's moral qualities was an unexpected finding. It helps explain why many divorcing people speak so vehemently of losing respect for their former partner. The love that people feel in a good marriage goes with the conviction that the person is worthy of being loved.

These people were realists. No one denied that there were serious differences—conflict, anger, even some infidelity—along the way. No one envisioned marriage as a rose garden, but all viewed its satisfactions as far outweighing the frustrations over the long haul. Most regarded frustrations, big and small, as an inevitable aspect of life that would follow them no matter whom they married. Everyone had occasional fantasies about the roads not taken, but their commitment to the marriage withstood the impulse to break out.

Above all, they shared the view that their partner was special in some important regard and that the marriage enhanced each of them as individuals. They felt that the fit between their own needs and their partner's responses was unique and probably irreplaceable. In this they considered themselves very lucky, not entitled.

Their marriages had benefited from the new emphasis in our society on equality in relationships between men and women. However they divided up the chores of the household and of raising the children, the couples agreed that men and women had equal rights and responsibilities within the family. Women have taken many casualties in the long fight to achieve equality, and many good men have felt beleaguered, confused, and angry about this contest. But important goals have been achieved: marriages today allow for greater flexibility and greater choice. Relationships are more mature on both sides and more mutually respectful. A couple's sex life can be freer and more pleasurable. Today's men and women meet on a playing field that is more level than ever before.

Unlike many unhappy families, these couples provided no evidence for the popular notion that there is a "his" marriage and a "her" marriage. On the contrary, the men and women were very much in accord. I did not see significant differences between husbands and wives in their goals for the marriage, in their capacity for love and friendship, in their interest in sex, in their desire to have children, or in their love and commitment to the children. They fully shared the credit for the success of the marriage and the family. Both men and women said, "Everything we have we did together."

Although some men were inhibited in their expression of feelings at the beginning of the marriage, as compared with their wives, I did not find much difference between the sexes in their ability to express emotions over the course of their relationship. Both spoke easily of their love for their partner. In response to my questioning, both men and women cried when they contemplated losing the other.

The children were central, both as individuals and as symbols of a shared vision, giving pleasure and sometimes unexpected meaning to the parents' lives and to the marriage. As the couples reported to me in detail, the children reflected their love and pride. And this powerful bond did not diminish when the children left home.

As I compared the happily married couples with the thousands of divorcing couples I have seen in the past twenty-five years, it was clear that these men and women had early on created a firm basis for their relationship and had continued to build it together. Many of the couples that divorced failed to lay such a foundation and did not understand the need to reinforce it over the years. Many marriages broke because the structure was too weak to hold in the face of life's vicissitudes. The happy couples regarded their marriage as a work in progress that needed continued attention lest it fall into disrepair. Even in retirement they did not take each other for granted. Far too many divorcing couples fail to understand that a marriage does not just spring into being after the ceremony. Neither the legal nor the religious ceremony makes the marriage. *People* do, throughout their lives.

As I write these final paragraphs, my thoughts turn to my grandmother and to Nikki, my youngest grandchild. My grandmother, who brought her three young children to the new land in the hold of a ship and raised them by herself, knew exactly what she wanted for me. When I was growing up, she used to sing Yiddish folk songs about love and marriage, about mysterious suitors from distant lands. Whom will you marry? the songs asked. Her hopes for me were built on her own tears. My future happy marriage and my unborn healthy children made her sacrifice worthwhile.

Nikki has just turned four. She has recently demoted her twenty or so stuffed bears, puppies, kittens, even her beloved tiger, to the foot of her bed. They who were her special joy hardly have her attention now. She has entered a new phase. I am to address her as "Princess" when I call. (The great advantage of grandmothers, I have discovered, is that they follow instructions, whereas mothers issue instructions.) She is Princess Jasmine, and she awaits Aladdin. She is practicing at being a grown-up young lady, preparing for the future with all the energy and devotion that she brought to caring for her animals. No one works harder or with greater purpose than a child at play.

What do I want for Nikki? The roads that were so clear to my grandmother have become harder to follow. They fork often and sometimes lead to a dead end. Some directions, however, are still visible. I, too, want my granddaughter to be strong and brave and virtuous. I want her to love and be loved passionately and gently and proudly by a man worth loving. I want her to experience the joys and terrors of raising children. But far beyond what my grandmother envisioned for me, I want Nikki to have the choices in life that I and many others had to fight for, real choices that the community will respect and support. And I want her to know how to choose wisely and understand how to make it all work. I hope that Nikki finds the Aladdin that she has started to look for. If he comes flying into her life on a magic carpet, so much the better.

JOURNAL PROMPT:

If you could select only *one* quality of a good marriage, which quality would you assert holds the most significance? Why? (The authors discuss several throughout the essay.)

COLLABORATIVE EXERCISE:

Working in small groups, discuss ways in which parents (and other adults) can offer positive impressions of marriage to young children and adolescents. In your discussion, remember how especially vulnerable and receptive young children are to what they see, hear, and even read.

ESSAY ASSIGNMENT:

1. Examine the ways in which a marriage might or might not survive infidelity, either by one or both partners.
2. In the course of their research (published in their full-length book, *The Good Marriage*), the authors of this piece have interviewed many couples. Only five people wanted a marriage like their parents', even though many genuinely loved their parents. "The men consciously rejected the role models provided by their fathers. The women said that they could never be happy living as their mothers did." Write an essay in which you explain your desire to have a marriage similar to your parents' or in which you desire a different sort of marriage from your parents'.
3. Write a review of this article in which your audience consists of single men and women contemplating marriage. Your goal in this review is to emphasize the authors' positive, realistic approach to marriage.

ADDITIONAL ESSAY PROMPTS

1. Marriage, found in all cultures, has been the basic social institution since very early times. However, recently many young people have chosen not to get married, and the number of children raised in single-parent families has risen dramatically. Write an essay in which you debate the institution of marriage and its function in our society today.

2. Write an essay in which you explain how to have a happy marriage. (You must research and use at least five outside sources.) Include in your paper at least six key elements you believe sustain a relationship.

3. The authors of "The Good Marriage" suggest that, "All long-lasting marriages change, if simply because we all change as we grow older." One woman is quoted as admitting that she and her husband "have had at least six different marriages." Changes, or rites of passage, can often cause a married couple to grow apart, particularly when they begin to raise children. Write an essay in which you research the effect of having children on a marriage. What do the experts suggest as a way to maintain a strong marriage while raising children?

4. Jean Piaget, in a study of moral development, wrote, "The tendency to tell lies is a natural tendency . . . spontaneous and universal." Respond to Piaget's claim. Do you agree or disagree?

5. Eventually, most of us encounter situations in life about which we feel strongly while someone we care about feels just the opposite. Using dialogue only, try to re-create a conversation you had with someone where the two of you disagreed. Let the words, without background description (much like Hemingway did in "Hills like White Elephants"), capture the essence of that incompatibility.

6. Many couples make the conscious decision to remain childless. In your opinion, what are some of the advantages and disadvantages a childless couple may encounter or experience?

7. Peruse several different newspapers for articles about couples that have celebrated a significant wedding anniversary. What information is given about the couple and their lives? What can you surmise from the photographs and descriptions of their lives? What do you think is the real story of their marriage? What do you think attributes to the longevity of the marriage?

8. Are parents solely responsible for how their children turn out? Adopt a position on this issue, and support your assertions with your own observations, experiences, and possibly information from other sources.

9. Rosalie Riegle Troester, in an article published in *Sage: A Scholarly Journal on Black Women,* writes: "African and African-American communities have recognized that vesting one person with full responsibility for mothering a child may not be wise or possible. As a result, *othermothers*—women who assist *bloodmothers* by sharing responsibilities—traditionally have been central to the institution of Black motherhood." Explore this concept of *othermothers*. What are the pros and cons of such a philosophy and practice?

ADDITIONAL RESEARCH QUESTIONS

1. Research the topic of homosexual unions in the United States. Include a brief history, and include up-to-date information on the current state of homosexual marriages and rights. Provide your own prediction of how laws and regulations might change in the future.

2. Explore the origin of the bridal shower. What was the original purpose for this rite of passage that a young woman often experiences before marriage? Has this tradition changed over the years? Explain.

3. Explore the origin of the bachelor party. What was the original purpose for this rite of passage that a young man often experiences before marriage? Has this tradition changed over the years? Explain.

4. Select **one** of the many "methods" available to a pregnant woman for the birth of her child. (For example: underwater birth, hospital delivery, birthing center, home birth, midwife-assisted birth, etc.) Explore the advantages and

disadvantages of the method, and include case histories of couples who have chosen this particular choice in birthing.

5. Do you believe that the media influences how we view gender roles, particularly in marriage? Explore this notion by spending time observing how gender roles are presented on your favorite television show or movie, or pay close attention to the series of commercials during a half-hour viewing of television. Does the media accurately or inaccurately reflect your understanding of a man's and woman's roles in marriage? Explain.

7

FAMILY

What is family? Is the definition different for each of us, or are there common elements in all families, traditional or otherwise? How does our family of origin impact our future behavior?

Traditional families suffer enormous pressure in today's rapidly changing world. One in every five American births is to an unmarried mother, usually a teenager. While many believe a family to be related by blood, marriage, or adoption, many more define family in a larger emotional context as a "group of people who love and care for one another." All of the selections included in this unit explore our traditional definitions and offer a glimpse of family rites. Chester Higgins Jr., for example, takes his son on a journey to Africa, where they create a moving ritual designed to bring them closer together and closer to their roots as African American men. In "Station," a poem by Eamon Grennan, the author explores the pain that divorce inflicts on both parent and child.

If the large extended families of our ancestors are now more fancy than reality, still we cling to a nostalgic view of happiness that for most no longer exists. This rift between an idealized picture of home and the rootless present-day nuclear version most of us live with is cause for much alienation and pain, examined in full by the authors in this section, who recognize that for most families life is not as portrayed in a Hallmark card advertisement.

When poet **RITA DOVE** was awarded the Pulitzer Prize for Poetry in 1987, she became one of the youngest writers ever to receive the honor and only the second black poet to do so, following Gwendolyn Brooks. She was born in 1951 in Akron, Ohio. Rita Dove served as poet laureate of the United States from 1993 to 1995 and is Commonwealth Professor of English at the University of Virginia in Charlottesville.

RITA DOVE

Daystar

She wanted a little room for thinking:
but she saw diapers steaming on the line,
a doll slumped behind the door.

So she lugged a chair behind the garage
to sit out the children's naps.

Sometimes there were things to watch—
the pinched armor of a vanished cricket,
a floating maple leaf. Other days
she stared until she was assured
when she closed her eyes
she'd see only her own vivid blood.

She had an hour, at best, before Liza appeared
pouting from the top of the stairs.
And just *what* was mother doing
out back with the field mice? Why,

building a palace. Later
that night when Thomas rolled over and
lurched into her, she would open her eyes
and think of the place that was hers
for an hour—where
she was nothing,
pure nothing, in the middle of the day.

JOURNAL PROMPT:

In this poem the woman seeks to regain a sense of herself. If you have ever felt stifled or trapped, how did *you* cope with similar feelings?

COLLABORATIVE EXERCISE:

Working in small groups, decide what this poem is about. What lines point to the author's intent? How do the descriptive words in the poem play to that intent? Explain.

ESSAY ASSIGNMENT:

1. In chapter 3, author Linda Seger discusses archetypes in her essay "Creating the Myth." Specifically, Seger writes about the female counterpart of the wise old man—the *good mother*. In what ways might the myth of the good mother parallel the description of the mother in Dove's poem?
2. Compare and contrast this poem to Yeats's well-known poem "The Lake Isle of Innisfree." Both poems focus on a place to which the narrator desires to escape.

Ellen Goodman is a nationally recognized columnist who writes for the *Boston Globe*. Her columns are syndicated by the *Washington Post* Writers' Group and appear in over four hundred newspapers across the country. In 1980, Goodman was awarded the Pulitzer Prize for her columns.

ELLEN GOODMAN

The Family Legacy

It is my turn now: My aunt, the keeper of Thanksgiving, has passed the baton, or should I say the drumstick? She has declared this a permanent legacy.

Soon, according to plan, my grandmother's dishes will be delivered by cousin-courier to my dining room. So will the extra chairs and the communal chafing dishes. The tradition will also be transplanted.

But this morning, she has come over to personally deliver a piece of this inheritance. She is making stuffing with me.

In one hand, she carries the family Thanksgiving "bible," a small blue book that bears witness to the recipes and shopping lists and seating plans of decades past. In the other hand, she carries three loaves of bread, a bag of onions, and the appropriate spices.

It must be said that my aunt does not quite trust me to do this stuffing the right way, which is, of course, her way, and her mother's way. She doesn't quite trust my spices or my Cuisinart or my tendency to cut corners. So, like a tribal elder, she has come to instruct me, hands on, to oversee my Pilgrim's progress every step of the way.

Together we peel the onions and chop them. Not quite fine enough for her. I chop some more. Together we pull the bread apart and soak it and squeeze it. Not quite dry enough for her. I squeeze again.

Gradually I, the middle-aged mother of an adult child standing in the kitchen of the home I make mortgage payments on, feel myself again a child. Only this time I find amusement in taking such exacting instructions from my elder. More than amusement. I find comfort in still being somebody's young.

But sautéing the onions until they are perfectly brown (my aunt doesn't like white onions in the stuffing), I start divining a subtext to this recipe sharing. It says: Time is passing. Generations pass. One day I will be the elder.

"I don't think I like this whole thing," I say aloud, sounding like the child I am now. My aunt, who is about to be threescore years and ten, stops stirring the pan for a moment and looks at me. She understands. And for a while it isn't just the fumes of onions that come into our eyes.

The moment passes; I go back to mixing, and my aunt goes back to her favorite activity: bustling. But I no longer feel quite so much the child.

Adulthood arrives in these small sudden exchanges more than in well-heralded major crises. And the final moment of assuming adulthood may be when we inherit the legacy, become the keeper of traditions, the curator of our family's past and future memories. When the holidays are at our houses. The reunions at our instigation. When the traditions are carried on, or cast aside, because of choices that we make.

When we were small, my sister and I used to giggle at assorted holiday tables ruled over by our elders. We would at times squirm under the rule of imposed traditions and best behaviors. A certain prayer, an unfamiliar dish, an eccentric relative could send us to the bathroom laughing.

In time, when we were teenagers and then young parents, we were occasionally rebellious conformists, critical participants at family celebrations. We maintained a slight distance of humorous affection for the habits that the older generation carried on.

We were the ones who would point out that no one really liked mincemeat, that the string beans were hopelessly mushy, the onion-ring topping simply passé, that there was altogether too much chicken fat in the stuffing. It was easy to rebel against the things we could count on others maintaining.

Now I see this from another vantage point, that of almost-elder. I see that tradition is not just handed down but taken up. It's a conscious decision, a legacy that can be accepted or refused. Only once it's refused, it disappears.

How fragile is this sinew of generations. How tenuous the ceremonial ties that hold families together over time and generations, while they change as imperceptibly and inevitably as cells change in a single human body.

So it is my turn to accept the bequest, the dishes, the bridge chairs, the recipe book. This year there will be no string beans. Nor will there be ginger snaps in the gravy, forgive me. But the turkey will come with my grandmother's stuffing, my aunt's blessing, and my own novice's promise.

JOURNAL PROMPT:

Write about a family tradition. What is the history of the tradition—who initiated it and why?

COLLABORATIVE EXERCISE:

Goodman writes that "tradition is not just handed down but taken up. It's a conscious decision, a legacy that can be accepted or refused." In your groups, discuss the value of keeping traditions alive. Is a tradition something that should always be honored? When, if ever, should a tradition be broken or changed? Start by creating a list of at least ten traditions that your group knows of that are important to the United States, to your country of origin, to your family, etc.

ESSAY ASSIGNMENT:

1. Write a letter to a family member, either committing yourself to carrying on a family tradition or suggesting a new way of doing things. Be sure to be diplomatic yet assertive in your explanation, no matter what path you follow in this letter. Pay careful attention to word choice, tone, and voice.
2. Share a favorite family recipe. Along with an ingredient list and a step-by-step explanation, include any history or anecdotes connected with this recipe.

THOMAS SIMMONS graduated from Stanford University and attended graduate school at the University of California at Berkeley. Simmons's love affair with motorcycles began at a very early age. This essay is part of his memoir about struggling with the religious teachings and beliefs of his family, *The Unseen Shore: Memoirs of a Christian Science Childhood* (1991).

THOMAS SIMMONS

MOTORCYCLE TALK

My father, who suffered from so many private griefs, was not an easy man to get along with, but in one respect he was magnificent: he was unfailing in his devotion to machines of almost any variety. When he chose to, he could talk to me at length on the virtues of, say, the 1966 Chevrolet four-barrel carburetor or the drawbacks of the Wankel rotary engine. Talking, however, was not his strongest suit: he was a man of action. As he liked to point out, talking would never make an engine run more smoothly.

On weekends sometimes, or on his rare summer days of vacation, he would encourage me in my first and last steps toward automotive literacy. He would allow me to stand beside him as he worked on the car, and when he needed a simple tool—a crescent wrench or needlenose pliers—I would be allowed to hand them to him. And when I was 12, he and my daring mother bought me a motorcycle.

It was a 50cc Benelli motocross bike—neither new, nor large, nor powerful, nor expensive. But it gave form and life to my imaginings. No longer did I have to confine myself wistfully to magazine photos of high-speed turns and hair-raising rides through rough country. I had the thing itself—the device that would make these experiences possible, at least to some degree.

And, although I did not know it at the time, I also had a new kind of lexicon. The motorcycle was a compendium of gears and springs and sprockets and cylinder heads and piston rings, which between my father and me acquired the force of more affectionate words that we could never seem to use in each other's presence.

Almost immediately the Benelli became a meeting ground, a magnet for the two of us. We would come down to look at it—even if it was too late in the day for a good ride—and my father would check the tension of the chain, or examine the spark plug for carbon, or simply bounce the shock absorbers a few times as he talked. He'd tell me about compression ratios and ways of down-shifting smoothly through a turn; I'd tell him about my latest ride, when I leaped two small hummocks or took a spill on a tight curve.

More rarely, he'd tell the stories of his youth. His favorite, which he recounted in slightly different versions about four times a year, had to do with the go-kart he built from scrap parts in his father's basement during the Depression. It was by any account a masterful performance: he managed to pick up a small, broken gasoline engine for free, and tinkered with it until it came back to life. The wheels, steering gear, axles, chassis—all were scrounged for a few cents, or for free, from junkyards and vacant lots in and around Philadelphia.

Winter was in full swing when my father had his go-kart ready for a test-drive; snow lay thick on the ground. But he'd built the go-kart in his father's large basement, and given the weather he felt it made sense to make the trial run indoors. His engineering skills were topnotch. Assembled from orphaned parts, the go-kart performed like a well-tuned race car. My father did what any good 13-year-old would have done: he got carried away. He laid on the power coming around the corner of the basement, lost control, and smashed head-on into the furnace. It was a great loss for him. The jagged wood and metal cut and bruised him; he had destroyed his brand-new car. Far worse was the damage to the furnace. In 1933 such damage was almost more than the family finances could sustain. Furious, my father's father called him names, upbraided him for his stupidity and irresponsibility, and made him feel worthless. Years later, as he would tell this story to me, my father would linger over those words—"stupid," "irresponsible"—as if the pain had never gone away.

In these moments he and I had a common stake in something. Though he might not know whether I was reading at the eighth-grade level or the twelfth-grade level—or whether my math scores lagged behind those of the rest of the class—he was delighted to see that I knew how to adjust a clutch cable or stop after a low-speed, controlled skid. These skills were a source of genuine adventure for me, and I came to life when he observed my progress.

But this was only part of our rapport with the motorcycle. My father found few occasions to be overtly tender with the family, but he could be tender with a machine. I began to notice this in the countless small adjustments he regularly made. His touch on the cranky carburetor settings for gas and air was gentle, even soothing; at least it seemed to soothe the motorcycle, which ran smoothly under his touch but not under mine.

I found that, from time to time, this tenderness buoyed me in its wake.

If my father was, in his dreams, a flat-track mechanic, then I was his driver: he owed me the best he could give me; that was his job. This dream of his bound us in a metaphor which, at its heart, was not so different from the kind of straightforward love another child might have received from a more accessible father. I did not know this then, not exactly. But I knew, when we both hovered over the Benelli's cylinder head or gearbox, adjusting a cam or replacing a gasket, that he would not have worked on this machine for himself alone.

Yet there was a secret to our new language, a secret that only slowly revealed itself. What we shared through the motorcycle contradicted most of our other encounters in the family. It was almost as if we lived in another world when we came together over this machine, and for a time I hoped that that world might be the new one, the ideal on the horizon. I was wrong. The bands of our words were strong, but too narrow to encompass the worlds rising before me.

Almost without knowing it I began to acquire other vocabularies—the tough, subtle speech of girls, the staccato syllables of independence, the wrenching words of love and emptiness. In this I began to leave him behind. He could not talk of these things with me. He remained with his engines; and long after I had ceased to ride it, he would occasionally open the gas jets, prime the carburetor, and take my motorcycle for a spin around the block.

But as it seems that nothing is ever wholly lost, this vocabulary of the garage and the flat-track speed-way has a kind of potency, a place in the scheme of things. When, recently, I had dinner with my father, after not having seen him for nearly a year, we greeted each other with the awkwardness of child cousins: we hardly knew what to say. I had almost given up on the possibility of a prolonged conversation until I happened to mention that my car needed a new clutch. Suddenly we were safe again, as we moved from the clutch to the valves on his souped-up VW and the four-barrel carburetor on the '66 Chevrolet Malibu, still pouring on the power after all these years. We had moved back to the language of our old country. And though one of us had journeyed far and had almost forgotten the idioms, the rusty speech still held, for a time, the words of love.

JOURNAL PROMPT:

Is there a person in your family with whom you have difficulty communicating?

COLLABORATIVE EXERCISE:

Closely examine the writer's opening paragraph. Does it invite the reader into the essay? Why or why not? Does it offer the reader a thesis or theme? If it does not, at what point in the essay does the author's purpose become clear?

ESSAY ASSIGNMENT:

1. The motorcycle seems to be the impetus for bringing father and son together and encouraging the easy flow of conversation. Write about a relationship you have with someone in your immediate or extended family that mirrors the relationship in the essay—one in which the basis of the relationship is reliant on something both of you have in common. How does this common denominator help "orchestrate" the relationship?
2. Write an essay called "________ Talk" in which you fill in the blank with an item that could represent the relationship between a mother and her daughter. Then, discuss the ways in which mothers and daughters communicate. What activities often draw mother/daughter relationships closer? Compare them to the relationship between father and son in this piece.

CHESTER HIGGINS JR. works as a photographer with *The New York Times* and is the author of several books, including *Some Time Ago* (1980) and *Feeling the Spirit: Searching the World for the People of Africa* (1994). In this essay, Higgins writes about a very powerful rite of passage with his son and how it changed his life in unexpected ways.

CHESTER HIGGINS JR.

A FATHER'S RITE

I took my son to Africa this year. For three weeks my 20-year-old son and I explored the past and present of our people in Egypt and Ethiopia. I wanted him to see what I regard as the land of his heritage; I wanted him to experience the ecstasy I felt on my first visit to Africa when I was in my 20's.

I had envisioned a kind of rite of passage for my son; what transpired between us became a turning point—in our relationship, for me as his father and I hope for him as well.

Being a father seems to require skills never taught to me. Throughout my son's 20 years and my daughter's 22 years, I have often felt as if I were in a boat slipping along the water in a dark night without a lamp or a lighthouse to guide me. I felt like an impostor. I was reared by my stepfather, a distant man, and at 19 I sought out my biological father, whom I had never known. Those experiences made me determined to take the role of a father seriously.

When my son was 9 years old and my daughter was 11, their mother and I divorced, and it nearly sank the already adrift boat. With divorce often comes anger, a welter of conflicting feelings and much pain for everybody. New York State court-restricted visitations for a father can reduce his relationship with his children to that of an uncle. Having been deprived of my own father, I was determined to maintain as much contact with my children as the law would allow.

For my 15th trip to Africa, in July, to photograph the reinterment of His Majesty Haile Selassie[1] on what would have been his 100th birthday, I decided to ask my son, Damani, to come along as my assistant. Damani, who has dreadlocked his hair, shares my love of His Majesty and of reggae, the music of the Rastafarians[2] who worship Selassie. I added to our itinerary a stopover in Egypt so that my son could also see the pyramids, temples and tombs of our ancestors.

Haile Selassie's reinterment was postponed by the new Ethiopian regime about two weeks before we were to arrive. Though deeply disappointed, neither Damani nor I considered canceling our trip, nor did the thousands of Rastafarians who annually gather for Selassie's birthday. While we were in Ethiopia, my son in his dreadlocks blended into the population; his enthusiasm for this venerable African country warmed my heart. On a four-day trip to visit the ancient sacred city of Lalibala, where, in the 12th century, churches were hewn out of the surrounding mountains, I had a dream. In my dream, I saw two men, one older and one younger, facing one another against a background of temples and pyramids. The father was speaking as he anointed the head of his son.

I became enamored of the possibility of enacting a ceremony with my son in Africa. For the next six days I privately wondered what words to use in such a ceremony. Gradually the words came to me. By the time we arrived in Cairo, I was ready. I told my son that there was a ceremony I wanted to perform with him in the tombs at Luxor, Egypt. His eyes shone with anticipation. But I wondered if he would still be receptive after my next statement. In the dream I remembered that the son was anointed, as it were, with a dry substance. I took this to

---

[1] Ruler of Ethiopia from 1916 to 1974.—Eds.

[2] Members of a religious and political movement who believe that Ethiopia is heaven and Haile Selassie is a god.—Eds.

mean that powder rather than oil was used. But what powder? I ruled out ground herbs and flowers, and finally settled on sand. Sand represents the Sahara, and sand also contains the remains of the ancient people of Pharaonic Egypt. That made metaphysical sense to me, but in the real world, young adults or almost anybody for that matter, are disinclined to have sand poured on their hair.

"I will need sand to anoint your head," I told my son.

"Sand?" he asked, hesitantly. "How much?"

"Just a little; you can put some in a film canister," I said hastily. We both knew a 35-millimeter film canister wouldn't hold much sand. "Take the canister and find sand you feel special about and I'll use that."

Once he was in control of the amount of sand, and where it would come from, he decided to take some from the desert in the shadow of the pyramids in Cairo. Days later, when we reached Luxor, he collected more from around the remains of the Temple of Karnak—one of the largest, oldest stone temples in the world.

The next afternoon we sailed across the Nile to Thebes and to the Valley of the Kings, a basin formed by towering mountains. From the heavenly perch of the ancient Egyptian gods, the valley resembles a huge bowl to which there is one narrow entrance, flanked by more tall peaks. The tombs of the Pharaohs are hewn into the lower part of the mountains that form the basin. Inside each tomb, 12-foot-square passageways lead down several thousand feet into the solid rock. The scene that greets modern-day visitors to these sacred chambers is astonishing: Ornately painted walls reveal images of animals, people and scenes that were part of the real and imaginary lives of Pharaonic Egyptians. It was here, inside one of the tombs of an 18th Dynasty Pharaoh, that I chose to perform the ceremony revealed to me in my dream in Ethiopia.

In front of an enormous wall painting of Osiris, the god of resurrection, my son and I faced each other. I poured the sand he had collected into the palm of my left hand, and with my right, I anointed the top of his head with this sand. Looking into his eyes, I said:

"I, your father, anoint the crown of your head with the soil of Africa. This piece of earth is a symbol of the lives of your ancestors. It is a bonding of their lives to yours. Like your father, you, too, are African. We are Africans not because we were born in Africa, but because Africa was born in us. Look around you and behold us in our greatness. Greatness is an African possibility; you can make it yours. Just as the great ones before you have, by their deeds, placed their names on history, so can you by your deeds place your name on tomorrow. . . . So here, in the company of those great ones who have waited patiently for your visit—you are loved, you are encouraged. Our faces shine toward yours. Go forward; may you live long, may you prosper and have health."

We hugged each other, enjoying the specialness of the moment. Leaving him alone inside the tomb to meditate, I walked back toward the light and waited for him outside on the valley floor.

Here in the land of our ancient fathers, in the tomb of one of the great fathers of the ancient Egyptian empire, my perception of what it means to be a father was unalterably expanded and enhanced.

JOURNAL PROMPT:

Are there people in your life with whom you might like to share a rite similar to the one described in the essay? Write about that person and what you hope to achieve by sharing an experience similar to the one devised by the author and his son.

COLLABORATIVE EXERCISE:

Higgins likens parenting to being "in a boat slipping along the water in a dark night without a lamp or a lighthouse to guide me." Keeping in mind the symbolic significance of the sand used in the author's ritual, create a ritual for two-parent families, designed to bond all immediate family members. Defend whether or not you think such a ritual is necessary.

ESSAY ASSIGNMENT:

1. Chester Higgins Jr. and his son travel to Africa, the home, he says, "of our ancient fathers." In fact, they perform their ritual ceremony in the tomb of an Egyptian pharaoh. Investigate the belief system of the ancient Egyptians concerning the afterlife. What caused them to create such elaborate burial ceremonies?
2. In this essay the author describes a journey he made with his son. Think of a trip you have taken in which you learned something important about yourself. Did you learn something significant about family or a part of the world once inhabited by your ancestors?
3. What is the author's purpose in writing this essay? Does his theme move beyond the subject matter to create a larger view of life? Defend your response.

Author **BARBARA KINGSOLVER** was born in 1955 in eastern Kentucky. Kingsolver has always been a storyteller: "I used to beg my mother to let me tell her a bedtime story." She received an M.S. from the University of Arizona in Tucson. She credits her careers in scientific writing and journalism for giving her a writer's discipline and broadening her fictional possibilities. She is the author of several essays, short stories, and novels. The necessity of a broader definition of family is Kingsolver's goal in this essay, which originally appeared in *Parenting* magazine (1995).

BARBARA KINGSOLVER

STONE SOUP

In the catalog of family values, where do we rank an occasion like this? A curly-haired boy who wanted to run before he walked, age seven now, a soccer player scoring a winning goal. He turns to the bleachers with his fists in the air and a smile wide as a gap-toothed galaxy. His own cheering section of grown-ups and kids all leap to their feet and hug each other, delirious with love for this boy. He's Andy, my best friend's son. The cheering section includes his mother and her friends, his brother, his father and stepmother, a stepbrother and stepsister, and a grandparent. Lucky is the child with this many relatives on hand to hail a proud accomplishment. I'm there too, witnessing a family fortune. But in spite of myself, defensive words take shape in my head. I am thinking: I dare *anybody* to call this a broken home.

Families change, and remain the same. Why are our names for home so slow to catch up to the truth of where we live?

When I was a child, I had two parents who loved me without cease. One of them attended every excuse for attention I ever contrived, and the other made it to the ones with higher production values, like piano recitals and appendicitis. So I was a lucky child too. I played with a set of paper dolls called "The Family of Dolls," four in number, who came with the factory-assigned names of Dad, Mom, Sis, and Junior. I think you know what they looked like, at least before I loved them to death and their heads fell off.

Now I've replaced the dolls with a life. I knit my days around my daughter's survival and happiness, and am proud to say her head is still on. But we aren't the Family of Dolls. Maybe you're not, either. And if not, even though you are statistically no oddity, it's probably been suggested to you in a hundred ways that yours isn't exactly a real family, but an impostor family, a harbinger of cultural ruin, a slapdash substitute—something like counterfeit money. Here at the tail end of our century, most of us are up to our ears in the noisy business of trying to support and love a thing called family. But there's a current in the air with ferocious moral force that finds its way even into political campaigns, claiming there is only one right way to do it, the Way It Has Always Been.

In the face of a thriving, particolored world, this narrow view is so pickled and absurd I'm astonished that it gets airplay. And I'm astonished that it still stings.

Every parent has endured the arrogance of a child-unfriendly grump sitting in judgment, explaining what those kids of ours really need (for example, "a good licking"). If we're polite, we move our crew to another bench in the park. If we're forthright (as I am in my mind, only, for the rest of the day), we fix them with a sweet imperious stare and say, "Come back and let's talk about it after you've changed a thousand diapers."

But it's harder somehow to shrug off the Family-of-Dolls Family Values crew when they judge (from their safe distance) that divorced people, blended families, gay families, and single parents are failures. That our children are at risk, and the whole arrangement is messy and embarrassing. A marriage that ends is not called "finished," it's called *failed.* The children of this family may have been born to a happy union, but now they are called *the children of divorce.*

I had no idea how thoroughly these assumptions overlaid my culture until I went through divorce myself. I wrote to a friend: "This might be worse than being widowed. Overnight I've suffered the same losses—companionship, financial and practical support, my identity as a wife and partner, the future I'd taken for granted. I am lonely, grieving, and hard-pressed to take care of my household alone. But instead of bringing casseroles, people are acting like I had a fit and broke up the family china."

Once upon a time I held these beliefs about divorce: that everyone who does it could have chosen not to do it. That it's a lazy way out of marital problems. That it selfishly puts personal happiness ahead of family integrity. Now I tremble for my ignorance. It's easy, in fortunate times, to forget about the ambush that could leave your head reeling: serious mental or physical illness, death in the family, abandonment, financial calamity, humiliation, violence, despair.

I started out like any child, intent on being the Family of Dolls. I set upon young womanhood believing in most of the doctrines of my generation: I wore my skirts four inches above the knee. I had that Barbie with her zebra-striped swimsuit and a figure unlike anything found in nature. And I understood the Prince Charming Theory of Marriage, a quest for Mr. Right that ends smack dab where you find him. I did not completely understand that another whole story *begins* there, and no fairy tale prepared me for the combination of bad luck and persistent hope that would interrupt my dream and lead me to other arrangements. Like a cancer diagnosis, a dying marriage is a thing to fight, to deny, and finally, when there's no choice left, to dig in and survive. Casseroles would help. Likewise, I imagine it must be a painful reckoning in adolescence (or later on) to realize one's own true love will never look like the soft-focus fragrance ads because Prince Charming (surprise!) is a princess. Or vice versa. Or has skin the color your parents didn't want you messing with, except in the Crayola box.

It's awfully easy to hold in contempt the straw broken home, and that mythical category of persons who toss away nuclear family for the sheer fun of it. Even the legal terms we use have a suggestion of caprice. I resent the phrase "irreconcilable differences," which suggests a stubborn refusal to accept a spouse's little quirks. This is specious. Every happily married couple I know has loads of irreconcilable differences. Negotiating where to set the thermostat is not the point. A nonfunctioning marriage is a slow asphyxiation. It is waking up despised each morning, listening to the pulse of your own loneliness before the radio begins to blare its raucous gospel that you're nothing if you aren't loved. It is sharing your airless house with the threat of suicide or other kinds of violence, while the ghost that whispers, "Leave here and destroy your children," has passed over every door and nailed it shut. Disassembling a marriage in these circumstances is as much *fun* as amputating your own gangrenous leg. You do it, if you can, to save a life—or two, or more.

I know of no one who really went looking to hoe the harder row, especially the daunting one of single parenthood. Yet it seems to be the most American of customs to blame the burdened for their destiny. We'd like so desperately to believe in freedom and justice for all, we can hardly name that rogue bad luck, even when he's a close enough snake to bite us. In the wake of my divorce, some friends (even a few close ones) chose to vanish, rather than linger within striking distance of misfortune.

But most stuck around, bless their hearts, and if I'm any the wiser for my trials, it's from having learned the worth of steadfast friendship. And also, what not to say. The least helpful question is: "Did you want the divorce, or didn't you?" Did I want to keep that gangrenous leg, or not? How to explain, in a culture that venerates choice: two terrifying options are much worse than none at all. Give me any day the quick hand of cruel fate that will leave me scarred but blameless. As it was, I kept thinking of that wicked third-grade joke in which some boy comes up behind you and grabs your ear, starts in with a prolonged tug, and asks, "Do you want this ear any longer?"

Still, the friend who holds your hand and says the wrong thing is made of dearer stuff than the one who stays away. And generally, through all of it, you live. My favorite fictional character, Kate Vaiden (in the novel by Reynolds Price), advises: "Strength just comes in one brand—you stand up at sunrise and meet what they send you and keep your hair combed."

Once you've weathered the straits, you get to cross the tricky juncture from casualty to survivor. If you're on your feet at the end of a year or two, and have begun putting together a happy new existence, those friends who were kind enough to feel sorry for you when you needed it must now accept you back to the ranks of the living. If you're truly blessed, they will dance at your second wedding. Everybody else, for heaven's sake, should stop throwing stones.

Arguing about whether nontraditional families deserve pity or tolerance is a little like the medieval debate about left-handedness as a mark of the devil. Divorce, remarriage, single parenthood, gay parents, and blended families simply are. They're facts of our time. Some of the reasons listed by sociologists for these family reconstructions are: the idea of marriage as a romantic partnership rather than a pragmatic one; a shift in women's expectations, from servility to self-respect and independence; and longevity (prior to antibiotics no marriage was expected to last many decades—in Colonial days the average couple lived to be married less than twelve years). Add to all this, our growing sense of entitlement to happiness and safety from abuse. Most would agree these are all good things. Yet their result—a culture in which serial monogamy and the consequent reshaping of families are the norm—gets diagnosed as "failing."

For many of us, once we have put ourselves Humpty-Dumpty-wise back together again, the main problem with our reorganized family is that other people think we have a problem. My daughter tells me the only time she's uncomfortable about being the child of divorced parents is when her friends say they feel sorry for her. It's a bizarre sympathy, given that half the kids in her school and nation are in the same boat, pursuing childish happiness with the same energy as their married-parent peers. When anyone asks how *she* feels about it, she spontaneously lists the benefits: our house is in the country and we have a dog, but she can go to her dad's neighborhood for the urban thrills of a pool and sidewalks for roller-skating. What's more, she has three sets of grandparents!

Why is it surprising that a child would revel in a widened family and the right to feel at home in more than one house? Isn't it the opposite that should worry us—a child with no home at all, or too few resources to feel safe? The child at risk is the one whose parents are too immature themselves to guide wisely; too diminished by poverty to nurture; too far from opportunity to offer hope. The number of children in the U.S. living in poverty at this moment is almost unfathomably large: twenty percent. There are families among us that need help all right, and by no means are they new on the landscape. The rate at which teenage girls had babies in 1957 (ninety-six per thousand) was twice what it is now. That remarkable statistic is ignored by the religious right—probably because the teen birth rate was cut in half mainly by legalized abortion. In fact, the policy gate-keepers who coined the phrase "family values" have steadfastly ignored the desperation of too-small families, and since 1979 have steadily reduced the amount of financial support available to a single parent. But, this camp's most outspoken attacks seem aimed at the notion of families getting too complex, with add-ons and extras such as a gay parent's partner, or a remarried mother's new husband and his children.

To judge a family's value by its tidy symmetry is to purchase a book for its cover. There's no moral authority there. The famous family comprised of Dad, Mom, Sis, and Junior living as an isolated economic unit is not built on historical bedrock. In *The Way We Never Were,* Stephanie Coontz writes, "Whenever people propose that we go back to the traditional family, I always suggest that they pick a ballpark date for the family they have in mind." Colonial families were tidily disciplined, but their members (meaning everyone but infants) labored incessantly and died young. Then the Victorian family adopted a new division of labor, in which women's role was domestic and children were allowed time for study and play, but this was an upper-class construct supported by myriad slaves. Coontz writes, "For every nineteenth-century middle-class family that protected its wife and child within the family circle, there was an Irish or German girl scrubbing floors . . . a Welsh boy mining coal to keep the home-baked goodies warm, a black girl doing the family laundry, a black mother and child picking cotton to be made into clothes for the family, and a Jewish or an

Italian daughter in a sweatshop making ladies' dresses or artificial flowers for the family to purchase."

The abolition of slavery brought slightly more democratic arrangements, in which extended families were harnessed together in cottage industries; at the turn of the century came a steep rise in child labor in mines and sweatshops. Twenty percent of American children lived in orphanages at the time; their parents were not necessarily dead, but couldn't afford to keep them.

During the Depression and up to the end of World War II, many millions of U.S. households were more multigenerational than nuclear. Women my grandmother's age were likely to live with a fluid assortment of elderly relatives, in-laws, siblings, and children. In many cases they spent virtually every waking hour working in the company of other women—a companionable scenario in which it would be easier, I imagine, to tolerate an estranged or difficult spouse. I'm reluctant to idealize a life of so much hard work and so little spousal intimacy, but its advantage may have been resilience. A family so large and varied would not easily be brought down by a single blow: it could absorb a death, long illness, an abandonment here or there, and any number of irreconcilable differences.

The Family of Dolls came along midcentury as a great American experiment. A booming economy required a mobile labor force and demanded that women surrender jobs to returning soldiers. Families came to be defined by a single breadwinner. They struck out for single-family homes at an earlier age than ever before, and in unprecedented numbers they raised children in suburban isolation. The nuclear family was launched to sink or swim.

More than a few sank. Social historians corroborate that the suburban family of the postwar economic boom, which we have recently selected as our definition of "traditional," was no panacea. Twenty-five percent of Americans were poor in the mid-1950s, and as yet there were no food stamps. Sixty percent of the elderly lived on less than $1,000 a year, and most had no medical insurance. In the sequestered suburbs, alcoholism and sexual abuse of children were far more widespread than anyone imagined.

Expectations soared, and the economy sagged. It's hard to depend on one other adult for everything, come what may. In the last three decades, that amorphous, adaptable structure we call "family" has been reshaped once more by economic tides. Compared with fifties families, mothers are far more likely now to be employed. We are statistically more likely to divorce, and to live in blended families or other extra-nuclear arrangements. We are also more likely to plan and space our children, and to rate our marriages as "happy." We are less likely to suffer abuse without recourse, or to stare out at our lives through a glaze of prescription tranquilizers. Our aged parents are less likely to become destitute, and we're half as likely to have a teenage daughter turn up a mother herself. All in all, I would say that if "intact" in modern family-values jargon means living quietly desperate in the bell jar, then hip-hip-hooray for "broken." A neat family model constructed to service the Baby Boom economy seems to be returning gradually to a grand, lumpy shape that human families apparently have tended toward since they first took root in the Olduvai Gorge. We're social animals, deeply fond of companionship, and children love best to run in packs. If there is a *normal* for humans, at all, I expect it looks like two or three Families of Dolls, connected variously by kinship and passion, shuffled like cards and strewn over several shoeboxes.

The sooner we can let go the fairy tale of families functioning perfectly in isolation, the better we might embrace the relief of community. Even the admirable parents who've stayed married through thick and thin are very likely, at present, to incorporate other adults into their families—household help and baby-sitters if they can afford them, or neighbors and grandparents if they can't. For single parents, this support is the rock-bottom definition of family. And most parents who have split apart, however painfully, still manage to maintain family continuity for their children, creating in many cases a boisterous phenomenon that Constance Ahrons in her book *The Good Divorce* calls the "binuclear family." Call it what you will—when ex-spouses beat swords into plowshares and jump up and down at a soccer game together, it makes for happy kids.

Cinderella, look, who needs her? All those evil stepsisters? That story always seemed like too much cotton-picking fuss over clothes. A childhood tale that fascinated me more was the one called "Stone Soup," and the gist of it is this: Once upon a time, a pair of beleagured soldiers straggled home to a village empty-handed, in a land ruined by war. They were famished, but the villagers had so little they shouted evil words and slammed their doors. So the soldiers dragged out a big kettle, filled it with water, and put it on a fire to boil. They rolled a clean round stone into the pot, while the villagers peered through their curtains in amazement.

"What kind of soup is that?" they hooted.

"Stone soup," the soldiers replied. "Everybody can have some when it's done."

"Well, thanks," one matron grumbled, coming out with a shriveled carrot. "But it'd be better if you threw this in."

And so on, of course, a vegetable at a time, until the whole suspicious village managed to feed itself grandly.

Any family is a big empty pot, save for what gets thrown in. Each stew turns out different. Generosity, a resolve to turn bad luck into good, and respect for variety—these things will nourish a nation of children. Name-calling and suspicion will not. My soup contains a rock or two of hard times, and maybe yours does too. I expect it's a heck of a bouillabaisse.

JOURNAL PROMPT:

Describe your family. Is it a "Family of Dolls" or one of the many other blends Kingsolver writes about?

COLLABORATIVE EXERCISE:

Kingsolver appears to have written this essay for an audience who believes families are disintegrating. (The author suggests that families are simply reorganizing as a function of changes in society.) How do her personal experiences strengthen her argument? Point out at least three places where she says, in essence, "You see, it's not true what they say, and I have *proof.*"

ESSAY ASSIGNMENT:

1. Kingsolver writes that "it seems to be the most American of customs to blame the burdened for their destiny." Discuss this concept. From your perspective, is it accurate? Give examples to support your claim.
2. Write a letter to the author of the essay either commending her for her insight or offering an alternative point of view for improving the family unit.
3. Examine the essay's use of rhetorical strategies. For example, can you find a successful use of description, narration, comparison and contrast, cause and effect, classification, or definition? Which strategy seems to be the most effective for advancing the author's purpose, and why?

Poet and writer ALICE WALKER received her B.A. from Sarah Lawrence College in 1965. She was active in the civil rights movement of the 1960s. She has spoken for the women's movement, the antiapartheid movement, and the antinuclear movement, and against female genital mutilation. She received the Pulitzer Prize in 1983 for her novel *The Color Purple.* Among her numerous awards and honors are the Lillian Smith Award from the National Endowment for the Arts, a nomination for the National Book Award, a Guggenheim Fellowship, and the Front Page Award for Best Magazine Criticism from the Newswoman's Club of New York. She currently resides in Northern California.

ALICE WALKER

EVERYDAY USE

I will wait for her in the yard that Maggie and I made so clean and wavy yesterday afternoon. A yard like this is more comfortable than most people know. It is not just a yard. It is like an extended living room. When the hard clay is swept clean as a floor and the fine sand around the edges lined with tiny, irregular grooves, anyone can come and sit and look up into the elm tree and wait for the breezes that never come inside the house.

Maggie will be nervous until after her sister goes: she will stand hopelessly in corners, homely and ashamed of the burn scars down her arms and legs, eying her sister with a mixture of envy and awe. She thinks her sister has held life always in the palm of one hand, that "no" is a word the world never learned to say to her.

You've no doubt seen those TV shows where the child who has "made it" is confronted, as a surprise, by her own mother and father, tottering in weakly from backstage. (A pleasant surprise, of course: What would they do if parent and child came on the show only to curse out and insult each other?) On TV mother and child embrace and smile into each other's faces. Sometimes the mother and father weep, the child wraps them in her arms and leans across the table to tell how she would not have made it without their help. I have seen these programs.

Sometimes I dream a dream in which Dee and I are suddenly brought together on a TV program of this sort. Out of a dark and soft-seated limousine I am ushered into a bright room filled with many people. There I meet a smiling, gray, sporty man like Johnny Carson who shakes my hand and tells me what a fine girl I have. Then we are on the stage and Dee is embracing me with tears in her eyes. She pins on my dress a large orchid, even though she has told me once that she thinks orchids are tacky flowers.

In real life I am a large, big-boned woman with rough, man-working hands. In the winter I wear flannel nightgowns to bed and overalls during the day. I can kill and clean a hog as mercilessly as a man. My fat keeps me hot in zero weather. I can work outside all day, breaking ice to get water for washing; I can eat pork liver cooked over the open fire minutes after it comes steaming from the hog. One winter I knocked a bull calf straight in the brain between the eyes with a sledge hammer and had the meat hung up to chill before nightfall. But of course all this does not show on television. I am the way my daughter would want me to be: a hundred pounds lighter, my skin like an uncooked barley pancake. My hair glistens in the hot bright lights. Johnny Carson has much to do to keep up with my quick and witty tongue.

But that is a mistake. I know even before I wake up. Who ever knew a Johnson with a quick tongue? Who can even imagine me looking a strange white man in the eye? It seems to me I have talked to them always with one foot raised in flight, with my head turned in whichever way is farthest from them. Dee, though. She would always look anyone in the eye. Hesitation was no part of her nature.

"How do I look, Mama?" Maggie says, showing just enough of her thin body enveloped in pink skirt and red blouse for me to know she's there, almost hidden by the door.

"Come out into the yard," I say.

Have you ever seen a lame animal, perhaps a dog run over by some careless person rich enough to own a car, sidle up to someone who is ignorant enough to be kind to them? That is the way my Maggie walks. She has been like this, chin on chest, eyes on ground, feet in shuffle, ever since the fire that burned the other house to the ground.

Dee is lighter than Maggie, with nicer hair and a fuller figure. She's a woman now, though sometimes I forget. How long ago was it that the other house burned? Ten, twelve years? Sometimes I can still hear the flames and feel Maggie's arms sticking to me, her hair smoking and her dress falling off her in little black papery flakes. Her eyes seemed stretched open, blazed open by the flames reflected in them. And Dee. I see her standing off under the sweet gum tree she used to dig gum out of; a look of concentration on her face as she watched the last dingy gray board of the house fall in toward the red-hot brick chimney. Why don't you do a dance around the ashes? I'd wanted to ask her. She had hated the house that much.

I used to think she hated Maggie, too. But that was before we raised the money, the church and me, to send her to Augusta to school. She used to read to us without pity; forcing words, lies, other folks' habits, whole lives upon us two, sitting trapped and ignorant underneath her voice. She washed us in a river of make-believe, burned us with a lot of knowledge we didn't necessarily need to know. Pressed us to her with the serious way she read, to shove us away at just the moment, like dimwits, we seemed about to understand.

Dee wanted nice things. A yellow organdy dress to wear to her graduation from high school; black pumps to match a green suit she'd made from an old suit somebody gave me. She was determnined to stare down any disaster in her efforts. Her eyelids would not flicker for minutes at a time. Often I fought off the temptation to shake her. At sixteen she had a style of her own: and knew what style was.

I never had an education myself. After second grade the school was closed down. Don't ask me why: in 1927 colored asked fewer questions than they do now. Sometimes Maggie reads to me. She stumbles along good naturedly but can't see well. She knows she is not bright. Like good looks and money, quickness passed her by. She will marry John Thomas (who has mossy teeth in an earnest face) and then I'll be free to sit here and I guess just sing church songs to myself. Although I never was a good singer. Never could carry a tune. I was always better at a man's job. I used to love to milk till I was hooked[1] in the side in '49. Cows are soothing and slow and don't bother you, unless you try to milk them the wrong way.

I have deliberately turned my back on the house. It is three rooms, just like the one that burned, except the roof is tin; they don't make shingle roofs any

---

[1] I.e., by the horn of the cow being milked.

more. There are no real windows, just some holes cut in the sides, like the portholes in a ship, but not round and not square, with rawhide holding the shutters up on the outside. This house is in a pasture, too, like the other one. No doubt when Dee sees it she will want to tear it down. She wrote me once that no matter where we "choose" to live, she will manage to come see us. But she will never bring her friends. Maggie and I thought about this and Maggie asked me, "Mama, when did Dee ever *have* any friends?"

She had a few. Furtive boys in pink shirts hanging about on washday after school. Nervous girls who never laughed. Impressed with her they worshiped the well-turned phrase, the cute shape, the scalding humor that erupted like bubbles in lye. She read to them.

When she was courting Jimmy T she didn't have much time to pay to us, but turned all her faultfinding power on him. He *flew* to marry a cheap city girl from a family of ignorant flashy people. She hardly had time to recompose herself.

When she comes I will meet—but there they are!

Maggie attempts to make a dash for the house, in her shuffling way, but I stay her with my hand. "Come back here," I say. And she stops and tries to dig a well in the sand with her toe.

It is hard to see them clearly through the strong sun. But even the first glimpse of leg out of the car tells me it is Dee. Her feet were always neat-looking, as if God himself had shaped them with a certain style. From the other side of the car comes a short, stocky man. Hair is all over his head a foot long and hanging from his chin like a kinky mule tail. I hear Maggie suck in her breath. "Uhnnnh," is what it sounds like. Like when you see the wriggling end of a snake just in front of your foot on the road. "Uhnnnh."

Dee next. A dress down to the ground, in this hot weather. A dress so loud it hurts my eyes. There are yellows and oranges enough to throw back the light of the sun. I feel my whole face warming from the heat waves it throws out. Earrings gold, too, and hanging down to her shoulders. Bracelets dangling and making noises when she moves her arm up to shake the folds of the dress out of her armpits. The dress is loose and flows, and as she walks closer, I like it. I hear Maggie go "Uhnnnh" again. It is her sister's hair. It stands straight up like the wool on a sheep. It is black as night and around the edges are two long pigtails that rope about like small lizards disappearing behind her ears.

"Wa-su-zo-Tean-o!" she says, coming on in that gliding way the dress makes her move. The short stocky fellow with the hair to his navel is all grinning and he follows up with "Asalamalakim,[2] my mother and sister!" He moves to hug Maggie but she falls back, right up against the back of my chair. I feel her trembling there and when I look up I see the perspiration falling off her chin.

---

[2] Phonetic rendering of a Muslim greeting. "Wa-su-zo-Tean-o" is a similar rendering of an African dialect salutation.

"Don't get up," says Dee. Since I am stout it takes something of a push. You can see me trying to move a second or two before I make it. She turns, showing white heels through her sandals, and goes back to the car. Out she peeks next with a Polaroid. She stoops down quickly and lines up picture after picture of me sitting there in front of the house with Maggie cowering behind me. She never takes a shot without making sure the house is included. When a cow comes nibbling around the edge of the yard she snaps it and me and Maggie *and* the house. Then she puts the Polaroid in the back seat of the car, and comes up and kisses me on the forehead.

Meanwhile Asalamalakim is going through motions with Maggie's hand. Maggie's hand is as limp as a fish, and probably as cold, despite the sweat, and she keeps trying to pull it back. It looks like Asalamalakim wants to shake hands but wants to do it fancy. Or maybe he don't know how people shake hands. Anyhow, he soon gives up on Maggie.

"Well," I say. "Dee."

"No, Mama," she says. "Not 'Dee,' Wangero Leewanika Kemanjo!"

"What happened to 'Dee'?" I wanted to know.

"She's dead," Wangero said. "I couldn't bear it any longer, being named after the people who oppress me."

"You know as well as me you was named after your aunt Dicie," I said. Dicie is my sister. She named Dee. We called her "Big Dee" after Dee was born.

"But who was *she* named after?" asked Wangero.

"I guess after Grandma Dee," I said.

"And who was she named after?" asked Wangero.

"Her mother," I said, and saw Wangero was getting tired. "That's about as far back as I can trace it," I said. Though, in fact, I probably could have carried it back beyond the Civil War through the branches.

"Well," said Asalamalakim, "there you are."

"Uhnnnh," I heard Maggie say.

"There I was not," I said, "before 'Dicie' cropped up in our family, so why should I try to trace it that far back?"

He just stood there grinning, looking down on me like somebody inspecting a Model A car. Every once in a while he and Wangero sent eye signals over my head.

"How do you pronounce this name?" I asked.

"You don't have to call me by it if you don't want to," said Wangero.

"Why shouldn't I?" I asked. "If that's what you want us to call you, we'll call you."

"I know it might sound awkward at first," said Wangero.

"I'll get used to it," I said. "Ream it out again."

Well, soon we got the name out of the way. Asalamalakim had a name twice as long and three times as hard. After I tripped over it two or three times he told me to just call him Hakim-a-barber. I wanted to ask him was he a barber, but I didn't really think he was, so I didn't ask.

"You must belong to those beef-cattle peoples down the road," I said. They said "Asalamalakim" when they met you, too, but they didn't shake hands. Always too busy: feeding the cattle, fixing the fences, putting up salt-lick shelters, throwing down hay. When the white folks poisoned some of the herd the men stayed up all night with rifles in their hands. I walked a mile and a half just to see the sight.

Hakim-a-barber said, "I accept some of their doctrines, but farming and raising cattle is not my style." (They didn't tell me, and I didn't ask, whether Wangero (Dee) had really gone and married him.)

We sat down to eat and right away he said he didn't eat collards and pork was unclean. Wangero, though, went on through the chitlins and corn bread, the greens and everything else. She talked a blue streak over the sweet potatoes. Everything delighted her. Even the fact that we still used the benches her daddy made for the table when we couldn't afford to buy chairs.

"Oh, Mama!" she cried. Then turned to Hakim-a-barber. "I never knew how lovely these benches are. You can feel the rump prints," she said, running her hands underneath her and along the bench. Then she gave a sigh and her hand closed over Grandma Dee's butter dish. "That's it!" she said. "I knew there was something I wanted to ask you if I could have." She jumped up from the table and went over in the corner where the churn stood, the milk in it clabber by now. She looked at the churn and looked at it.

"This churn top is what I need," she said. "Didn't Uncle Buddy whittle it out of a tree you all used to have?"

"Yes," I said.

"Uh huh," she said happily. "And I want the dasher, too."

"Uncle Buddy whittle that, too?" asked the barber.

Dee (Wangero) looked up at me.

"Aunt Dee's first husband whittled the dash," said Maggie so low you almost couldn't hear her. "His name was Henry, but they called him Stash."

"Maggie's brain is like an elephant's," Wangero said, laughing. "I can use the churn top as a centerpiece for the alcove table," she said, sliding a plate over the churn, "and I'll think of something artistic to do with the dasher."

When she finished wrapping the dasher the handle stuck out. I took it for a moment in my hands. You didn't even have to look close to see where hands pushing the dasher up and down to make butter had left a kind of sink in the wood. In fact, there were a lot of small sinks; you could see where thumbs and fingers had sunk into the wood. It was beautiful light yellow wood, from a tree that grew in the yard where Big Dee and Stash had lived.

After dinner Dee (Wangero) went to the trunk at the foot of my bed and started rifling through it. Maggie hung back in the kitchen over the dishpan. Out came Wangero with two quilts. They had been pieced by Grandma Dee and then Big Dee and me had hung them on the quilt frames on the front porch and quilted them. One was in the Lone Star pattern. The other was Walk Around the Mountain. In both of them were scraps of dresses Grandma Dee had worn fifty and more years ago. Bits and pieces of Grandpa Jarrell's Paisley shirts. And one teeny faded blue piece, about the size of a penny matchbox, that was from Great Grandpa Ezra's uniform that he wore in the Civil War.

"Mama," Wangero said sweet as a bird. "Can I have these old quilts?"

I heard something fall in the kitchen, and a minute later the kitchen door slammed.

"Why don't you take one or two of the others?" I asked. "These old things was just done by me and Big Dee from some tops your grandma pieced before she died."

"No," said Wangero. "I don't want those. They are stitched around the borders by machine."

"That'll make them last better," I said.

"That's not the point," said Wangero. "These are all pieces of dresses Grandma used to wear. She did all this stitching by hand. Imagine!" She held the quilts securely in her arms, stroking them.

"Some of the pieces, like those lavender ones, come from old clothes her mother handed down to her," I said, moving up to touch the quilts. Dee (Wangero) moved back just enough so that I couldn't reach the quilts. They already belonged to her.

"Imagine!" she breathed again, clutching them closely to her bosom.

"The truth is," I said, "I promised to give them quilts to Maggie, for when she marries John Thomas."

She gasped like a bee had stung her.

"Maggie can't appreciate these quilts!" she said. "She'd probably be backward enough to put them to everyday use."

"I reckon she would," I said. "God knows I been saving 'em for long enough with nobody using 'em. I hope she will!" I didn't want to bring up how I had offered Dee (Wangero) a quilt when she went away to college. Then she had told me they were old-fashioned, out of style.

"But they're *priceless!*" she was saying now, furiously; for she has a temper. "Maggie would put them on the bed and in five years they'd be in rags. Less than that!"

"She can always make some more," I said. "Maggie knows how to quilt."

Dee (Wangero) looked at me with hatred. "You just will not understand. The point is these quilts, *these* quilts!"

"Well," I said, stumped. "What would *you* do with them?"

"Hang them," she said. As if that was the only thing you *could* do with quilts.

Maggie by now was standing in the door. I could almost hear the sound her feet made as they scraped over each other.

"She can have them, Mama," she said, like somebody used to never winning anything, or having anything reserved for her. "I can 'member Grandma Dee without the quilts."

I looked at her hard. She had filled her bottom lip with checkerberry snuff and it gave her a face a kind of dopey, hangdog look. It was Grandma Dee and Big Dee who taught her how to quilt herself. She stood there with her scarred hands hidden in the folds of her skirt. She looked at her sister with something like fear but she wasn't mad at her. This was Maggie's portion. This was the way she knew God to work.

When I looked at her like that something hit me in the top of my head and ran down to the soles of my feet. Just like when I'm in church and the spirit of God touches me and I get happy and shout. I did something I never had done before: hugged Maggie to me, then dragged her on into the room, snatched the quilts out of Miss Wangero's hands and dumped them into Maggie's lap. Maggie just sat there on my bed with her mouth open.

"Take one or two of the others," I said to Dee.

But she turned without a word and went out to Hakim-a-barber.

"You just don't understand," she said, as Maggie and I came out to the car.

"What don't I understand?" I wanted to know.

"Your heritage," she said. And then she turned to Maggie, kissed her, and said, "You ought to try to make something of yourself, too, Maggie. It's really a new day for us. But from the way you and Mama still live you'd never know it."

She put on some sunglasses that hid everything above the tip of her nose and her chin.

Maggie smiled; maybe at the sunglasses. But a real smile, not scared. After we watched the car dust settle I asked Maggie to bring me a dip of snuff. And then the two of us sat there just enjoying, until it was time to go in the house and go to bed.

JOURNAL PROMPT:

Is there a particular item, similar to the quilts in the story, that has been handed down in your family from generation to generation? What is this item? What is the story behind it, and where is it kept? Is it used on a daily basis?

COLLABORATIVE EXERCISE:

In this story, Walker implies that Dee's attitude about the quilts has changed drastically from what it was previously. In your groups, define this attitude in specific terms. Then, go on to list ways in which this change of attitude reflects Dee's feelings about the significance of family and her roots as an African American.

ESSAY ASSIGNMENT:

1. Write about what you believe to be the importance, if any, of keeping family heirlooms.
2. In the persona of Mama, respond in letter format to author Ellen Goodman's first-person narrative "The Family Legacy." Explain why you agree with Goodman's assessment of the importance of family, tradition, and heritage.

3. In the persona of author Ellen Goodman, respond in letter format to the character Dee. Explain why you believe family heirlooms have more than an aesthetic importance.

MEL LAZARUS is the author of several books and plays and is also a nationally syndicated cartoonist ("Miss Peach" and "Momma"). In this introspective piece, Lazarus explains how a childhood event helped him define and understand his relationship with his father.

MEL LAZARUS

ANGRY FATHERS

"Daddy's going to be very angry about this," my mother said. It was August 1938, at a Catskill Mountains boarding house. One hot Friday afternoon three of us—9-year-old city boys—got to feeling listless. We'd done all the summer-country stuff, caught all the frogs, picked the blueberries and shivered in enough icy water. What we needed, on this unbearably boring afternoon, was some action.

To consider the options, Artie, Eli and I holed up in the cool of the "casino," the little building in which the guests enjoyed their nightly bingo games and the occasional traveling magic act.

Gradually, inspiration came: the casino was too new, the wood frame and white Sheetrock walls too perfect. We would do it some quiet damage. Leave our anonymous mark on the place, for all time. With, of course, no thought as to consequences.

We began by picking up a long, wooden bench, running with it like a battering ram, and bashing it into a wall. It left a wonderful hole. But small. So we did it again. And again. . . .

Afterward the three of us, breathing hard, sweating the sweat of heroes, surveyed our first really big-time damage. The process had been so satisfying we'd gotten carried away; there was hardly a good square foot of Sheetrock left.

Suddenly, before even a tweak of remorse set in, the owner, Mr. Biolos, appeared in the doorway of the building, Furious. And craving justice: When they arrived from the city that night, he-would-tell-our-fathers!

Meantime, he told our mothers. My mother felt that what I had done was so monstrous she would leave my punishment to my father. "And," she said, "Daddy's going to be very angry about this."

By 6 o'clock Mr. Biolos was stationed out at the driveway, grimly waiting for the fathers to start showing up. Behind him, the front porch was jammed, like a sold-out bleacher section, with indignant guests. They'd seen the damage to their bingo palace, knew they'd have to endure it in that condition for the rest of the summer. They, too, craved justice.

As to Artie, Eli and me, we each found an inconspicuous spot on the porch, a careful distance from the other two but not too far from our respective mothers. And waited.

Artie's father arrived first. When Mr. Biolos told him the news and showed him the blighted casino, he carefully took off his belt and—with practiced style—viciously whipped his screaming son. With the approbation, by the way, of an ugly crowd of once gentle people.

Eli's father showed up next. He was told and shown and went raving mad, knocking his son off his feet with a slam to the head. As Eli lay crying on the grass, he kicked him on the legs, buttocks and back. When Eli tried to get up he kicked him again.

The crowd muttered: Listen, they should have thought of this before they did the damage. They'll live, don't worry, and I bet they never do that again.

I wondered: What will my father do? He'd never laid a hand on me in my life. I knew about other kids, had seen bruises on certain schoolmates and even heard screams in the evenings from certain houses on my street, but they were those kids, their families, and the why and how of their bruises were, to me, dark abstractions. Until now.

I looked over at my mother. She was upset. Earlier she'd made it clear to me that I had done some special kind of crime. Did it mean that beatings were now, suddenly, the new order of the day?

My own father suddenly pulled up in our Chevy, just in time to see Eli's father dragging Eli up the porch steps and into the building. He got out of the car believing, I was sure, that whatever it was all about, Eli must have deserved it. I went dizzy with fear.

Mr. Biolos, on a roll, started talking. My father listened, his shirt soaked with perspiration, a damp handkerchief draped around his neck; he never did well in humid weather. I watched him follow Mr. Biolos into the casino. My dad—strong and principled, hot and bothered—what was he thinking about all this?

When they emerged, my father looked over at my mother. He mouthed a small "Hello." Then his eyes found me and stared for a long moment, without expression. I tried to read his eyes, but they left me and went to the crowd, from face to expectant face.

Then, amazingly, he got into his car and drove away! Nobody, not even my mother, could imagine where he was going.

An hour later he came back. Tied onto the top of his car was a stack of huge Sheetrock boards. He got out holding a paper sack with a hammer sticking out of it. Without a word he untied the Sheetrock and one by one carried the boards into the casino.

And didn't come out again that night.

All through my mother's and my silent dinner and for the rest of that Friday evening and long after we had gone to bed, I could hear—everyone could hear—the steady bang bang bang bang of my dad's hammer. I pictured him sweating, missing his dinner, missing my mother, getting madder and madder at me. Would tomorrow be the last day of my life? It was 3 A.M. before I finally fell asleep.

The next morning, my father didn't say a single word about the night before. Nor did he show any trace of anger or reproach of any kind. We had a regular day, he, my mother and I, and, in fact, our usual, sweet family weekend.

Was he mad at me? You bet he was. But in a time when many of his generation saw corporal punishment of their children as a God-given right, he knew "spanking" as beating, and beating as criminal. And that when kids were beaten, they always remembered the pain but often forgot the reason.

And I also realized years later that, to him, humiliating me was just as unthinkable. Unlike the fathers of my buddies, he couldn't play into the conspiracy of revenge and spectacle.

But my father had made his point. I never forgot that my vandalism on that August afternoon was outrageous.

And I'll never forget that it was also the day I first understood how deeply I could trust him.

JOURNAL PROMPT:

Write about an incident from your past when you did something foolish. Did your peers influence you, or did you act alone?

COLLABORATIVE EXERCISE:

Many parents today still struggle with the issue of spanking as a means of discipline. Imagine you must write an argumentative essay, which requires you to include a discussion of the pros and cons of spanking. In your group, complete all the preparatory work for an essay such as this. You will want to do some brainstorming and compile a pro and con list with supports for each side. Also, be sure to craft a thesis statement that is assertive and debatable.

ESSAY ASSIGNMENT:

1. In what ways does this essay approach, although very subtly, the issue of family values? What are the values that appear to orchestrate this particular family and their priorities?
2. Recall a time from your childhood or adolescence when you were punished. At the time, did you feel that the punishment was fair and appropriate? Explain. Do you feel any differently now as you reflect on the incident? Finally, as the adult delivering the punishment, would you go about it differently?

Poet EAMON GRENNAN was born in Dublin, Ireland, and has been a resident of the United States for over twenty years. His poetry volumes include *What Light There Is* (1989), which was a finalist for the *LA Times* Book Award; *As If It Matters* (1991); and *So It Goes* (1995). He won a 1996 Pushcart Prize for his poem "Stone Flight."

EAMON GRENNAN

STATION

We are saying goodbye
on the platform. In silence
the huge train waits, crowding the station
with aftermath and longing
and all we've never said
to one another. He shoulders
his black dufflebag and shifts
from foot to foot, restless to be off, his eyes
wandering over tinted windows where he'll sit
staring out at the Hudson's platinum dazzle.

I want to tell him he's entering into the light
of the world, but it feels like a long tunnel
as he leaves one home, one parent
for another, and we both
know in our bones it won't ever
be the same again. What is the air at,
heaping between us then
thinning to nothing? Or those slategrey birds
that croon to themselves in an iron angle
and then take flight—inscribing
huge loops of effortless grace
between this station of shade and the shining water?

When our cheeks rest glancing against each other,
I feel mine scratchy with beard and stubble, his
not quite smooth as a girl's, harder, a faint fuzz
starting—those silken beginnings I can see
when the light is right, his next life
in bright first touches. What ails our hearts? Mine

aching in vain for the words
to make sense of our life together; his
fluttering in dread
of my finding the words, feathered syllables
fidgeting in his throat.

In a sudden rush of bodies
and announcements out of the air, he says
he's got to be going. One quick touch
and he's gone. In a minute
the train—ghostly faces behind smoked glass—
groans away on wheels and shackles, a slow glide
I walk beside, waving
at what I can see no longer. Later,
on his own in the city, he'll enter the underground
and cross the river, going home
to his mother's house. And I imagine
that pale face of his
carried along in the dark glass, shining
through shadows that fill the window
and fall away again
before we're even able to name them.

JOURNAL PROMPT:

Write about a time you said good-bye to someone you love.

COLLABORATIVE EXERCISE:

Working in small groups, discuss the effect of Grennan's use of imagery to enhance and advance the mood and purpose of this poem. To get started, consider the following lines:

1. "the huge train waits, crowding the station / with aftermath and longing"
2. "his eyes / wandering over tinted windows"
3. "syllables / fidgeting in his throat"
4. "ghostly faces behind smoked glass"

ESSAY ASSIGNMENT:

1. The subject matter of Grennan's poem is communication: the painful awkwardness that often exists between a parent and child, especially in this situation of divided homes. Write about a time when you found it difficult to communicate how you really felt to someone you loved.

What was the situation? Explain why it was uncomfortable or even impossible to express your feelings.

2. Discuss the nature images in "Station," as well as in three other poems in this textbook: "Cinderella," "Twelve," and "Sitting at Night on the Front Porch." In what ways do the nature images advance the themes of each work?

Additional Essay Prompts

1. Love is rarely verbally expressed between father and son in "Motorcycle Talk." What holds the relationship together, and what creates the silences?

2. Both the father in the poem "Station" and the father in the essay "A Father's Rite" are single, divorced parents who desire to strengthen their relationships with their sons. How are the father/son relationships similar and/or different? How does each of the two fathers communicate with his son? What does each want and need from the relationship?

3. Discuss the advantages and disadvantages of having one parent at home with the children while the other parent works outside the home. How does this arrangement help and/or hinder the home environment?

4. Write an essay in which you define the ideal father and what his role should be in the family. Clarify the reasons why you assign particular traits, activities, and responsibilities to the father. What experiences and observations in your life help to shape your opinion?

5. Write an essay in which you define the ideal mother and what her role should be in the family. Clarify the reasons why you assign particular traits, activities, and responsibilities to the mother. What experiences and observations in your life help to shape your opinion?

6. Consider a family from a television show, either from the past or present, with which you are familiar. Describe the family members and the home environment in detail. Then, analyze how Barbara Kingsolver (author of "Stone Soup") might view this family.

7. Write an essay in which you support or refute homosexuals raising children.

8. Does your home have one room that seems to be a "gathering place" for family members? Describe this room. What events and activities take place here? To what do you attribute its "magnetism" for your family?

9. In your opinion, are there situations when divorce is the very best decision? Explain your response, using personal experiences and observations.
10. What factors should a couple consider before having children?

ADDITIONAL RESEARCH QUESTIONS

1. An increasing number of families are choosing to homeschool their children. Explore the effect that homeschooling has on the family. You many want to consider such issues as roles within the family, relationships between family members, time management, etc.
2. Humans are not the only mammals who live within a particular family structure. Select a primate, and research its family structure.
3. Because of the large number of divorces and remarriages in this country, stepfamilies are probably the fastest growing *new* family structure. What problems do parents and children encounter when a stepfamily is created? What are the adjustments that must be made in order for stepfamilies to live in harmony?
4. In 1995, Francine Du Plessix Gray wrote an essay about changes in the American family for *The New Yorker* magazine. She wrote: "Kids . . . never seem to sit down to a proper meal at home anymore. This is not another pious harangue on 'spiritual starvation'; this is about the fact that we may be witnessing the first generation in history that has not been required to participate in that primal rite of socialization, the family meal." Write an essay in which you research the family meal. Why is it a ritual that is fast disappearing? Interview older adults to find out their experiences of the family dinner; then, interview young people to hear their current experiences. Based on what you find, analyze why this ritual may become extinct.
5. Investigate the current surge of interest in genealogy and research into family trees. (There are even magazines devoted entirely to the search for ancestors.) What are the reasons for the intense popularity of looking for "our past"?

8

The Mature Years: As We Age

Many of us are uncomfortable discussing death. Years ago, when Grandma died in the upstairs back bedroom, even young children knew that death is but a part of life. Today we ship the terminally ill off to die in a hospital; we are divorced from death because it is something we as a society don't want to see, to comprehend, and to confront.

Most traditional cultures have formalized rites to mark a life's passing; we have, according to Jessica Mitford, a commercialized mortuary business anxious to capitalize upon our fears. We have, according to Richard Selzer, insensitive health providers anxious to be rid of patients who cause trouble. Fortunately, we also have, according to E. B. White's essay "Once More to the Lake," the revelation that all life is cyclical and death is but a part of the wheel.

Students can examine their preconceived notions about death as they read these entries; they may come to a further understanding of how our society "protects" us from one of the most basic aspects of our communal journey.

E. B. White is best known as the author of *Stuart Little* (1945), and *Charlotte's Web* (1952), classic children's books. For many years, White was also an essayist for *The New Yorker* magazine. In this selection, White contemplates the cyclical patterns of our lives, as well as our psychological connection to the past.

E. B. WHITE

Once More to the Lake

One summer, along about 1904, my father rented a camp on a lake in Maine and took us all there for the month of August. We all got ringworm from some kittens and had to rub Pond's Extract on our arms and legs night and morning, and my father rolled over in a canoe with all his clothes on; but outside of that the vacation was a success and from then on none of us ever thought there was any place in the world like that lake in Maine. We returned summer after summer—always on August 1st for one month. I have since become a salt-water man, but sometimes in summer there are days when the restlessness of the tides and the fearful cold of the sea water and the incessant wind which blows across the afternoon and into the evening make me wish for the placidity of a lake in the woods. A few weeks ago this feeling got so strong I bought myself a couple of bass hooks and a spinner and returned to the lake where we used to go, for a week's fishing and to revisit old haunts.

I took along my son, who had never had any fresh water up his nose and who had seen lily pads only from train windows. On the journey over to the lake I began to wonder what it would be like. I wondered how time would have marred this unique, this holy spot—the coves and streams, the hills that the sun set behind, the camps and the paths behind the camps. I was sure the tarred road would have found it out and I wondered in what other ways it would be desolated. It is strange how much you can remember about places like that once you allow your mind to return into the grooves which lead back. You remember one thing, and that suddenly reminds you of another thing. I guess I remembered clearest of all the early mornings, when the lake was cool and motionless, remembered how the bedroom smelled of the lumber it was made of and of the wet woods whose scent entered through the screen. The partitions in the camp were thin and did not extend clear to the top of the rooms, and as I was always the first up I would dress softly so as not to wake the others, and sneak out into the sweet outdoors and start out in the canoe, keeping close along the shore in the long shadows of the pines. I remembered being very careful never to rub my paddle against the gunwale for fear of disturbing the stillness of the cathedral.

The lake had never been what you would call a wild lake. There were cottages sprinkled around the shores, and it was in farming country although the shores of the lake were quite heavily wooded. Some of the cottages were owned by nearby farmers, and you would live at the shore and eat your meals at the farmhouse. That's what our family did. But although it wasn't wild, it was a fairly large and undisturbed lake and there were places in it which, to a child at least, seemed infinitely remote and primeval.

I was right about the tar: it led to within half a mile of the shore. But when I got back there, with my boy, and we settled into a camp near a farmhouse and into the kind of summertime I had known, I could tell that it was going to be pretty much the same as it had been before—I knew it, lying in bed the first morning, smelling the bedroom, and hearing the boy sneak quietly out and go off along the shore in a boat. I began to sustain the illusion that he was I, and therefore, by simple transposition, that I was my father. This sensation persisted, kept cropping up all the time we were there. It was not an entirely new feeling, but in this setting it grew much stronger. I seemed to be living a dual existence. I would be in the middle of some simple act, I would be picking up a bait box or laying down a table fork, or I would be saying something, and suddenly it would be not I but my father who was saying the words or making the gesture. It gave me a creepy sensation.

We went fishing the first morning. I felt the same damp moss covering the worms in the bait can, and saw the dragonfly alight on the tip of my rod as it hovered a few inches from the surface of the water. It was the arrival of this fly that convinced me beyond any doubt that everything was as it always had been, that the years were a mirage and there had been no years. The small waves were the same, chucking the rowboat under the chin as we fished at anchor, and the boat was the same boat, the same color green and the ribs broken in the same place, and under the floor-boards the same fresh-water leavings and débris—the dead hellgrammite, the wisps of moss, the rusty discarded fishhook, the dried blood from yesterday's catch. We stared silently at the tips of our rods, at the dragonflies that came and went. I lowered the tip of mine into the water, tentatively, pensively dislodging the fly, which darted two feet away, poised, darted two feet back, and came to rest again a little farther up the rod. There had been no years between the ducking of this dragonfly and the other one—the one that was part of memory. I looked at the boy, who was silently watching his fly, and it was my hands that held his rod, my eyes watching. I felt dizzy and didn't know which rod I was at the end of.

We caught two bass, hauling them in briskly as though they were mackerel, pulling them over the side of the boat in a business-like manner without any landing net, and stunning them with a blow on the back of the head. When we got back for a swim before lunch, the lake was exactly where we had left it, the same number of inches from the dock, and there was only the merest suggestion of a breeze. This seemed an utterly enchanted sea, this lake you could leave to its own devices for a few hours and come back to, and find that it had not stirred, this constant and trustworthy body of water. In the shallows, the dark, water-soaked sticks and twigs, smooth and old, were undulating in clusters on the bottom against the clean ribbed sand, and the track of the mussel was plain. A school of minnows swam by, each minnow with its small individual shadow, doubling the attendance, so clear and sharp in the sunlight. Some of the other campers were in swimming, along the shore, one of them with a cake of soap, and the water felt thin and clear and unsubstantial. Over the years there had been this person with the cake of soap, this cultist, and here he was. There had been no years.

Up to the farmhouse to dinner through the teeming, dusty field, the road under our sneakers was only a two-track road. The middle track was missing, the one with the marks of the hooves and the splotches of dried, flaky manure. There had always been three tracks to choose from in choosing which track to walk in; now the choice was narrowed down to two. For a moment I missed terribly the middle alternative. But the way led past the tennis court, and something about the way it lay there in the sun reassured me; the tape had loosened along the backline, the alleys were green with plantains and other weeds, and the net (installed in June and removed in September) sagged in the dry noon, and the whole place steamed with midday heat and hunger and emptiness. There was a choice of pie for dessert, and one was blueberry and one was apple, and the waitresses were the same country girls, there having been no passage of time, only the illusion of it as in a dropped curtain—the waitresses were still fifteen; their hair had been washed, that was the only difference—they had been to the movies and seen the pretty girls with the clean hair.

Summertime, oh summertime, pattern of life indelible, the fade-proof lake, the woods unshatterable, the pasture with the sweetfern and the juniper forever and ever, summer without end; this was the background, and the life along the shore was the design, the cottagers with their innocent and tranquil design, their tiny docks with the flagpole and the American flag floating against the white clouds in the blue sky, the little paths over the roots of the trees leading from camp to camp and the paths leading back to the outhouses and the can of lime for sprinkling, and at the souvenir counters at the store the miniature birch-bark canoes and the post cards that showed things looking a little better than they looked. This was the American family at play, escaping the city heat, wondering whether the newcomers in the camp at the head of the cove were "common" or "nice," wondering whether it was true that the people who drove up for Sunday dinner at the farmhouse were turned away because there wasn't enough chicken.

It seemed to me, as I kept remembering all this, that those times and those summers had been infinitely precious and worth saving. There had been jollity and peace and goodness. The arriving (at the beginning of August) had been so big a business in itself, at the railway station the farm wagon drawn up, the first smell of the pine-laden air, the first glimpse of the smiling farmer, and the great importance of the trunks and your father's enormous authority in such matters, and the feel of the wagon under you for the long ten-mile haul, and at the top of the last long hill catching the first view of the lake after eleven months of not seeing this cherished body of water. The shouts and cries of the other campers when they saw you, and the trunks to be unpacked, to give up their rich burden. (Arriving was less exciting nowadays, when you sneaked up in your car and parked it under a tree near the camp and took out the bags and in five minutes it was all over, no fuss, no loud wonderful fuss about trunks.)

Peace and goodness and jollity. The only thing that was wrong now, really, was the sound of the place, an unfamiliar nervous sound of the outboard motors. This was the note that jarred, the one thing that would sometimes break the illusion and set the years moving. In those other summertimes all motors were inboard; and when they were at a little distance, the noise they made was a sedative, an ingredient of summer sleep. They were one-cylinder and two-cylinder engines, and some were make-and-break and some were jump-spark, but they all made a sleepy sound across the lake. The one-lungers throbbed and fluttered, and the twin-cylinder ones purred and purred, and that was a quiet sound too. But now the campers all had outboards. In the daytime, in the hot mornings, these motors made a petulant, irritable sound; at night, in the still evening when the afterglow lit the water, they whined about one's ears like mosquitoes. My boy loved our rented outboard, and his great desire was to achieve singlehanded mastery over it, and authority, and he soon learned the trick of choking it a little (but not too much), and the adjustment of the needle valve. Watching him I would remember the things you could do with the old one-cylinder engine with the heavy flywheel, how you could have it eating out of your hand if you got really close to it spiritually. Motor boats in those days didn't have clutches, and you would make a landing by shutting off the motor at the proper time and coasting in with a dead rudder. But there was a way of reversing them, if you learned the trick, by cutting the switch and putting it on again exactly on the final dying revolution of the flywheel, so that it would kick back against compression and begin reversing. Approaching a dock in a strong following breeze, it was difficult to slow up sufficiently by the ordinary coasting method, and if a boy felt he had complete mastery over his motor, he was tempted to keep it running beyond its time and then reverse it a few feet from the dock. It took a cool nerve, because if you threw the switch a twentieth of a second too soon you would catch the flywheel when it still had speed enough to go up past center, and the boat would leap ahead, charging bull-fashion at the dock.

We had a good week at the camp. The bass were biting well and the sun shone endlessly, day after day. We would be tired at night and lie down in the accumulated heat of the little bedrooms after the long hot day and the breeze would stir almost imperceptibly outside and the smell of the swamp drift in through the rusty screens. Sleep would come easily and in the morning the red squirrel would be on the roof, tapping out his gay routine. I kept remembering everything, lying in bed in the mornings—the small steamboat that had a long rounded stern like the lip of a Ubangi, and how quietly she ran on the moonlight sails, when the older boys played their mandolins and the girls sang and we ate doughnuts dipped in sugar, and how sweet the music was on the water in the shining night, and what it had felt like to think about girls then. After breakfast we would go up to the store and the things were in the same place—the minnows in a bottle, the plugs and spinners disarranged and pawed over by the youngsters from the boys' camp, the fig newtons and the Beeman's gum. Outside, the road was tarred and cars stood in front of the store. Inside, all was just as it had always been, except there was more Coca-Cola and not so much Moxie and root beer and birch beer and sarsaparilla. We would walk out with a bottle of pop apiece and sometimes the pop would backfire up our noses and hurt. We explored the streams, quietly, where the turtles slid off the sunny logs and dug their way into the soft bottom; and we lay on the town wharf and fed worms to the tame bass. Everywhere we went I had trouble making out which was I, the one walking at my side, the one walking in my pants.

One afternoon while we were there at that lake a thunderstorm came up. It was like the revival of an old melodrama that I had seen long ago with childish awe. The second-act climax of the drama of the electrical disturbance over a lake in America had not changed in any important respect. This was the big scene, still the big scene. The whole thing was so familiar, the first feeling of oppression and heat and a general air around camp of not wanting to go very far away. In midafternoon (it was all the same) a curious darkening of the sky, and a lull in everything that had made life tick; and then the way the boats suddenly swung the other way at their moorings with the coming of a breeze out of the new quarter, and the premonitory rumble. Then the kettle drum, then the snare, then the bass drum and cymbals, then crackling light against the dark, and the gods grinning and licking their chops in the hills. Afterward the calm, the rain steadily rustling in the calm lake, the return of light and hope and spirits, and the campers running out in joy and relief to go swimming in the rain, their bright cries perpetuating the deathless joke about how they were getting simply drenched, and the children screaming with delight at the new sensation of bathing in the rain, and the joke about getting drenched linking the generations in a strong industructible chain. And the comedian who waded in carrying an umbrella.

When the others went swimming my son said he was going in too. He pulled his dripping trunks from the line where they had hung all through the shower, and wrung them out. Languidly, and with no thought of going in, I watched him, his hard little body, skinny and bare, saw him wince slightly as he pulled up around his vitals the small, soggy, icy garment. As he buckled the swollen belt suddenly my groin felt the chill of death.

JOURNAL PROMPT:

Patricia Hampl in "Memory and Imagination" writes that "what is remembered is what *becomes* reality." She claims that whether or not something really happened the way we remember it is not the important thing; rather, it is what the memory gives us that is important. One of the messages of E. B. White's essay also has to do with the role of memory in our lives. Write about a time when you discovered that your childhood memories were not accurate.

COLLABORATIVE EXERCISE:

What do you think is the significance of the last sentence of this essay? Find in the essay examples of foreshadowing of the statement.

ESSAY ASSIGNMENT:

1. Write an essay in which you analyze what "Once More to the Lake" suggests about the issues of past and present, youth and age, life and death. Include a detailed discussion of how these issues reflect the cyclical patterns of our lives.

2. Is there a place from your childhood that remains timeless in memory? Do you think a return there might destroy the specialness of that place for you, or as it was for E. B. White, could it be the source of new insights about your life?

American poet **Charles Wright** was born in Tennessee in 1935 and educated at Davidson College and the University of Iowa. His many honors include the American Academy of Arts and Letters Award of Merit Medal and the Ruth Lilly Poetry Prize. Wright was elected a Chancellor of the Academy of American Poets in 1999. He has written several collections of poetry, including *Black Zodiac* (1997), which won the Pulitzer Prize and the *LA Times* Book Prize. Charles Wright is Souder Family Professor of English at the University of Virginia in Charlottesville.

CHARLES WRIGHT

Sitting at Night on the Front Porch

I'm here, on the dark porch, restyled in my mother's chair.
10:45 and no moon.
Below the house, car lights
Swing down, on the canyon floor, to the sea.

In this they resemble us,
Dropping like match flames through the great void
Under our feet.
In this they resemble her, burning and disappearing.

Everyone's gone
And I'm here, sizing the dark, saving my mother's seat.

JOURNAL PROMPT:

A familiar adage is that we become our parents. Have you observed this in your own life? How does Wright's poem support or deny this belief?

COLLABORATIVE EXERCISE:

Why do you think Wright uses the images he does to reflect on and honor his mother's passing? Be specific.

ESSAY ASSIGNMENT:

1. How does Charles Wright's poem mirror the theme of "Once More to the Lake"?
2. Write an essay about a favorite person from your past. Describe things this person loved and places this person inhabited. As in Wright's poem, let the images you choose reveal the character of the person.

In this essay a doctor examines the way one patient deals with his imminent death. **RICHARD SELZER**, a surgeon and writer, is the recipient of many awards, including a Guggenheim Fellowship and an American Medical Writers Award. His essays have appeared in many nationwide magazines. Selzer's work, while often graphic, is compassionate and filled with wonder for the mystery of the human body.

RICHARD SELZER

THE DISCUS THROWER

I spy on my patients. Ought not a doctor to observe his patients by any means and from any stance, that he might the more fully assemble evidence? So I stand in the doorways of hospital rooms and gaze. Oh, it is not all that furtive an act. Those in bed need only look up to discover me. But they never do.

From the doorway of Room 542 the man in the bed seems deeply tanned. Blue eyes and close-cropped white hair give him the appearance of vigor and good health. But I know that his skin is not brown from the sun. It is rusted, rather, in the last stage of containing the vile repose within. And the blue eyes are frosted, looking inward like the windows of a snowbound cottage. This man is blind. This man is also legless—the right leg missing from midthigh down, the left from just below the knee. It gives him the look of a bonsai, roots and branches pruned into the dwarfed facsimile of a great tree.

Propped on pillows, he cups his right thigh in both hands. Now and then he shakes his head as though acknowledging the intensity of his suffering. In all of this he makes no sound. Is he mute as well as blind?

The room in which he dwells is empty of all possessions—no get-well cards, small, private caches of food, day-old flowers, slippers, all the usual kick-shaws of the sickroom. There is only the bed, a chair, a nightstand, and a tray on wheels that can be swung across his lap for meals.

"What time is it?" he asks.

"Three o'clock."

"Morning or afternoon?"

"Afternoon."

He is silent. There is nothing else he wants to know.

"How are you?" I say.

"Who is it?" he asks.

"It's the doctor. How do you feel?"

He does not answer right away.

"Feel?" he says.

"I hope you feel better," I say.

I press the button at the side of the bed.

"Down you go," I say.

"Yes, down," he says.

He falls back upon the bed awkwardly. His stumps, unweighted by legs and feet, rise in the air, presenting themselves. I unwrap the bandages from the stumps, and begin to cut away the black scabs and dead, glazed fat with scissors and forceps. A shard of white bone comes loose. I pick it away. I wash the wounds with disinfectant and redress the stumps. All this while, he does not speak. What is he thinking behind those lids that do not blink? Is he remembering a time when he was whole? Does he dream of feet? Of when his body was not a rotting log?

He lies solid and inert. In spite of everything, he remains impressive, as though he were a sailor standing athwart a slanting deck.

"Anything more I can do for you?" I ask.

For a long moment he is silent.

"Yes," he says at last and without the least irony. "You can bring me a pair of shoes."

In the corridor, the head nurse is waiting for me.

"We have to do something about him," she says. "Every morning he orders scrambled eggs for breakfast, and, instead of eating them, he picks up the plate and throws it against the wall."

"Throws his plate?"

"Nasty. That's what he is. No wonder his family doesn't come to visit. They probably can't stand him any more than we can."

She is waiting for me to do something.

"Well?"

"We'll see," I say.

The next morning I am waiting in the corridor when the kitchen delivers his breakfast. I watch the aide place the tray on the stand and swing it across his lap. She presses the button to raise the head of the bed. Then she leaves.

In time the man reaches to find the rim of the tray, then on to find the dome of the covered dish. He lifts off the cover and places it on the stand. He fingers across the plate until he probes the eggs. He lifts the plate in both hands, sets it on the palm of his right hand, centers it, balances it. He hefts it up and down slightly, getting the feel of it. Abruptly, he draws back his right arm as far as he can.

There is the crack of the plate breaking against the wall at the foot of his bed and the small wet sound of the scrambled eggs dropping to the floor.

And then he laughs. It is a sound you have never heard. It is something new under the sun. It could cure cancer.

Out in the corridor, the eyes of the head nurse narrow.

"Laughed, did he?"

She writes something down on her clipboard.

A second aide arrives, brings a second breakfast tray, puts it on the nightstand, out of his reach. She looks over at me shaking her head and making her mouth go. I see that we are to be accomplices.

"I've got to feed you," she says to the man.

"Oh, no you don't," the man says.

"Oh, yes I do," the aide says, "after the way you just did. Nurse says so."

"Get me my shoes," the man says.

"Here's oatmeal," the aide says. "Open." And she touches the spoon to his lower lip.

"I ordered scrambled eggs," says the man.

"That's right," the aide says.

I step forward.

"Is there anything I can do?" I say.

"Who are you?" the man asks.

In the evening I go once more to that ward to make my rounds. The head nurse reports to me that Room 542 is deceased. She has discovered this quite by accident, she says. No, there had been no sound. Nothing. It's a blessing, she says.

I go into his room, a spy looking for secrets. He is still there in his bed. His face is relaxed, grave, dignified. After a while, I turn to leave. My gaze sweeps the wall at the foot of the bed, and I see the place where it has been repeatedly washed, where the wall looks very clean and very white.

JOURNAL PROMPT:

Why does the patient ask for his shoes when he has no legs? How is his request connected to his throwing of the plate?

COLLABORATIVE EXERCISE:

Selzer's description of the nurse is not an attractive one. Why does she seem so unsympathetic to her patient? What is the doctor's view of this dying man? How does the title play to this?

ESSAY ASSIGNMENT:

1. What do you think Selzer's purpose was in calling his essay "The Discus Thrower"? (Hint: How did the ancient Greeks view their athletes?) What tone does the title suggest for the essay? What is your response to the title and its effectiveness in symbolically revealing the doctor's attitude toward his patient?
2. Research and compare the treatment of a dying person in a hospital with the care received in a hospice.
3. View an hour of the Bill Moyers documentary "On Death and Dying." What are some of the suggestions made to create a humane death for the terminally ill?

The author of this selection was born and raised in New York City, where he earned a Ph.D. from Columbia University. He also holds a law degree from the University of Virginia. **Melvin Urofsky** has written and edited over fifteen books. In *Letting Go: Death, Dying, and the Law* (1993), he examines the complex relationships between patients, their families, the law, and physicians, as well as the role medical ethics plays in medical decision making.

MELVIN I. UROFSKY

Two Scenes from a Hospital

Two things a person does alone, the ancient maxim held, are come into the world and leave it. It is true that for most of human existence, people died by themselves, the victims of predators, war, disease, or aging. As civilization tamed humanity, people died at home, in their own beds, surrounded by loving family who might ease the final pains but could do nothing to delay death. Only in the recent past have people gone to hospitals to die, and only within the last decade or so has medicine developed drugs, procedures, and technology to hold off death.

These developments raise a host of questions, but in the end they all come down to what does the individual want, and if the individual is incapable of deciding, what does the family want. But there are others who now demand a voice in the decision—doctors, nurses, hospital administrators, insurance companies, and, very often, agents of the state. In most instances, the person dies without interference, since there is still little that medicine can do when age or disease [has] taken [its] ultimate toll. But in other situations, instead of death coming peacefully and with dignity, there is conflict and suffering, rage and public controversy.

In these cases, the key issue is who will decide whether or not care should be provided or withheld, whether enormous energy and resources should be expended to delay death, or whether nothing should be done, so that death may have its way. Who decides, and what role, if any, should the law play in this process? These are not easy questions, as can be seen in the following stories.

Rocco Musolino was a big man, one who enjoyed good food and drink and people, a gregarious man who had run a liquor store in College Park, Maryland, until his retirement. He also hated hospitals, and never wanted to end his days in one.

To avoid that possibility, Musolino wrote a living will in 1989 in which he specifically declared that if he were terminally ill, he did not want to be kept alive by machine. Aware that if he were really sick he might not be able to make decisions on his own, he also signed a durable power of attorney giving his wife of fifty years, Edith, the authority to make decisions about his care. Repeatedly he told his family he did not want to be hooked up to any "damn machine" or "kept alive as a vegetable."

Rocco Musolino had drawn up his living will shortly after he had suffered a major heart attack in 1988. While he was in the hospital at that time doctors had performed a catheterization procedure that revealed that he had severe blockages in the coronary arteries and that one-fourth of his heart muscle was already dead. The damage was so extensive that doctors ruled out coronary bypass surgery.

Musolino had no illusions as to the prognosis of the disease, nor the fact that his diabetes seriously compounded the problem. In the two years following his heart attack, his condition deteriorated to the point that he had difficulty moving around his house. "If he made it to the bathroom, that was a big deal," his daughter Edith Scott said. "He couldn't shave. He would get all out of breath."

On October 24, 1990, following a night of chest pains and difficulty in breathing, he told his wife he couldn't stand the pain anymore. She called an ambulance to take him to Georgetown University Medical Center. There his regular cardiologist, Dr. Richard Rubin, examined Musolino, and then called in a surgeon, Dr. Nevin Katz, who told the family that Rocco's only hope lay in bypass surgery, the same procedure that had been ruled out two years earlier.

"He'll die without an operation," Katz told Edith Musolino. "He's got a 50-50 chance with it." The family agreed reluctantly, since it appeared that potential kidney failure would also require dialysis, the type of machine treatment that Musolino had always feared. Musolino stayed in the hospital to undergo tests and build up his strength, and the medical staff scheduled him for bypass surgery on November 12. The night before the operation, Dr. Rubin went in to visit his patient, and later said that Rocco expressed a strong desire to live, even if it meant he might have to go onto dialysis for the rest of his life.

Later that night, Musolino suffered two cardiac arrests but survived, and Rubin and Katz decided to go ahead with the surgery. Rubin called to get Edith Musolino's consent and then wrote in the patient's record: "He is awake and wishes to proceed. He is aware of the risk. I have reviewed the high risk of death (40 percent), high risk of renal failure (long term about 50 percent) with wife and daughter." His daughter later said she could not recall any such discussion.

The operation appeared successful, at least in relieving strain on the heart, but Musolino's kidneys failed, and he required dialysis several times a week. Since he could not breathe without a respirator, his wife reluctantly agreed to a tracheotomy, in which doctors inserted a breathing tube into his neck. In addition to causing constant pain, the breathing tube left Rocco unable to talk.

Musolino remained conscious and aware of what was happening, but his family claims he was never fully alert, and his medical records seemed to bear this out. Doctors' notes show that he slept a lot, and often responded to questions only with a grimace. A neurologist who examined him noted that his fluctuating state of consciousness resulted from severe medical problems; if he overcame them, he would probably regain full mental clarity.

But Rocco Musolino did not improve, and as the weeks went on his family concluded he would never recover. In late November they asked the doctors to put a "Do Not Resuscitate" order on his chart, so that he would not be treated if he suffered another cardiac arrest. Dr. Katz refused. When the family requested that he stop some of the medication, he angrily told them: "I stay awake at night trying to keep your father alive, and you want me to kill him. What is wrong with you people?" Only after his patient's condition deteriorated further did Katz agree to a "DNR" order.

Edith Musolino watched her husband's condition worsen. "Everything that could be wrong with him was wrong with him. I knew he was dying. I knew his body couldn't take any more." She made up her mind in December to ask the hospital to stop the dialysis sessions and to let her husband die in peace.

On December 21, 1990, the hospital's ethics committee met to consider the request, and recommended a psychiatric examination to determine whether Musolino was mentally competent. Under District of Columbia law, if he were declared incompetent, then the durable power of attorney would become operative, and his wife would have the authority to make the medical decisions.

The hospital named Dr. Steven A. Epstein to do the evaluation, and he visited Musolino twice at times when the patient seemed to rally a bit. Epstein's initial report, dated December 27, was inconclusive, and the family pushed for a second evaluation. This time the doctor reported the patient "lethargic and barely responding to voice. Today he clearly cannot make health care decisions on his own." Musolino, he told the family, was not mentally competent.

On New Year's Day 1991, Edith Musolino filed a note in her husband's medical record withdrawing her consent for dialysis. According to her, doctors, hospital administrators, and the hospital's lawyers agreed that she had the authority, they ordered dialysis stopped and removed the tube used to connect Musolino to the machine. Advised that without the treatment he would probably die within a few days, she and her children went to a funeral home to make the necessary arrangements.

They returned to the hospital to learn that Katz had changed his mind, and wanted to restart dialysis. He wrote on January 2, "I cannot in good conscience carry out their request," and he asked the hospital's lawyers and the chairman of the ethics committee to reopen the case.

The family now tried to find another physician or to have Musolino transferred to another hospital that would honor their requests. Katz agreed to turn over the case if the family could find a heart specialist with intensive-care experience. As Scott Musolino reported, "I called so many doctors. No one was willing to touch my father."

The next day Georgetown Hospital's lawyers wrote to the family's attorney informing him that the hospital would seek "emergency temporary guardianship" unless the family agreed to resume dialysis. Edith Musolino felt she had no choice but to agree.

Ten days later, her husband's condition deteriorating, her frustration and anger at the indignities that had been heaped upon him in spite of his express wishes finally erupted in a confrontation with Katz at Rocco's bedside. With her husband's legs and arms twitching, his face grimacing, she demanded of Katz: "What are you trying to prove here? You have made him suffer so much."

Katz asked her what she wanted. She said she wanted another doctor, Taveira Da Silva, the head of the hospital's intensive-care unit, who had earlier agreed to take the case on condition that dialysis be continued. Katz agreed, and the next morning nurses wheeled Rocco to the ICU, where the staff gradually began treating him as a dying patient. While Da Silva described Musolino as "terminal," he nonetheless continued dialysis, even though by this point the patient had become totally disoriented and his arms had to be tied down during the procedure.

His family had reached the end of their patience as well and had agreed that the only way to save Rocco from further indignity was to take him home. At a meeting on January 24, Dr. Da Silva agreed to stop the dialysis if they wanted to do that. A few days later, however, Da Silva finally came to the conclusion the family had reached much earlier—Rocco Musolino had "virtually a fatal, irreversible disease," that no medical care could help, and that the living will, which the hospital and doctors had ignored for three months, should be enforced. He told Edith that he would stop the dialysis and let her husband die in the hospital.

Instead of relief that her husband's long ordeal would soon be over, Edith Musolino felt only anger. "You know, Doctor," she said, "I was beginning not to know who to pray to anymore. Do I pray to you, or do I pray to God?"

On February 2, 1991, Rocco Musolino died, after a stay of 102 days in Georgetown University Medical Center, a place he had never wanted to be and where he and his family had lost all power to decide his fate.

While Rocco Musolino's wife fought to get hospital authorities to stop treating him, halfway across the continent hospital officials were trying to get a patient's family to consent to cessation of treatment.

On December 14, 1989, Helga Wanglie, an eighty-six-year-old retired schoolteacher, tripped on a scatter rug in her home in Minneapolis and fractured her hip. After surgery in a small private hospital, she developed breathing problems and was transferred to Hennepin County Medical Center. There, although on a respirator, she remained fully conscious and alert, writing notes to her husband, since the breathing tube prevented her from talking.

After five months, the hospital weaned her from the respirator in May 1990, and she entered Bethesda Lutheran Hospital across the river in St. Paul, a facility specializing in the care of respiratory ailments. A few days later, her heart stopped suddenly, and by the time doctors and nurses could resuscitate her, she had suffered severe brain damage. An ambulance brought her back to Hennepin Medical in a comatose state, her breathing sustained by a ventilator. When it became clear that doctors could do nothing for Mrs. Wanglie, they spoke with her husband of fifty-three years, Oliver, a retired attorney, about turning off the ventilator.

Although her husband and sons recognized that Helga had no cognition and might never regain consciousness, they would not hear of turning off the machine. His wife had strong religious convictions, Oliver told reporters, and they had talked about the possibility that if anything happened to her, she wanted "everything" done to keep her alive. "She told me, 'Only He who gave life has the right to take life.' . . . It seems to me [the hospital officials] are trying to play God. Who are they to determine who's to die and who's to live? I take the position that as long as her heart is beating there's life there."

Eight months after readmitting Helga Wanglie and trying to convince her family to stop treatment, Hennepin Medical Center officials announced they would go to court seeking the appointment of a guardian to determine Helga Wanglie's medical treatment. The hospital did not request that the court authorize discontinuing treatment. To the best of my knowledge, no hospital has ever made such a request, nor has there been any case law on it. Rather, the hospital sought the appointment of a "stranger" conservator, that is, one independent of both family and hospital, to make decisions based on the best interests of the patient. The hospital believed that a neutral party would agree with its position.

While in most right-to-die cases it is the patient or the family that wants the hospital to stop treatment, the Wanglie case is the rarely seen other side of the coin. Dr. Michael B. Belzer, the hospital's medical director, said he sympathized with the Wanglie family, but a heartbeat no longer signified life, since machines could artificially do the heart's work. The real question, he believed, was whether the hospital had an obligation to provide "inappropriate medical treatment."

Mrs. Wanglie's medical bills were paid in full by her insurance company, so money was not an issue in the hospital's decision. "This is a pure ethics case," said Dr. Arthur Caplan, director of the Center for Biomedical Ethics at the University of Minnesota. For years, he explained, we've used the "smokescreen of 'Can we afford to do this?' There's been a harder question buried under that layer of blather about money, namely: 'What's the point of medical care?'"

Dr. Belzer noted that Hennepin had the facilities and "the technology to keep fifty Helga Wanglies alive for an indefinite period of time. That would be the easy thing to do. The harder thing is to say just because we can do it, do we have to do it?"

Hennepin Medical Center is a public hospital, one of the best in the upper midwest, and before it could petition a court to appoint a conservator or guardian for Mrs. Wanglie (in order to have consent for turning off the life support), it needed the approval of the county's Board of Commissioners. The board members gave the hospital permission by a 4–3 vote, with the tiebreaker cast by a member who had known the Wanglie family for more than thirty years. It took him a month to make up his mind.

The commissioner, Randy Jackson, said that he finally voted to let the hospital go to the courts because "I don't think this is a decision to be made by a board of elected commissioners who happen to be trustees of the hospital. These are issues that we're going to be confronted with more and more often as medical machinery becomes more and more able to keep people alive."

Hospital attorneys presented their case to county judge Patricia Belois on May 28, 1991, asking her to appoint a conservator to decide Mrs. Wanglie's fate. They did not question her husband's sincerity, but argued instead that her condition was hopeless, and respirators had never been intended to prolong life in such cases.

On July 1, Judge Belois ruled against the hospital and left power to decide questions on Helga's medical treatment in her husband's hands. "He is in the best position to investigate and act upon Helga Wanglie's conscientious, religious, and moral beliefs." After the decision Oliver Wanglie said "I think she'd be proud of me. She knew where I stood. I have a high regard for the sanctity of human life."

A little while after this decision, Helga Wanglie died.

[T]he key issue is that of who decides what is best for a terminally ill person and what role the law and the courts have in that process. In an ideal world, perhaps, the interests of patients, families, doctors, hospitals, and courts would all coincide. But aside from the fact that this is an imperfect world, the interests of these groups are not necessarily congruent.

For centuries doctors have sworn to uphold life, and now for the first time they are being asked, openly and at times defiantly, what gives them the right to decide other people's fate? Hospitals, caught in a crunch between escalating expenses and new technology, must weigh costs that never before mattered. Moreover, in a society as litigious as ours, doctors and hospitals walk in constant fear that a "wrong" judgment will lead to a ruinous lawsuit. While elective bodies are responsible for broad policy decisions, it is difficult if not impossible to frame legislation in such a way as to cover all contingencies, and so courts must step in to interpret not only what the laws say and mean, but also what the limits of self-autonomy are under both the common law and constitutional protection.

Two things a person does alone, the ancient maxim held: come into the world and leave it. But at the end of the twentieth century, before one can leave this world, he or she may find it necessary to traverse a bewildering legal, moral, and medical maze.

JOURNAL PROMPT:

Imagine that you are a close member of the Musolino or Wanglie family. How would you have reacted to the treatment rendered your relative?

COLLABORATIVE EXERCISE:

This essay examines how medical and legal issues make dying a complex matter in our society today, one in which our own interests are not always honored. Brainstorm some solutions to the dilemma.

ESSAY ASSIGNMENT:

1. Compare this essay with "I Want to Die at Home." How are the two works similar? How are they different? (Think in terms of subject matter, theme, and writing style.)
2. Write about a personal experience of having someone close to you die.
3. Do you believe either of the doctors' actions in the Musolino case to be justified? What about the behavior of the Wanglie family? Were they justified in taking the stance they did, refusing further treatment to keep Helga alive?

Gwendolyn Brooks was born in Topeka, Kansas, in 1917 and raised in Chicago. She wrote over twenty collections of poetry, including *Anne Allen* (1949) for which she received a Pulitzer Prize. In 1968, she was named poet laureate for the state of Illinois. She lived in Chicago until her death on December 3, 2000.

GWENDOLYN BROOKS

THE BEAN EATERS

They eat beans mostly, this old yellow pair.
Dinner is a casual affair.
Plain chipware on a plain and creaking wood,
Tin flatware.

Two who are Mostly Good.
Two who have lived their day,
But keep on putting on their clothes
And putting things away.

And remembering . . .
Remembering, with tinklings and twinges,
As they lean over the beans in their rented back room that is full of
beads and receipts and dolls and cloths, tobacco crumbs, vases
and fringes.

JOURNAL PROMPT:

Describe an older couple you know well.

COLLABORATIVE EXERCISE:

What do we know about this couple's lives? Draft a detailed description of both the man and the woman, and include the impressions the words suggest. Because we each come to a poem with our own experiences, each group member may have very different ideas about this couple.

ESSAY ASSIGNMENT:

1. Two different philosophies seem to emerge while reading this poem: both the value of holding on to *things* and the idea of living a life free of clutter. Write a three- to four-page essay in which you take a side and argue for one "approach" to life versus the other. Support your opinion with logical details from your own life and observations.
2. Daniel Schacter, author of *Searching for Memory: The Brain, the Mind and the Past,* explains the importance of memory: "We are constantly making use of information acquired in the past." In this poem, how does Schacter's belief in the vitality of memory explain this couple's lives? What useful purpose does memory serve them? How does memory play a role in your own life?

In this essay, **ANNE RICKS SUMERS,** an ophthalmologist, examines her brother's last days in a hospital and makes a plea that people should be allowed to die at home surrounded by family and friends. This essay was first printed in *Newsweek* in April 1994.

ANNE RICKS SUMERS

I WANT TO DIE AT HOME

Last week my brother Rick died at home. I am so proud that we helped him die at home. Everyone should have as beautiful a death. Don't get me wrong—it is tragic and wrong that he should be dead. Rick was only 40, a nice, funny guy, a good husband, a dedicated lawyer, a father of a little boy who needs him. He didn't "choose death"; he wanted desperately to live, but a brain tumor was killing him and the doctors couldn't do a thing. He had only one choice: die in the hospital or die at home.

Three months ago, doctors discovered cancer in both of Rick's kidneys. The kidneys were removed and he and his wife coped well with home dialysis. He returned to work, took care of his son, remodeled his kitchen and went to a Redskins game.

Then disaster struck. It all happened so quickly. On a Tuesday his wife noticed Rick was confused. By Wednesday he was hallucinating and an MRI showed that his brain was studded with inoperable cancer. Doctors said chemotherapy or radiation might buy him a few more weeks of life, but they couldn't predict whether he would become more lucid. When Rick was coherent, his only wish was to go home.

"Where are you, Rick?" said the intern, testing Rick's mental status.

"I don't know," he answered politely, "but I want to go home."

Rick was confused and disoriented, but he was fully aware that he was confused and disoriented. I showed him pictures of my children I keep on my key chain; he shook my keys and gently put them back in my hand: "You better drive. I'm too f---ed up to drive."

My brother was a strong guy. He kept getting up out of bed. The hospital staff tied him down. He was furious, humiliated, embarrassed, enraged, confused and frightened.

A hospital is no place to die. It's noisy and busy and impersonal; there's no privacy anywhere for conversation or a last marital snuggle; there's no place for the family to wait and nap; only one or two people can be with the dying person. The rest of the family hovers unconnected in a waiting room, drinking bad coffee, making long phone calls on pay phones in lobbies. It was exhausting.

Please don't misunderstand me; I like hospitals. Hospitals are great places to live, to struggle for life, to undergo treatments, to have surgery, to have babies. But not to die. If it's at all possible, people should die in familiar surroundings in their own beds.

Rick begged to go home. The doctors could offer us nothing more. Hospice care wasn't available on such short notice. We all knew it would be an enormous responsibility to take him home.

But Rick's wife is the most determined person I know. He wanted to go home and she wanted to take him home. Rick's doctor was empathetic and efficient; in less than two hours after we came to this decision, we were on the road in an ambulance, heading to his house. Rick's last evening was wild, fun, tragic and exhilarating. Rick walked from room to room in his house, savoring a glass of red wine, eating a cookie, talking with his best friend, our mother and dad, our sisters and brothers. Neighbors stopped in with food and stayed for the conversation. Friends from the Quaker Meeting House stopped by. Cousins arrived.

It was like a Thanksgiving—good food, lots of conversation, but the guest of honor would be dead in a few days, or hours.

Although Rick was confused he wasn't frightened. Rick knew he was in his home, surrounded by friends and family. He was thrilled to be there. He ate. He cleaned. He was busy all evening, reminiscing, telling fragments of stories, neatening up, washing dishes, giving advice and eating well.

At the end of the evening he brushed his teeth, washed his face, lay down in his wife's arms in his own bed and kissed her goodnight. By morning he was in a deep coma.

All that long Saturday my family was together and we grieved. We watched over Rick. My father planted bulbs, daffodils and tulips, to make the spring beautiful for his grandson. My mother washed Rick's hair. My brothers and sisters and in-laws painted the porch banisters. Family, friends and neighbors came by to see him sleeping in his bed. Sometimes as many as 10 people were in his bedroom, talking, crying, laughing or telling stories about him, or just being with him—other times it was just his wife.

He took his last breath with his wife and his best friend beside him, his family singing old folk songs in the living room. He was peaceful, quiet, never frightened or restrained. Rick died far too young. But everyone should hope to die like this; not just with dignity, but with fun and love, with old friends and family.

Over the past week I have told friends about my brother's death. A few friends shared with me their regret about their parents dying prolonged and painful deaths alone in the hospital, sedated or agitated, not recognizing their children. Other people express fear of a dead body in the house—"Wasn't it ugly?" they ask. No, it looked like he was sleeping.

Rick's death was as gentle as a death can be. It worked because all parties—doctors, family, Rick and Rick's wife—were able to face facts and act on them. His doctors had the sense to recognize that no more could be done in the way of treatment and had the honesty to tell us. Rick's wife was determined to do right by him, whatever the burden of responsibility she was to bear. Our families were supportive of all her decisions and as loving and helpful as we could be.

Doctors must learn to let go—if there's nothing more to offer the patient then nothing more should be done—let patients go home. We all should plan for this among ourselves—preparing our next of kin. Families, husbands, wives need not be fearful. If a family member is dying in a hospital and wants to return home, try to find the means to do it.

And to all of the nurses, doctors and social workers in hospices: continue to do your good work. You have the right idea.

JOURNAL PROMPT:

How do you feel about dying at home rather than in a hospital? Did Sumers's article in any way alter your position on this issue?

COLLABORATIVE EXERCISE:

What clues do we have as to Sumers's family's economic and social background? Evaluate any clues you find about their professions, lifestyles, and belief systems. Does your understanding of their social position make the argument more or less valid?

ESSAY ASSIGNMENT:

1. Psychologists claim that all our fears stem from the one great fear: the fear of death. Explore how at least two other societies prepare for and deal with death.
2. How does the author explore "dying with dignity" in her essay? What does "to die with dignity" mean to you?

NORMAN COUSINS, after having been stricken with a life-threatening condition, has written extensively about health matters. His *Anatomy of an Illness* (1979) chronicles his journey of healing and recovery. In the late seventies, Cousins became affiliated with the UCLA School of Medicine while he explored the power of positive thinking (and laughter) as a means of combating illness. This essay, first published in the *Saturday Review* in 1975, is Cousins's argument for people's right to choose death with dignity.

NORMAN COUSINS

The Right to Die

The world of religion and philosophy was shocked recently when Henry P. Van Dusen and his wife ended their lives by their own hands. Dr. Van Dusen had been president of Union Theological Seminary; for more than a quarter-century he had been one of the luminous names in Protestant theology. He enjoyed world status as a spiritual leader. News of the self-inflicted death of the Van Dusens, therefore, was profoundly disturbing to all those who attach a moral stigma to suicide and regard it as a violation of God's laws.

Dr. Van Dusen had anticipated this reaction. He and his wife left behind a letter that may have historic significance. It was very brief, but the essential point it made is now being widely discussed by theologians and could represent the beginning of a reconsideration of traditional religious attitudes toward self-inflicted death. The letter raised a moral issue: does an individual have the obligation to go on living even when the beauty and meaning and power of life are gone?

Henry and Elizabeth Van Dusen had lived full lives. In recent years, they had become increasingly ill, requiring almost continual medical care. Their infirmities were worsening, and they realized they would soon become completely dependent for even the most elementary needs and functions. Under these circumstances, little dignity would have been left in life. They didn't like the idea of taking up space in a world with too many mouths and too little food. They believed it was a misuse of medical science to keep them technically alive.

They therefore believed they had the right to decide when to die. In making that decision, they weren't turning against life as the highest value; what they were turning against was the notion that there were no circumstances under which life should be discontinued.

An important aspect of human uniqueness is the power of free will. In his books and lectures, Dr. Van Dusen frequently spoke about the exercise of this uniqueness. The fact that he used his free will to prevent life from becoming a caricature of itself was completely in character. In their letter, the Van Dusens sought to convince family and friends that they were not acting solely out of despair or pain.

The use of free will to put an end to one's life finds no sanction in the theology to which Pitney Van Dusen was committed. Suicide symbolizes discontinuity; religion symbolizes continuity, represented as its quintessence by the concept of the immortal soul. Human logic finds it almost impossible to come to terms with the concept of nonexistence. In religion, the human mind finds a larger dimension and is relieved of the ordeal of a confrontation with nonexistence.

Even without respect to religion, the idea of suicide has been abhorrent throughout history. Some societies have imposed severe penalties on the families of suicides in the hope that the individual who sees no reason to continue his existence may be deterred by the stigma his self-destruction would inflict on loved ones. Other societies have enacted laws prohibiting suicide on the grounds that it is murder. The enforcement of such laws, of course, has been an exercise in futility.

Customs and attitudes, like individuals themselves, are largely shaped by the surrounding environment. In today's world, life can be prolonged by science far beyond meaning or sensibility. Under these circumstances, individuals who feel they have nothing more to give to life, or to receive from it, need not be applauded, but they can be spared our condemnation.

The general reaction to suicide is bound to change as people come to understand that it may be a denial, not an assertion, of moral or religious ethics to allow life to be extended without regard to decency or pride. What moral or religious purpose is celebrated by the annihilation of the human spirit in the triumphant act of keeping the body alive? Why are so many people more readily appalled by an unnatural form of dying than by an unnatural form of living?

"Nowadays," the Van Dusens wrote in their last letter, "it is difficult to die. We feel that this way we are taking will become more usual and acceptable as the years pass.

"Of course, the thought of our children and our grandchildren makes us sad, but we still feel that this is the best way and the right way to go. We are both increasingly weak and unwell and who would want to die in a nursing home?

"We are not afraid to die. . . ."

Pitney Van Dusen was admired and respected in life. He can be admired and respected in death. "Suicide," said Goethe, "is an incident in human life which, however much disputed and discussed, demands the sympathy of every man, and in every age must be dealt with anew."

Death is not the greatest loss in life. The greatest loss is what dies inside us while we live. The unbearable tragedy is to live without dignity or sensitivity.

JOURNAL PROMPT:

How does the author's particular choice of words contribute to his argument?

COLLABORATIVE EXERCISE:

Discuss with your classmates what the standard objections to suicide are. How does the author counter these objections? Poll your group. Do your personal attitudes about suicide change when you consider someone who is not aged, infirm, or terminally ill? (For your discussion, consider that the highest suicide rates in the United States belong to teenagers, the aged, and the sick.)

ESSAY ASSIGNMENT:

1. Explore what two different philosophers have to say about free will. Compare and contrast their views.
2. What is your reaction to this essay? Are your feelings about suicide influenced by deep moral and/or religious attitudes? Explore, if you can, how your attitude toward this subject developed. Has it changed over time or become more solidified?
3. What is the author's thesis? How does he use the behavior of the Van Dusen couple to argue his point of view?

MALCOLM COWLEY, a literary critic, spent his formative years in western Pennsylvania. In 1917, Cowley interrupted his studies at Harvard to volunteer to drive a truck in France during World War I. He is known for his "spectatorial attitude" and as a recorder of his generation's experiences.

MALCOLM COWLEY

THE VIEW FROM 80

Even before he or she is 80, the aging person may undergo another identity crisis like that of adolescence. Perhaps there had also been a middle-aged crisis, the male or the female menopause, but for the rest of adult life he had taken himself for granted, with his capabilities and failings. Now, when he looks in the mirror, he asks himself, "Is this really me?"—or he avoids the mirror out of distress at what it reveals, those bags and wrinkles. In his new makeup he is called upon to play a new role in a play that must be improvised. André Gide, that long-lived man of letters, wrote in his journal, "My heart has remained so young that I have the continual feeling of playing a part, the part of the 70-year-old that I certainly am; and the infirmities and weaknesses that remind me of my age act like a prompter, reminding me of my lines when I tend to stray. Then, like the good actor I want to be, I go back into my role, and I pride myself on playing it well."

In his new role the old person will find that he is tempted by new vices, that he receives new compensations (not so widely known), and that he may possibly achieve new virtues. Chief among these is the heroic or merely obstinate refusal to surrender in the face of time. One admires the ships that go down with all flags flying and the captain on the bridge.

Among the vices of age are avarice, untidiness, and vanity, which last takes the form of a craving to be loved or simply admired. Avarice is the worst of those three. Why do so many old persons, men and women alike, insist on hoarding money when they have no prospect of using it and even when they have no heirs? They eat the cheapest food, buy no clothes, and live in a single room when they could afford better lodging. It may be that they regard money as a form of power; there is a comfort in watching it accumulate while other powers are dwindling away. How often we read of an old person found dead in a hovel, on a mattress partly stuffed with bankbooks and stock certificates! The bankbook syndrome, we call it in our family, which has never succumbed.

Untidiness we call the Langley Collyer syndrome. To explain, Langley Collyer was a former concert pianist who lived alone with his 70-year-old brother in a brownstone house on upper Fifth Avenue. The once fashionable neighborhood had become part of Harlem. Homer, the brother, had been an admiralty lawyer, but was now blind and partly paralyzed; Langley played for him and fed him on buns and oranges, which he thought would restore Homer's sight. He never threw away a daily paper because Homer, he said, might want to read them all. He saved other things as well and the house became filled with rubbish from roof to basement. The halls were lined on both sides with bundled newspapers, leaving narrow passageways in which Langley had devised booby traps to catch intruders.

On March 21, 1947, some unnamed person telephoned the police to report that there was a dead body in the Collyer house. The police broke down the front door and found the hall impassable, then they hoisted a ladder to a second-story window. Behind it Homer was lying on the floor in a bathrobe; he had starved to death. Langley had disappeared. After some delay, the police broke into the basement, chopped a hole in the roof, and began throwing junk out of the house, top and bottom. It was 18 days before they found Langley's body, gnawed by rats. Caught in one of his own booby traps, he had died in a hallway just outside Homer's door. By that time the police had collected, and the Department of Sanitation had hauled away, 120 tons of rubbish, including besides the newspapers, 14 grand pianos and the parts of a dismantled Model T Ford.

Why do so many old people accumulate junk, not on the scale of Langley Collyer, but still in a dismaying fashion? Their tables are piled high with it, their bureau drawers are stuffed with it, their closet rods bend with the weight of clothes not worn for years. I suppose that the piling up is partly from lethargy and partly from the feeling that everything once useful, including their own bodies, should be preserved. Others, though not so many, have such a fear of becoming Langley Collyers that they strive to be painfully neat. Every tool they own is in its place, though it will never be used again; every scrap of paper is filed away in alphabetical order. At last their immoderate neatness becomes another vice of age, if a milder one.

The vanity of older people is an easier weakness to explain, and to condone. With less to look forward to, they yearn for recognition of what they have been: the reigning beauty, the athlete, the soldier, the scholar. It is the beauties who have the hardest time. A portrait of themselves at twenty hangs on the wall, and they try to resemble it by making an extravagant use of creams, powders, and dyes. Being young at heart, they think they are merely revealing their essential persons. The athletes find shelves for their silver trophies, which are polished once a year. Perhaps a letter sweater lies wrapped in a bureau drawer. I remember one evening when a no-longer athlete had guests for dinner and tried to find his sweater. "Oh, that old thing," his wife said. "The moths got into it and I threw it away." The athlete sulked and his guests went home early.

Often the yearning to be recognized appears in conversation as an innocent boast. Thus, a distinguished physician, retired at 94, remarks casually that a disease was named after him. A former judge bursts into chuckles as he repeats bright things that he said on the bench. Aging scholars complain in letters (or one of them does), "As I approach 70 I'm becoming avid of honors, and such things—medals, honorary degrees, etc.—are only passed around among academics on a *quid pro quo* basis (one hood capping another)." Or they say querulously, "Bill Underwood has ten honorary doctorates and I have only three. Why didn't they elect me to . . .?" and they mention the name of some learned society. That search for honors is a harmless passion, though it may lead to jealousies and deformations of character, as with Robert Frost in his later years. Still, honors cost little. Why shouldn't the very old have more than their share of them?

To be admired and praised, especially by the young, is an autumnal pleasure enjoyed by the lucky ones (who are not always the most deserving). "What is more charming," Cicero observes in his famous essay *De Senectute,*[1] "than an old age surrounded by the enthusiasm of youth! . . . Attentions which seem trivial and conventional are marks of honor—the morning call, being sought after, precedence, having people rise for you, being escorted to and from the forum. . . . What pleasures of the body can be compared to the prerogatives of influence?" But there are also pleasures of the body, or the mind, that are enjoyed by a greater number of older persons.

Those pleasures include some that younger people find hard to appreciate. One of them is simply sitting still, like a snake on a sun-warmed stone, with a delicious feeling of indolence that was seldom attained in earlier years. A leaf flutters down; a cloud moves by inches across the horizon. At such moments the older person, completely relaxed, has become a part of nature—and a living part, with blood coursing through his veins. The future does not exist for him. He thinks, if he thinks at all, that life for younger persons is still a battle royal of each against each, but that now he has nothing more to win or lose. He is not so much above as outside the battle, as if he had assumed the uniform of some small neutral country, perhaps Lichtenstein or Andorra. From a distance he notes that some of the combatants, men or women, are jostling ahead—but

---

[1] *On Old Age.*

why do they fight so hard when the most they can hope for is a longer obituary? He can watch the scrounging and gouging, he can hear the shouts of exultation, the moans of the gravely wounded, and meanwhile he feels secure; nobody will attack him from ambush.

Age has other physical compensations besides the nirvana of dozing in the sun. A few of the simplest needs become a pleasure to satisfy. When an old woman in a nursing home was asked what she really liked to do, she answered in one word: "Eat." She might have been speaking for many of her fellows. Meals in a nursing home, however badly cooked, serve as climactic moments of the day. The physical essence of the pensioners is being renewed at an appointed hour; now they can go back to meditating or to watching TV while looking forward to the next meal. They can also look forward to sleep, which has become a definite pleasure, not the mere interruption it once had been.

Here I am thinking of old persons under nursing care. Others ferociously guard their independence, and some of them suffer less than one might expect from being lonely and impoverished. They can be rejoiced by visits and meetings, but they also have company inside their heads. Some of them are busiest when their hands are still. What passes through the minds of many is a stream of persons, images, phrases, and familiar tunes. For some that stream has continued since childhood, but now it is deeper: it is their present and their past combined. At times they conduct silent dialogues with a vanished friend, and these are less tiring—often more rewarding—than spoken conversations. If inner resources are lacking, old persons living alone may seek comfort and a kind of companionship in the bottle. I should judge from the gossip of various neighborhoods that the outer suburbs from Boston to San Diego are full of secretly alcoholic widows. One of those widows, an old friend, was moved from her apartment into a retirement home. She left behind her a closet in which the floor was covered wall to wall with whiskey bottles. "Oh, those empty bottles!" she explained. "They were left by a former tenant."

Not whiskey or cooking sherry but simply giving up is the greatest temptation of age. It is something different from a stoical acceptance of infirmities, which is something to be admired. At 63, when he first recognized that his powers were failing, Emerson wrote one of his best poems, "Terminus":

It is time to be old,
To take in sail:—
The god of bounds,
Who sets to seas a shore,
Came to me in his fatal rounds,
And said: "No more!
No farther shoot
Thy broad ambitious branches, and thy root.
Fancy departs: no more invent;
Contract thy firmament
To compass of a tent."

Emerson lived in good health to the age of 79. Within his narrowed firmament, he continued working until his memory failed; then he consented to having younger editors and collaborators. The givers-up see no reason for working. Sometimes they lie in bed all day when moving about would still be possible, if difficult. I had a friend, a distinguished poet, who surrendered in that fashion. The doctors tried to stir him to action, but he refused to leave his room. Another friend, once a successful artist, stopped painting when his eyes began to fail. His doctor made the mistake of telling him that he suffered from a fatal disease. He then lost interest in everything except the splendid Rolls-Royce, acquired in his prosperous days, that stood in the garage. Daily he wiped the dust from its hood. He couldn't drive it on the road any longer, but he used to sit in the driver's seat, start the motor, then back the Rolls out of the garage and drive it in again, back twenty feet and forward twenty feet; that was his only distraction.

I haven't the right to blame those who surrender, not being able to put myself inside their minds or bodies. Often they must have compelling reasons, physical or moral. Not only do they suffer from a variety of ailments, but also they are made to feel that they no longer have a function in the community. Their families and neighbors don't ask them for advice, don't really listen when they speak, don't call on them for efforts. One notes that there are not a few recoveries from apparent senility when that situation changes. If it doesn't change, old persons may decide that efforts are useless. I sympathize with their problems, but the men and women I envy are those who accept old age as a series of challenges.

For such persons, every new infirmity is an enemy to be outwitted, an obstacle to be overcome by force of will. They enjoy each little victory over themselves, and sometimes they win a major success. Renoir was one of them. He continued painting, and magnificently, for years after he was crippled by arthritis; the brush had to be strapped to his arm. "You don't need your hand to paint," he said. Goya was another of the unvanquished. At 72 he retired as an official painter of the Spanish court and decided to work only for himself. His later years were those of the famous "black paintings" in which he let his imagination run (and also of the lithographs, then a new technique). At 78 he escaped a reign of terror in Spain by fleeing to Bordeaux. He was deaf and his eyes were failing; in order to work he had to wear several pairs of spectacles, one over another, and then use a magnifying glass; but he was producing splendid work in a totally new style. At 80 he drew an ancient man propped on two sticks, with a mass of white hair and beard hiding his face and with the inscription "I am still learning."

Giovanni Papini said when he was nearly blind, "I prefer martyrdom to imbecility." After writing sixty books, including his famous *Life of Christ,* he was at work on two huge projects when he was stricken with a form of muscular atrophy. He lost the use of his left leg, then of his fingers, so that he couldn't hold a pen. The two big books, though never to be finished, moved forward slowly by dictation; that in itself was a triumph. Toward the end, when his voice had become incomprehensible, he spelled out a word, tapping on the table to indicate letters of the alphabet. One hopes never to be faced with the need for such heroic measures.

"Eighty years old!" the great Catholic poet Paul Claudel wrote in his journal. "No eyes left, no ears, no teeth, no legs, no wind! And when all is said and done, how astonishingly well one does without them!"

JOURNAL PROMPT:

Write about someone you know who is at least seventy years old. How is this person facing the challenges of aging? Is this person an inspiration to you? Why or why not? Explain.

COLLABORATIVE EXERCISE:

Working in small groups, compile a list of at least ten issues that men and women encounter as they become senior citizens.

ESSAY ASSIGNMENT:

1. This is an opportunity to write a narrative in which you take on the persona of Malcolm Cowley, the author of "The View from 80." Write a letter to Karla Cole, the author of "We Don't Want to Grow Old." What advice might you offer Cole? In Cowley's voice, offer some insights on the aging process that might help her understand what it means to grow old.
2. How does the U.S. government help or hinder an elderly person's efforts to remain independent? Include in your discussion some suggestions on how the government might contribute to the dignity of growing older.
3. Interview a person in his or her eighties. Discuss some of the issues Cowley takes up in his essay. Ask the person to comment on these matters, and then record his or her response.

KARLA COLE, as an education major at the University of Southern Mississippi, wrote the following piece for a freshman English assignment. She presents a very intriguing observation of her peers at high school reunions.

KARLA COLE

WE DON'T WANT TO GROW OLD

Something has happened in my own generation that hasn't happened in my parents', or in any generation that I know of before that. It appears we forgot to grow up. Baby-boomers are the ones I'm referring to, a group that I identify strongly with, because I am one.

For those of you too young to understand, baby-boomers are those people born between 1946 and 1964, during the population explosion after World War II. This growth had far-reaching effects upon education, politics, culture, and economics. Nothing was left unchallenged or unchanged. There was one change to be avoided at all costs though: aging. And no amount of time, money, or effort was too great a sacrifice to delay the appearance of getting older.

Have you ever looked at pictures of your grandparents when they were in their thirties? Didn't they look middle aged? It seems they didn't even try to look otherwise, as if they aspired to old age. Now look at today's thirty-somethings. The difference is alarming.

Older generations lived through some very difficult times: world wars, economic depression, lack of luxury items that we call necessities, such as televisions and VCRs. Life was hard, and people earned their maturity at a young age. My grandmother, who was born at the turn of the century, says people identified with their elders. "We knew we were getting older, and it never occurred to us to try to hide it."

But trying to hide it is what baby-boomers excel at. As a group we are now at least thirty years old with the oldest being dangerously close to fifty. With the ever increasing life expectancy, thanks to the miracles of modern medicine, we are still quite young. And don't we look it? Compare us to the way we looked ten or fifteen years ago, and don't be surprised if we look younger now. A look at our past contains some clues as to why the sudden shift in attitudes toward aging.

Ours was a generation set apart from the rest of society—from nursery school all the way through college. Prior to the fifties, families had the most influence in shaping the values and behavior of children. There seemed to be nothing wrong with that until the experts, like Dr. Benjamin Spock, taught parents to relax and replace firmness and discipline with freedom. And so we were emancipated to associate mainly with each other.

But the biggest influence on our generation was the media, namely television. Baby-boomers were the first to grow up with it. Our values were largely determined by advertisers who told us what we wanted and our parents gladly supplied as much as they could. It was a prosperous time compared to our parents' childhood, and they made sure we would not suffer the hardships they had endured. So it was our collective buying power that made fads overnight, and entire industries were built to meet our wants and needs. Parents and society focused on us and we focused on ourselves. Life was easy.

For that reason, no one was prepared for what happened in the sixties and seventies. A counterculture emerged, and it seems we rebelled against everything. We were held together by a "don't trust anyone over thirty" mentality. Our government lied to us, materialism proved shallow and unfulfilling, and our televisions brought to us all the world's problems and none of the solutions. It's no wonder we "tuned in, turned on, and dropped out." Our innocence had been taken from us, and our parents were often more naive about the world we lived in than we were. So maybe we started growing up too fast and missed something important in our growing up years that we continually try to recapture. If we're still growing up, how could we possibly be growing old?

Whatever the reasons, we think younger, we act younger, and many of us look younger. And with a little help from our friends in the fitness, cosmetics, and plastic surgery industries, maybe we can postpone the aging process indefinitely. Maybe we don't have to grow old.

JOURNAL PROMPT:

What are your thoughts and feelings about growing older? Include a discussion about anyone who may have influenced or inspired your attitude about the aging process.

COLLABORATIVE EXERCISE:

In her article, Cole includes a discussion of the media and its influence on our attitudes toward aging. Examine the following forms of media and their techniques of promoting a "postponement" of the aging process:

1. television programs
2. television commercials
3. magazine articles/covers
4. billboards

ESSAY ASSIGNMENT:

1. Write an essay in which you convince the reader of one of the following statements:
   A. It is perfectly normal and acceptable to postpone the aging process as much as possible in any way possible.
   B. It is unwise and unacceptable to postpone the inevitable process of aging.
2. Do you think the author's attitude toward aging is shared by the young adults you know?
3. In general, how are elderly people depicted by advertisers? Give examples.

Poet and novelist **May Eleanor Sarton** was born in Belgium on May 3, 1912, and immigrated to the United States at age four. Sarton taught and lectured on poetry at several universities, including Bryn Mawr, Wellesley College, and Harvard. Her numerous publications include such personal works as *Journal of a Solitude, The House by the Sea,* and *After the Stroke: A Journal* (1988).

MAY SARTON

MONDAY, MAY 3RD, 1982

Such a peaceful, windless morning here for my seventieth birthday—the sea is pale blue, and although the field is still brown, it is dotted with daffodils at last. It has seemed an endless winter. But now at night the peepers are in full fettle, peeping away. And I was awakened by the cardinal, who is back again with his two wives, and the raucous cries of the male pheasant. I lay there, breathing in spring, listening to the faint susurration of the waves and awfully glad to be alive.

The table is set downstairs, all blue and white, with a tiny bunch of miniature daffodils, blue starflowers, and, glory be, two fritillaries. They always seem unreal with their purple-and-white-checkered bells, and I have never succeeded with a real show of them.

Then at each corner of the square table I have put a miniature rose, two white and two pale yellow, part of a bounty of miniature roses that have come for my birthday and will go along the terrace wall when the nights are not quite so cold. They are from Edythe Haddaway, one of the blessings of the last five years, for she comes when I am away to take care of Tamas and Bramble, feels at peace in this house, she tells me, and makes it peaceful for me to know that she is in residence and all is well at home when I am off on poetry-reading trips.

What is it like to be seventy? If someone else had lived so long and could remember things sixty years ago with great clarity, she would seem very old to me. But I do not feel old at all, not as much a survivor as a person still on her way. I suppose real old age begins when one looks backward rather than forward, but I look forward with joy to the years ahead and especially to the surprises that any day may bring.

In the middle of the night things well up from the past that are not always cause for rejoicing—the unsolved, the painful encounters, the mistakes, the reasons for shame or woe. But all, good or bad, painful or delightful, weave themselves into a rich tapestry, and all give me food for thought, food to grow on.

I am just back from a month of poetry readings, in and out through all of April. At Hartford College in Connecticut I had been asked to talk about old age—"The View From Here," I called the reading—in a series on "The Seasons of Womanhood." In the course of it I said, "This is the best time of my life. I love being old." At that point a voice from the audience asked loudly, "Why is it good to be old?" I answered spontaneously and a little on the defensive, for I sensed incredulity in the questioner, "Because I am more myself than I have ever been. There is less conflict. I am happier, more balanced, and" (I heard myself say rather aggressively) "more powerful." I felt it was rather an odd word, "powerful," but I think it is true. It might have been more accurate to say "I am better able to use my powers." I am surer of what my life is all about, have less self-doubt to conquer, although it has to be admitted that I wrote my new novel *Anger* in an agony of self-doubt most of the year, the hardest subject I have attempted to deal with in a novel since *Mrs. Stevens Hears the Mermaids Singing.* There I was breaking new ground, giving myself away. I was fifty-three and I deliberately made Mrs. Stevens seventy, and now here I am at what then seemed eons away, safely "old."

I have always longed to be old, and that is because all my life I have had such great exemplars of old age, such marvelous models to contemplate. First of all, of course, was Marie Closset (her pen name, Jean Dominique), whom I celebrated in my first novel and with whom I exchanged lives through letters and meetings from my twenty-fifth year until her death. I turn to her bound volumes of poetry this minute and open to the line "Au silence léger des nuits près de la mer," but I am bound to look for and find the long lyric addressed to Poetry, and as I write it here, I hear very clearly her light, grave voice, and we are sitting in her study, side by side:

Poésie! Je t'ai portée a mes lèvres
Comme un caillou frais pour ma soif,
Je t'ai gardée dans ma bouche obscure et sèche
Comme une petite pierre qu'on remasse
Et que l'on mâche avec du sang sur les lèvres!

Poésie, ah! je t'ai donné l'Amour,
L'Amour avec sa face comme une aube d'argent
Sur la mer,—et mon âme, avec la mer dedans,
Et la tempête avec le ciel du petit jour
Livide et frais comme un coquillage luisant.

How happy Jean-Do would be to know that at seventy I live by the sea, and all those images are newly minted for me today "like a cool pebble for my thirst," "and my soul with the sea in it, and the tempest at dawn, pale and fresh as a shining shell." (But where is the music in English?)

Then Lugné-Poë, my father in the theater, was a constant challenger and giver of courage during the theater years. I see his immense devouring smile and remember my pet name for him, "mon éléphant." So he always signed his letters with an elephant head and a long trunk waving triumphantly at the end of a page.

Basil de Selincourt, my father in poetry, fierce as a hawk (and he looked rather like a hawk), wrote the first really good review I ever had (in the London *Observer* on *Encounter in April,* my first book of poems) and that was before we became friends. He taught me many things, not least how to garden into very old age by working at an extremely slow tempo—but I never did really learn it. That is still to come when, like Basil, I hope to put in a vegetable garden in my late eighties.

Then there is Eva Le Gallienne, who was only thirty when I first knew her as the star and creator of the Civic Repertory Theatre, and who has again triumphed in her eighties and shown a whole new generation what great acting is. She is proof that one can be eighty-three and still young. She too is a great gardener, so perhaps a good old age has to do with being still a friend of the earth.

I think also of Camille Mayran, who has written a magnificent book in her nineties, *Portrait de Ma Mère en Son Grand Âge.* She tells me that now, well over ninety, she sees no change in herself except for a "slight slowing down." She is all soul and mind, not a gardener at all! So one cannot generalize. But Eleanor Blair has just telephoned to wish me a happy birthday, as I write, and she says her garden is flourishing. Her voice sounded so young on the phone!

Perhaps the answer is not detachment as I used to believe but rather to be deeply involved in something, is to be attached. I am attached in a thousand ways—and one of them compels me now to leave this airy room high up in the house to go down and get ready for my guests.

JOURNAL PROMPT:

Can you imagine yourself "old"? How do you anticipate you'll react to physical changes?

COLLABORATIVE EXERCISE:

The author states that at seventy, she is . . . "happier, more balanced, and . . . more powerful." What do you suppose she means by "more powerful"?

ESSAY ASSIGNMENT:

1. How has our longevity changed since the 1900's? To what do we attribute these changes? What impact does increased longevity have on society? (Be sure to explore the realms of work, leisure, and health.)
2. Sarton suggests that for her, age has brought newfound awareness. From your observations, do you agree that age brings wisdom?
3. Sarton suggests that old age begins when one looks backward rather than forward. Discuss when you consider that old age begins. What makes one person old at sixty and another still young at eighty?

As the fifth daughter of the second Baron Redesdale, **JESSICA MITFORD** grew up in England with her brother and five sisters, one of whom was the novelist Nancy Mitford. She moved to the United States in 1939 and began to write in the late 1950's. Mitford is known worldwide for her witty and irreverent investigations of various aspects of American society. Her book *The American Way of Death* (1963), a caustic examination of unscrupulous practices in the

American funeral industry, became a best-seller. Other publications include examinations of the civil rights movement, prisons, and American birth practices.

JESSICA MITFORD

BEHIND THE FORMALDEHYDE CURTAIN

The drama begins to unfold with the arrival of the corpse at the mortuary.

Alas, poor Yorick! How surprised he would be to see how his counterpart of today is whisked off to a funeral parlor and is in short order sprayed, sliced, pierced, pickled, trussed, trimmed, creamed, waxed, painted, rouged, and neatly dressed—transformed from a common corpse into a Beautiful Memory Picture. This process is known in the trade as embalming and restorative art, and is so universally employed in the United States and Canada that the funeral director does it routinely, without consulting corpse or kin. He regards as eccentric those few who are hardy enough to suggest that it might be dispensed with. Yet no law requires embalming, no religious doctrine commends it, nor is it dictated by considerations of health, sanitation, or even of personal daintiness. In no part of the world but in Northern America is it widely used. The purpose of embalming is to make the corpse presentable for viewing in a suitably costly container; and here too the funeral director routinely, without first consulting the family, prepares the body for public display.

Is all this legal? The processes to which a dead body may be subjected are after all to some extent circumscribed by law. In most states, for instance, the signature of next of kin must be obtained before an autopsy may be performed, before the deceased may be cremated, before the body may be turned over to a medical school for research purposes; or such provision must be made in the decedent's will. In the case of embalming, no such permission is required nor is it ever sought.[1] A textbook, *The Principles and Practices of Embalming,* comments on this: "There is some question regarding the legality of much that is done within the preparation room." The author points out that it would be most unusual for a responsible member of a bereaved family to instruct the mortician, in so many words, to "embalm" the body of a deceased relative. The very term

[1] Partly because of Mitford's attack, the Federal Trade Commission now requires the funeral industry to provide families with itemized price lists, including the price of embalming, to state that embalming is not required, and to obtain the family's consent to embalming before charging for it.—Eds.

embalming is so seldom used that the mortician must rely upon custom in the matter. The author concludes that unless the family specifies otherwise, the act of entrusting the body to the care of a funeral establishment carries with it an implied permission to go ahead and embalm.

Embalming is indeed a most extraordinary procedure, and one must wonder at the docility of Americans who each year pay hundreds of millions of dollars for its perpetuation, blissfully ignorant of what it is all about, what is done, how it is done. Not one in ten thousand has any idea of what actually takes place. Books on the subject are extremely hard to come by. They are not to be found in most libraries or bookshops.

In an era when huge television audiences watch surgical operations in the comfort of their living rooms, when, thanks to the animated cartoon, the geography of the digestive system has become familiar territory even to the nursery school set, in a land where the satisfaction of curiosity about almost all matters is a national pastime, the secrecy surrounding embalming can, surely, hardly be attributed to the inherent gruesomeness of the subject. Custom in this regard has within this century suffered a complete reversal. In the early days of American embalming, when it was performed in the home of the deceased, it was almost mandatory for some relative to stay by the embalmer's side and witness the procedure. Today, family members who might wish to be in attendance would certainly be dissuaded by the funeral director. All others, except apprentices, are excluded by law from the preparation room.

A close look at what does actually take place may explain in large measure the undertaker's intractable reticence concerning a procedure that has become his major *raison d'être*. Is it possible he fears that public information about embalming might lead patrons to wonder if they really want this service? If the funeral men are loath to discuss the subject outside the trade, the reader may, understandably, be equally loath to go on reading at this point. For those who have the stomach for it, let us part the formaldehyde curtain. . . .

The body is first laid out in the undertaker's morgue—or rather, Mr. Jones is reposing in the preparation room—to be readied to bid the world farewell.

The preparation room in any of the better funeral establishments has the tiled and sterile look of a surgery, and indeed the embalmer-restorative artist who does his chores there is beginning to adopt the term *dermasurgeon* (appropriately corrupted by some mortician-writers as "demi-surgeon") to describe his calling. His equipment, consisting of scalpels, scissors, augers, forceps, clamps, needles, pumps, tubes, bowls, and basins, is crudely imitative of the surgeon's, as is his technique, acquired in a nine- or twelve-month post-high-school course in an embalming school. He is supplied by an advanced chemical industry with a bewildering array of fluids, sprays, pastes, oils, powders, creams, to fix or soften tissue, shrink or distend it as needed, dry it here, restore the moisture there. There are cosmetics, waxes, and paints to fill and cover features, even plaster of Paris to replace entire limbs. There are ingenious aids to prop and stabilize the cadaver: a Vari-Pose Head Rest, the Edwards Arm and Hand Positioner, the Repose Block (to support the shoulders during the embalming), and the Throop Foot Positioner, which resembles an old-fashioned stocks.

Mr. John H. Eckels, president of the Eckels College of Mortuary Science, thus describes the first part of the embalming procedure: "In the hands of a skilled practitioner, this work may be done in a comparatively short time and without mutilating the body other than by slight incision—so slight that it scarcely would cause serious inconvenience if made upon a living person. It is necessary to remove the blood, and doing this not only helps in the disinfecting, but removes the principal cause of disfigurements due to discoloration."

Another textbook discusses the all-important time element: "The earlier this is done, the better, for every hour that elapses between death and embalming will add to the problems and complications encountered. . . ." Just how soon should one get going on the embalming? The author tells us, "On the basis of such scanty information made available to this profession through its rudimentary and haphazard system of technical research, we must conclude that the best results are to be obtained if the subject is embalmed before life is completely extinct—that is, before cellular death has occurred. In the average case, this would mean within an hour after somatic death." For those who feel that there is something a little rudimentary, not to say haphazard, about this advice, a comforting thought is offered by another writer. Speaking of fears entertained in early days of premature burial, he points out, "One of the effects of embalming by chemical injection, however, has been to dispel fears of live burial." How true; once the blood is removed, chances of live burial are indeed remote.

To return to Mr. Jones, the blood is drained out through the veins and replaced by embalming fluid pumped in through the arteries. As noted in *The Principles and Practices of Embalming,* "every operator has a favorite injection and drainage point—a fact which becomes a handicap only if he fails or refuses to forsake his favorites when conditions demand it." Typical favorites are the carotid artery, femoral artery, jugular vein, subclavian vein. There are various choices of embalming fluid. If Flextone is used, it will produce a "mild, flexible rigidity. The skin retains a velvety softness, the tissues are rubbery and pliable. Ideal for women and children." It may be blended with B. and G. Products Company's Lyf-Lyk tint, which is guaranteed to reproduce "nature's own skin texture . . . the velvety appearance of living tissue." Suntone comes in three separate tints: Suntan; Special Cosmetic Tint, a pink shade "especially indicated for female subjects"; and Regular Cosmetic Tint, moderately pink.

About three to six gallons of a dyed and perfumed solution of formaldehyde, glycerin, borax, phenol, alcohol, and water is soon circulating through Mr. Jones, whose mouth has been sewn together with a "needle directed upward between the upper lip and gum and brought out through the left nostril," with the corners raised slightly "for a more pleasant expression." If he should be bucktoothed, his teeth are cleaned with Bon Ami and coated with colorless nail polish. His eyes, meanwhile, are closed with flesh-tinted eye caps and eye cement.

The next step is to have at Mr. Jones with a thing called a trocar. This is a long, hollow needle attached to a tube. It is jabbed into the abdomen, poked around the entrails and chest cavity, the contents of which are pumped out and replaced with "cavity fluid." This done, and the hole in the abdomen sewn up, Mr. Jones's face is heavily creamed (to protect the skin from burns which may be caused by leakage of the chemicals), and he is covered with a sheet and left unmolested for a while. But not for long—there is more, much more, in store for him. He has been embalmed, but not yet restored, and the best time to start the restorative work is eight to ten hours after embalming, when the tissues have become firm and dry.

The object of all this attention to the corpse, it must be remembered, is to make it presentable for viewing in an attitude of healthy repose. "Our customs require the presentation of our dead in the semblance of normality . . . unmarred by the ravages of illness, disease, or mutilation," says Mr. J. Sheridan Mayer in his *Restorative Art.* This is rather a large order since few people die in the full bloom of health, unravaged by illness and unmarked by some disfigurement. The funeral industry is equal to the challenge: "In some cases the gruesome appearance of a mutilated or disease-ridden subject may be quite discouraging. The task of restoration may seem impossible and shake the confidence of the embalmer. This is the time for intestinal fortitude and determination. Once the formative work is begun and affected tissues are cleaned or removed, all doubts of success vanish. It is surprising and gratifying to discover the results which may be obtained."

The embalmer, having allowed an appropriate interval to elapse, returns to the attack, but now he brings into play the skill and equipment of sculptor and cosmetician. Is a hand missing? Casting one in plaster of Paris is a simple matter. "For replacement purposes, only a cast of the back of the hand is necessary; this is within the ability of the average operator and is quite adequate." If a lip or two, a nose, or an ear should be missing, the embalmer has at hand a variety of restorative waxes with which to model replacements. Pores and skin texture are simulated by stippling with a little brush, and over this cosmetics are laid on. Head off? Decapitation cases are rather routinely handled. Ragged edges are trimmed, and head joined to torso with a series of splints, wires, and sutures. It is a good idea to have a little something at the neck—a scarf or a high collar—when time for viewing comes. Swollen mouth? Cut out tissue as needed from inside the lips. If too much is removed, the surface contour can easily be restored by padding with cotton. Swollen necks and cheeks are reduced by removing tissue through vertical incisions made down each side of the neck. "When the deceased is casketed, the pillow will hide the suture incisions . . . as an extra precaution against leakage, the suture may be painted with liquid sealer."

The opposite condition is more likely to present itself—that of emaciation. His hypodermic syringe now loaded with massage cream, the embalmer seeks out and fills the hollowed and sunken areas by injection. In this procedure the backs of the hands and fingers and the under-chin area should not be neglected.

Positioning the lips is a problem that recurrently challenges the ingenuity of the embalmer. Closed too tightly, they tend to give a stern, even disapproving expression. Ideally, embalmers feel, the lips should give the impression of being ever so slightly parted, the upper lip protruding slightly for a more youthful appearance. This takes some engineering, however, as the lips tend to drift apart. Lip drift can sometimes be remedied by pushing one or two straight pins through the inner margin of the lower lip and then inserting them between the two front upper teeth. If Mr. Jones happens to have no teeth, the pins can just as easily be anchored in his Armstrong Face Former and Denture Replacer. Another method to maintain lip closure is to dislocate the lower jaw, which is then held in its new position by a wire run through holes which have been drilled through the upper and lower jaws at the midline. As the French are fond of saying, *il faut souffrir pour être belle.*[2]

If Mr. Jones has died of jaundice, the embalming fluid will very likely turn him green. Does this deter the embalmer? Not if he has intestinal fortitude. Masking pastes and cosmetics are heavily laid on, burial garments and casket interiors are color-correlated with particular care, and Jones is displayed beneath rose-colored lights. Friends will say "How *well* he looks." Death by carbon monoxide, on the other hand, can be rather a good thing from the embalmer's viewpoint: "One advantage is the fact that this type of discoloration is an exaggerated form of a natural pink coloration." This is nice because the healthy glow is already present and needs but little attention.

The patching and filling completed, Mr. Jones is now shaved, washed, and dressed. Cream-based cosmetic, available in pink, flesh, suntan, brunette, and blond, is applied to his hands and face, his hair is shampooed and combed (and, in the case of Mrs. Jones, set), his hands manicured. For the horny-handed son of toil special care must be taken; cream should be applied to remove ingrained grime, and the nails cleaned. "If he were not in the habit of having them manicured in life, trimming and shaping is advised for better appearance—never questioned by kin."

Jones is now ready for casketing (this is the present participle of the verb "to casket"). In this operation his right shoulder should be depressed slightly "to turn the body a bit to the right and soften the appearance of lying flat on the back." Positioning the hands is a matter of importance, and special rubber positioning blocks may be used. The hands should be cupped slightly for a more lifelike, relaxed appearance. Proper placement of the body requires a delicate sense of balance. It should lie as high as possible in the casket, yet not so high that the lid, when lowered, will hit the nose. On the other hand, we are cautioned, placing the body too low "creates the impression that the body is in a box."

Jones is next wheeled into the appointed slumber room where a few last touches may be added—his favorite pipe placed in his hand or, if he was a great

---

[2] You have to suffer to be beautiful.—Eds.

reader, a book propped into position. (In the case of little Master Jones a Teddy bear may be clutched.) Here he will hold open house for a few days, visiting hours 10 A.M. to 9 P.M.

All now being in readiness, the funeral director calls a staff conference to make sure that each assistant knows his precise duties. Mr. Wilber Kriege writes: "This makes your staff feel that they are a part of the team, with a definite assignment that must be properly carried out if the whole plan is to succeed. You never heard of a football coach who failed to talk to his entire team before they go on the field. They have drilled on the plays they are to execute for hours and days, and yet the successful coach knows the importance of making even the bench-warming third-string substitute feel that he is important if the game is to be won." The winning of *this* game is predicated upon glass-smooth handling of the logistics. The funeral director has notified the pallbearers whose names were furnished by the family, has arranged for the presence of clergyman, organist, and soloist, has provided transportation for everybody, has organized and listed the flowers sent by friends. In *Psychology of Funeral Service* Mr. Edward A. Martin points out, "He may not always do as much as the family thinks he is doing, but it is his helpful guidance that they appreciate in knowing they are proceeding as they should. . . . The important thing is how well his services can be used to make the family believe they are giving unlimited expression to their own sentiment."

The religious service may be held in a church or in the chapel of the funeral home; the funeral director vastly prefers the latter arrangement, for not only is it more convenient for him but it affords him the opportunity to show off his beautiful facilities to the gathered mourners. After the clergyman has had his say, the mourners queue up to file past the casket for a last look at the deceased. The family is *never* asked whether they want an open-casket ceremony; in the absence of their instruction to the contrary, this is taken for granted. Consequently well over 90 per cent of all American funerals feature the open casket—a custom unknown in other parts of the world. Foreigners are astonished by it. An English woman living in San Francisco described her reaction in a letter to the writer:

> I myself have attended only one funeral here—that of an elderly fellow worker of mine. After the service I could not understand why everyone was walking towards the coffin (sorry, I mean casket), but thought I had better follow the crowd. It shook me rigid to get there and find the casket open and poor old Oscar lying there in his brown tweed suit, wearing a suntan makeup and just the wrong shade of lipstick. If I had not been extremely fond of the old boy, I have a horrible feeling that I might have giggled. Then and there I decided that I could never face another American funeral—even dead.

The casket (which has been resting throughout the service on a hydraulically operated device called Porto-Lift to a balloon-tired, Glide Easy casket carriage which will wheel it to yet another conveyance, the Cadillac Funeral Coach. This may be lavender, cream, light green—anything but black. Interiors, of course, are color-correlated, "for the man who cannot stop short of perfection."

At graveside, the casket is lowered into the earth. This office, once the prerogative of friends of the deceased, is now performed by a patented mechanical lowering device. A "Lifetime Green" artificial grass mat is at the ready to conceal the sere earth, and overhead, to conceal the sky, is a portable Steril Chapel Tent ("resists the intense heat and humidity of summer and the terrific storms of winter . . . available in Silver Gray, Rose, or Evergreen"). Now is the time for the ritual scattering of earth over the coffin, as the solemn words "earth to earth, ashes to ashes, dust to dust" are pronounced by the officiating cleric. This can today be accomplished "with a mere flick of the wrist with the Gordon Leak-Proof Earth Dispenser. No grasping of a handful of dirt, no soiled fingers. Simple, dignified, beautiful, reverent! The modern way!" The Gordon Earth Dispenser (at $5) is of nickel-plated brass construction. It is not only "attractive to the eye and long wearing"; it is also "one of the 'tools' for building better public relations" if presented as "an appropriate non-commercial gift" to the clergyman. It is shaped something like a saltshaker.

Untouched by human hand, the coffin and the earth are now united.

It is in the function of directing the participants through this maze of gadgetry that the funeral director has assigned to himself his relatively new role of "grief therapist." He has relieved the family of every detail, he has revamped the corpse to look like a living doll, he has arranged for it to nap for a few days in a slumber room, he has put on a well-oiled performance in which the concept of *death* has played no part whatsoever—unless it was inconsiderately mentioned by the clergyman who conducted the religious service. He has done everything in his power to make the funeral a real pleasure for everybody concerned. He and his team have given their all to score an upset victory over death.

JOURNAL PROMPT:

Have you contemplated your own demise? Has reading this essay changed your view of the funeral industry?

COLLABORATIVE EXERCISE:

For some students the subject matter of this essay is simply too gruesome to contemplate. With your peers, discuss some of the factors that influence our modern Western attitudes about death.

ESSAY ASSIGNMENT:

1. Jessica Mitford was an investigative reporter who imbued her work with humor and irony. Investigate some of the other subjects she explored: the prison system, birth in America, creation of celebrities.

Choose one of these subjects, and find passages in which her sense of the ironic shines through.

2. Analyze how Mitford develops her portrayals of particular industries in this country.
3. In what ways does investigative writing have the power to create change? Compare Mitford's essay, which relies on facts, with one of the other selections in this chapter that creates an argument using emotion to persuade. For you, which is stronger?

This essay, an argument against euthanasia, was taken from a speech that MATTHEW CONOLLY delivered to the Hemlock Society, a group that favors a person's right to choose his or her own moment of death.

MATTHEW E. CONOLLY

EUTHANASIA IS NOT THE ANSWER

From the moment of our conception, each of us is engaged in a personal battle that we must fight alone, a battle whose final outcome is never in any doubt, for, naked, and all too often alone, sooner or later we *all* must die.

We do not all make life's pilgrimage on equal terms. For some the path is strewn with roses, and after a long and healthy life, death comes swiftly and easily, for others it is not so. The bed of roses is supplanted by a bed of nails, with poverty, rejection, deformity, and humiliation the only lasting companions they ever know.

I know that many people here today carry this problem of pain in a personal way, or else it has been the lot of someone close to you. Otherwise you would not be here. So let me say right at the outset, that those of us who have not had to carry such a burden dare not criticize those who have, if they should plead with us for an early end to their dismal sojourn in this world.

Hard Cases Make Bad Laws

Society in general, and the medical profession in particular, cannot just turn away. We must do *something;* the question is—what?

The "what" we are being asked to consider today, of course, is voluntary euthanasia. So that there be no confusion, let me make it quite clear that to be opposed to the active taking of life, one does not have to be determined to keep the heart beating at all costs.

I believe I speak for all responsible physicians when I say that there clearly comes a time when death can no longer be held at bay, and when we must sue for peace on the enemy's terms. At such a time, attending to the patient's comfort in body, mind, and soul becomes paramount. There is no obligation, indeed no justification, for pressing on at such a time with so-called life-sustaining measures, be they respirators, intravenous fluids, CPR, or whatever. I believe that there is no obligation to continue a treatment once it has been started, if it becomes apparent that it is doing no good. Also, withholding useless treatment and letting nature take its course is *not* equivalent to active euthanasia. Some people have attempted to blur this distinction by creating the term "passive euthanasia." The least unkind thing that can be said about this term is that it is very confusing.

Today's discussion really boils down to the question—do hard and tragic cases warrant legalization of euthanasia? There can be no doubt that hard and tragic cases do occur. However, the very natural tendency to want to alleviate human tragedy by legislative change is fraught with hazard, and I firmly believe that every would-be lawmaker should have tattooed on his or her face, where it can be seen in the mirror each morning, the adage that HARD CASES MAKE BAD LAWS.

If we take the superficially humane step of tailoring the law to the supposed wishes of an Elizabeth Bouvia (who, incidentally, later changed her mind), we will not only bring a hornet's nest of woes about our own ears, but, at a stroke, we will deny many relatives much good that we could have salvaged from a sad situation, while at the same time giving many *more* grief and guilt to contend with. Even worse, we will have denied our patients the best that could have been offered. Worst of all, that soaring of the human spirit to heights of inspiration and courage which only adversity makes possible will be denied, and we will all, from that, grow weaker, and less able to deal with the crisis of tomorrow.

Unleashing Euthanasia

Let's look at these problems one by one. The first problem is that once we unleash euthanasia, once we take to ourselves the right actively to terminate a human life, we will have no means of controlling it. Adolf Hitler showed with startling clarity that once the dam is breached, the principle somewhere compromised, death in the end comes to be administered equally to all—to the unwanted fetus, to the deformed, the mentally defective, the old and the unproductive, and thence to the politically inconvenient, and finally to the ethnically unacceptable. There is no logical place to stop.

The founders of Hemlock no doubt mean euthanasia only for those who feel they can take no more, but if it is available for one it must be available for all. Then what about those precious people who even to the end put others before themselves? They will now have laid upon them the new and horrible thought that perhaps they ought to do away with themselves to spare their relatives more trouble or expense. What will they feel as they see their 210 days of Medicare hospice payments run out, and still they are alive. Not long ago, Governor Lamm of Colorado suggested that the old and incurable have a *duty* to get out of the way of the next generation. And can you not see where these pressures will be the greatest? It will be amongst the poor and dispossessed. Watts will have sunk in a sea of euthanasia long before the first ripple laps the shore of Brentwood. Is that what we mean to happen? Is that what we want? Is there nobility of purpose there?

It matters to me that my patients trust me. If they do so, it is because they believe that I will always act in their best interests. How could such trust survive if they could never be sure each time I approached the bed that I had not come to administer some coup de grace when they were not in a state to define their own wishes?

Those whose relatives have committed more conventional forms of suicide are often afterwards assailed by feelings of guilt and remorse. It would be unwise to think that euthanasia would bring any less in its wake.

A Better Way

Speaking as a physician, I assert that unrelieved suffering need never occur, and I want to turn to this important area. Proponents of euthanasia make much of the pain and anguish so often linked in people's minds with cancer. I would not dare to pretend that the care we offer is not sometimes abysmal, whether because of the inappropriate use of aggressive technological medicine, the niggardly use of analgesics, some irrational fear of addiction in a dying patient, or a lack of compassion.

However, for many, the process of dying is more a case of gradually loosing life's moorings and slipping away. Oftentimes the anguish of dying is felt not by the patient but by the relatives: just as real, just as much in need of compassionate support, but hardly a reason for killing the patient!

But let us consider the patients who do have severe pain, turmoil, and distress, who find their helplessness or incontinence humiliating, for it is these who most engage our sympathies. It is wrong to assert that they must make a stark choice between suicide or suffering.

There is another way.

Experience with hospice care in England and the United States has shown repeatedly that in *every* case, pain and suffering can be overwhelmingly reduced. In many cases it can be abolished altogether. This care, which may (and for financial reasons perhaps must) include home care, is not easy. It demands infinite love and compassion. It must include the latest scientific knowledge of analgesic drugs, nerve blocks, antinausea medication, and so on. But it can be done, it can be done, it can be done!

Life Is Special

Time and again our patients have shown us that life, even a deformed, curtailed, and, to us, who are whole, an unimaginable life, can be made noble and worth living. Look at Joni Earickson—paraplegic from the age of seventeen—now a most positive, vibrant and inspirational person who has become world famous for her triumph over adversity. Time and time again, once symptoms are relieved, patients and relatives share quality time together, when forgiveness can be sought and given—for many a time of great healing.

Man, made in the image of his Creator, is *different* from all other animals. For this reason, his life is special and may not be taken at will.

We do not know why suffering is allowed, but Old and New Testament alike are full of reassurances that we have not been, and will not ever be, abandoned by our God. "Yea, though I walk through the valley of the shadow of death, I will fear no evil *for thou art with me.*"

Call to Change Direction

Our modern tragedy is that man has turned his back on God, who alone can help, and has set himself up as the measure of all things. Gone then is the absolute importance of man, gone the sanctity of his life, and the meaning of it. Gone too the motivation for loving care which is our responsible duty to the sick and dying. Goodbye love. Hello indifference.

With our finite minds, we cannot know fully the meaning of life, but though at times the storms of doubt may rage, I stake my life on the belief that to God we are special, that with Him, murder is unacceptable, and suicide (whatever you call it) becomes unnecessary.

Abandon God, and yes, you can have euthanasia. But a *good* death it can never be, and no subterfuge of law like that before us today can ever make it so.

My plea to the Hemlock Society is: Give up your goal of self-destruction. Instead, lend your energy, your anger, your indignation, your influence and creativity to work with us in the building of such a system of hospice care that death, however it come, need no longer be feared. Is not this a nobler cause? Is not this a better way?

JOURNAL PROMPT:

How much have you read about euthanasia? Has your reading in any way changed your mind about this subject?

COLLABORATIVE EXERCISE:

In his speech, Conolly suggests that "once we unleash euthanasia, once we take to ourselves the right actively to terminate a human life, we will have no means of controlling it. Adolph Hitler showed with startling clarity that once the dam is breached . . . death in the end comes to be administered equally to all." Discuss the logic of Connolly's comparison of euthanasia getting out of control to the atrocities of World War II. Is his assertion reasonable, or does it reflect some of the fallacies discussed in class?

ESSAY ASSIGNMENT:

1. Imagine that you were in the audience when Conolly delivered his speech. Write a detailed response, addressed to Conolly, in which you offer your opinion about his assertions. Don't just praise or criticize him, but be articulate and specific in responding to each of his main points.
2. When we think about euthanasia, we often think first of the painful burden this situation creates for relatives and loved ones. With this in mind, do you think it should be mandatory that people indicate in writing what their wishes are if they were in a situation where euthanasia might be seriously considered, if euthanasia were legal? Explain your answer.

ADDITIONAL ESSAY PROMPTS

1. Imagine that you are an ailing senior citizen, whose family has decided to place you in an assisted-living facility. How do you think you would react to the sudden loss of control over your life?
2. Investigate how another culture (one of your choosing) cares for its elderly persons. Compare the care given to the elderly in this culture with that of the United States.
3. At what age do you think a person should start planning for retirement? Write about how you would like to spend your retirement years and how you plan on making those dreams a reality.
4. Investigate the role of diet and exercise on the aging process.
5. Study the current Social Security situation. Do you think the program should be retained? If so, what are some measures that might be implemented to ensure its continuation?
6. Today, more than ever before, many grandparents are raising their grandchildren. What are some of the specific difficulties (and rewards) for both children and adults with such an arrangement?

7. Do you think it's possible to be a successful long-distance grandparent? Brainstorm and write about some unique ways grandparents can stay in touch with their grandchildren who live far away.

8. How do you feel about people in their seventies and eighties marrying? Do you know couples who have married—or remarried—late in life? How did other family members respond to the union?

9. Read May Sarton's novel *As We Are Now,* which chronicles the life of a seventy-six-year-old woman who has suffered a heart attack and is committed by family members to a nursing home. How do you respond to this portrait of a woman's helplessness and despair? Can you think of alternatives for someone in similar circumstances?

10. The essay by May Sarton reveals an author who is fully involved with life. She offers proof that although our physical activities may be somewhat curtailed as we age, it is still possible to maintain an active intellectual life. In fact, recent research suggests that an active mind wards off senility. How do you plan to remain intellectually alive?

ADDITIONAL RESEARCH QUESTIONS

1. Explore the issue of national health care. (In your research you might want to investigate the national health plans of other countries, such as Canada or Sweden.) What are some of the arguments for or against a national health-care program in this country?

2. Assume you are writing for an audience with a strong social agenda. Argue for or against euthanasia, keeping in mind the political leanings of your audience.

3. Write an essay in which you compare a community you know to one with which you are not familiar (some suggestions for exploration: retirement communities, gated communities, mobile home parks, religious communities, communes, small towns, housing projects). How are your two communities alike? How are they different?

4. It is your job to investigate placement of an aging relative who can no longer live alone. Research some of the issues you might explore when looking for a nursing home (for example: cost, activities, facilities, health care, etc.).

5. Research the effects of senility and dementia on family members as they struggle to cope with the sadness, frustration, and time limitations often placed on their personal lives.

Author/Title Index

Credits

Anonymous
"The Mountain Where Old People Were Abandoned" by Anonymous from *Folktales of Japan*. Copyright © 1963. Reprinted by permission of The University of Chicago Press.

Anonymous
"The Seal's Skin" by Anonymous from *Icelandic Folktales and Legends* by Jacqueline Simpson. Copyright © 1972 Jacqueline Simpson. Reprinted by permission of the University of California Press.

Bruno Bettelheim
"Life Divided from Inside" from *The Uses of Enchantment* by Bruno Bettelheim, copyright © 1975, 1976 by Bruno Bettelheim. Used by permission of Alfred A. Knopf, a division of Random House, Inc.

Robert Bly
The Sibling Society. Reading, MA: Addison-Wesley Publishing Company, Inc. 1996.

Robert Bly
Iron John: A Book About Men. Reading, MA: Addison-Wesley Publishing Company, Inc. 1990.

Jennifer Bojorquez
"Spare the Chores, Spoil the Child" by Jennifer Bojorquez from *The Sacramento Bee*, August 21, 1995. Copyright, The Sacramento Bee, 1995. Reprinted by permission.

T. Coraghessan Boyle
"Greasy Lake" by T. Coraghessan Boyle from *Greasy Lake and Other Stories* by T. Coraghessan Boyle, copyright © 1979, 1981, 1982, 1983, 1984, 1985 by T. Coraghessan Boyle. Used by permission of Viking Penguin, a division of Penguin Putnam Inc.

Rosemary L. Bray
"So How Did I Get Here?" by Rosemary L. Bray from *The New York Times Magazine*, 1992. Reprinted by permission of Elaine Markson Literary Agency, Inc.

Gwendolyn Brooks
"The Bean Eaters" by Gwendolyn Brooks from *Blacks*. Reprinted by permission of The Estate of Gwendolyn Brooks.

Barbara S. Cain
"Older Children and Divorce" by Barbara S. Cain from *The New York Times Magazine*, February 18, 1990. Copyright © 1990 by The New York Times Co. Reprinted by permission.

Mary Cantwell
"The Burden of a Happy Childhood" by Mary Cantwell from *The New York Times Magazine*, February 1, 1998. Copyright © 1998 by The New York Times Co. Reprinted by permission.

Judith Ortiz Cofer
"Quinceañera" by Judith Ortiz Cofer is reprinted with permission from the publisher of *Terms of Survival* (Houston: Arte Publico Press—University of Houston, 1987). "Advanced Biology" from *The Latin Deli: Prose and Poetry* by Judith Ortiz Cofer. Reprinted by permission of The University of Georgia Press.

Matthew Conolly
"Euthanasia Is Not the Answer" by Matthew Conolly. Reprinted by permission.

Malcolm Cowley
"The View from 80," from *The View from 80* by Malcolm Cowley, copyright © 1976, 1978, 1980 by Malcolm Cowley. Used by permission of Viking Penguin, a division of Penguin Putnam Inc.

Norman Cousins
"The Right to Die" by Norman Cousins. Reprinted by permission.

Sara Davidson
"The Wedding Dress: What Do Women Want?," from *Real Property* by Sara Davidson, copyright © 1980 by Sara Davidson. Used by permission of Doubleday, a division of Random House, Inc.

James Dickey
"Cherrylog Road" by James Dickey from *Poems 1957–1967*. Reprinted by permission of Wesleyan University Press.

Joan Didion
"On Self-Respect" from *Slouching Towards Bethlehem* by Joan Didion. Copyright © 1966, 1968, renewed 1996 by Joan Didion. Reprinted by permission of Farrar, Straus and Giroux, LLC.

Rita Dove
"Daystar," from *Thomas and Beulah,* Carnegie-Mellon University Press, © 1986 by Rita Dove. Reprinted by permission of the author.

Kieran Egan
"The Mythic Stage" by Kieran Egan from *Educational Development.* Reprinted by permission of the author.

Louise Erdrich
"*Z:* The Movie That Changed My Life" by Louise Erdrich as appeared in *The Movie That Changed My Life* by David Rosenberg.

Clarissa Pinkola Estes
"Sealskin, Soulskin" from *Women Who Run With the Wolves* by Clarissa Pinkola Estes, Ph.D., copyright © 1992, 1995 by Clarissa Pinkola Estes, Ph.D. Used by permission of Ballantine Books, a division of Random House, Inc.

Ellen Goodman
"The Family Legacy" from *Value Judgments* by Ellen Goodman. Copyright © Ellen Goodman. Reprinted by permission of International Creative Management, Inc.

Joan Young Gregg and Beth M. Pacheco
"Love's Role in Marriage" by Susan M. Garfield as appeared in *The Human Condition: A Rhetoric with Thematic Readings,* 1/e by Joan Young Gregg and Beth M. Pacheco. Reprinted by permission.

Linda Gregg
"The Conditions" copyright 1991 by Linda Gregg. Reprinted from *The Sacraments of Desire* with the permission of Graywolf Press, St. Paul, Minnesota.

Eamon Grennan
"Station" copyright 1998 by Eamon Grennan. Reprinted from *Relations: New & Selected Poems* with the permission of Graywolf Press, St. Paul, Minnesota.

Joy Harjo
"Three Generations of Native American Women's Birth Experience" by Joy Harjo from *Ms.* magazine, July/August 1991. Reprinted by permission of Ms. magazine, © 1991.

Ernest Hemingway
"Hills like White Elephants" reprinted with permission of Scribner, a division of Simon & Schuster, Inc., from *Men Without Women* by Ernest Hemingway. Copyright 1927 by Charles Scribner's Sons. Copyright renewed 1955 by Ernest Hemingway.

David Hicks and Margaret A. Gwynne
From *Cultural Anthropology,* 2/e by David Hicks and Margaret A. Gwynne. Copyright © 1997 by Allyn & Bacon. Reprinted by permission.

Chester Higgins Jr.
"A Father's Rite" by Chester Higgins Jr. from *The New York Times Magazine,* December 27, 1992. Copyright © 1992 by The New York Times Co. Reprinted by permission.

John Holt
"Three Kinds of Discipline" is reprinted from *Freedom and Beyond* by John Holt. Copyright © 1995, 1972 by Holt Associates. Published by Boynton/Cook, a subsidiary of Reed Elsevier Inc., Portsmouth, NH. Reprinted by permission of the publisher.

Langston Hughes
"Salvation" from *The Big Sea* by Langston Hughes. Copyright 1940 by Langston Hughes. Copyright renewed 1968 by Arna Bontemps and George Houston Bass. Reprinted by permission of Hill and Wang, a division of Farrar, Straus and Giroux, LLC.

Kay S. Hymowitz
"The Teening of Childhood" reprinted with the permission of The Free Press, a division of Simon & Schuster, Inc., from *Ready or Not: Why Treating Children as Small Adults Endangers Their Future and Ours* by Kay S. Hymowitz, a condensation of Chapter 4. Copyright © 1999 by Kay S. Hymowitz.

Edward P. Jones
"The First Day" from *Lost in the City* by

Edward P. Jones. Copyright © 1992 by Edward P. Jones. Reprinted by permission of HarperCollins Publishers, Inc.

Barbara Kingsolver

"Stone Soup" from *High Tide in Tucson* by Barbara Kingsolver. Copyright © 1995 by Barbara Kingsolver. Reprinted by permission of HarperCollins Publishers, Inc.

Dorianne Laux

"Twelve" from *What We Carry*. Copyright © 1994 by Dorianne Laux. Reprinted with the permission of BOA Editions, Ltd.

Mel Lazarus

"Angry Fathers" was first published in *The New York Times Magazine,* 1995. Reprinted courtesy of Mel Lazarus.

Anne Morrow Lindbergh

"Channeled Whelk" from *Gift from the Sea* by Anne Morrow Lindbergh, copyright © 1955, 1975, renewed 1983 by Anne Morrow Lindbergh. Used by permission of Pantheon Books, a division of Random House, Inc.

Devorah Major

"Little Girl Days" by Devorah Major from *California Childhood: Recollections and Stories of the Golden State.* Reprinted by permission of the author. Devorah Major is also author of *Brown Glass Windows* (Curbstone Press, Spring 2002) and *With More Than Tongue* (Creative Arts Book Company, Fall 2002). She is currently working on a book of essays, *Cooking and Other Everyday Rituals.*

Bobbie Ann Mason

"Shiloh" from *Shiloh & Other Stories.* Reprinted by permission of International Creative Management, Inc. Copyright Bobbie Ann Mason.

Rollo May

"In Search Of Our Roots" from *The Cry for Myth* by Rollo May. Copyright © 1991 by Rollo May. Used by permission of W. W. Norton & Company, Inc.

Nathan McCall

From *Makes Me Wanna Holler* by Nathan McCall, copyright © 1994 by Nathan McCall. Used by permission of Random House, Inc.

Jessica Mitford

"The American Way of Death" by Jessica Mitford from *The American Way of Death.* Reprinted by permission of Jessica Mitford. Copyright © 1963, 1978 by Jessica Mitford, all rights reserved.

Charles Mungoshi

From *The Setting Sun and the Rolling World* by Charles Mungoshi. Copyright © 1972, 1980 by Charles Mungoshi. Reprinted by permission of Beacon Press, Boston.

Michele L. Norris

"A Child of Crack" by Michele L. Norris from *The Washington Post,* 1989. Copyright © 1989, The Washington Post. Reprinted with permission.

Tim O'Brien

"On a Rainy River" from *The Things They Carried* by Tim O'Brien. Copyright © 1990 by Tim O'Brien. Reprinted by permission of Houghton Mifflin Company. All rights reserved.

Sharon Olds

"Rites of Passage" from *The Dead and the Living* by Sharon Olds, copyright © 1987 by Sharon Olds. Used by permission of Alfred A. Knopf, a division of Random House, Inc.

Linda Pastan

"Ethics," from *Waiting for My Life* by Linda Pastan. Copyright © 1981 by Linda Pastan. Used by permission of W. W. Norton & Company, Inc.

Melvin I. Urofsky

Letting Go: Death, Dying and the Law. New York, NY: Charles Scribner's Sons, 1993.

Anne Roiphe

"Why Marriages Fail" by Anne Roiphe. Reprinted by permission of International Creative Management, Inc. Copyright © 2000 by Anne Roiphe.

Theodore Roethke

"My Papa's Waltz," copyright 1942 by Hearst Magazines, Inc., from *The Collected Poems of Theodore Roethke* by Theodore Roethke. Used by permission of Doubleday, a division of Random House, Inc.

John A. Rush

"Rites, Ritual and Responsibility" by John A. Rush, Ph.D. Reprinted by permission.

Tepilit Ole Saitoti

Excerpts from *The Worlds of a Maasai Warrior* by Tepilit Ole Saitoti, copyright © 1986 by Tepilit Ole Saitoti. Used by permission of Random House, Inc.

May Sarton
"Monday May 3rd," from *At Seventy* by May Sarton. Copyright © 1984 by May Sarton. Used by permission of W. W. Norton & Company, Inc.

Linda Seger
"Creating the Myth" from *Making a Good Script Great* by Linda Seger. Reprinted by permission of Samuel French.

Richard Selzer
"Four Appointments with the Discus Thrower" from *Confessions of a Knife* by Richard Selzer. Copyright © 1979 by David Goldman and Janet Selzer, trustees. Reprinted by permission of Georges Borchardt, Inc., for the author.

Anne Sexton
"Pain for a Daughter" from *Live or Die* by Anne Sexton. Copyright © 1966 by Anne Sexton. Reprinted by permission of Houghton Mifflin Company. All rights reserved. "Cinderella" from *Transformations* by Anne Sexton. Copyright © 1971 by Anne Sexton. Reprinted by permission of Houghton Mifflin Company. All rights reserved.

Gail Sheehy
"Predictable Crises of Adulthood," from *Passages* by Gail Sheehy, copyright © 1974, 1976 by Gail Sheehy. Used by permission of Dutton, a division of Penguin Putnam Inc.

Thomas Simmons
From *The Unseen Shore* by Thomas Simmons. Copyright © 1991 by Thomas Simmons. Reprinted by permission of Beacon Press, Boston.

Steven Stark
"Where the Boys Are" by Steven Stark as appeared in *The Atlantic Monthly,* September 1994. Reprinted by permission of the author.

Ann Ricks Sumers
"I Want to Die at Home" by Ann Ricks Sumers from *Newsweek,* April 4, 1994, p. 13. Copyright © 1994 by Newsweek. All rights reserved. Reprinted by permission.

Jill Tweedie
In the Name of Love: Love and Theory and Practice Throughout the Ages. New York, NY: Pantheon Books, 1979.

Anne Tyler
"Teenage Wasteland" by Anne Tyler. Reprinted by the permission of Russell & Volkening as agents for the author. Copyright © 1983 by Anne Tyler. Story originally appeared in *Seventeen* magazine, November 1983.

Mona Van Duyn
"Cinderella's Story" from *If It Be Not I* by Mona Van Duyn, copyright © 1959 by Mona Van Duyn. Used by permission of Alfred A. Knopf, a division of Random House, Inc.

Alice Walker
"Everyday Use" from *In Love & Trouble: Stories of Black Women,* copyright © 1973 by Alice Walker, reprinted by permission of Harcourt, Inc.

Judith S. Wallerstein and Sandra Blakeslee
Excerpt from *The Good Marriage* by Judith S. Wallerstein and Sandra Blakeslee. Copyright © 1995 by Judith S. Wallerstein and Sandra Blakeslee. Reprinted by permission of Houghton Mifflin Company. All rights reserved.

E. B. White
"Once More to the Lake" from *One Man's Meat,* text copyright 1941 by E. B. White. Copyright renewed. Reprinted by permission of Tilbury House, Publishers, Gardiner, Maine.

Marie Winn
"The End of Play" from *Children Without Childhood* by Marie Winn, Viking Penguin 1984. Reprinted by permission of the author.

Charles Wright
"Sitting at Night on the Front Porch" by Charles Wright. Reprinted by permission of Wesleyan University Press.

Naomi Wolf
Promiscuities: The Secret Struggle Toward Womanhood. New York, NY: Random House, 1998.